The New Sociology

# The New Sociology

ESSAYS IN SOCIAL SCIENCE AND SOCIAL THEORY

IN HONOR OF C. WRIGHT MILLS

EDITED BY
**IRVING LOUIS HOROWITZ**

 **A GALAXY BOOK**

**New York  Oxford University Press**
**1965**

**To the American graduate students
of Social Science**

Copyright © 1964 by Oxford University Press, Inc.
Library of Congress Catalogue Card Number: 64-15013
First published 1964
First published as a Galaxy Book 1965
Second printing, 1966

Printed in the United States of America

# Contents

# Preface

This volume, which is presented as a memorial tribute to the late C. Wright Mills, did not take shape after but rather before Mills died. The old canard about a man being "ahead of his time" did not obtain in Mills' case. Mills was of his times and in his times. Precisely for this reason he was a leader of the present generation—or at least of the present generation of social science workers. And in simple truth is this not usually the case? Thorstein Veblen may have had his troubles in the institutes of "higher learning," but his social and economic thought was as vital during his lifetime no less than afterwards.

That sort of romanticism in which "fame is the spur" has an intrinsic corruptness—an egotistic belief in one's oracular powers. Mills was no egotist in this sense, whatever his self-image as the carrier of the "classic tradition" may have seemed to critics. His "spur" was to understand the world better, and perhaps, toward the end of his life, to connect knowledge and action in a new way. Mills paid the strictest attention to the points in question, and for that reason, however dramatic his analysis, it never reeked of that wooly-headed prescriptiveness that too often characterized "philosophical anthropology" on the abstract level and social reform on the practical level.

Not that Mills was a contented man—far from it. But his discontent was a consequence of both private and social disenchantment. His political radicalism was a consequence of the general radicalization of that suppressed part of the world hitherto called "underdeveloped." His sociological radicalism was an expression of displeasure at the backing away from the big-scale tasks of analysis that characterized most sociology of the 'fifties.

In March of 1960, a trifle more than two years before Mills died, I asked him how he would feel about a series of studies discussing his work and examining a select series of social problems utilizing his approach. He was clearly flattered by the idea but very doubtful that it could be brought to fruition in what was then the dominant climate of the sociological profession in the United States. In any event he suggested that I draw up a proposal for such a volume as a preliminary. My letter, which accompanied a proposed list of topics such a volume would cover, read in part as follows:

> I am writing to you concerning your interest in a volume of studies in sociology and social theory which would be dedicated to you. Of course, you might justifiably decline on any number of grounds, not the least of which is that you might feel rather young to be so permanently "enshrined." However, it is my opinion that the situation in sociology warrants such a volume now. A statement of those dedicated to a sociology of larger meanings and bigger problems is due, maybe overdue, if *The Sociological Imagination* is indicative of the present status of the profession in the United States. While I cannot swear allegiance to every statement you have made—of course, I am sure you would not want anyone to do so—it is already clear that you are the leading American sociologist, an erstwhile successor to Veblen. I see no viable reason to wait for posterity to render a judgment already self-evident. As I see it, such a volume should not be a Mills celebration, but rather, in the British tradition, a series of studies and topics on themes you have opened up. Each contributor should stand on his own two feet, and not on your shoulders. In that way, we can assure ourselves of a permanent contribution to the kind of social science we both stand for.

Even before my letter, Mills indicated his doubts whether an appropriate group of scholars and intellectuals could be gathered for such a project. He pointed out that he was under heavy criticism

by leading members of the academic establishment, vilified by political opponents, and at the same time, being accused of everything
from naïveté to Machiavellism by orthodox Marxists and Communists. The Russians—ironically enough—were less critical of his concept of the Power Elite than might be imagined, given its essential
and basic non-Marxist view of the relationship of power to economy
in American society. But the lagging left of Western Europe more
than made up for things with their priggish smugness and their certainty that Mills was "on the right road . . . and by avoiding a few
theoretical errors . . . would yet get there." Just where "there" was
remained unexplained. Presumably, "there" was the Marxism of the
Russians. Despite this solid phalanx of opposition—with leading sociologists playing at secular popery, and "excommunicating" Mills
from the profession, and politicians playing at sociology by attempting to drown out Mills' voice when it was addressed to public issues
—Mills replied in a most gratifying way:

> I am very grateful to you for having written up your idea. But
> the truth is I do not know how to answer it. You see, I do not
> really know much about American sociologists—as a whole I
> mean; I do know that some find what I have written useful,
> and that others may detest it. It's my own view you might have
> quite a time getting together a "respectable" group that thought
> such a dialogue worthwhile.

Doubts registered and fears discussed, we nevertheless met later
in the year to map out strategy for the volume. The basic accomplishments of this meeting were to give a more concrete turn to the
type of essays we would want and to discuss the potential contributors to such a volume. It was most intriguing to compare the names
we had in mind and when the meeting ended we were both delighted to find that there were too many people we had mentioned
as "absolutely essential" to such a volume rather than too few. I
never saw Mills in a more amenable and relaxed state than that
autumn day. He was genuinely enthusiastic about the possibilities
of such a volume although he continued to harbor misgivings. He
sent a follow-up note telling me that he was still giving the matter
some thought and suggested as a title, *The Sociology of Our Times:
Critical Appraisals of the Work of C. Wright Mills.*
After this, the matter remained under advisement. Mills was not

quite sure but that he was too young and had too many things to
write, before such a volume would be truly appropriate. Tragedy
quickly intervened to cancel this objection. In the same letter suggesting a title for the volume, Mills mentioned that he was "working
hard now on Latin America and Cuba because of the N.B.C. television debate with A. A. Berle." That debate never came to pass.
Mills suffered a relapse of his coronary condition. And while he re-
covered from that attack, he was forced to go on a reduced work
schedule, and it was all he could do to complete tasks he was in the
midst of, much less undertake consideration of yet new enterprises.
On March 21, 1962, Mills died.

The irony of the situation is that we are all too ready to pay
homage to the dead. Mills received no awards which sociologists
make annually for books deserving or otherwise—while now an
annual award is to be made in his name. After *Power Elite* he was
turned down for every request for a grant from the great institutions
of the "philanthropoids" with but a single honorable exception—
while now sponsorship for work *on* Mills is available. I am reminded of Langston Hughes' marvelous character Jesse B. Semple,
when he overheard a lecture in which the honored antiquarian of
the evening had this to say:

> You think you are honoring me, ladies and gentlemen of the
> Athenyannie Arts Club, when you invited me here tonight? You
> are *not* honoring me a damned bit! I said, not a bit . . . not a one
> of you from Sugar Hill to Central Park ever offered me a pig's
> foot. Then when the *New York Times* said I was a genius last
> month, here you come now giving a banquet for me when I'm
> old enough to fall over in my grave—if I was able to walk to the
> edge of it—which I am not . . . Now, to tell you the truth, I don't
> want no damned banquet. I don't want no honoring where *you*
> eat as much as me, and enjoy yourselves more, besides making
> some money for your treasury.

It is not difficult to picture Mills saying something like this. Even
a casual acquaintance would make plain his deep contempt for
ritual and ceremony. That is why this volume concentrates on carrying forth the tradition of the new and not "honoring" in any redundant and sentimental way. The volume celebrates the maturation
of classical sociological theory into a crystallized *scientific* position—

stripped of inherited ideological and metaphysical pretenses. From this stance, perhaps Mills would have understood the undertaking of such a book.

There would be little point in listing separately those who helped me. From the conceptual stage until the final preparation of this manuscript this has been a co-operative venture. The comments and suggestions of our contributors, and also of those interested in this memorial volume not included here, is, I sincerely hope, reflected in the final results. Mills was an independent man. The scholars in this volume have a shared value—they too have proven resourceful and independent. Each contributor has given freely of his time, his intellectual energies, and his belief in the intrinsic *and* utilitarian worth of *The New Sociology*. Such dedication cannot be repaid by a simple perfunctory acknowledgment. The orientation of the volume and of the contributors is that this memorial volume should accomplish two objectives: to pay our intellectual respects with the most powerful weapon at our disposal—quality of mind; to break new ground and retrieve valuable old territory, the better to carve out a social science of present meaning.

Irving Louis Horowitz

*Washington University, St. Louis*
*November 1963*

IRVING LOUIS HOROWITZ

# An Introduction to *The New Sociology*

**I**

There can be little doubt that the prevailing tendency in American sociology during the past two decades between 1940 and 1960 has put this discipline into a *cul de sac*. This tendency has been to package sociology, its tendencies, its tangents, and its theorists, in an institutional setting that is more concerned with the presentation of a social image than with the forging of a sociological imagination. Within this institutional framework arguments rage over the trivial; reputations are established over the personal; and ideas flourish over the organizational. The rationalists, or "macroscopic" tendency, concerned with developing "general theories" of human behavior, has managed to survive more because of the brilliance and tenacity of its leading advocates than due to any general acceptance of the logic or results derived from "grand theory." The public image of sociology derives from the efforts stimulated from empiricism, crystallized in institutes and research bureaus, and centering upon the notion that sociology establishes "truths" rather than "meanings," and that the master task of sociology is to distinguish between factual information and operational models.

The rise of empiricism in American sociology is customarily explained by emphasizing the pitfalls of approaching sociology in any other way. Thus, its practitioners will speak of empiricism as a reaction to an exaggerated historicism. Some might offer an explanation based on the growing secularization of the social sciences in general. Others offer the grim view that sociological empiricism coincides with the *Zeitgeist*, with the analytical nature of this age. Finally, there are those who see in this view the best method for obtaining factual results independent of ideological or valuational claims or considerations.

In these remarks it is not my intention to challenge or confront any of these hypotheses directly. I should like to restrict myself to the question "how" rather than "why." That is, I shall examine the subsidiary issue of how, for the past two decades, sociological empiricism has retained its pre-eminence in the face of challenges from all quarters. Many working within the field have not found the conversion from empirical sociology to sociological empiricism either simple or necessary.

It is my contention that in answering the question how, we are also offering a causal explanation, albeit a partial one, for the pre-eminence of one style of sociological research. And beyond this, we are perhaps presenting an inventory of the practical barriers which will have to be overcome if there is to be a freeing of what C. Wright Mills aptly termed the "sociological imagination." By saying practical barriers, I do not wish to minimize theoretical objections, only to indicate that such abstract objections seem directly connected to a complex of concrete factors.

It is clear from an investigation in professional social science journals of the annual listings of higher degrees in progress and already awarded, that, while there is a sharp numerical rise over the years, there is no corresponding growth in the number of higher-degree-granting institutions. By far the highest proportion of degrees granted in sociology, and in social science generally, is made by a highly selective and restrictive group of universities. This observation is confirmed in studies made by Wilson, Barber, and Berelson.[1] Thus the power and prestige of these selective universities, and, more specifically, the departments in which this power is directly lodged, show a growth pattern far in excess of the increase in higher education as such. "Team work," the drive for consensus, the pressure to state findings exclusively in quantitative terms, are reinforced by the financial and occupational need for the graduate student to get his degree. This power of the large department is not diminished after graduation. The communications network is kept open in terms of grants and awards, university press publications, journal articles, efforts of promotion and relocation—all of which in some measure require the sanction of the major institutions and their various departments. Barr offers this interesting account in "fictional" form: "The fact that his desk [the head of the economics department] was a clearing house for teaching posts with swank research organizations and private business corporations gave him absolute control of his graduate students. They knew that they would be taken care of if they won his favor. They knew likewise that, if they failed to win it, they would not even get a degree, no matter how strong a dissertation they wrote." [2] With such a situation, the younger men are under obvious constraint not to do violence to the prevailing group norms. The most serious criticism of value premises is thus confined to the upper echelons of the discipline, or to those scholars working in the different areas of social science.

What Mills has called the "feudal structure" of graduate education in itself encourages empiricism—first as a degree-getting posture substituting means for ends, and later on as a theoretical position. Solotaroff describes this as a general process. It does not have to be emphasized that this process holds even more firmly in sociology where empiricism is king. The graduate student "learns to go along with the acceptable style of scholarly thinking, in which 'originality' means mainly finding a problem, or segment of one, that is still to be explored, 'pertinence' means mainly the amount of fresh factual documentation that can be accumulated, and 'soundness' means mainly working within the existing body of 'scholarly opinion.' Moreover, he begins to find satisfaction in the close, skeptical examination of evidence, in the thoroughness of research, in accumulating a great deal of knowledge about a particular question. He develops a respect for factuality and for careful arguments that remain within clearly defined terms." [3] In brief, the process of recruitment emphasizes the mechanical values of working in areas where information is already available and, by the same token, discourages research into problems where evidence is lacking or where information is tentative. Such an approach assiduously avoids potential resistance to entrenched attitudes, a situation which might create difficulties for graduate students interested in graduation, promotion, and eventual career placement.

The total institution pattern is simulated, with emphasis on "working the system" replacing the older canons or systems of intellectual work. Empiricism is thus not simply a sociological methodology, but a social ideology.

Closely allied to recruitment practices is a sociological orientation in which there is excessive concentration on experiment as something apart from constructing theories. Specialized techniques of questionnaire design, codification, and compartmentalizing often make the interviewing process into the end of research rather than merely its instrument. The spate of literature on survey design and sampling techniques has encouraged a strict methodological view of the purposes of sociology. That this is not confined to any one branch of social science is confirmed by a UNESCO survey of political science. The editor of this survey indicates that "a good deal of political research carried on in universities today is aloof from the real problems of political life. Too often research seems to be conducted for the sake of research. The topics chosen have no apparent significance, and the investigation does not throw light on any contemporary problem of importance. There is no driving force behind such research, no vital motives inspiring the work, no useful potentialities in the conclusions which emerge." [4] There seem here to be two intertwined problems: establishing criteria of significance and, no less, an unwillingness to break through the data barrier. There are obviously a multitude of reasons for this. Lerner and Hilgard have caught the essence of the problem when they note that "the prestige of the natural scientist is high in American culture, where the developed industrial civilization and high standard of living are commonly attributed to scientific advances. This fact may lie behind the self-conscious wish of social scientists to become scientists like other natural scientists (chemists, physicists, biologists). Hence, those in the social disciplines turn to the natural sciences for their models of system-building. They wish to attain the generally accepted criteria of good science: objective and reproducible observations; precise and valid instruments for refining observations; hypotheses that help to initiate inquiry and direct research; general theories; and laws that satisfy the esthetic demand for an articulated and harmonious system." [5]

Policies and orientations in social science are clearly related to the reconstruction of the image of sociology held in the past.

While Lerner and Hilgard have indicated some of the major reasons for the attempt at mimetic reproduction of natural science methods, there remains the matter of the lingering identification of sociology with social reform (or something less applicable). The peer group in sociology has thus felt a special obligation to cleanse the word of its inherited "socialist" connotations. This could be done either through the substitution of methodology for actual useful results, or by direct appeals to members of the profession to abandon moral residues or biases which still persist—especially any bias against the business and industrial world. The manipulative values of sociology, which for a while were viewed as a necessary, if discomforting, byproduct of research, have now become something of a matter of principle. Institutionally oriented sociologists are bemoaning the lack of interest—it could be called the historic antipathy—of the professional social scientist for the business calling. The mutuality of interests between sociologists and businessmen has been reflected in the statement that it is businessmen who have done most of the scholarly work, based on a content analysis comparing the *Harvard Business Review* and the *American Journal of Sociology*.[6] It will be interesting to see if a parallel analysis of the contents of the "official" periodical literature for the corresponding decade beginning with 1960 will show an appropriate response to this plea for tolerance, understanding, and fair-play. As social research began to take place in an atmosphere frequently resembling International Business Machines Corporation, the status possessed by the latter was presumably to reflect on the former. This simply has not happened. As Robert K. Merton has pointed out in reply to the anti-sociologists, sound judgment is still the critical pivot.

It might be argued that a commitment to a business-like way of doing sociology is not necessarily a commitment to business values as such. Nonetheless, if the early researches of Elton Mayo and Chester Barnard betoken anything at all, it is that "industrial" sociology does indeed start with assumptions of the parity of labor and management, the need to further class consensus, and the essential insignificance of economic divisions in society. When we add these to the empiricist redefinition of authority as legitimate power, the results are disastrous for any serious "reflections on business." Such a call amounts to absorption of business values, not reflections on such values.

In line with the growing emphasis on sociology as a heuristic device has come the notion of "applied" sociology that can service the customers who purchase the commodity. In this way the subsidization of sociology has increasingly come to be underwritten by corporate elites. The extraordinary expansion of business interest in sociological research is underscored by the Institute for Social Research at the University of Michigan: "The staff of the Institute for Social Research has grown from the original group of 12 persons who established the Institute in 1946 to over 450 individuals in 1961." In a list of sponsors of this Institute, which is typical of like institutes elsewhere, we are presented with a "who's who" of the business world. Especially well represented are chemicals, oil and refining, communications, public utilities, banking and investment, philanthropic foundations, food and drug manufacturers, auto, steel, aircraft, insurance corporations, and leading federal agencies.[7] Interestingly enough, the list does not contain a single labor union, and, with the exception of the Boy Scouts of America, no non-corporate agencies or societies.

This makes plain that, first, the selective subsidization of sociology has developed at an extremely rapid rate; second, that, although the research findings are open to all in theory, they are open only to corporate wealth in fact; and, finally, that the center of gravity in sociology has shifted away from "pure" or academic research to "applied" or institutional research. To term this development the "secularization" of the field is simply to provide a misanthropic label for the fact that tenacious clinging to "value-free" empiricism is a consequence of the sales value of a nihilistic method in actual research undertakings.

The hovering of the corporate image over the activities of sociology has caused a considerable shift in the subject matter treated by the discipline. Such areas as sociological theory, the history of sociology, the sociology of religion, and the sociology of education have been outflanked in the course of the development of sociology as a heuristic discipline. "Who pays how much for what," not any imagined "revulsion" with traditional content, best explains the dominant motif in American sociology. And what pays is survey design, communication and influence analysis, studies of leadership and organizational behavior, etc. The slogan is to separate facts from values; the substance, however, is to suppress values at the expense of facts. For it is no more the case that studies in the social structure of Mormonism are more "value laden" than studies in the structure of inter-personal relations in an automobile factory. But it has been precisely this assumption of certain aspects of social life as being "sacred" and others "profane" that has driven a wedge in the sociological establishment between the academic departments and the corporate-sponsored institutes.[8]

For the post-war, post-depression generation of American sociologists, talk of the valuational ground of social science seemed a path long since trodden. There came into focus a strong current that identified social science not only with value neutrality but with scholarly aloofness from moral issues. Whereas in the 'thirties there was a tempered and qualified acceptance of the disjunction of fact and values, we now find this disjunction turned into a veritable law of sociology. This position considers "sociology 'value-free' in general and politically neutral in particular, and one finally that emphasizes, rather than erases, the distinction between sociology on the one hand and social and political philosophy on the other."[9] Empiricist methodology gives vigorous assent to this, informing us that we cannot, even in principle, provide an accounting of value alternatives. "Science can only tell us *how* to achieve goals; it can never tell us *what* goals should be sought."[10] This, of course, marks a profound retreat even from Weber's disclaimers. Instead of being considered a heuristic device informing sociological theory, methodology becomes a substitute for social problems as such.

The epitome of such efforts is the transformation of sociology into scientism. It exhibits not just indifference to values but open hostility to the existence of a plurality of values. It succeeds in re-tooling the "culture-lag" doctrine by making it conform to its own reductionist image of society. One writer has even suggested: "The fact that there are differences of opinion in a large society as to what these values are [present-day values] itself represents an unnecessary social lag. For in such recent developments as scientific public opinion polling, the values of a population and the unanimity and relative intensity with which they are held can also be determined."[11] The confusion between consensus and conformism is made complete. We are left with the impression that we ought not to be laggards; that resistance to a social consensus is tantamount to being backward, if not deviant. This "natural science" approach reduces morality to making sure that the number of police does not lag behind population shifts.[12]

The echoes of a neutralist posture are well illustrated in recent studies of nuclear war made by the new civilian militarists. The question of moment for the sociologist, it seems, is not the feasibility, or necessity of nuclear conflict, but rather how rapidly it will take the survivors of such a war to reconstruct their social patterns. The cupidity of this "crackpot realism" is so complete that the possibility that people might actually have learned something from a total hydrogen war (aside from ways of preventing it) is not raised.[13] As Von Wiese prophesied: "Value judgments, adieu." [14] The truth of course is not that values have actually disappeared from the social sciences, rather that the social scientist has become so identified with the going value-system. This phenomenon serves to reinforce the view that sociological empiricism is indeed the only form of useful sociology, since it alone confirms the dominant American attitude of regarding the morally uncommitted as the necessary counterpart to the scientifically objective.

The process of professionalization, which involves a gamut of sub-processes—from being *au courant* with the vernacular of the moment, to an appreciation of the number of variables the latest calculator can deal with in a single computation—serves the classic purpose of distinguishing peer-group membership from outsiders. Fossils and deviants of older generations, or those who have come through the educative process with a concern for value questions intact, must still face the resistance of the highly organized professional societies. An English sociologist has pointed out the situation with respect to professionalization: "A professional association seeks privileges at the expense of the common good. It attaches more importance to respect for seniority, conformity to professional rules of conduct and the growth of tradition than it does to individual freedom and inventiveness. Its members are conditioned to interpret their duties more in terms of professional skills than in terms of the needs of clients." [15] Clearly, the basis of professionalization has increasingly come to rest on a notion of consensus that often carries over into conformism. The social scientist is asked to comport himself as a physicist or physician, yet unlike the former he dare not establish a *Bulletin of Atomic Scientists,* lest the charge of meddling in political affairs come back to haunt him; and unlike the latter he is not authorized to make prescriptions (only descriptions and perhaps recommendations), lest the charge of moral involvement be raised.

An examination of the concept of sociological neutrality might begin by devising a test for distinguishing how much is based on indifference to policy problems, the desire to achieve a higher scientific ranking in the eyes of policy makers, or simply a belief that non-neutrality might result in a loss of position and professional ranking. Such a study might be extended to include information on whether or not ethical and political neutrality is simply a manifested pose which reveals a latent antipathy or sympathy for certain movements and ideals. For this purpose it might be well to start with a typology of social science attitudes toward specific social classes, occupational groupings, and ethnic affiliations. The work of Lazarsfeld and Thielens on *The Academic Mind* [16] and that of Caplow and McGee on *The Academic Marketplace* [17] provide useful anchor-points.

In addition to those who adopted empiricism for "practical" reasons, there are many, and by no means the least able, whose empiricism reflected a profound rejection of oracular and ideological distortions in the name of value. The inherited European currents reflected a lack of patience with scientific controls. We might just mention their impressionist approach to evidence, intense individualistic appraisals, attempts at exclusively long-range predictions (particularly on matters of "decline and fall"), absence of specific surveys to settle specific issues localized in time and space, the failure to establish any organized pressure toward information reliability, etc.[18] But with the solution, at least partial, of these methodological considerations, attempts at a more coherent picture of the function of value premises in social science can be made. It would do violence to the facts to consider the present situation without due regard to this current in American sociology.

The forging of a valuable sociology depends in part on the creation of a social science of values. Here we come to the greatest impediment to an advance in sociological research—the empiricist refusal to view the social sciences as essentially a human enterprise bound at one end by the biological-psychological constitution of men and at the other by the historical career of mankind. In a most important statement Redfield has summed up the reasons for considering anthropology a human science. His observations, which I shall paraphrase, seem to me to hold true for sociology as well: [19] (a) However clever the design of an experiment, there is a clear difference between humanity and non-humanity, between history at the upper level and physics at the lower level. (b) To reduce culture to physics is to decompose humanity into parts, and thus into something other than the study of man or society. (c) The dominance in the social sciences of natural science models and methods is not matched by any corresponding success in executing studies based on these models and methods. (d) The basis of any one social science is the study of some portion of humanity. It thus shares with the other social sciences, with the humanities, and with philosophy a common frame of reference. (e) The development of an explicit concern with values, with the values of those doing the investigation no less than those who are under investigation, makes even the striving, much less the realization, of a pure "natural science" of man devoid of value functions quite out of the question.

## II

But we have thus far only examined the sources of the crisis in empiricist sociology. It does not explain the reason for the present state of its discontent. While the reasons are numerous, the peculiar demands of the business and professional communities on the sociologist are basic to this problem. It is very difficult to tell an individual who requests aid on a research project: "Very well, we'll help you, we'll do more research on it." When a man (particularly a businessman) requests professional help and guidance, you have to offer both. You cannot give him highly particularized results having no general validity, nor an abstract theory which may or may not be usable in his area of enterprise. In consequence, empiricism has deteriorated into one-upmanship: it cures the social ailments by discovering more diseases.

Discontented empiricists insist that sociology ought to be more like psychoanalytic practice: that this is really the "tough-minded" solution.[20] We ought to sit down with businessmen, discuss their problems, work from our limited resources of knowledge, and develop answers to specific problems that arise. The deviant empiricist feels entitled to do this because he holds that there is only a finite number of laws involved in social science. He simplifies "laws" of society so that they become tautological statements. We are feted on a plethora of "laws" such as: "the older a conservative is, the more conservative does he become"; or that, "if you maximize the size of an audience, you maximize the size of its response." These "laws" are posed with such assurance that, no matter who comes to you, and whatever the problem, you can rely on them for solutions.

These kinds of "laws" confuse law with observable recurrences; e.g. every "time John returns home from work his dog wags his tail." But the implied generalization that, "every time a man comes home his dog wags his tail," does not follow. When we speak of a law in social science, we are usually talking about invariant relationships which enable the researcher to assemble not only information about the past, but to establish that kind of reliable information which will yield insight into future contingencies. In other words, if you take the situation of the master who keeps coming home to a dog wagging his tail you have still not accounted for the general behavior of pets to people. If you have cats, would the master's return produce the same response? Would the dog yield the same reaction to a different person? Would another dog respond differently? Would the dog wag his tail if the master were absent for any extended period of time? A procedural fallacy seems to underscore sociological empiricism: the size of a research project comes to determine the character of the theory.

Even if we grant the legal status of such statements, they are of such a low level of generalization that their applicability to any major problem is severely circumscribed. To offer consultation or advice as a scientist is quite out of the question. What is lacking in empiricism is a methodological apparatus which would enable one to give answers to specific questions which are at variance with the law statement itself. If you are dealing with cats and not with dogs, attempts to generalize responses may well break down. If you are dealing with carpetbaggers and not museum curators, the attempt may also bog down. Low level generalizations do not therefore make for a useful scientific yield.

While the search for law is a healthy sign, it is a reflection of the crisis within empiricism. The significant revolt within empiricism is relatively ineffectual and fraught with even greater dangers; namely, of converting sociology into couch-therapy for the businessman and for the ills of bureaucratic organization.[21] The supreme dilemma in the empiricist's approach is that they devise soothing forms of policy recommendations but are either barred or methodologically dissuaded from the realm of policy decisions and policy responsibilities. There is a difference between being "on tap" rather than "on top," and, as Alvin W. Gouldner indicates in his paper, the distinction between technical competence and moral responsibility only intensifies the cleft in social science.

If we take the grand theorists, the rationalistic sector of American sociology, who work at the level of the general theory of action, the problem seems to be in reverse. Their problem is, and traditionally has been, that it is not possible to apply a general theory of action to specific events. There have been attempts made, particularly by Marion Levy, that translate theories of affectivity and affective neutrality into observation statements about traditional and advanced societies. But in the translation process the "general theory" is completely dropped. Few claims have been substantiated that proposals expressed in any general theory of action scheme have been verified or are even open to verification. The most ambitious projects thus far only attempt to develop a model for the workings of society (any society) and its effects on the behavior of people (any people) for the purposes of proving the functionality of group life (any group). Rationalistic sociology has multiplied concepts and in so doing has blunted even the search for an applied sociology. From the idea of society as rational has come the idea that all societal parts are rational. The life-cycle of one society has been generalized to mean the life-cycles of all societies. The sociologist has only to put the pieces together and account for "dysfunctional" elements. Too often the rationalist's dependence on equilibrium models spills over into a faith in social consensus; this in turn is carried over into a general neglect of problems of social change.[22] The "conservative" bent of the leading rationalistic sociologists is therefore not accidental but a direct consequence of a sociological approach which emphasizes struc-

tural elements of a society over those features revealing contradictory norms and values. Both Parsons and the philosopher Hegel
start from the idea of reason. The general theory of action is really
a general theory of how the parts mesh to form a whole. But to
say that a society is reasonable is a truism, and to say that everything within a society is rational is an absurdity. The long trek
from an action context to a paradigm for describing all types of
action in a four-part pattern variable is no better (but surely no
worse) than Hegel starting with the idea of thought and ending
with the perfect category, the perfect equation of Reason equal-
ing itself. This kind of sociologist is forever infatuated with the
concept of orderliness in human affairs. When regicide occurs the
equilibrium lover is quick to note the rapidity with which political
order is restored. When revolutions break out, this same soul immediately discounts the possibility that any serious economic reorganization is entailed. When extreme personal or cultural disorganization is present, he immediately offers reassurances of the
capacity of society to manage, if not reduce, disorganization. The
macroscopic may be a response to an absence of generalizations
in the empiricist trends, but it remains an unscientific response.
The desire for harmony is not quite proof of the existence of
orderliness in society. The intoxication with the idea of social
order too often spills over into a celebration of *our* social order.

A consequence of the deep dilemmas of the rationalists and
empiricists is that the same leading figures have dominated the
field for the past two decades. They have not been able to create a
scientific tradition—a critical climate of opinion. The same arguments concerning the utility of functionalism, the same standards
of bureaucratized research procedures, the same emphasis on
paradigms and model construction prevail now as they did when
sociology was in its righteous revolt against the earlier sociology
of social service on the one side and speculation on the other.
Younger men have not emerged from these institutes to challenge
their tenets and reappraise the gnawing issues which exist. Brilliance has become suspect. You can measure the value of a system
by what its offspring and offshoots produce. Whatever the reasons,
the fact remains that the sociological "sons" are simply not as good
as the fathers. If this were not the case, there would be a considerable number of leading men present today who were not around

in the 'thirties. But this is not the case. The "generational struggle" is present everywhere but in "official" sociology.

There are of course exceptions to this rule. But these "exceptions" reflect the crisis in empiricism—it has become so completely anti-ideological that it has remained defenseless in the face of criticism. Its posture has become administrative rather than intellectual. More often than not, the "old guard" has power and prestige rather than knowledge and imagination. Their administrative power disguises their intellectual flabbiness. Their arguments are few; their will to resist alternative positions feeble; their scholarly ammunition meager. It is a wonder and a tribute to bureaucratic power that empiricism survives. The professional "role" of those who argue the end of ideology thesis, as Stephen W. Rousseas and James Farganis make clear, is to supply the ideological bastions for the empiricist camp. The "ideologists" of sociology were needed in the critical period of the mid-'fifties when empiricism was showing the infirmities of age.

There is no question of the integrity or good intentions of the sociologists concerned; but ideological demands tend to generate and locate an intellectual supply. Empiricism had a need for an ideological front. Some saw fit to fill that need. Yet literary skills and philosophic acumen did not resolve the problems of the empiricist posture. They continue to be very severe for the reasons mentioned. Empiricists are still wresting methodology from pyrrhic rationalist opposition.[23] They still refer to functionalism as the unique sociological method; as if scholars like Nagel, Braithwaite, and Hempel had not thoroughly discredited the whole notion. This kind of sociologist addresses himself to problems of method as if the philosophers of science had never written on functionalism. Those in the area of political and industrial sociology are still talking about Michels and Weber, about power and bureaucracy, in the same way.[24] Scholars in the area of social stratification are still arguing the question of the "necessity" of stratification versus mobility in the same sterile way.[25]

No recent breakthroughs on the major sociological fronts have been made either by empiricists or rationalists. As a matter of fact, one would have to regard it as the other way around: the empiricists have turned their eyeballs inward while the rationalists have become increasingly abstract and abstruse. The size of the social group studied is constantly being diminished. In the decade of the 'twenties, large-sized cities like Chicago were being tackled *en bloc* by the famed ecological school. In the decade of the 'thirties, it was middle-sized cities that were studied, as in the Middletown studies of the Lynds. In the decade of the 'forties, small towns became the fashion, as the work of Hollingshead and Kaufman revealed. By the decade of the 'fifties, the size of the community had been reduced to dormitories, hospital wards, and laboratories.

By the present decade, even this sociological range has shrunk to the minutia of two-person groups. We now have "atom smashers" in the form of data processing equipment, but we find ourselves using them only to crack walnuts. The paradox now would seem to be that to go further, to enter "one person" analysis, is to be out of sociology altogether and into psychology pure and simple. The recent work in some quarters, ostensibly critical of excessive sociologism, seems to point precisely in the direction of the self-liquidation of sociology.[26] But if for no other reason than the prestige of sociology as a discipline and the institutional framework from which it now gains support, one should expect the "range" of sociological inquiry to get larger rather than smaller.

The only difficulty encountered is that empiricists and rationalists alike have moved themselves into a methodological monad without windows. They are bound by a theory of verification and procedural rules which are unsuited to large-scale analysis. The emphasis on data reliability, on the simulation of events, and on the recreation of the experimental situation, simply cannot be called upon for certain types of research. Is it appropriate to settle matters by designing models which presumably account for all possible social contingencies? The study of slogans and symbols, of revolutionary changes, of spontaneous events such as crowd behavior, of changing distribution of political power, of economic sectors in the competition between nations, etc.—these major spheres tended to be left unexamined. And by default, economists, anthropologists, and political scientists have been left to take up the slack.

At this point a sociology of wide range, an historically anchored sociology, became the desperate need of the profession. And at this point, the unique contribution of C. Wright Mills came into focus. As Anatol Rapoport has suggested: "The strongest feature of Mills' sociology is his attack against ossified method. The creative aspect of this critique resides in his suggested *sociological* reasons for this ossification." It is also evident, as the essays by Ralph Miliband and Andrew Hacker make clear, that those working in allied social science disciplines welcomed the addition of a sociological dimension to the major political questions of the age. But officialdom was not quite prepared to receive a dark prophet who was willing to take risks by working in areas abandoned by the leading professionals.

What Mills was arguing for was the imperative need, not only for social consciousness, but also consciousness by sociologists of basic premises and principles—what the classic tradition in sociology has always viewed as significant. In a critical sense, Mills was a conservative sociologist in the true meaning of the words, for he was interested in preserving the heritage of the area. He referred to his own position as being in the "classic tradition," in the mainstream of the work done by Pareto, Durkheim, Weber, Znaniecki, Simmel, and Marx. These for him were the pivotal sociologists; and indeed they are so over and above Mills' vision of them, because it is to them that we owe the firm distinction between science as clarification and information as manipulation.

### III

Any step forward in sociology must be based on a new awareness of our intellectual-scientific tradition. We must learn to pick up the threads of the past and develop a sense of identity with it if we are to escape being area-centered and time-bound. The sociology of knowledge needs to be supplemented by a knowledge of sociology. The kind of differentiations made by Sidney M. Willhelm certainly offers great possibilities in relating social science to social consciousness.

Professional sociological journals show a great preponderance of citations of articles done the previous year, this year, and even those yet to be published, but rarely of articles written ten or twenty years ago. This kind of mimesis of the natural sciences abounds. In journals of physics references to older articles rarely appear, since information is in a genuine process of being resifted. Physicists, however, do not dismiss their heritage from Newton to

Einstein simply because they are old-fashioned. The sociologist has been quick to hide behind his expertise, and too frequently he employs the mystique of numbers rather than relying on the special methodological demands of his discipline.

The problem is then: what is the nature of the discipline called sociology? What is the relationship between the past and present in the area? Do human sciences of the same type, operative at the same level of discourse, bear the same significance as the natural sciences? It is question-begging to take for granted that old information should not be cited because it is old. Entailed (unconsciously or otherwise) is an assumption which is yet to be proven: that the distinction between natural and social science is purely a convention—methodological and not structural.

Presumptions such as these drove Mills further and further into a different and sometimes exaggerated posture. Nonetheless, as Pablo Gonzáles Casanova indicates, Mills decisively pointed out the dilemmas in the established ways of doing sociology. Even those contributors to The New Sociology who make no direct references to Mills' work undertake to examine the direction and impulses of the new sociology, the new effort to forge a sociology of the big range. This effort is hardly idiosyncratic; nor does it stem from any single political bias. It is not the private property of any one man, nor even of any one group of contributors. Men like Costa Pinto, Germani, Powell, and Fox spell out the meaning of this position in detail. Big-range sociology is a public sociology —open to inspection, subject to criticism, anxious for improvement. While it is thoroughly justified in its claim that this represents a new turn, it represents no less than a continuity with the intellectual tradition in sociology as against narrow academicism.

The ceaseless barrage of criticism caused Mills to think himself a "lone wolf." He was mistaken in his romantic notion of being one and isolated. Any authentic movement or authentic sociological method invites many people; and since the new turn in sociology is intrinsically broad in scope, many scholars (from all of the human sciences and humanities) have been attracted by it. Only thus can the "new turn" become a major prevailing force in social science institutions and organizations. The first thing we have to do is recapture what Robert Park called the sense of the "big news" and entertain what Robert Lynd has called the "outrageous hypotheses." We have spent twenty years convincing ourselves that the solution of the middle-range problems would pave the way to a more sober treatment of large-range problems. The fact of the matter is that problems of the middle range have never been further from solution.

We are presently confronted with contradictory findings ostensibly derived from the same kinds of evidence. Mass culture is said to be a cause of mass society and a consequence of mass society. It is held to be a unique product of the post-industrial epoch, and also to be as old as Athenian society. Crime is said to be a consequence of economic divisions in society and also to be uniquely determined by familial, psychological, and even ecological factors. The criminal is said by some to be distinctly different in his behavior patterns, and is said by others to reproduce the ongoing social norms of the outside world. Social disorganization is defined by some in terms of standards of mental health, while for others it represents a form of essential norm deviation. While all agree that anomie is defined by a "condition of normlessness," just which social classes are subject to anomic pressures remains as confused as ever. Ecology is said by some city planners to prove the need for urban redevelopment, while for others social ecology is held to be a matter of inter-personal adjustments first and urban renewal last. Authoritarian behavior is said by some political sociologists to be more characteristic of the lower classes, while for others the evidence indicates that lower classes are less subject to authoritarian pressures because they are less subject to the demands of upward mobility. Television habits are held to illustrate the social isolation of the masses, the detachment from social norms, or, conversely, television viewing is seen as a high form of socialization, since it "keys" the viewers to changing societal patterns. One group of sociologists may speak of the breakdown of family relations, while others just as assuredly cite the same evidence to prove that all is well with the American family system. This list can be extended tenfold—as any sociologist can attest. What seems clear is that the "reorientation" and "secularization" of sociology, which have come about at the expense of new developments in fundamental theory, have not produced satisfactory results.

While in its origins middle-range research was an attempt to escape both from small group theory and from oracular theorizing, it has only obscured the problem areas by converting sociology into a magnificent ambiguity, into a bookkeeping system of "on the one hand . . . but then again on the other." It has not actually solved, or even located specifically, middle-range problems. Demography, criminology, gerontology, etc., the comfortable spheres of limited research, have developed precisely to the degree that studies have been carried out in a comparative and historical context. Hermann Mannheim's world-wide survey of patterns of crime has yielded substantial results both for criminologists and for penologists. David Glass' work on demographic patterns has opened up new vistas of the problem of underdevelopment and overpopulation. Albert Meister's work on comparative community voluntary associations has raised this particular sphere of middle-range rerearch to new levels of sophistication. While some sociologists are seeking safety in smaller range approaches to miniature problems, social science is being charged with understanding ever larger issues. And this requires just the sort of intellectual scope which professional rivalries and departmental jealousies effectively serve to limit.

The master problems for a modern sociology—the multiplication of social forms of capitalism and socialism, the social costs and benefits of economic development, the new nationalism and the rise of polycentric doctrines of socialism, the relation of racial competition to democratic norms, the connection between industrial life and anomic responses, the problems of world population and human health, and, above all, the question of world conflict and conflict resolution—these are large-scale problems. They are not simply newspaper headlines, but are, in fact, matters which occupy the attention of many and diverse professional publics. Sociology has an obligation, first and foremost, to reflect upon the problems dealt with at the level they occur, and to provide the information and the theory for social solutions to human problems. Problems of capitalism and socialism, underdevelopment and overdevelopment, or anomie, alienation, and anxiety, have to be met head on. One has to accept complex problems as entities in the world, to be solved at the level at which people encounter them. If we confront problems of social development, we cannot rest content with their institutionalization in one miniscule town and imagine that this satisfies the requirements of the scope of development. As William McCord and Peter Worsley demonstrate, you simply cannot solve problems of a little village without encountering agrarian problems as such, or problems of class, caste, and colonialism as such. To think otherwise is to reduce applied sociology to social work, to compel the sociologist to operate only within a framework of politically imposed circumstances. Sociology is not necessarily a tool of policy but functions more ably as a critic of policy. When it becomes otherwise, it turns into a hypocritical extension of special interests—an ideology.

The point to note is that the practice of large-range sociology does not lack for brilliant adherents. To simply recount such recent works as Erich Fromm's *Escape From Freedom*, Daniel Z. Friedenberg's *The Vanishing Adolescent*, William H. Whyte, Jr.'s *The Organization Man*, E. Franklin Frazier's *Black Bourgeoisie*, Erving Goffman's *Asylums*, David Riesman's *The Lonely Crowd*, Anatol Rapoport's *Fights, Games and Debates*, Arthur J. Vidich and Joseph Bensman's *Small Town in Mass Society*, among others, should make it perfectly clear that Mills was not the intellectual isolate he pictured himself to be. On the other hand, what thus far has been missing, and what is quite clearly needed to make a comparative-historical sociology professional, is the theory and the method of this style of sociology. Mills' own work is distinguished by this awareness that a theoretical option to narrow empiricism and grand-scale rationalism would have a double advantage: solidify the gains made, and stimulate new forms of big-range thinking, such as the application of statistical methods to problems of the developing nations. In this sense, the cross-disciplinary theoretical essays of Abraham Edel, Ernest Becker, and Marvin Scott may prove particularly fertile in expanding the horizons of the sociological range.

On the other hand, big-range sociology does not necessarily require an immense frame of reference. In studying *The Children of Sanchez*, Oscar Lewis has shown how it is possible to focus problems of underdeveloped and transitional societies through the words, thoughts, and deeds of a single family. Such impressive community studies as those of S. M. Miller and Elwin H. Powell reveal a similar awareness that large problems can be telescoped in terms of rural and urban affairs. Mills' own formula "private ills and public troubles" may be used to characterize this type of sociological inquiry. What is decisive is the quality of mind of the investigator, no less than the object of investigation. The implication in Rose K. Goldsen's remarks is that a fool with a method will still yield foolish results, and an intelligence without a method will yield oracular results. These are clearly false alternatives: and just as clearly, alternatives which ought to be resisted.

The new turn in sociology is thus an examination of large-scale problems. It also means a projection of solutions possible, whether they happen to coincide with public policy or not. This must come to be increasingly reflected in professional social science journals and in styles of sociological research and theory as such. After a half century of intellectual effort, criminologists have come to distinguish social policy from social pathology, incarceration from illness. In consequence of this hard-won understanding that social psychiatry is not a justification for legal oppression, but its direct opposite, has come the breakthrough in theory registered by Erving Goffman, Thomas Szasz, and Ernest Becker. This understanding of sociology as science, not rationalization, must become general.

Without this double vision of insight and criticism, it is hardly possible for the sociologist to escape the trivialization that has taken place over the past twenty-five years. A society cannot long endure scientific cant when there is better sociology being written in the popular press than in the professional journals. This is plainly an absurdity. What does one read to find out about problems of unemployment in West Virginia—of what happens to coal miners in an affluent society where oil and gas have replaced coal as a fuel source? Must we turn to popular media for an analysis of the costs as well as the benefits of social change? Must we become a tail-end discipline gaining a public hearing by virtue of our superb journalists? Instead of sniping at the sociological "popularizers" and "journalists," we might well start appreciating them. Darwin had his Huxley, and, happily, sociology has Dan Wakefield, Howard Coughlin, Michael Harrington, and W. H. Whyte.

**IV**

A main consequence of capturing the sense of the big news, the important event, is the reclamation of social history. Empiricists in sociology are always fond of talking about concreteness and specificity. They do not like abstraction; they like facts, scenes to observe, and models to build. One then turns to their articles and searches in vain for these virtuous methodological properties. That which is most lacking is precisely the sense of specificity. And those who possess it are more criticized than read.

Take the biggest issue of the post-war world—the question of arms control and disarmament. Special issues of outstanding quality have appeared on this matter from journals ranging from *Business Week* to *The Nation,* from *Daedalus* to *Foreign Affairs.* But where is the sociological reflection of the public concern over any aspect of this social problem? Surely not in the professional journals of sociology. McCarthyism came and went before professional journals took cognizance of this social phenomenon—and then only as a result of Edward Shils' *The Torment of Secrecy.* Must World War III also come and go before a similar recognition of the problems of thermonuclear annihilation reflect themselves in sociological research? The answer in part will be the type of support given to sociologists by their professional societies, and by the character of work undertaken by sociological institutes. It is interesting and gratifying to know that, with the entrance onto the sociological horizons of such new periodicals as *New Society* in England; *Social Problems, The Sociological Quarterly, Journal of Arms Control, The Correspondent* in the United States; *Sociologie du Travail* and *International Review of Community Development* in France; *Revista Brasileira de Ciências Sociais* and *International Journal of Comparative Sociology* in Third World nations, some real energies are being spent on connecting social science and social policy.

Self-conscious apologies for methodological imprecision supposedly cover the sins of pride and omission. There is a timelessness and ambiguity to much sociological research that would make proud the most abstruse metaphysician. If one were to remove the dates from what passes as research articles it would make little difference, for the research is intended to be time*less.* But if sociology is timeless and society operates in a sequence of events called the passage of time, then either social man is in a state of permanent equilibrium or the sociologist is living in a minus-one dimension. Too many sociologists live in a space-bound three-dimensional Newtonian world. The fourth dimension, history, is missing from our work. On this ground, the work of Mills, and the further advances made by Oliver Cox and Lewis Copeland, among others, are particularly instructive. Too often sociologists mean by history simply subjective history, the changing opinions of informants or the personal biographies of individuals. Even at the level of group life, at the level of small-group research, time must be recorded: as adolescence, obsolescence, aging, stagnation, death, and the continuing struggle of culture to survive and transcend itself. Subjective beliefs must be tested against objective circumstances.

We need to recapture the sense of the relationship of sociology to historical time, of life spans to life chances, of science to history. Although brilliant steps have been taken in this direction by men like Robert K. Merton and Hans H. Gerth, these remain isolated bursts. We do not have large-range sociology because we lack familiarity with historical sources. We are not dealing with "news," either of the past or the present. We ought not to lose the journalistic appreciation of immediately pressing issues as a concrete expression of history. People read a newspaper every day because they have an acute sense that what happens one day is both continuous with past events and discrete with respect to those same events. And that sense of the "present as history," of time and of journalism, is still held to be a negative value in the sociological profession. The social scientist who successfully penetrates historical realities is more likely to be criticized for being tendentious than praised for his achievements.

But the very idea of imputing negative values to journalism is a grotesque misreading of the essence of good sociology. The journalist is a chronicler of events. When he is successful, he offers the sociologist an enormous amount of data. The sociologist must give theoretical body to these events. Society has a temporal dimension, thus time must perforce be understood. We cannot study all historical monographs, or all news documents, but certainly we can draw, as Rex Hopper and Elwin H. Powell do, upon the information available from the historian and the journalist to forge a time-centered sociology.

Let us see how this would work in the problem of stratification. Sociologists too often resolve questions in stratification by resorting to an eternal theory (it is called a "functional-structural" approach, to be sure). No matter what kind of social change, there will always be the "inevitable psychological law" of the ruler and the ruled. Some have converted this into a technique for describing change. Social life is an eternal *corso* and *ricorso:* moving from one set of rulers, one set of elites, or one set of iron laws, to another. But whatever reversal of positions occurs, the "law" of ruler and ruled goes on. Real history, as development, is subverted by shallow concepts of "cycles." The cyclical theory of history is suspicious precisely because we no longer have to come to terms with the actual facts, with social trajectories and tendencies. At every point of investigation, if one makes the assumption that there is a natural process moving round and round, then time is indeed irrelevant and only structural factors become relevant.

How does this operate? "Comparative techniques" indicate that there is social stratification in the United States, in the Soviet Union, and in India. Therefore social stratification is eternal. Therefore a basic principle of sociology is that every society exhibits the hierarchical division of those who rule and those who are ruled. This hoary formulation made by sociologists as early as Spencer, Sumner, and Gumplowicz, and repeated from Brinton to Burnham, only reinforces a disregard for the socially novel. It is quite unimpressive and unimportant whether there is stratification in India, the Soviet Union, or the United States, unless at the same time it is made clear just what the thrust and direction of a society is and the measures by which stratification is either enforced or its effects minimized. Unless sociological facts are regarded in their historical specificity, it is not possible to deal with problems of social stratification and social equality in a realistic way. The precise nature of the "mix" between subordination and superordination, the relationship between coercion and terrorism on one side and consensus and conformism on the other, these are the sociological problems which enter directly into a meaningful consideration of stratification. The simple assertion that stratification is universal is at best a platitude, and at worst a way of obscuring legitimate and basic differences between social structures.

When you break the cycle, when you make the assumption that men do not necessarily tread the same circle but are creatures whose public and private histories have a rise and decline, then you must take up the matter of the degree of stratification, the kinds of power distribution consonant with change, the varieties of planning which minimize or maximize bureaucratic control, etc. The absence of perfect equality no more prevents a theoretical formulation of democratic social systems than the absence of perfect equilibrium prevents engineers from planning and building bridges and tunnels.

The same holds true of the sociology of religion. The pomp, the rhetoric, the apologias that pour forth as the sociology of religion defy imagination.[27] Our sociological textbooks assume that the "functional" character of religion guarantees its future. It is acknowledged that all societies have supported some kind of religion; therefore, it is held to be a permanent feature of all societies to come as well. But the real questions for sociologists are the social functions and the social dysfunctions of a religious code. Is it possible for a society to exist without organized religious institutions? Does the religious leader survive in modern industrial life because of his profane psychiatric advice or his sacred theological wisdom? Are there forms of substitution for gratification of security strivings which openly reject supernatural belief? These kinds of questions are difficult and dangerous. But these are the only kinds of questions worth asking. There is nothing of value in the soothing platitude that religion is functional in American society.

The writing on "Marriage and the Family" in sociological texts is similarly innocuous, bland, and unquestioning. Exceedingly high divorce rates, rising sexual freedom for women in and out of marriage, various social means of child care impinging on a sacred function of the family, the rising and seething egotistic pressures for individual romance—all is more or less resolved in the texts, where the ubiquitous family moves on to "changing patterns" but never declines. It is left to psychologists to manage in embarrassing explicitness the range and patterns of sexual activity. It is left to the brilliant and radical among the literati to mingle analysis with protest, as in Simone de Beauvoir's *Second Sex*. A really professional attitude, though, is cool and unperturbed, measuring gains and losses, full of confidence that there is nothing unmanageable in a tense situation.

If functionalism becomes an escape from providing an insight into social change, then we can expect little beyond apologetics and convenient excuses. Those sociologists in search of an "image" are so sensitive to criticism, particularly from religious and business sources, that they would prefer to cut off their writing hands rather than offer a damaging word about Protestantism, Capitalism, and their sacred bastion the Family (naturally atheism and socialism are exempt from this taboo). With the exception of William H. Whyte, and sociologically trained theologians like Kenneth W. Underwood and Peter Berger, not even the contradictions between a Protestant work ethic and a new Capitalist leisure ethic (which has thoroughly reshaped Weber's image of the classical capitalist model) have merited sufficient attention. Any person of sensitivity can observe the contradiction within American behavior between labor and leisure—between the needs of social production and the status requirements of private consumption. In addition to which there are problems within labor and leisure activities—the problem of alienation in the social careers of men and the problem of taking leisure so seriously that it indeed becomes destructive of such social careers. The emphasis of the papers by Ephraim Mizruchi and Marvin Scott on these themes is indicative of the new problems generated by the inherent absurdity of the poverty of culture beneath the tinsel of affluence.

## V

For a new turn in American sociology, we also need to restore intellect and imagination. Too many technicians are emerging from graduate schools and too few intellectuals. One reason we are inadequately preparing students is that we leave them as we find them—philosophically illiterate. We encourage the fiction that every time a student understands a problem, he has *ipso facto* made some discovery. Sociology students (and sometimes their instructors as well) imagine that the theory of elites was first formulated by Mosca or Michels at the turn of the twentieth century; Plato and Aristotle never enter the picture.

This unconsciousness of intellectual antecedents has even more serious repercussions in the sphere of methodology. The science of logic—the basis of scientific inquiry—is absent from the required curriculum of too many schools, and sociological logics of the type advocated by Herbert Hochberg and Llewellyn Gross are viewed as being of marginal significance. The methodology given in its place is watered down; and it cannot even begin to comprehend the level of the work done in multivalued logic or in modern epistemology. The weaknesses of this anti-philosophic tendency in sociology have become manifestly clear in the last decade. While the sociologists were congratulating one another on having found the "true" method, the functional method (and going so far as to assume that functionalism absorbs both logical and dialectical reasoning), philosophers of science revealed functionalism to be at best a heuristic device and at worst a series of tautologies. We have the philosophers of science to thank for the present openness and experimental atmosphere in sociology. Because of them sociologists have been better able to penetrate method more deeply through logic. It is therefore necessary to study the philosophy of science thoroughly. Any forfeiture along these lines will leave sociologists calcified and ossified in terms of real scientific advances. To recite with impunity the shibboleths of functionalism as if they were a child's first catechism in the face of serious criticism is to ignore alternative methodological tools. To teach sociology as if functional method is the exclusive method is to convert sociology into a higher theology. Methodological dogmatism will tend to debilitate further possibilities for cross-disciplinary researches in a unified language for the social sciences.

Not only in the sphere of methodology but also at the level of ethical analysis do we have much to learn from philosophy. As Gouldner points out, we have altogether too much faith in proud little inherited slogans on the separation of fact and value, and the man of action from the man of thought. We have lived for so long with the dualism of fact and value that we have lost sight of the need to study values, not to celebrate their vagaries. Scholars like Abraham Edel in philosophy, Ephraim Mizruchi in sociology, Ernest Becker in psychiatry, and the late Robert Redfield in anthropology have investigated the facts about values. This, while many still speak of the impossibility of bringing them together. As long as we choose to deem useless logical and empirical studies of value theory, we will continue to be scientific delinquents. To have empirical sociology, as distinct from empiricism, is precisely to confront questions of values, choices, and decisions and to work out the distinctions and the sources of cognitive and emotive claims in the beliefs and actions of men. Sociology cannot be a "policy science" until and unless there is a sociology of ethics and a sociology of sociology plugged into social research as such.

There is a third and deeper level of philosophic sophistication that we must acquire. The problem of meaning inheres in every sociologically significant concept and is at the same time a moral dilemma. The social world is one in which it is not right against wrong, or good against evil, but alternative systems of values fighting each other. It was the poet Goethe and Hegel who first pointed out this great truth. If the world exhibited only a conflict between good and evil, how simple and rapid choices would be. We would always know where to stand, at the side of righteousness and goodness. But then again, of what use would the sociologist be? In a world of the good versus the good, where do we stand? The simple fact of moral dilemma does not absolve one from moral responsibilities; it only intensifies them. Sociologists have been too willing to assume a neutralist posture in the face of ethical choices. Confronting a world of conflicting standards, some sociologists have decided to take the courageous leap to the top of the fence! Equivocation will not suffice. "Objectivity" is not a consequence of standing between two subjective truths. As Robert B. Notestein and Douglas Dowd remind us, it was Mills' importance to see that scientific truth may just as easily reside at the extremes as in the middle. Truth is the intellectual explanation of facts. Belief is a consequence of interests. It takes courage as well as intelligence to distinguish facts from interests. It takes more courage still to see where they intersect and how to proceed from that point on. Sociology in this sense requires courage no less than caution.

Every sociological question is at the same time a moral paradox. Consider the Durkheim theorem that in order to have social mobility it is necessary to accept a certain level of criminality (normbreaking). Social deviance or social violation of law is an essential ingredient in any firm sociological theory of change. The degree of deviant behavior may well indicate the rapidity and extent of social change and mobility. As Merton has pointed out, social alienation and *anomie* may likewise have positive functions. This confronts us with an intriguing moral problem. In treating the problem of the costs of social change as against the benefits of stability, how much deviance ought to be tolerated? And by whom and under what conditions? Consider the significant problems raised by Edward A. Shils.[28] One may want to find out the role of policy-making or decision-making at the juridical level. A microphone is introduced into the jury room to discover first hand, through the juror's deliberations, the decision-making process. Overheard are remarks that indicate the presence of a considerable subjective element. Here is solid information about the way jurors make their decisions about people on trial. Then Shils points out a most interesting moral paradox. The microphone in a jury room violates a sacred norm of modern society: the absolute privacy of the jury room. Now the sociological investigation was clearly legitimate from a methodological point of view. The sociologists wanted to find out the decision-making process at the courtroom level. On the other hand, is it not also legitimate to protect certain myths, norms, laws, and sacred values about the society? Can a sociologist afford to be so insensitive to ordinary life as to fail to take into account the importance of such sacred values as the sanctity of the courtroom? What is "right" and "wrong" in this situation? When does independence slip into irresponsibility? When does the absence of independence slip into sheer conformism? Should the sociologist break the norm to study decision-making processes in the American court system? Should the sociologist be punished for breaking the legal procedure established by precedent and prudence? Whatever the "answer," the fact is clear that ethical deliberation is integral to sociological research. And problems of this kind can be multiplied a hundredfold—in every sphere of sociology, from poll-taking to theory-making.

Take another dilemma: the relationship between social conformity and personal liberty. Generally speaking, sociologists as citizens tend to want to minimize conformity and maximize liberty. But without stipulating specific conditions of social life this desire is a simple platitude. If the extremes are the *Anarch* on one side and the *Behemoth* on the other, and personal liberty threatens the *Behemoth* and its sovereignty, how many sociologists as professionals are then willing to stand by their frequently heard assertions against conformity?

We often criticize the Soviets for their policy of forced allocation of manpower in needed areas, but does not the American policy of monetary incentives for the natural sciences and deprivation for the humanities function to gain the same ends, if not by force, then by bribery? The defense of national sovereignty and the defense of personal liberty may work at cross purposes. The sociologist would be a hypocrite to say that the answer is "in the middle somewhere," and he would be a coward to insist that his studies (and therefore obligations) cease at a purely descriptive level. The hard and fast distinction between psychological motivations for research and research results as such cannot be maintained. It is not the case that "morality" directly enters into the analytical process itself? Is there not a touch of immorality in a secret microphone in a jury room? Is there not a touch of hypocrisy in the jury system? What are the social criteria of legitimacy? What are the needs of a society over and against the needs of a particular institution? Why do people choose rapid industrialization with its attendant psychological turmoil over social stability and norm adherence? Social questions? Yes. Moral questions? Certainly.

## VI

There is a myth extant that "society" begins at Maine and ends at Miami Beach, begins again in New York and ends in California. This notion is doubly peculiar because it is never made explicit. Nevertheless it is reflected by implication and omission in sociological text and theme. The social world, and that of scholarly reference, has become miniscule. It is as if sociology has shriveled up into a form of senile domesticity. The same sociologists who are always impressing upon us the need for comparative study are often least cognizant of their own ethnocentric bias. How can you compare what you exclude from your range of vision? What can be compared? The relationship between the Norton Street Gang and the Hawthorne workers? Or Middletown and Elmtown? These are important but they hardly exhaust the range of even selective comparative measurement. *You can no longer settle any major sociological problem within the boundaries of the United States.* S. M. Miller has indicated as much in relation to "minority problems." Is it possible to treat Negro mass movements with a consideration of the "colored man's religion" (Buddhism or Mohammedanism) as against the "white man's religion" (Christianity)? How can a full treatment be achieved without accounting for the developing African nations or the growth of "negritude." How can you go far in such a field without indicating the extent to which official United States policy has been pushed into democratic channels by a general fear of hostile world reaction to white supremacy? Should not the Negro problem be seen as an illustration of industrial underdevelopment of the South in the United States? Lacking an overall accounting of such questions as the nature of development, nationalism, and racialism, can intelligent results proceed from discussions of the Negro in America? There is an inherited tendency, acutely reflected in the sociological literature on the Negro, to become apolitical in approaching sensitive and delicate problems. When Negroes are discussed, the emphasis is likely to turn excessively psychological. Negro-white interaction is too often examined at the level of parochial values (rarely at the level of international values). We ought not to lag behind the popular consciousness. The American Negro has joined the world. The American sociologists studying "minority questions" can scarcely avoid doing likewise.

The work of Woytinsky and Woytinsky indicates that we cannot examine demography without basing our analysis on some definite correlation of underpopulated and industrialized or under-industrialized and overpopulated. We eventually arrive at a new series of variables in handling huge dimensions of the earth on the basis of interesting and useful models. It is important to bear in mind that models devised to deal with two- or three-person groups need not lead to the trivialization of sociology. The work started by Simmel and continued by probability theory may prove a starting point in developing a method for dealing with two- or three-nation groups. From the point of view of methodology, you can construct a dyadic or triadic model to cover nations as well as persons or groups. *Quantification need not imply trivialization.* International issues can perhaps be handled by available methodological tools. Simmel's general theory of conflict is quite serviceable. His observation that triadic groups tend to be unstable and quadratic groups even more so leads to a general theory of coalitions. Coalitions can be formed at any level of abstraction in interaction. Numbers or quantities are therefore not an inhibiting factor in the formation of social theory. The very tool which is useful at the level of two-person games is also potentially useful at the level

of two- or three-nation involvement. Mills' formula, "IBM plus
Reality plus Humanism equals Sociology," may be a useful slogan
to overcome headcounting and connect sociology to the mainstream of international development.

The ethnocentric properties of American sociology contain a
chauvinistic byproduct. Textbook sociology speaks of European
and American styles of approaching the subject. One gets the impression that the Europeans are inept and incapable of doing
empirical research and that meaningful sociology is strictly an
American preserve, that it rises in righteous revolt against the
European tradition. Too many famous papers have resorted to
these stereotyped characterizations. And yet the very scholars
held to be the leaders of empiricism often emigrated from Europe,
from France, Germany, Austria, Italy, and Poland. Other American
sociologists were trained in Europe and imbibed Pareto, Durkheim,
Marx, and Weber naturally, without recourse to nationalistic sentiment. Even in the early formative period of American sociology
there was a high degree of interaction between European and
American styles in social science. This present ethnocentricity reflects a fascination with machines at the expense of minds. It is a
self-imposed boundary drawn around American sociology as a
special entity. Yet there is a great howl when Russians speak of
Soviet physics. How crude and how obvious of the Russians! Do
they not know that science is international? Have they no idea
then that there is no such thing as Soviet physics? But in sociology
the very people who laugh hardest seem to be willing to speak
of the unique character of American sociology. When Khrushchev
speaks of Soviet scientific achievements, it grates; it offends the
American scientific mind. Rightfully one does not connect nationalism with science. But in the name of "American" sociology there
are those who would perpetrate the same nationalistic myth. Yet
communication in the area of sociology is as swift today as in other
areas, and international conferences as numerous.

If there is the need for increased attention to the history of
philosophy among sociologists, there is perhaps an even more urgent need for greater attention to the history of sociology. This
might lead us out of our prejudices and thrust us headlong into an
international sociology, into what sociologists are doing all over
the world. There are too few of us who know or care about what

sociologists in Paris or Karachi are working on. We scarcely know what the Centre of Urban Studies in London has turned up in the way of a theory of social stratification, or what the work studies program at the Sorbonne has done on Western European patterns of industrial organization. Fewer still know of what social science institutes in Mexico City, Rio de Janeiro, and Buenos Aires have produced on the vital subject of the movement from ruralization to urbanization in Latin America. Too many American sociologists fail to command skills in foreign languages (as do European and Latin American sociologists). They cannot travel without being embarrassed. And they rarely discuss events in terms other than "American interest" versus "other interests." This must cease if American sociology is to be transformed in depth and scope to belong to and reflect the variety and dynamics of the world.

## VII

Finally there is the phenomenon that is termed sociological imperialism. Some of our sociological rationalists regard this benignly, as useful for everyone in the social sciences, and phrase it in pleasant verbal form: "economics and politics as sub-systems of society." It causes some wonder among economists, political scientists, and anthropologists that we regard ourselves as master over all we survey, all the more so since we do not pay particular attention to the findings in their fields. We tend to confine ourselves to the view of sociology as an isolated discipline, or waxing egotistic we imagine sociology to be a synthetic summation of all spheres of social life. We do not treat human problems as large areas needing the investigation of all the social sciences. We will not develop a big-range sociology unless sociology departments help lead the other human sciences to join forces in common scientific tasks. It is only when we have the development of a unified theory of human behavior, when men in various fields of research are brought together who share a common concern for the actual, observable behavior of men in society, that monumental scientific advances will be forthcoming. When study becomes fragmented into superficially delineated specialties, when study "outside the specialty" is held to be a liability rather than an asset, formal rigidities of departmental policy contribute to a distortion of applied social research. It becomes one more factor blocking the passage from social science to social responsibility. There is considerable frustration over the jargon of the special social sciences and the obfuscation that jargonized language helps to reinforce. But to attempt to establish sociological jargon as imperial and supreme is surely not a step in the direction of overcoming problems of professional vocabulary, any more than the question of improving international relations will be resolved by making English the compulsory world language.

Nevertheless progress is being made. Scholarship and journalism have been splendidly bridged by the American Universities Field Staff. Youth development centers, Peace Research Institutes, overseas programs in developing nations, etc., are all moves to integration. Significant interaction will be materially assisted by abolishing rigid departmental boundaries in the social sciences. Professionalism is becoming increasingly dysfunctional.

There are two distinct ways in which sociology can meet the challenge of specialization through inter-disciplinary research. We can take the lead in the redevelopment and reorientation of social science or we can bury ourselves in the higher trivialities. To take the latter path is to run the risk of ending up in an academic museum along with phrenology and alchemy. This may seem shocking and unbearable to contemplate but it is hardly improbable. Every day, business and foundation monies make sociologists richer. We multiply journals quarterly and new recruits annually. How can catastrophe befall us?

The contents of a science are even more subject to change than its forms, to combination and recombination. No professional interests, however adept at preserving present moorings, can stave off such changes. In the one-hundred-year history of sociology, major revolutions have taken place in social existence. But by comparison only slender developments have occurred in sociology proper. Let anyone who doubts the existence of a sociological lag compare the classic figures in sociology with any current survey of the field. The differences are less than spectacular, and not all differences can be said to be for the better.

## VIII

We are entering an age in which the need for international cooperation will either be met, or we will be victimized by a permanent war economy and a perennial cold war. Sociology is being called upon to commit its human and intellectual forces to help solve international friction, with the same patience and perseverance with which it has historically addressed itself to problems of race and community. The past offers guidelines (not mandates) to the present and future. Those whose intellectual horizons are exclusively fixed upon small-group and middle-range problems will either shrivel up and vanish or, what is worse, cause the social sciences to shrivel up. Established sociological ideologies must give way to more sophisticated and democratic norms. The classic tradition of large-range sociology can be employed to help uncover, and thus remove, stagnating vested disciplinary interests and to advance and develop the sources of sociological knowledge.

Interdisciplinary social science does not entail a parochial combination of sociological, anthropological, and psychological verbiage. There is little point to a "unified" system of linguistic nonsense based on eclecticism. Social science is interdisciplinary because social problems are transcultural. Andrew Hacker clearly shows the bearing of political science on Mills' theory of power. How can national boundaries and national pride be consonant, with international communications and transportation already an organized and systematic phenomenon? How can democratic political norms be safeguarded in an era of the fifteen-minute technological war? How will traditional Christian values fare in a technological world of immediacy which reduces every man to the passions of the flesh and the thirst for power? Sociology as a "style of research" can add a major illumination of the problems of man, problems which do not stop at professional boundaries.

The task of science is to lessen the pain of encountering the future by anticipating its problems. In the glow of affluence for the few, our sociology has too frequently deteriorated into cynical apathy. In the chimeric strength of professional exclusivity, sociology has too often lost the qualities that made its ancestry so vital—the impulse to shape a future that is more viable for more people. In the endless duplication of mechanical models we have forgotten that a certain amount of adventurism, fighting spirit, and even insecurity is healthy for the growth of a science. Russell L. Ackoff has put the matter well: "We must stop acting as though nature were organized into disciplines in the same way that universities are." [29]

It might be objected that these remarks are rhetorical and ministerial, in that they apply to an earlier period in sociological history in which the secularization of science was not yet a fact. Pride may lead some to think that ideological commitments have been made superfluous, while prejudice may lead others to believe that ethical guidelines only hamper research projects and prospects. The purpose of these remarks, and of the contributions to this memorial to C. Wright Mills, is to show that nothing could be further from the truth. While it may be the case that shortcomings involving ideological blindness and moral cowardice pervade the social scientific world in general, the burden this places on sociology in consequence is all the more imposing. For the "pragmatists" and "poets" of sociology alike have as an essential obligation the understanding of the social bases of the human condition. Only when we return to a "classic" view of social science can we really get on with the task of forging a "new" view of the field.

Continuity with sociological tradition will assure meaningful departures from that tradition, rather than simplistic and egotistic attempts at being different by being diffident. The past can either obfuscate the future by beclouding the clear needs of the moment or it can illuminate that future by providing signposts for the roads we now traverse. The case for a sociology of the large range rests, like any scientific claim, on utility; in this case the utility of linking past and present in an effort to shape the future with confidence. A science is judged by how much it gives to the world not by how much it extracts from it. Let sociology uphold the scientific tradition of clarification and not the mythic tradition of manipulation. That sociology which rests on "descriptive studies involving random ratlike movements" has had its chance [30]—an opportunity fudged by the anti-humanism of its sociological assumptions, and by cowardice disguised as modesty. When intellect is restored to social science and the cutting edge is put back into social programs, the behavioral sciences will deserve and receive the plaudits which are now reserved for the physical sciences.

## IX

Since this is not simply a volume of essays on social theory and research, but one which has the ulterior purpose of rendering a professional tribute to C. Wright Mills, I should like to conclude this introduction by indicating the kind of sociological work he was engaged in toward the close of his life. It is well known that Mills became increasingly interested in Marxism in the last decade of his work. But what is insufficiently realized is the extent to which he sought in sociology certain answers to, no less than embodiments of, Marxism as an intellectual tradition. While an initial confrontation with the problem of how social science is related to socialism is made in his reader on *The Marxists,* he was well aware of the inadequacies of what was, after all, an introductory analysis.

Mills certainly did not intend to embark upon an anti-Marxist crusade. Yet, he deeply believed that, while Marxism was a basic and fundamental part of the classic tradition in the social sciences, it was only part and not the whole. As such, he felt an ever-deepening need to move beyond Marxism—not by a process of evasion and withdrawal, as had become customary in American social scientific circles, but rather by a confrontation of ideas, a dialogue which was to be a mutually enriching one rather than an ideological free-for-all. As one of the fragments of *Comparative Sociology* (the proposed title of his last work) makes plain, Marxism remained a stimulant and an essential ingredient in any reformulation of the tasks of modern sociology, but it was not to be construed as anything more than that.

> The most revealing *intellectual* terms of our crisis are the conditions and practices of social inquiry and reflection, in particular the abandonment of the classic tradition in sociological thinking. There is much fruitful discussion these days of the humanities vis à vis the natural sciences (in the Soviet Union it is taking the shape of a controversy between physicists and poets over what type of Soviet Man). But in the West, and certainly doubly so in the United States, there has not been an appropriate discussion of the social sciences as a political problem, as a problem for policy-makers. The simple fact is that if we do not develop more adequate sociological theories of the character of present-day varieties in social systems, of the ways in which history is now being made and extended, then the varieties of marxism will fill the vacuum by default.

The essential task therefore was to "fill the vacuum" created by a sociology of false alternatives. Mills was satisfied that he had "settled accounts" with classical Marxism, and he was in the process of preparing an examination of present political and cultural barriers preventing an overall East-West settlement (begun in the *Causes of World War Three* and to have ended with *The New Left*). What remained was a deepening of scientific knowledge about the social world. And in the projected volume on *Comparative Sociology* he aimed at a *magnum opus* that would raise social theory to a social science. The work of G. D. H. Cole on socialist history, E. H. Carr and Isaac Deutscher on Russian political history and social biography, and Joseph Needham on Chinese civilization convinced Mills that he would require a large-scale format if his wide-ranging sociology was not to become superficial and hence unconvincing.

*Comparative Sociology* was both a title and a label which Mills gave to a projected "six to nine volume study of the world range of present-day social structures." Unfortunately Mills never got beyond a few select scenarios of this panorama. He worked up a brief section on the methodology which was to guide *Comparative Sociology*. While it is reminiscent of the last section of *The Sociological Imagination,* it is more sophisticated, revealing a deep awareness of the epistemological issues at stake in methodology. He made four points on how an empirical sociology could overcome the shortcomings of both an empiricism which suffered from the fallacy of misplaced concreteness and a rationalism which suffered from being "abstracted" from experience as such. Mills wanted to employ empirical materials without involving himself in an empiricist methodology, and he insisted upon the need for abstraction in social science without becoming entangled in a network of undemonstrable premises.

The substance of his remarks is as follows: It is not possible to be concerned with the empirical realities without the use of abstraction. One cannot empty one's mind and just see what is what. Even the most fanatical views are put forth in the name of fact or assumed to be self-evident. In selecting what one sees and what one makes of it, therefore, there are meanings, abstractions, and not mere events. The suppression of abstractions only means that they will be smuggled in as general propositions among detailed observations and anecdotes. It is not possible to make sense of what one observes or is told during brief visits without a grasp of at least recent history. What one sees is not just suddenly there. At least part of its meaning lies in its development. And all historical knowledge is abstract—inferences about past events from still-surviving signs and reports. In observing a society, or any specific features of it, one inevitably compares it with other societies one knows. This is a source of standards of perception, but it is crucial for the observer to clarify to himself and in his work just what comparative standards are being employed.

The lectures Mills gave at the London School of Economics in 1960 provided him with the jumping-off point for *Comparative Sociology*.[31] Especially significant to him were the distinctions between the "modern era" or the "Third Epoch" and the "postmodern era" or the "Fourth Epoch." The Enlightenment was symbolic and yet characterized the Third Epoch. Out of it came the ideas of economic rationality (or socialism, broadly speaking) and political libertarianism (or democracy). But the Third Epoch gave way to the Fourth because of the seeming incompatibilities of the two master ideological strains. Rousseau, Marx, and Weber seemed to offer the paradox in stark terms: increased rationality may not be assumed to make for increased freedom. The existence of mass alienation among workers, anxiety among professionals, and anomie among the middle sectors, invalidated the "modern" period. The price of rationality is nothing short of a suspension of freedom (bureaucratized socialism and state capitalism), while the price of freedom is nothing short of rationality—of the suspension of a balanced, developing society.

Thus in the West (and here Mills never quite made up his mind whether the Soviet Union was part of his "West" or not, or if so, to what extent) there is a common cluster of issues which are "epochal" in character. And Mills saw his comparative sociology as entailing a multilinear rather than an unilinear theory of history. Each major world region has its own historic form of development:

> In the course of studying the historical contour of each world region, the impact of extraneous world states will be stated, but to quite varying events. For my contention is that the need for historical analysis varies greatly in importance according to the nature of the social structure that we are trying to understand and explain.

History was to be seen in terms of macroscopic social systems, rather than social systems in terms of history—as one finds in the great historicists from Marx to Toynbee. This emerges in the two root questions Mills feels should be asked by the sociologist:

> What is the nature of our epoch and how best can we define it for study? In short, what are the tasks of a theory of history and how can we best use it to delineate the structure of the present world and the past world? What are the major units of the world's social structure and how best can we define them? In short, what are the tasks of a comparative social science and how best can we set up a comparative accounting?

Mills was confronted by the problem of just what was to be compared with what; and no less, what constituted the basis of selection. For a solution of this problem, he turned to the work of the new "Chicago school" and primarily to the brilliant Sylvia L. Thrupp, a founder of *Comparative Studies in Society and History.* The idea of comparative sociology, borrowed as it is from the science of anatomy, brought new enthusiasm into the kind of social science which Mills came to see as necessary, if a parochial and debilitating nationalism was to be overcome. This fitted in well with the kind of Weberian historical analysis of social character offered by Hans Gerth in an earlier period of Mills' intellectual formation.

What was needed was some way to break the arbitrariness, not simply of ethnocentric accounts of history based on national prestige, but also accounts of history that in their high degree of abstractness and generality were at best "ideal-typologies" with strong subjective biases. The reason for the multi-volume character of *Comparative Sociology* was precisely to avoid making ideal types which are of little scientific relevance and are at best heuristic devices for compelling men to act in a certain way. Therefore Mills' comparative analysis would begin by taking selective areas—demography, economic output, forms of social control, types of decision-making agencies, etc.—and provide an exhaustive account of these selective areas, rather than an exhaustive area with a selective account, as was characteristic of the oracular historicist tradition.

The first volume was intended to provide information on all that could systematically be said about the externals of all world regions. Exhaustion of all relevant statistical and systematic knowledge was a necessary prologemena to set forth key classifications and master trends. Mills intended to deal with 100 nations in terms of an "area code" not unlike that provided by Norton Ginsburg in his *Atlas of Economic Development*. The "area code" was to be reinforced by a study of two phases: the transformation from ruralism to urbanism in each area, and the revolutionary pivots and main drifts in each area. This kind of exhaustive account of developing man could be made possible by the theoretical premise that what happens in one nation powerfully affects immediately surrounding nations within the common region. Presumably, Mills believed that the fact that when "France sneezed, Europe coughed" is conceptually expandable. So that when China flexes its muscles, the Southeast Asian countries do more than just observe. Indeed, the coalescence of geographic, ethnic, and linguistic clustering is one which needs considerably greater amplification before its analytic utility can be established. But the worth of the attempt, whatever the outcome, is incontestable. It would, in Mills' mind, be the first real breakthrough out of ethnocentric "Western" or "American sociology" into a "World Sociology."

The cultural relativism of Malinowski and Benedict in social anthropology was a primitive effort in the direction of a nonethnocentric social science. But since, for Mills, it remained encumbered by the ideological and intellectual commitments of the West, its breakthrough was partial, and intrinsically restricted; i.e. the study of kinship relations in a small Amazon town was exhaustively taken up, while the entire Northeast of Brazil, in revolutionary ferment, went unexamined. The frequent penciled allusions to the work of Linton, Kroeber, and other anthropologists indicate that Mills was not unaware of the possibilities cultural anthropology opened up for the study of world regions. Likewise Mills' growing interest in geographic, demographic, and especially economic problems emphasized his belief that a comparative sociology was indeed possible, if not inevitable.

The only other volume which Mills had sketched out even in preliminary form was one which would take select sociological issues as they manifested themselves in the "four epochs" (ancient, medieval, industrial, and post-industrial); in terms of the regional codes (by continental areas, and by the power blocs: Western, Communist, and Third World), and in terms of economic development (underdeveloped, developed, and overdeveloped). The precise variables he envisioned as necessary for study are: (a) symbol spheres; (b) ascendant modes of communication; (c) public help and social services; (d) world horizons, e.g. manor, nation, cosmopolitan, international; (e) reaches of political power; (f) societal images (God, Reason, Bureaucracy); (g) public relevance and the role of intellectuals; (h) types of personality; (i) forms of legitimation; (j) and, finally, types of anxiety and psychological problems. One can only conjecture about what Mills would have done with his "epochal sociology." For the present, it might be useful to sketch his position on what such an approach entailed structurally.

The idea of an epoch is, as Mills well appreciated, a construction. It is a suggested way of thinking about contemporary society and about the place of this society in the course of history. It is a rather far-reaching idea, for, if taken seriously, it requires the scientist to summarize the pivotal events and decisive trends which characterize contemporary society. More than that, he must do so in such a way as to make plain just how this society differs from other epochs. This means that the construction of an epoch can escape temporal location within a view or theory of human history as a whole. Mills is specific on his recommendations here.

> External events and historical trends are not enough. To make our point that we are indeed being moved into a new epoch of human history requires, first, that we show a shift or a change in the psychological bearings of the individual's biography and character; and second, intellectually, moreover, we must show that the very categories of explanation which served to orient men in past epochs no longer are satisfactory in the present epoch. It is this fact that is perhaps most central in defining an epoch. For the explanations on which men lean set up for them what they expect and what they hope for. And it is by means of the "hoped for" that we can most readily enter into the meaning of an epoch for human and psychological values.

The profound and lasting interest Mills had in the sociology of knowledge, in the study of the ideological and utopistic apparatus that leads to consciousness of society and of interests, is strongly reflected in his final observations on the problem of social epochs. In this, his final discussion of the maximum problem in social history, Mills reaches both sociological and literary heights which inspire conjecture as to what he might have produced. It stands as a powerful description of the relationship between social change and human consciousness.

Men become acutely aware of historic change only when it occurs within the short span of a generation or two. But even when the conditions of their everyday life change very swiftly, even when they come to see that their children face a world which they as children never faced, they come only grudgingly to a consciousness of epochal change. The pace of change however need not be revolutionary, although in our generation it has been. It need not be violent or sudden, although in our generation it has been. More than the mere fact of rapid change is needed. Most men do not feel deeply and completely affected by the fact that since World War II, Asia has again stood up in world affairs, that since World War I, Russia has demonstrated to the world an alternative form of industrialization—the first since the seventeenth century—that the long ascendency of the British has decisively ended, as well as the score of other pivotal facts of the present world. It takes a certain imagination and a certain memory to grasp something of the meaning of these shifts before the meaning comes into your own daily life and you are carted off to war or thrown into an economic slump, or urgently asked to believe new beliefs or to hate new enemies. More than the mere eventful change, even those as fast and prolific and almost total as in our generation, is needed for the consciousness of epoch.

Some men have longer memories and more imagination than others. They are aware of a wider range of everyday milieus, and believe that they understand more of their own times. Such men are likely to become more puzzled, beyond the mere shoulder shrug, when historical change is fast paced. They become puzzled because their explanations break down; then it is that their expectations collapse and sometimes they become more puzzled: they become disoriented. This means, that those who had expectations, those that thought they could explain what was happening in the world came to see that they could not, and hence to sense on every side a new epoch rising. It is in terms of ideology that such men become aware of crisis;

when these crises become more than merely partial, when their whole view of life becomes upset, they experience anxiety. It is out of such anxiety that the epochal consciousness arises.

Beneath anxiety of men with ideology, and the everyday fetishism of men without it, there is more than personal troubles and there is more than ideological confusion in the face of change. Troubles and confusions there may be, but they, in turn, do not spring only from the biographies of individuals. These biographies themselves, the plan of life and the ideological view of things, in various and intricate ways are an intrinsic part of the structure of society. Beneath the consciousness of epochal change, beneath the anxiety and confusion and bewilderment that indicate it, there are changes in the very structure of whole societies inside the entire modern epoch.

This, then, represents the last point reached by Mills in his description of the world, and no less in his own intellectual development. He perceived a great Rousseauian truth at the modern level: every real development involves real social costs; every penetration of the fog of ideology creates new forms of social anxieties.

In these final and agonizing years, Mills addressed himself to the open secrets of society. He candidly recognized the rise of a *Tiers Monde;* he revealed the inner corruption of American deterrence policy; he saw the horrible truth that only the Soviets seemed desperately in need of emulating the American dream world of consumer affluence; he showed that the break-up in the "classic tradition" occurs when men of knowledge render their exclusive services to men of power. Alexander Herzen once wrote that "one has to have great courage to speak out loudly, to say the things secretly known to everyone." Mills had that sort of courage. His audacity stemmed from a capacity to organize and clarify the obvious. The cowardice of his age stemmed from a capacity to trivialize and obfuscate the obvious. For this reason the final and unfinished writings of C. Wright Mills must be seen, as he himself saw them, as part of the ongoing scientific struggle between clarification and manipulation, or, if one prefers, the Faustian struggle between moral tribulation and intellectual treason.

Whether Mills possessed the architectural skills to pick up and structure all the images that enter into a social, political, and historical construction of the modern world (for example, how the "politics of truth" can be linked to ideological awareness) has to remain a moot point. Death at the age of 45 has decreed that no answer can be given. But whether he, or any other man, can any longer scale the heights of social analysis and synthesis is perhaps less important than his willingness to make the attempt. Perhaps the final judgment on Mills will be: Here was a man whose integrity made it easier for the rest of us to speak out; whose honesty made it easier for the rest of us to be honest. When social science is tied to social responsibility, the legacy of Mills will be realized.

NOTES:

1. Cf. Logan Wilson, *The Academic Man* (New York, 1942), p. 33; Bernard Barber, *Science and the Social Order* (Glencoe, 1952), pp. 142-3; and Bernard Berelson, *Graduate Education in the United States* (New York, 1962), p. 226.

2. Stringfellow Barr, *Purely Academic* (New York, 1958), pp. 51-2.

3. Theodore Solotaroff, "The Graduate Student: A Profile," *Commentary*, 32, 1961, pp. 482-90. For an earlier estimate, see C. Wright Mills, *White Collar: The American Middle Classes* (New York, 1951), pp. 129-36.

4. William A. Robson, *The University Teaching of Social Sciences: Political Science* (Paris, 1954), p. 116.

5. Ernest P. Hilgard and Daniel Lerner, "The Person: Subject and Object of Science and Policy," *The Policy Sciences: Recent Developments in Scope and Method*, eds. D. Lerner and H. D. Lasswell (Stanford, 1951), p. 38.

6. Paul F. Lazarsfeld, "Reflections on Business," *American Journal of Sociology*, LXV, July 1959, pp. 1-26.

7. *Institute for Social Research, 1946-1961* (Ann Arbor, 1962), pp. 35-7.

8. Irving L. Horowitz, "Social Science Objectivity and Value Neutrality: Historical Problems and Projections," *Diogenes: International Review of Philosophy and Humanistic Studies*, No. 39, Fall 1962, pp. 17-44.

9. Robert Bierstedt (ed.), *The Making of Society: An Outline of Sociology* (New York, Rev. Ed., 1959), p. v.

10. William J. Goode and Paul K. Hatt, *Methods in Social Research* (New York, 1952), p. 27.

11. George A. Lundberg, C. C. Schrag, and O. N. Larsen, *Sociology* (New York, Rev. Ed., 1958), pp. 722-3.

12. Ibid. p. 721.

13. Cf. in particular, Herman Kahn, *On Thermonuclear War* (Princeton, 1960); and Thomas C. Schelling, *The Strategy of Conflict* (Cambridge, 1960). In this connection see Irving L. Horowitz, "Arms, Policies and Games," *The American Scholar*, 31, 1961-62, pp. 94-107.

14. Leopold von Wiese, *Systematic Sociology*, ed. Becker (New York, 1932), p. 8, also pp. 64-8.

15. Peter Townsend, "A Society For People," *Conviction*, ed. N. MacKenzie (London, 1958), p. 105.

16. Paul Lazarsfeld and Wagner Thielens, *The Academic Mind* (Glencoe, 1958).

17. Theodore Caplow and Reece J. McGee, *The Academic Marketplace* (New York, 1958).

18. Cf. Robert K. Merton, "The Sociology of Knowledge and Mass Communications," *Social Theory and Social Structure* (Glencoe, Rev. Ed., 1957), pp. 439-55; see also, Kurt H. Wolff, "The Sociology of Knowledge and Sociological Theory," *Symposium on Sociological Theory*, ed. L. Gross (Evanston, Ill., 1959), pp. 567-92.

19. Robert Redfield, "Relations of Anthropology to the Social Sciences and to the Humanities," *Anthropology Today: An Encyclopedic Inventory*, ed. A. L. Kroeber (Chicago, 1953), pp. 728-38.

20. Hans L. Zetterberg, *Social Theory and Social Practice* (New York, 1962), esp. pp. 135-62.

21. Cf. Irving L. Horowitz, "Sociology for Sale," *Studies on the Left*, 3, Summer, 1963.

22. Irving L. Horowitz, "Consensus, Conflict and Cooperation: A Sociological Inventory," *Social Forces*, 41, Dec. 1962, pp. 177-88.

23. See in particular, Kingsley Davis, "The Myth of Functional Analysis as a Special Method in Sociology and Anthropology," *American Sociological Review*, 24, 1959, pp. 757-73.

24. Seymour M. Lipset, "Political Sociology," *Sociology Today: Problems and Prospects*, eds. R. K. Merton, L. Broom, and L. S. Cottrell, Jr. (New York, 1959), pp. 89-91.

25. Kingsley Davis and Wilbert E. Moore, "Some Principles of Stratification," *American Sociological Review*, 10, 1945, pp. 242-9.

26. Cf. Theodore Newcomb, "The Study of Consensus," *Sociology Today*, op. cit. pp. 279-84.

27. Kingsley Davis, *Human Society* (New York, 1949), esp. pp. 519-20. Arnold W. Green, *Sociology: An Analysis of Life in Modern Society* (New York, Third Ed., 1960). For an analysis see Irving L. Horowitz, "Sociology and Politics: The Myth of Functionalism Revisited," *Journal of Politics*, 25, May 1963, pp. 248-64.

28. Cf. Edward A. Shils, "Social Inquiry and the Autonomy of the Individual," *The Human Meaning of the Social Sciences*, ed. Daniel Lerner (New York, 1959), pp. 114-57.

29. Russell L. Ackoff, as quoted in Alfred Kuhn, *The Study of Society: A Unified Approach* (Homewood, Ill., 1963).

30. Cf. Samuel A. Stouffer, "Some Observations on Study Design," *American Journal of Sociology*, 55, 1950, pp. 355-61.

31. Cf. Irving L. Horowitz (ed.), *Power, Politics and People: The Collected Essays of C. Wright Mills* (New York, 1963), pp. 221-62.

# I

## C. Wright Mills as a Social Scientist:
## A Collective Portrait

# 1

**ROBERT B. NOTESTEIN**

## The Moral Commitment of C. Wright Mills

In the morally neutral world of contemporary social science, we move through the conceptual corridors of "grand theory" and practice the art of throwing away information systematically. Our trained incapacity to realize that we may be spending our days in an intellectual Utopia [1] or that we are only facing the walls of Plato's cave makes us uncomfortable in the presence of a C. Wright Mills. But if as a result of our distress we on occasion re-examine the social role of the man of knowledge, both our disciplines and our world will be well served. C. Wright Mills served us well. The atmosphere of urgency and concern that pervades his writings can be better understood if we examine the objects of his commitment.

Mills' moral commitment was to reason and freedom. If these values were to be implemented by Mills, the sociologist, what was he to do? As a scholar he would study the "objective chances available for given types of men within given types of social structure to become free and rational as individuals. Another of his themes has to do with what chances, if any, men of different positions in differing types of societies have, first by their reason and experience, to transcend their everyday milieux, and second, by virtue of their power, to act with consequence for the structure of their society and their period." [2] As an instructor he must address three audiences: those who are well aware of the power they

exercise; those who have power but are unaware of the consequences of their actions; and those who are without power and
without awareness of structural changes in their society which may
be the causes of their personal troubles.[3] He must attempt to edu-
cate each public in the consequences of their action or inaction,
and he will then hold them publically accountable.

Assuming we acted in terms of Mills' model of the sociologist,
what does he believe are our chances of influencing any of these
audiences? The chances are poor. The conditions that would have
to be present before we could wield this power would be the existence of "parties and movements and publics having two characteristics: (1) within them ideas and alternatives of social life
are truly debated, and (2) they have a chance really to influence
decisions of structural consequence." [4]

These two conditions of effective teaching are, viewed from another point of view, Mills' definition of democracy. "Democracy
implies that those vitally affected by any decision men make have
an effective voice in that decision. This in turn, means that all
power to make such decisions be publicly legitimated and that
the makers of such decisions be held publicly accountable." [5]

From still another point of view these two conditions constitute
a model of a social structure that ordered his description of twentieth-century American society in *White Collar* and *The Power
Elite*. Mills was a successful American practitioner of the sociology
of knowledge.[6] He conceived of the "sociological imagination" as
designed to examine issues raised by the intersection of history and
biography. This conception of the "sociological imagination" was in
turn formed by his belief that "it is the felt threat to cherished
values—such as those of freedom and reason—that is the necessary
moral substance of all significant problems of social inquiry, and
as well of all public issues and private troubles." [7] *The Power
Elite* is his outline of the nation's public issues, while *White Collar*
is his outline of the private troubles of a significant proportion of
our population. The issues and troubles are seen as a threat to the
values of freedom and reason.

The values of Mills as a person and sociologist were not derived
from the culture of scientific endeavor. The community of social
scientists was not his spiritual home. I would suggest that his
values were molded and fixed by the events in the late 1920's and

early 1930's in the United States, events that led to an "elective affinity" between the interests of Mills and the ideas of his two mentors, Thorstein Veblen and John Dewey. I would agree with the statement of Hans Gerth, "Coming from the open spaces of Texas with five persons per square mile he responded with all the compassion and righteous indignation of the middle class man out for a better world and smarting in impotent agony." [8]

In order to find a time, a place, and a social structure where his concept of freedom and reason was relevant, Mills, like other insurgent middle class Americans, turned back to the image of a time already constructed for us by other American critics from the Middle Border: Frederick Jackson Turner, Vernon Parrington, and John R. Commons. Daniel Bell has contradicted this view by saying, "The peculiar fact is that, while all the illustrations Mills uses are drawn from American life, the key concepts are drawn from European experiences," [9] and he refers, among others, to Marx, Pareto, Mosca, Balzac, and Mannheim. If Bell means that Mills, as a result of his alienation from the America of the depression years, took over not only the conceptual tools of these Europeans but also their perspectives in the manner of a T. S. Eliot or Henry Adams, I believe him wrong. To suggest that concepts drawn from European experience will necessarily distort the "reality" of the American experience is to imply a theory of American "exceptionalism" which Mills certainly did not share.

In *White Collar*, Mills introduces his chapters on the Old Middle Classes with a quotation from the English economic historian R. H. Tawney: "Whatever the future may contain, the past has shown no more excellent social order than that in which the mass of the people were the masters of the holdings which they plowed and of the tools with which they worked, and could boast . . . it is a quietness to a man's mind to live upon his own and to know his heir certain." [10] For Mills, the place was the United States west of the Appalachians. The time was "between mercantilism and subsistence farming in the beginning, and monopoly and high finance at the end . . ." [11] or what the historian has called the Middle Period or the Jacksonian Period delimited by the end of the War of 1812 and the outbreak of the Civil War. The American social structure of this era can be divided into the institutional orders of economy, religion, polity, kinship, and military.

In the economy the small entrepreneur was central. A majority of the population owned the property with which they worked. They held not merely an investment but controlled the conditions of their work, and hence were independent men. The economy was self-balancing, with authority exerted by impersonal regional markets. The ordering of market relations was left to "wide-flung traditions." In the polity the constitutional division of authority both between and within state and federal government was a fact, not an ideology. Party competition for the votes of individuals involved public debate in regional or community voluntary associations. In religion there was a variety of sects and denominations which engaged in open competition for larger congregations. The institutional order of kinship took its form from an open marriage market where individuals chose one another. In the military order there were relatively autonomous state militias composed of farmers with rifles available for duty until crops needed harvesting, not a hierarchy of ranks co-ordinated by sudden commands and military deference.

"The principle of integration—which is also the basic legitimation of this society—is the ascendancy within each order of the institution of the free initiative of independent men in competition with one another." [12] Each institutional order is believed to be autonomous—and is to be free from the co-ordination by other orders. "In this society, the elite becomes a plurality of top groups quite loosely made up." [13] No one of them is sovereign. Within each order claims to status are validated, not by appeal to family dynasties, but by individual accomplishment.

This era of classic liberalism was for Mills not merely a time when economic and political competition held the society together; it was also a time when the exercise of freedom and rationality by the individual was possible. *The Power Elite* and *White Collar* represent, in my view, portraits of a society which has fallen away from what Mills considered a state of "social grace."

Mills cannot be classified as a radical of the stamp of either a Herbert Croly or a Louis D. Brandeis. He states quite specifically that he does not know what is to be done. "I do not know the answer to the question of political irresponsibility in our time or to the cultural and political question of the cheerful Robot." [14] What was Mills' concern may be judged from an assessment he made of Thorstein Veblen which might apply to him as well: "His criticisms of institutions and the personnel of American society was based on his belief that they did not adequately fulfill American values. If he was, as I believe, a Socratic figure, he was in his own way as American as Socrates in his was Athenian." [15]

NOTES:

1. Ralf Dahrendorf, "Out of Utopia: Toward a Reorientation of Sociological Analysis," *American Journal of Sociology*, 64, 1958, 115-27.
2. C. Wright Mills, *The Sociological Imagination* (New York, 1959), pp. 184-5.
3. Ibid. p. 185.
4. Ibid. p. 190.
5. Ibid. p. 188.
6. "Language, Logic and Culture," *American Sociological Review*, 4, 1939, 670-80; "Methodological Consequences of the Sociology of Knowledge," *American Journal of Sociology*, 46, 1940, 316-30; "The Professional Ideology of Social Pathologists," *American Journal of Sociology*, 49, 1943, 165-80; the previously unpublished paper "The Language and Ideas of Ancient China." All of these have been reprinted in *Power, Politics and People: The Collected Essays of C. Wright Mills*, ed. Irving L. Horowitz (New York, 1963).
7. *The Sociological Imagination*, p. 175.
8. Hans Gerth, "Charles Wright Mills, 1916-1962," address given at memorial service at Columbia University on April 16, 1962.
9. Daniel Bell, "The Power Elite—Reconsidered," *American Journal of Sociology*, 64, 1958, 244.
10. C. Wright Mills, *White Collar* (New York, 1951), p. 1.
11. Ibid. p. 6.
12. *Sociological Imagination*, p. 45.
13. C. W. Mills, *The Power Elite* (New York, 1956), p. 271. *The Sociological Imagination*, p. 176.
14. *The Sociological Imagination*, p. 176.
15. *The Power Elite*, p. 108.

# 2

DOUGLAS F. DOWD

## Thorstein Veblen and C. Wright Mills: Social Science and Social Criticism

This essay comments on one vital aspect of C. Wright Mills' complex life and work: his role as a radical social critic. In doing so, it will compare Mills with Thorstein Veblen, another academic radical, in the hope that a perspective can be gained on the limitations of, and the need for, academic social criticism today.

On personal grounds, Mills and Veblen stood in seemingly sharp contrast: Mills was gregarious, Veblen a virtual anchorite; Mills was outspoken and political, Veblen oblique and (or so he presumed) politically aloof; Mills was aggressive in life and muscular in print, Veblen retiring and, as a writer, involute. Mills was unusually knowledgeable, but not, by temperament, a scholar. Veblen was a "born" scholar, but found himself drawn into combat—in his way—with the hurly-burly of his day. Even aside from the linguistics involved, Mills would not have worked through *The Laxdaela Saga;* Veblen could not have written a *Listen, Yankee*.

There still remain many points of similarity between the two. If not with quite the same style or method, Veblen could have written *The New Men of Power, White Collar,* or *The Power Elite;* similarly, Mills could have written *The Theory of Business Enterprise, The Nature of Peace,* or *Absentee Ownership*. Even more clearly, what Veblen attempted in economics in the essays collected in *The Place of Science in Modern Civilization*, Mills later at-

54

tempted in sociology in *The Sociological Imagination*. What ties the two men together, despite their differences, is the similarity of their values, their aims, and their function as social critics.

Although Veblen repeatedly dissociated himself from any involvement in the matters on which he commented; and although Mills may have fancied himself at times as a detached scholar; the nature and consequences of their work—in different ways, because of their different contexts—were the same: they stood as beacons of systematic social criticism in a Saragossa Sea of academic insipidity. Whatever their influence or lack of it on their colleagues, both Veblen and Mills were read widely by a public who expected social criticism from social scientists. There were no limits of breadth or depth to the scope of Veblen and Mills: they were radicals.

The two were much alike, then, in the comprehension and coherence they attempted, in the degree to which they were willing to probe, and, it must be added, in the degree to which they failed. If others have matched their failure, none has matched their reach—or their grasp.

Neither Veblen nor Mills was a radical in a programmatic sense; neither had a program. They did not accept society as it was. Both had a single commitment, barely disguised in Veblen and less so or not at all in Mills, to the well-being of mankind. The bedrock of their commitment was composed of the same elements: democracy and individual liberty, peace, and material well-being. If they both believed there were limits to what these values could achieve, only those limits imposed by time, technology, and the painful evolution of social consciousness were legitimate. All other limits were irrational and should be eliminated as quickly as possible; all else was sand in the gears.

They saw these impediments as the institutional foundations of modern society, for Veblen "the vested interests," for Mills "the power elite." Even more was implied in the existence of an ideology and substructure of privilege and irrationality which supported these foundations. Both of them felt that human betterment required profound changes in the political, economic, military, and social framework of American society. No specific program was required to qualify them as radicals; these views were sufficient in themselves.

Indeed, given the dimensions of the problem of social progress, as delineated by Veblen and Mills, a program would have been a premature expression of hope. For them, as earlier for Marx, the point was not to "concoct kitchen recipes for the future" but to lay bare the anatomy, the physiology, and the nervous system of the present for those who, armed with understanding and intention, could, as Veblen put it, "save themselves alive."

The notion of a "commitment to the well-being of mankind" has been used here to distinguish Veblen and Mills from the bulk of their colleagues, and this will perhaps be taken as a net large enough to catch all but a few social scientists—not to mention, these days, politicians, businessmen, and even generals. The liberal rhetoric is the air we breathe; but as it is usually meant, like the air we breathe, it is polluted. The pollution consists of the unconscious or conscious adjectives that almost universally precede "mankind." These adjectives designate class, nation, color, religion, or similar divisions. They are adjectives, as Veblen would say, of invidiousness. Where they are relevant, they are in the nature of things taken for granted, beyond dispute: even beyond conversation. It may of course be hoped that adjectives denoting color and religion are slowly diminishing in frequency; perhaps, in a confused way, the same may be said of class; but nationality still remains a repository of invidiousness.

Neither Veblen nor Mills prefaced "mankind" with any adjective. Neither could abide exclusiveness or privilege; neither could find any class or group to hail. Both were democrats; both, though American to the core, eschewed patriotism; both, though middle class in origin, status, and function, were repelled by the feudalization of status and the commercialization of values of "middle-class society."

If these things were true of Veblen and Mills, what is the case with other social scientists; where do they stand? On the urgent analytical and practical issues of our day, academic social scientists tend overwhelmingly either to conform to the popular view or help to create it; they avoid issues and submerge their audience and themselves in technicalities.

Veblen and Mills went to the roots of society to seek the source of its diseases; and they proclaimed their findings to the literate public, as well as to their colleagues. They did so, not without fault, and not without error; not, in Veblen, without obscurity. But they made the attempt. They developed systematic analysis that searched and roamed, cutting across time, place, "problem," and discipline. This was the strength they shared; and it was their mutual weakness.

It took strength, and determination, to stand against the onrushing, bloodless specialization and trivialization of the social sciences —a trend which, just beginning to emerge in Veblen's time, now approaches the limits of credibility. The weakness of Veblen and Mills was not particularly theirs; it resided in the fact that they attempted so much, in almost a lone endeavor—and in a society that, because it needs serious analysis, erects towering obstacles for those who would make the attempt.

Progress in science requires well-trained minds working diversely and freely, and as specialists, toward a common end of understanding. The end sought by Veblen and Mills—an understanding of the conditions for a viable and humane world society —would be difficult to attain under the best of circumstances. But when the surest means of success in the world of the social sciences lies in technical obscurantism—in, for all practical purposes, raising walls against knowledge—then a Veblen or a Mills can hardly be condemned for falling short of his goal. The economist Rothschild, in a related context, once remarked that "it is better to be vaguely right than precisely wrong." Veblen and Mills were, at their best and at their worst, vaguely right.

It is, of course, impossible to be precisely "right" about the larger dimensions of the human condition. But even to be tolerably "right"—that is, to have an adequate framework of social theory— clearly requires considerable specialization within the social sciences. It was not specialization as such against which Veblen and Mills reacted. Specialization is frequently a necessary foundation for systematic analysis. But they did react against specialization developed without conscious reference to or adequate training in the larger body of knowledge and purposes of one's presumed discipline.

Veblen and Mills, working too much alone, did well to be as vaguely right as they were. The least that can be done by those who share their commitment is to reduce that vagueness by using the available energy and skills to fill in the many gaps they left.

If social theory in its youth was too grandiose to be entirely mean-ingful, its present tendency is toward a chaotic pulverization. For society to be understood, it must be appreciated as well as studied —which is to say that specialized studies and analyses, indispensa-ble though they are to understanding, will achieve meaning and coherence only if unified by consciously held values. The social scientist who reaches for this goal faces formidable problems, most of which were faced in one way or another by Veblen and Mills.

Among the relevant personal and practical problems, those that have to do with career, or even livelihood, loom large. Even Veb-len and Mills, who were possessed of talent to a high degree, paid a price in this area for their ideas and their stance. Veblen's diffi-culties in gaining and keeping a first-rate academic post, his slow promotion, and his low salary, need no recounting here. And, if Mills did not have the same difficulties, this may be explained in part by his location within one of the bastions of academic free-dom in America, and in part by the fact that his role as an unremit-ting social critic did not become apparent until late in his life. When that did become apparent, his professional life became combative, and, in some unfortunate degree, warped.

Both Veblen and Mills were outsiders by birth—given their career choices. Both became, in addition, professional outsiders, standing off to view society critically. In fact or in effect, they withdrew from their colleagues, from their profession, even from their professional responsibilities, as their work and views fell into a persistently critical pattern. Their ability, and finally their desire, to communicate with professional associates suffered in this respect.

The path of social criticism, for both Veblen and Mills, was strewn with the sharp stones of bitterness, and it produced, to-ward the end of their lives, a quality of shrillness in their writings missing in their earlier years. Living in a society that seemed al-most eager to verify their gloomiest observations, and surrounded by colleagues who viewed them with a combination of tolerant amusement, hostility, and obliviousness to the import of their theories, both men became increasingly intemperate, and have been judged by what they had become.

Need this be so? If the conventional become mellow to the

point of blandness as they age, must the unconventional become all bile? Only, I think, if to be unconventional means to work alone; to become, as a tendency, an intellectual gunfighter, or a recluse. Veblen and Mills had professional defects and were less than perfect as persons; but surely much of this resulted from working under conditions of too little professional co-operation and recognition, and too much professional hostility—conditions conducive to imbalance in manner as well as in analysis.

Social critics should not of course expect rewards from the society they dissect—although there is an important sense in which the affirmative could be made. But the personal cost of a critical stance might well be reduced, and the quality of its product improved, were the number of functioning social critics to expand, and to move toward the goal of a better understanding of society.

The academic profession in America is the social critic's refuge; even, in extreme cases, his foxhole—with all the limitations of such a vantage point. And, although academic freedom has had an honorable career in some American colleges and universities, the percentage of such cases has been small, and in recent years has shrunk. As a concept and an ideal, academic freedom—in some full sense of the term—is barely understood, let alone supported, in the larger community; within the academic community it has more frequently been identified with narrow considerations of job tenure than with creating and maintaining an atmosphere within which the free pursuit of understanding might prevail. But, like other freedoms, the stunted quality of academic freedom in America may be explained in part by the infrequency with which it is exercised.

There have been periods of vitality for the academic social critic in America, and during them social criticism and academic freedom have risen together. Social Criticism was rampant in the 'thirties and in the immediate postwar years, and not in college faculties alone. It was in this period that Veblen received his greatest success and firmest appreciation; that Mills himself received his education; when the social sciences most actively performed their function of social criticism; and, finally, serious social critics, though never as secure as their conventional counterparts, had more security than at any time before or since.

This did not happen just because the 'thirties were economically depressed years—however important the depression was—or because today follows upon McCarthyism. The problems of today's America are not less vital—the contrary is clearly true—than those of the 'thirties and the immediate postwar years. That they are less evident may be partly due to the fact that many of today's social scientists have become celebrants or defendants of their society. Certainly McCarthyism would not have had quite the impact it did if academics had stood together to argue the principles of a free society.

The few social critics of today stand isolated, etched against the horizon. Social criticism is less productive of useful results because the problems afflicting society are immense and ever more complicated, while simultaneously the number of those attacking these problems is reduced through specialization. The techniques of the social sciences have narrowed the training and the focus of the novice, while the institutions of modern society have infringed more and more in this field. These two developments complement each other: the economist can now work for business groups, for labor groups, or for the military, say, to the profit of both himself and his employer. Much the same is true of the sociologist, the political scientist, the psychologist, and even the anthropologist. "Society" in the social sciences becomes increasingly something to be manipulated for the benefit of one or another of its component parts—one or another of its "vested interests." None of this represents a conspiracy among evil men; it is a process as "natural" as the flooding of river valleys in the absence of dams and levees. But there has been a default among social scientists, whose function—if it is anyone's—is to construct the needed dams and levees.

The ranks of social critics in the social sciences, never thick, are steadily thinned out; the supply of recruits diminishes to the vanishing point. Potentially interested undergraduates are bored, and turn to more purposeful or coherent disciplines; or, they stay, they become steely-eyed, if amiable, technicians. The few critically-minded students who survive the undergraduate major in the social sciences, in the mistaken expectation that graduate work will at last introduce them systematically to the urgent social issues that first attracted them, find their frustrations compounded. They become part of a mindless procession that moves from sociology to sociometrics, from economics to econometrics, from economic history to—the term is careening into usage—cliometrics. The social sciences cannot make sense or progress without quantification and logic, to be sure; nor can they make sense or progress if their practitioners are informed by quantification and logic alone.

The manner in which the foregoing process has accelerated and spread might be likened to Gresham's Law in economics, where bad money drives out good. As the study of moral philosophy and social problems moved toward "social science," the process of specialization, and the development of usable quantitative techniques, have been natural and indispensable accompaniments. But, given the pattern of rewards in the academy, these indispensable developments have been debased, and the future of the social sciences is unseemly indeed if current trends are not interrupted.

One normally has to teach in the academy, and the better teacher—other things being equal—is preferred to the poorer. But rewards are meted out first and foremost for publication; publication, in turn, is hastened by a narrow focus. This in turn leads to quantification. There are, of course, elements of the picture that keep it from being entirely dismal: some who publish much, publish meaningfully; some quantified work is broad in focus, and some that is narrow in focus is valuable; generalists, who preserve breadth and imbue purpose as teachers are still rewarded, particularly in smaller colleges, although decreasingly so in the large universities. The trend remains a forbidding one.

This is the era of the research grant. The foundations and other institutions issuing grants, beset as they are by applications—and apart from any more insidious motivation—tend understandably to seek objective criteria as their guides. This quite naturally inclines them to the narrow, the quantifiable, and ordinarily the noncontroversial, for such projects are likely to be finished with dispatch. Those who receive the bulk of the available grants tend, in the course of time, to gain power in the best faculties of the land; they, in turn, set standards for admissions and curricula. The mastery of technique and the acquisition of perspective, both essential, become competitive; and the latter gives way to the former. In addition, the undergraduate curriculum is steadily infiltrated by attitudes and purposes and training that fit this process. Thus, specialization and quantification—necessary attributes of science—take on a life of their own which dangerously threatens the historic perspectives and purposes of the social sciences.

Today there are many social scientists, trained in an era before "the end of ideology" who still listen, and who seek ways to work honestly and effectively at the tasks cut out for them years ago. For Veblen, these tasks meant the study of institutions, whose very existence meant they were to some degree in need of reform; for Mills it meant "structural criticism" that emphasizes the qualitative aspects of existence, explores relationships, illuminates process, and brings value to bear on fact. Surely a return by social scientists to such purposes could stem the hemorrhage of bright and concerned students that has so weakened the vitality of the social sciences in recent years.

In considering the respective areas of teaching, research, and writing, we may learn something from the experience of Veblen and Mills, not all of it positive. As teachers, both Veblen and Mills had devoted students. Neither developed a "system" or an associated "school"; nor, it appears, was either inclined or able to do so. One consequence of their lack of system is that their "followers" have marched, or, rather, lurched, off into diverse and even contradictory directions. By comparison with their colleagues, both Mills and Veblen were defensive in their attitudes toward teaching. Veblen's defensiveness was hidden behind a mask of diffidence amounting to virtual hostility. Mills, in his last years, had despaired of graduate instruction; or, when he felt there were promising lines to follow on that level, he found himself blocked by unsympathetic colleagues. Both finally did battle with the academic establishment—Veblen doing battle against the "immature and reluctant" students and the "captains of erudition," and Mills against the "slavish" enmeshed in the coils of an "adaptive organism." So, literally or figuratively, Veblen mumbled and Mills shouted.

What, then, is the legitimate role of the social critic as teacher? Should the podium, for instance, be used as a soap-box? It should not, and it need not. The college teacher has two roles to play in the classroom: to convey knowledge and to stimulate thought. This is true in all fields; not least in the social sciences. Of the two functions, surely the latter is as important as the former; and, if the function of graduate instruction is more justifiably that of training specialists, the least that those so engaged can do is to insist that graduate students are given adequate general training.

To stimulate thought is to ask questions, even to provoke confusion; to distinguish myth from reality, cranks from theorists, the trivial from the vital. We need not be reminded that all teaching, thought, and writing is selective. Are the principles of selection for the conventional teacher more readily justified than those for the critical analyst? If anything, the teacher in the social sciences who implicitly or explicitly supports the "establishment" is as much in default of his professional obligations as a doctor who confines his diagnoses to cheerful comments about his healthy patients.

Nor is it necessary for the professor to have a program—at least, not in the classroom. To probe is not to preach; to ask is not to answer. The alternatives are not "neutrality" and "advocacy." To be uncommitted is not to be neutral, but to be committed—consciously or not—to the *status quo;* it is, in Mills' phrase, "to celebrate the present." To be committed in the classroom means to place the intelligence and energies of students at the disposal of their values through the employment of the procedures of science. And if in the process the social scientist must give up some precision for some vagueness, no one will be the worse for it. In a free society there need be no fear of minds being led down one path to the exclusion of others. Today, there is greater danger that minds will not pursue any path; that they will spin on dead center.

As for research and writing, it is not being proposed that social scientists be college debaters; or that they write general articles for *Harper's, The Nation,* or the *New York Times Sunday Magazine.* Those may be useful activities or not; but no particular focus on time, place, or issue, or any particular level of discourse is proposed as being more useful than another. What remains important is that the social scientist is committed and that his work is relevant to that commitment. This is as true of the classroom as it is of the study. Technique is vital, if it is related to integrity. Seemingly minute research projects are vital, if those engaged in them are aware of their relevance to the major problems of our society.

In this realm Veblen and Mills stand the critical social scientist in good stead. They left gaps; in the case of Veblen, they at times pursued a will-o'-the-wisp; they offered too many generalizations with too little support. But they did ask important questions, and they took long strides toward answering them. Mills and Veblen asked essentially the same questions, although their somewhat different societies and the passage of time required that each had to look in somewhat different corners, and had to emphasize different problems in their critical analyses.

It is illuminating to consider the number of matters which Veblen and Mills examined in common: war and peace, power, class, status, property, economic development—and, significantly, higher learning and methodology in the social sciences. Both men considered all these matters merely different aspects of the same problem—the achievement and maintenance of civilization as defined by the values they held. The confrontation of this problem today will require a vast range of social studies: large and small; statistical, historical, theoretical, and methodological; in sociology, political science, psychology, anthropology, and economics. The list can be extended. They are studies informed by our hopes, our fears, and our knowledge, given to us by our society and our values. They are studies the principal dimensions of which have already been sketched out and, to a significant but desperately inadequate degree, filled in by a handful of social scientists. We need not search for problems to investigate, and, indeed, in this world, with the serious problems at hand, we cannot afford to do so. We cannot afford, in Spender's words, to "lecture on navigation while the ship is going down."

There are doubtless many social scientists today to whom what has been stated above would appear as mere sentimental gibberish. For them, the larger problems of mankind seem to have been resolved, or put beyond resolution: ideology or even idealism among social scientists, whatever role they may have played in the past, may now seem to be unnecessary or possibly dangerous baggage, or whatever is left can be transmitted through a computer; or utopia, perhaps Nirvana, waits around a nearby corner. These arguments cannot sway such minds.

For those who share the values of Mills and Veblen—those who see civilization as yet to be achieved, except for some tiny percentage of the world's people—the job ahead requires the greatest diligence, co-operation, and good sense that can be mustered. In the forefront of those engaged in this work must come the social critic, who recognizes, in Veblen's words, that "the bonds of custom, prescription, principles, precedent," must be broken, lest history record another and perhaps ultimate "triumph of imbecile institutions over life and culture." Which bonds must be broken, where, why, and how, and which can and should be modified or even extended, the social scientist must try to understand. When he assumes that task, he becomes a critic of his society, as Veblen and Mills have been before him.

# 3

PABLO GONZÁLEZ CASANOVA

# C. Wright Mills: An American Conscience

Mills was a good writer: he knew how to write and concerned himself with writing well. He had a rich and finely shaded use of language. Mills studied sociology and philosophy in the United States and thus knew the techniques of research and analysis of North American sociology. He knew and mastered the bonds that link sociology and philosophy; his works include studies on sociological theory and political thought and others based on direct field work and grounded in statistical analysis. He did not always follow North American sociological techniques, and yet he was extremely faithful in the long run to his own philosophy and morality. He was inconsistent in technique and consistent in philosophy. Toward the end of his life, Mills embarked upon problems which could not be discussed in the United States and not only declared his position but pointed out a new path to his country. He was a man with an "extravagant" message—"a noble gadfly" like Socrates, who fluttered over his gigantic nation to warn it of dangers, to offer it modest success if it acted in accordance with reason and morality.

Perhaps on reading this portrait of Mills one may think that it has something of the rhetorical, like eulogies of the dead. Nevertheless, bearing in mind Mills' risks and re-reading his work one sees that this really is how he was. It seems inconceivable that it

could have been so; that he could have been the living image of a
romantic man—impulsive, reflective, and so consistent, for his entire life.

Mills' portrait does not correspond to the stereotype of a sociologist. The stereotyped sociologist has no nostalgia. He either
does not have or does not display any moral concern. He systematically eludes "politics" and is summed up—as Mills himself
observed—in the politics of the *status quo*. He is not ideological
because that is not scientific. He does not dig into the roots of
human problems, nor do big solutions appeal to him. He does not
know how to write well. He is not a non-conformist, a "deviant."
He is a methodologist, a technician, an expert, an experimental
investigator, a statistician; he is also assiduous about small problems and carefully controls all the variables, save those of the
corporations, the elites of business, politics or the military that pay
for his work, and those that serve his theoretical and mathematical
models, his field investigations, his prudent analysis, his sociological experiments. Or he merely executes studies that have no use
to anyone, with sociological "spleen"—à la Homans—with irritation
and without commitment or concern for reform or revolution.

Such is the patented sociologist's image, product of a search
for rigor in the study of man and in the process of rationalization
for the political weaknesses of the investigator. Mills did not fit
this image. As an anti-stereotype, Mills quite naturally was disqualified, unrecognized, and degraded, especially when he touched
upon forbidden themes, or failed to make criticisms more or less
pleasing to the governing elite, or firmly implanted in the North
American conscience a problem as serious as Cuba. A campaign of rumors and gossip began to disqualify him, to declare
him a journalist in the pejorative sense of the term. This campaign
has had results particularly among sociologists in the United States
and conservative sociologists everywhere. It is a tenacious and
irresponsible campaign, whose consequences are not so grave for
Mills' memory as for the ability of the social sciences to engage
in fruitful scientific analysis of contemporary social problems in a
time of crisis.

Mills could not be disqualified, punctured with a pin like an
insect and made to pass into the collection of political animals
that try unsuccessfully to be sociologists. And the patented so-

ciologists cannot pursue their course as if nothing happened, satisfied with their rhetoric and their reasons. The animus between the partisans of Mills and his detractors is difficult to resolve, since the arguments have not been carried to their ultimate conclusions. The official sociologists pursue a series of arguments that have great attraction and an indisputable validity. Heirs of the scientific spirit, of the experimental method, emulators of the techniques of analysis of the natural sciences, they walk into the twentieth century treading on favorable terrain, confronting the intuitionists, poets, philosophers, and politicians. From this point of view they are attractive. Moreover, the effective use of scientific method— reflective, skeptical, experimental, rigorous, quantitative, accumulative—gives to many of their investigations an indisputable value. For these reasons, it is difficult to destroy what is false in them on theoretical and academic grounds.

However compelling their undoubted rigor, the knowledge they obtain is open to serious question and the regions they fail to explore very large. No one doubts that the methods and techniques they profess and use may be valuable and useful for successful generalizing and for establishing precise relations of factors, but they do not realize that such techniques and methods are unusable for the treatment of the more important problems in the contemporary world.

Contemporary social science is at the level of "artisanry," of small enterprise, and of the monopolies. In its varied styles it reflects the folklore of the artisan; in the diversity of its models and measurements it confirms that at best it has contributed to the age of small enterprise; in its uniformity and in the artificial creation of demand it reflects monopolistic organization.

North American sociology is a curious mixture of these three forms. On no account, however, does it represent a really universal and objective science that attempts to rid itself of the folklore of capitalism. If North American sociology were concerned with consequences which were politically viable and realizable, it would not tie itself, when undertaking projects designed to enhance its prestige, to the giant corporations, with their documentary centers, equipment for field research, electronic machinery, model builders, researchers, enumerators, analysts—all of whose research plans or designs are controlled in advance. When undertaking such work, it would allow for rigor and uniformity, freedom of research, and investigation at an internal and international level of fundamental social phenomena.

The ideal projections of sociology are of course unrealizable. In the present state of research not even annual data and the most elemental statistics are universally employed or applied. Sociologists barely attend to the primary normative efforts. More important, with all the rules of scientific investigation at their disposal, all they study are the orthodox themes of sociology: stratification, mobility, social change, and conflict. This elaborate apparatus, however, is never used to study problems that are prohibited in sociology; those of social structure in a world dominated by monopolies. In such a state of affairs, folklore imposes itself; the small enterprise, with the small businessman-worker or the captain of industry, survives in the universities and institutes, while large-scale research works through the subsidy or in the service of the monopolies. No one escapes from this reality, and all discipline is reduced to artisan proportions, or to that of small business or the monopoly. That its findings may on occasion be laudable and individual studies valuable does not excuse its enormous limitations.

Under these circumstances the voice of Mills achieves a far greater transcendence and respectability than anyone is willing to recognize. Mills can and does have a scientific folklore, but it is that of an independent entrepreneur; he possessed the great audacity of a Civil War general, a conqueror of the Far West, or a railroad magnate of the nineteenth century. In curious form, his conservative characteristics—his attitude of the old world, his longing for America as a promised land, his undeniable admiration for small business and small owners (so evident in the first chapters of *White Collar*)—left him unsatisfied and moved him to commit himself to the new utopias of the socialist world.

But this nostalgic stance of impresario and romantic made him reject official sociology and violate the limits it imposed. It made him touch upon the forbidden themes in social science and American life. It made him look for the solutions to the problems of war and imperialism, of mass society and the society of hunger. The work of his final years takes on more and more of an emotional and accusing tone. It acquired more literary tone and less rigidity, especially when treading upon the forbidden, as in speaking important truths about the problem of the United States and Cuba. He then could be seen, not only as an impressionistic sociologist, but as a writer who knew the techniques of the interview. At the very moment that Mills spoke of "big truths"—his moment of "sin"—he tried to abandon the sociological nearsightedness and official politics of his own country and to gain knowledge of the fundamental problems that attracted him and made him the intransigent defender of the North American conscience.

His confrontation with the national mythology and with the monopolies did not lead him to an accurate appraisal of the role of political mythology in modern capitalism, that is to say, to the Marxist position. He could not follow through precisely because he was a liberal to the death and because he was North American to the marrow in both his individualism and his critical spirit.

The Marxist influence on Mills emerged through the intermediary of Max Weber. Marxism represented for him a more and more attractive alternative the more closely he approached forbidden areas; but his need to reject anything that was official brought him, as it had earlier in Cuba, to an attitude verging on revisionism and the European third force, an attitude that never left him. He moved into the position of the "new left," that position which has its base in the "third world" in which the conceptions and categories of Marxism undergo practical revision, designed to strip it of dogma and slogans and allow it to promote effectively revolution in the hungry countries of the world.

For a short time Mills regretted that he touched political ground, that he flavored his writing with politics. Nevertheless, he was not satisfied, because his really basic concern was to resolve the problem of this terrain, that of political life. On this ground he was a precursor—a great precursor.

When Mills wrote *Listen, Yankee*, he did not write it to be read by Cubans. He wrote it to be heard by Americans. His book was a warning to prevent an error in United States foreign policy. And he himself believed in power to prevent that error. He was a utopian, for when the United States government did not hear him, he did not despair. He upheld his ideals "in a utopian way, while waiting." Another book, *The Causes of World War III*, had a similar end. He knew he was a utopian, and he accepted his role in order to fulfill his intellectual mission. In both cases Mills stood firmly by the perspective of a North American non-conformist on the two great problems of the contemporary world: imperialism and war. He stood up to them like a utopian and a moralist, despite the fact that he was a good North American and a practical man.

Actually Mills was ingenuous; but he could find no other way. He could not move toward an impoverished proletariat nor to a hungry people. He could not believe that Marx's view that the proletariat was the force of history could be applied to the United States of 1960, nor did he believe in the support of the leaders of the third world. His people were opulent, overdeveloped, opposed to change. But he did not despair altogether; for he searched for help wherever he could find it, among the students, professors, intellectuals, scientists, clergy, and others who represented what was decent and moral in North America.

In political terms, he was a small force and he knew it. He came from a country of white-collar strata, workers, conformists, masses; he lacked the powerful instrument that might allow the change from an aggressive economy to a politics of development. The human resources that he counted on were very small. The moment had not arrived, and Mills was aware of this; he was a precursor. Like all precursors he was a realist politician without common sense.

The final years of his life revolved around an essential problem of contemporary society; the possibility of total destruction through atomic war. This possibility could not be contemplated by men before the two great powers established the "balance of terror" by which they could destroy themselves and the world. At the end of his life, Mills was deeply affected by this danger. All his work in his last years was directly or indirectly bound up with this concern. He struggled against the liberal rhetoric, Marxist dogma, and sociological dehumanization; he struggled for the North American conscience, for Cuba, and for the poor countries; above all, he struggled to define the true task of the intellectual in an international society with nuclear arms and to define the paths of liberalism and Marxism when there already exists the possibility of nuclear war. He saw these were the proper tasks of social science in the atomic age. It is not necessary to repeat here what Mills has already said on these problems. It is far more important to apply his findings to the solution of an existent problem and to define it in terms of how he set it forth and measured it for us.

The danger of atomic war put the problems of humanism in new terms. Mills approached this novel danger, which has no historical precedent, in an elemental way. His reactions to the danger manifested themselves mainly at the emotional level, psychologically and ideologically. Social theory had not kept up with the rapid, profound changes and the unexpected social situation that they had produced—namely, the actual possibility that man could end his own history. The two ideological currents of our time—liberalism and Marxism—had not followed these changes to their ultimate consequences, which would mean a total adjustment in the analytic concepts and the political focus of the modern world. All these forces had done was to register certain changes and collect some new data. Above all, this superficial ideological response, with its backwardness and suspicion of outsiders, was seen most clearly in the lack of support given to the great social reforms of the age, which in Mills' view represented the only way out of the present danger. He could also observe that the same Marxist or liberal phrases which had been used to explain social change—internal or international—before the danger of atomic war, were now inadequate and inconsequential for the new conditions.

Mills gave a clear account of everything preceding this present danger. It was only at the start of this century that in both liberalism and Marxism, it was considered desirable to reform capitalism. The typical liberalism of North America opposed reform because it clung to the old values emanating from the Yankee experience—absolute freedom of enterprise, freedom of commerce, no state intervention. Marxism opposed the capitalist reform because it was a form of "attenuating the class struggle," of "alienating the proletariat," and of "hiding the contradictions of capitalism." Reform was attacked by liberalism because it smashed "liberty," while Marxism contended that it would hold back the "social revolution." The reformists are stigmatized, either because they refused to come to terms with the existing situation, as the liberals urged, or because they refused to recognize that the only solution was the overturning of the existent order, as the Marxist contended.

The transformation of social structures in the twentieth century has brought both sides to make partial concessions to reformism:

within liberalism, the Keynesian current and the New Deal experience constitute a form of concession; within Marxist thought, the thesis that in some countries "a peaceful road to socialism" may be possible constitutes another concession. But these concessions are made reluctantly for pragmatic and theoretical reasons and are condemned as violations of the sacred principles of Liberty or Revolution, of Free Enterprise or Class Struggle. This mood of irritation and concession has not yet disappeared, notwithstanding the novelty of the danger human society faces from atomic war. The classic models of liberalism and Marxism still remain the theoretical and political conscience and models for our time, and all deviations from them are seen as diminishing the theoretical perfection and destroying the ethical and rational beauty of these models.

Nevertheless, the monopolistic and technological advance of modern society coincides with the burgeoning of a war economy, and depends on it for its moderating influence and anti-cyclical force, while, at the same time, the increased standard of living and the broadening tax base in the developed capitalist countries have destroyed much of the basis of the class struggle of the nineteenth century. The result has been a general conformity extending from the great masses to the leaders. The North American people know—as Mills says—that the war economy is the basis of their employment, and they tacitly support it. This dependence on a war economy has destroyed the relevance to their society of the classic model of liberalism. The working masses of North America are at the opposite pole from a revolutionary spirit, and, what is more, the working classes of Europe, including those affiliated with the Communist parties, are at the opposite pole from this revolutionary spirit and from the classic model of Marxism. Thus, only a mystical view of liberalism can claim any relevance for it in a world dependent upon the war economy and the society of war. And only a mystical view of the proletariat can conceive of it still as the motor force of the revolution. The intellectual and governing elites agree unwillingly to these violations of the ideal models, conform unwillingly, but refuse to recognize that only through profound social reforms can the way be discovered to prevent an atomic war.

The United States, for instance, cannot sustain itself and continue to develop while it remains tied to the war economy. This is a fact more than it is an accusation; a fact that Mills recognized and one that underlies the conformity of United States society today. North American society does not believe that these conditions can vary and that it can continue to develop social reform programs, similar or superior to those of England, France, Sweden, and Norway, which would make the war economy unnecessary. And for its part, Marxist thought and socialist societies continue maintaining that capitalism necessarily must go to war. Both worlds and theories go on viewing with apprehension, skepticism, or displeasure the idea of social reform in the capitalist countries and in the United States. Both have become converted—without wanting to be—to the "metaphysics of war."

This problem, directly linked to the survival of man, is an intellectual and political problem. Nor is anyone in a better situation than the North American to study what concerns him, and no one better situated to put an end to the "fetish of indecision," the provincialism, and the liberal rhetoric that—as Mills said—are irrelevant to the problems of today's world.

On their side, the socialist countries and the Marxist theoreticians have an equally important task; that is, if their primary objective is peace and they recognize the necessity for peaceful co-existence. If socialists recognize that there is small chance that the proletariat of the United States and the other developed countries will make a revolution, then it is only logical that they recognize the need for supporting reform in these countries. Similarly, they should stop bedeviling those Marxists who do advocate this reform and those who seek to investigate the possibilities of capitalism in a peace economy. The struggle against "official" or "orthodox" Marxism, in the religious and bureaucratic sense of the term, is then indispensable, and it is very irresponsible for Marxists to view thinkers like Mills as simple "revisionists" in the pejorative sense, or to accuse them of treason to Marxist theories.

On the other hand, the hungry peoples—the small and the large underdeveloped nations, semi-colonial or semi-independent—cannot ignore the fact that their struggle for independence and development is one of the strongest links in the struggle for peace, and that it represents their most important theoretical and political problem. Also, the theoretical and scientific instruments that these nations develop for dealing with their problems may form the basis for a new model of development whose ethical and theoretical beauty may surpass the classic models of Marxism and liberalism, allowing them to take their place in history without bringing about the end of history itself.

Mills, as a precursor of the theory and politics of our time, tackled all these problems and left us with an idea of what ought to constitute sociology in his formula: IBM + reality = Humanism. In the long run he stripped down the formula: he studied and applied the techniques; he eviscerated North American reality. He was a sociologist and the conscience of the United States. Because of this, Mills remains for a long time to come a model of why we think highly of North American sociology.

# 4

RALPH MILIBAND

## Mills and Politics

"Inside this country today, the Labor leaders are the strategic actors: they lead the only organizations capable of stopping the main drift towards war and slump." "What the U.S. does, or fails to do, may be the key to what will happen in the world. What the Labor leader does, or fails to do, may be the key to what will happen in the U.S."

I doubt that many people would recognize C. Wright Mills in these quotations: they are taken, among many similar statements, from *The New Men of Power*, the study of American labor leaders and American trade unionism which Mills published in 1948.

This is not one of the books upon which Mills's reputation as a social thinker is based—and it is true that it does not, for all its scholarship and depth, have the same originality and sweep as either *White Collar* or *The Power Elite*. Yet, *The New Men of Power* is a good point from which to begin an assessment of the nature of Mills' political commitments. The book provides a convenient and even indispensable point of reference for measuring the distance which Mills traveled in his mature political life; it also enables one to understand better the sombre mood of most of his subsequent work.

There are features of Mills' political evolution from *The New Men of Power* of 1948 to his writings in the 'fifties, particularly the late 'fifties, which are peculiar to him alone; but there are also aspects of that evolution which are obviously part of a much more general trend, particularly in the United States. Mills should not be cast as a "representative" figure, nor should he be stereotyped as a "hero of our times." But the political fears, the hopes and the anxieties which he articulated were scarcely his alone; in his own way, he provides an element, perhaps a significant element, in the biography of a generation.

From this view, *The New Men of Power* may be seen as one of the last expressions, before the big freeze set in, of the hopes engendered in and by the Roosevelt era, if not, as far as Mills was concerned, by the Roosevelt Administration itself; it marks one of the last expressions of that era's hope that America might be humanely turned into a progressive society by means of a political alliance between labor, white collar, and intellectuals.

The hope was already heavily mortgaged in 1948, and *The New Men of Power* hardly reads like a message of optimism and good cheer. Still, the hope, however faint and qualified, continued to stir: there did exist a way out for the United States.

A decade later, even such cautious optimism seemed absurdly starry-eyed, certainly to Mills. The intervening years, "the mindless years we have been enduring," as he bitterly called them in 1955, had left their creases on minds as well as on faces; the dirty gray of the 'fifties had seeped in everywhere, choking many, frightening others, corroding the spirit of all, even the boldest. These were bad years for good men. And they were the years in which Mills did his main work.

One feature of Mills' political commitment which immediately invites attention is that it is very difficult to give it an obviously appropriate name. Attempts to do so, often with ill-intent ("Texas Trotskyite" was one of the more colorfully inaccurate labels foisted on him), have not carried much conviction. He obviously belongs on the left, but his particular place there is not easily determined. To say that he was a socialist may be a beginning, but it is only in an exceptionally backward political and ideological context, such as that of the United States, where socialism is still invested with highly-charged meaning, that it can be said to afford a useful preliminary element of identification. However, since socialists come in all shapes and sizes, the question remains as to what this meant in Mills' case.

Nor is the difficulty made any easier by a review of Mills' political past, for the good and sufficient reason that he had no political past, that he never belonged to any socialist group, faction, or party, and that he does not appear to have been sufficiently in sympathy with any socialist tendency in America to identify specifically with any of them. He found the Communists morally, intellectually, and politically impossible; the various Trotskyite sects were too disputatiously futile for a serious man to bother with; and the social democrats were, so to speak, too social democratic for his robust political tastes.

Politically and temperamentally, Mills was a determined nonjoiner, with an intense dislike of togetherness, including political togetherness. This undoubtedly saved him from much political strain, not to speak of the waste of time, and it also saved him from the necessity of painful political disengagements. Even so, the political isolation which was willed upon him by circumstance and predilection was by no means all gain. Nor was his academic isolation. It seems best, at any rate, to forget about labels and tags and to look at Mills' political commitment from a rather different angle—to ask, for a start, what Mills was against.

Mills, as everybody knows, was a "critic of American society." But this is even less useful than the socialist ascription, since critics of America are two-a-penny; such criticism is in fact a major American industry—there is a good living in it, depending on the kind of criticism provided.

Unlike many critics of American society, Mills, in this as in many other respects, went the whole hog. He was not a critic of this or that particular aspect of American society, of this or that evil in American life—he was against the American condition as a whole, against the way America went about making a living, against the way it treated people, against the way it conducted its political affairs, against the values, rhetoric apart (indeed, rhetoric included), by which it was guided; he was against what America was doing to itself, and what it was doing to the world. The point must not be burked: in relation to American society, Mills was wholly alienated and utterly unsentimental; his commitment, in a negative sense, was total.

Yet, it is misleading to say that Mills hated America: the formula allows too much play to feeling and too little to rational opposition; and it also ignores that there was much in America which Mills liked. The point is rather that what Mills did like in America was of less importance than what he disliked. There was a balance, but it was unfavorable.

Nor had Mills transferred his affections from America to another country. He had no adopted country. He had no national affections. He was remarkably free from national commitments. He did not "believe" in America, nor did he "love" America. He did not feel that the nation-state, including his own, was a fit and proper object of allegiance, either in war or in cold war. "I cannot," he wrote in *Listen, Yankee*, "give unconditional loyalties to any institution, man, state, movement or nation. My loyalties are conditional upon my own convictions and my own values"; and these, he added, "lie more with the Cuban revolution than with the official United States reaction to it." This, it may be noted, is only a restatement of a classic liberal position: that it should have come to constitute so unusual a stance is a token of the nationalist emphasis which has so deeply marked this century. Mills couched his declaration of independence in extremely comprehensive terms, so comprehensive as to demand a degree of lonely rationality which is very hard indeed to live by, but by which he himself did try and live.

There was a personal, biographical element in Mills' attitude to America, obviously not sufficient in itself, yet significant in combination with other features of his personality; namely, the fact that he did not leave Texas until he was over twenty-one. Mills came to the big city as a stranger, and he saw it with the eyes of a stranger, sufficiently familiar with America-beyond-Texas not to be without bearings, not sufficiently familiar to take too much for granted; only a provincial could have written the extraordinary chapter on Macy's in *White Collar*. Mills himself believed that his particular reaction to American society had much to do with the fact that he only properly entered it after he had grown up. This would hardly have been enough to give him depth and understanding; but it did give him distance without a loss of focus, and freshness without bafflement. By a curious twist, his very provincialism helped him to escape the nationalist trap, and to avoid national sentimentality. He was indeed violently hostile to nationalist celebration, anywhere, to flag-waving, to the use of the past for the purpose of blackmail. He was a most historically-minded sociologist, but without any reverence for antiquity. He liked England, but what he liked least about it was its obsession with the day before yesterday; the dislike induced in him a perverse and ostentatious philistinism: he simply would not be moved by the grace and beauty of Cambridge, because it was old; in London, he knew well the area between Bloomsbury, where he usually stayed, and the London School of Economics; but he never actually went to see anything in London. His curiosity, which was insatiable, lay in other directions.

Mills himself was very conscious that his work had a critical, "negative" quality. But rejection can never be purely negative, least of all wholesale rejection. Denial entails affirmation and it is always in the name of values that values are buried. Even nihilism is an exceedingly positive commitment to a certain view of life. For Mills, the point of reference was the vision of a society where men might achieve control of their fate by the use of knowledge and reason, and where men's social and institutional setting would encourage self-cultivation and craftsmanship.

Mills' rejection of America has sometimes been construed as due to a nostalgic longing for a vanished, pre-industrial age, for a rural, small-town, one-man-one-gun America, with the lone ranger as the ideal human type. This is based on a confusion. If the frontier is taken to be synonymous with individuality and independence, Mills was undoubtedly for it, since he greatly admired both qualities and was greatly drawn to Whitman's "man in the open air." He had no wish, on the other hand, to idealize the frontier, and he was too good a sociologist to believe that only the frontier could produce individuality and independence. Himself a gifted technical man, he had due regard for technology. What he objected to in industrial capitalism was not industry but capitalism. He certainly did not believe that working with spinning wheels was the secret of the good life; on the contrary, he knew well that technology in a humane social setting was the key to man's liberation for the cultivation of individuality and craftsmanship. He knew, too, that his critique of America could only be relevant and

fruitful if it was made from the vantage point, not of a pre-industrial age, but with the projected hopes and ideals of a post-capital-
ist era, in which the claims of property and profit would have come
to be seen for the vulgar distraction that they are.

Mills was a moralist as well as a moral man. He somehow managed not to lose a rare capacity for sustained indignation. He was
the least resigned of men, either for himself or for others. At the
same time, he was well aware that unfocused indignation is harm-
less petulance and that moralism without social analysis is private
self-indulgence and public deception. With the right to denounce
crime goes the duty to locate the criminals, and to expose them.
To speak and act as if there can be crime without criminals, or to
pretend that all are equally guilty, is a dereliction which Mills
judged harshly, and which he fiercely denounced, never more eloquently than in his *Pagan Sermon to the Christian Clergy.*

The largest part of Mills' sociological work was concerned with
power, its contemporary nature, its location, and its sources. He
has been accused of being "obsessed," "haunted" by power, and by
hatred for men of power. This is in any case a strange charge in an
epoch which has seen power used and abused on an unprecedented
scale. But in truth, it was not so much by power that Mills was
haunted as by powerlessness. Fewer and fewer men, he believed,
had it in their power to make decisions of enormous consequence
for, or rather against, the mass of men. Indeed, they had it in their
power ultimately to decide life and death for untold millions. Not
only was that power growing irresponsible: it was also cumulative,
in that it included the power to manipulate opinion, to shape news,
to engineer acquiescence, to turn rational "publics" into apathetic
"masses." Had he only applied his analysis to the Soviet bloc, he
would not have raised a stir. Instead, Mills had the bad taste to
insist that it applied to the United States, that things were not
what they were reputed to be, that there existed a steadily widening gulf between democratic rhetoric and the reality of power, between democratic ceremonial, however elaborate, and elite decision-making.

Mills wrote about elites, but he was not a writer for the elite. He
did believe that concentration of power, generally for nefarious
ends, was one of the dominant characteristics of his times. But he

did not believe that elite rule was inevitable, and that the only important and worthwhile problem in relation to power was to find which elite would rule best. He did not wear his democratic beliefs on his sleeve, and in the formal sense in which the term has increasingly come to be used in liberal theory, he was not much of a democrat at all. But his political point of reference, inseparable from the others, was the need for democratic participation at all levels and at all points of decision-making, industrial as well as political, on the job as well as in the polling-booth. It is significant that he should have chosen the words of an unknown worker in Nevada as the epitome of *The New Men of Power:*

> When that boatload of wobblies come
> Up to Everett, the sheriff says
> Don't you come no further
> Who the hell's yer leader anyhow
> *Who's yer leader*
> And them wobblies yelled right back—
> *We ain't got no leader*
> *We're all leaders*
> And they kept right on comin'.

There was in Mills a not very dormant anarchist. His whole personal system of feeling was anti-elitist, anti-bureaucratic, anti-state. He himself reacted with raw intensity to other-imposed rules and regulations, and he had a passionate dislike of little men with large stamps. He knew the weaknesses of the anarchist position, and he was wary of the demagogic denunciation of authority. But he also believed that a constant emphasis on the libertarian and "utopian" element in socialism was essential. His first visit to Poland in 1957 coincided with the debate then going on between "revisionism" and official thought. In that debate, Mills found himself torn more than he would have expected, and more than he liked, between two tendencies, neither of which he felt himself able to endorse wholeheartedly. But in the conflict between authority and its critics, he could not help his sympathies being committed to the critics. He had, in the 'fifties, moved from his earlier view of Russia as a "bureaucratic tyranny." But he remained deeply suspicious of its bureaucratic bias. Precisely one of the reasons which caused him to place such high hopes in Castro's

Cuba was his belief that a fusion could occur there between revolutionary freedom and revolutionary authority.

Mills was very suspicious of lyrical upsurges and visionary evocations. But it is impossible to read him without being made aware of how seriously he took "the central goal of western humanism . . . the presumptuous control by reason of man's fate," of how untainted he was by smart cynicism about humane alternatives to the here-and-now. Like any serious man in the twentieth century, he found himself with dilemmas, ambiguities, and doubts. But he had no difficulty in knowing what he was against and in deciding what he was for. His difficulty lay elsewhere: in locating the means of radical change.

"There are no national parties," Mills wrote in *The Power Elite,* "to which the professional politicians belong and which by their debate focus national issues clearly and responsibly and continuously." This is one of the recurrent themes in Mills' writings on politics in the United States. He believed that the main political parties, far from offering any obstacle to what he called the "grim trivialization of public life," were themselves important channels of manipulated irrationality: association with them, or with their leaders in office, must entail more compromise than could ever be warranted by the likely results—intellectuals who see themselves as gray eminences usually end up as gray apologists.

Mills' alienation from the normal run of American political life was pushed to rather unusual lengths. The first election in which he was entitled to vote was the election of 1940: I think I am right in saying that he did not vote in that election, nor in any subsequent election, presidential, state, or local. To belong in a political sense, he wrote, meant "a belief in the purposes and in the leaders of an organization"; it was "to make the association a psychological center of one's self, to take into our conscience, deliberately and freely, its rules of conduct and its purposes, which we thus shape and which in turn shapes us." "We do not," he concluded, "have this kind of belonging to any political organization."

It is not at all certain that Mills could ever have found a political organization worthy of quite the kind of allegiance he described; and whether a political intellectual should accept so thorough a commitment to a political party is itself a matter for debate. Total identification may well be crippling to the mind, just as total homelessness is crippling to the spirit.

Homelessness may, however, be viewed as a temporary condition, in which case the absence of an effective agency of desired change is endurable, though frustrating; far worse is the belief that such an agency is most unlikely ever to come into being. This is the real change in Mills' political outlook and perspective between the 'forties and the 'fifties. He had thought, in the earlier period, that organized labor might form the basis for a new movement dedicated to radical pressure and change. "The American worker," he had written in *The New Men of Power*, "has a high potential militancy when he is pushed, and if he knows what the issue is"; "the American labor unions and a new American left," he had also written, "can release political energies, develop real hopefulness, open matters up for counter-symbols only if they are prepared to act boldly and win over the less bold by their success." The qualification did not belie the hopefulness of the prospect.

In *The New Men of Power*, Mills had also made a sharp distinction between organized workers and the "underdogs," "those who get least of what there is to get." The underdogs, he had written, "are ignorant and often too timid to judge the weighty questions which poll-takers and politicians offer them. Their withdrawal and isolation is literally of such an extent that they do not know what they might wish for. To endure this life requires a low level of aspiration which softens the will and creates apathy."

An essential element in Mills' political evolution is that he had come very near, in the 'fifties, to attributing to organized labor the characteristics, in political if not in economic terms, which he had earlier attributed to the underdog alone. Over the image of the potentially alert and politically involved worker, there was superimposed the terrible image of the "cheerful robot," as the typical product of advanced industrial society. One image spelled hope, however deferred; the other despair, however qualified.

Once Mills had dismissed as a "labor metaphysic" the belief that organized labor could provide the base of a new radical movement, what was there left to sustain belief in the possibility of structural, as distinct from marginal, change in American society, or for that matter in advanced industrial societies generally, since he thought that labor in all such societies was subject to the same debilitation which had, in his view, affected American labor? Who would there be to defeat the reactionary purpose of the men who determined America's role in the world? Mills answered that there remained the intellectuals.

Mills had always stressed the importance of the role which intellectuals must play in the shaping of a radical movement. "To have an American labor movement capable of carrying out the program of the Left, making allies among the middle class, and moving upstream against the main drift," he had written in 1948, "there must be a rank and file of vigorous workers, a brace of labor intellectuals, and a set of politically alert labor leaders." These, he had also insisted, could only hope to be effective in alliance with each other. But as he lost hope in the capacity of organized labor, so did he come to attribute an independent political role to "scientists and artists, ministers and scholars ... those who represent the human intellect ... who are part of the great discourse of inquiry and reason, of sensibility and imagination."

It is important to see clearly what is here involved. Mills was not asking intellectuals to "enter politics," as the term is commonly understood. On the contrary, he sometimes seemed to go right to the other extreme. The "joint political-cultural struggle," he wrote in 1959, "must be waged in intellectual and moral ways rather than in a more direct political way"; "we cannot," he also said, "create a Left by abdicating our roles as intellectuals to become working-class agitators or machine politicians, or by play-acting at any other direct political action." Far from inviting intellectuals to engage in political activism, he almost appeared to make a virtue of non-participation.

It was a position which he himself could not sustain, as was shown by his own involvement in the United States-Cuban conflict. But what he was concerned in stressing was that intellectuals must not allow themselves to be deflected by the lure of "practical" politics, that they must practice the "politics of truth," even though this might be called "unrealistic." As early as 1944, Mills had warned that "if he [i.e. the intellectual] approaches public issues 'realistically,' that is, in terms of the major parties, he has already so compromised their very statement that he is not able to sustain an enthusiasm for political action and thought." He was well entitled to think that the point had not lost its relevance fifteen years later.

It would be foolish to dismiss the "politics of truth" as of no consequence and equally foolish to underestimate the influence which intellectuals may wield in their society. Nor even should the notion be rejected out of hand that intellectuals might be, as he said in 1960, a "possible, immediate, radical agency of change." The difficulty is that Mills was not talking about any kind of change but of change in the basis and character, the tone and texture of the social order; and change also in the character of America's role in the world. As for this, it was Mills himself who, paradoxically, provided ground for thinking that he was pitching his hopes for intellectuals much too high.

This, it should be noted, is not because intellectuals are not "committed." Mills knew that this was not the question at all. For intellectuals and academics as a matter of fact are, when it comes to the point, quite definitely committed—not least, certainly, in the United States, probably the only country in the Western world where it is impossible to switch on a television set at any hour of the day or night without finding some academic sounding off on some officially consecrated scourge. Even those who preach the end of ideology are themselves highly committed: what they want is not the end of ideology, but conversion to their own very ideological form of social quietism. The question is not commitment as against non-commitment. The question is what intellectuals are committed to, and how seriously. The answer, which Mills himself gave, is that intellectuals, for the most part, were committed to low-temperature liberalism. In fact, that was exactly the trouble.

Mills' critique of American liberalism is one of the dominant themes of his work throughout. In one of his first published essays, *The Professional Ideology of Social Pathologists*, written in 1941, when he was twenty-five, he had already dissected with great skill the character and motivation of one facet of liberalism; namely, small-scale and small-minded social engineering, which he was later to call "liberal practicality," and whose quite deliberate and often explicit purpose was to search for adaptation and adjustment to social framework deemed beyond question and beyond probing. What Mills condemned in safety-valve welfarism was not the welfare, but the refusal to consider the possibility that it was the machine itself which ought to be scrapped.

Liberalism in the twentieth century, Mills said again and again, had gone flabby and conservative. It had become a rhetoric of apology, a way of masking reality, a means of clouding issues, an obstacle to understanding and to significant action. "As a rhetoric," he wrote in *The Power Elite*, "liberalism has become a mask of all political positions, as a theory of society it has become irrelevant, and in its optative mood, misleading."

This view of liberalism is quite obviously relevant to the discussion of the intellectuals' political role. For if liberalism was in fact the ideology of so many academics, intellectuals, and social scientists, indeed the intellectuals' very own form of false consciousness, it must also follow, quite apart from all other considerations pointing to the same conclusion, that intellectuals could not very well be expected to play the role which Mills had assigned to them. Intellectuals, it may be worth repeating, can play a role as intellectuals, and Mills was quite right to urge that they should. But they hardly play the role, all by themselves, of gravediggers of the old order. Despite all the disappointments of the years following *The New Men of Power*, I think that Mills was closer to reality, politically and sociologically, when he pinned his hopes to the alliance of radical labor, white collar, and left intellectuals.

True, such an alliance, for truly radical purposes, seems very unlikely in the United States. But it may at least be a beginning to see that the business of radical politics in the United States will not get properly under way until it does come on the agenda. The crowning paradox of Mills' contribution to American radicalism is that, when that alliance does come into being, when socialism does again become a serious as well as a subversive word in the United States, Mills, who had come to despair that it would, will be honored as one of those who, in the dark and hollow years, made the rebirth possible.

# 5

ROSE K. GOLDSEN

## Mills and the Profession of Sociology

As I reflect on C. Wright Mills, Swift's epitaph springs to mind:

> ... whose savage indignation can no longer lacerate his heart.
> Go, passerby, and imitate if you can
> This strenuous defender of virile liberty.

I am reminded, too, of Arthur Koestler's moving essay on "the screamers." [1] The term harks back to an old dream in which, Koestler says, "I scream for help but nobody hears me, the crowd walks past laughing and chatting." In the same way, he feels his written essays scream to attract the attention of those of us who refuse to face "the reality of horror" in the society we live in. "... perhaps it is we, the screamers, who react in a sound and healthy way to the reality which surrounds us, whereas you are the neurotics who totter about in a screened phantasy world because you lack the faculty to face facts. Were it not so, this war would have been avoided, and those murdered within sight of your day-dreaming eyes would still be alive." [2]

Mills was a strenuous defender of virile liberty and a screamer. He hit hard at the injustices of the social order. He chose to be a sociologist because he saw it as the profession that had the concepts and skills—and thus the responsibility—to expose and correct such injustices. He felt that the profession was abdicating this responsibility, and he criticized it most bitterly for this.

Mills told the profession: Just as the business of physicists is to understand matter, so the business of the sociologist is to understand social structures. At this point in history at least, the principal way to "get a fix" on social structures—if not the sole way—is to study power: where it resides, who wields it, how it is used, and how misused. The sociologist who avoids studying power in social structures seriously increases, if he does not in fact guarantee, the chance that he will end up with trivia. This summarizes Mills' stand on scientific policy.

Mills told the profession: Because the sociologist's product can be utilized in the manipulation of human beings, every sociologist has the obligation of interpreting his work and communicating his findings to the public. We must endeavor to make sociological knowledge as inescapable for men-on-the-street as are the doings of Li'l Abner or the virtues of the latest detergent. A discipline that yields knowledge and provides tools for the potential manipulation of men must make the possibilities of such manipulation clear, very clear, to its possible victims. This position confronts head on the matter of professional ethics.

Finally, Mills said to the profession: Anyone who studies the workings of power in today's social structures finds over and over again that the wielders of power are perpetrating injustices and endangering the safety, dignity, and even the human-ness of humanity. The sociologist must therefore persuade first the intellectuals and through them the citizenry to forestall and check these injustices by changing the social structures that misuse power: governments, corporations, armies, schools, churches, professional societies. This takes a position on the tactics of inducing social change.

Sociologists who do not follow these three principles were, for Mills, at best engaged in trivial mental exercises, at worst handing themselves and their science over (deliberately or by default) to the Establishment.

To his position on scientific policy the professional sociologists replied: "What we choose to study may seem trivial to you; but the peas Mendel studied were also trivial. When we discover the equivalent of genetic laws you'll see you do us an injustice."

To his argument that sociologists have a particular obligation to

join the ranks of "the screamers," the more unsympathetic members of the profession replied "yellow journalism," or "not our
style." The sympathetic ones said: "All right, but in a different role.
Not as a sociologist but as aroused citizen, journalist, publicist,
or propagandist."

To his point on the tactics of social change, those of the profession who consider themselves in the camp of the social reformers
said: "Your technique is the direct frontal attack of Rationalism and
the Enlightenment. There are other, indirect ways to bring about
social reform and social change that could turn out to be even
more effective than the one you propose. We can and do relent-
lessly and dispassionately accumulate hard evidence that gives
'injustice' concrete referents. The statistical techniques and random
samplings that you call trivial yield data on (for example) number
of hospital beds, patients, and doctors; infant deaths by social
class, dollars spent on illness by those over 65; race discrimination
and its social effects; bureaucratic bunglings. Bit by bit we make
so overwhelming a case in behalf of social reform that it cannot be
gainsaid."

To Mills all this was as if a musician composing television com-
mercials were to justify himself by declaring that you can still make
exciting harmonic experiments with *Pepsi-Cola Hits the Spot*.

I learned from Mills to ask the outrageous question, and I ask
it now of him: How did his three principles fit together? Which
took precedence over which?

In the days when we worked together on *Puerto Rican Journey*, I
found much pleasure and excitement in wandering around Harlem and the East Bronx, chatting, drinking coffee with Puerto
Ricans, questioning, arguing, wondering, commiserating, checking.
Mills rode around Harlem and the East Bronx in his impossible
open jeep. He did not interview migrants or try to share their
views. He interviewed English-speaking officials and intellectuals.
He took everything else in through his eyes and his pores. He also
read everything he could get hold of on migrations. His brilliance
when we discussed these works always gave me new insights and
ideas and understanding, and it raised even the most pedestrian
writings above their own level. Mills never felt he had to study
our interviews or analyze them. He culled them and quickly

pounced on the nuggets that would make the main points he had blocked out for his looking and reading. The staff did the detailed analysis.

In a sense he was right. One migration, after all, is very much like another. But in a sense I think he was wrong. So is one love affair very much like another—but for each new pair unique, and a source of wonder. Research in this respect is much like a love affair—always the same yet always unique. It builds on the researcher's sense of wonder more than on his foregone conclusions, however insightful they may be.

In 1946 a brilliant study by Mills and Melville J. Ulmer was published.[3] This research directed its attention to the important questions: How does concentration of economic power affect the general welfare of our cities and their inhabitants? Does economic concentration tend to raise or depress the level of civil welfare? The study carefully selected and examined three pairs of cities. Its findings indicated that big business tends to depress while small business tends to raise the level of civic welfare.

In 1954 Irving A. Fowler presented his doctoral research in a dissertation which paid Mills the compliment of replicating this study in 30 cities in New York State.[4] Fowler used some of the same measures Mills and Ulmer had employed; but, as a good researcher should, he went well beyond them, extending and expanding their work. It was a painstaking job of digging through reports and statistics; of legwork, interviewing, coding, correlating, testing, and retesting. It took him four years to analyze the data and write the report.

Fowler's study reversed the findings of Mills and Ulmer, whose earlier study is still being reprinted.[5] Fowler's thesis is on the shelf of the Cornell Library, and the copy I have indicates that I am the second person to have checked it out.

Mills never changed his mind about the relationship between big business and local welfare, nor did he repudiate or modify his earlier work with Ulmer. Was he wrong? After all, what is "welfare" and how do you measure it? Fowler had worked in the best tradition of sociology. He had examined and tested 48 indicators of eleven different facets of community welfare.[6] But the "welfare" that the sociologists' indicators measure is like an X-ray plate, a pale shadow of the welfare people-in-the-flesh enjoy or are deprived of. What about the psychological climate, the spirit, the sense that you are your own man, the sense of your own dignity and worth? What about confidence in the future for yourself, for your children and their children? What about the feeling that your existence is serious and meaningful? A study like Fowler's by no means settles the matter. The carefully woven net he had cast to capture the notion of "welfare" might still have been too wide-meshed. Some of these more elusive aspects could still have slipped through. Such results often turn up in social science research. The next step for an empirical sociologist like Fowler is for him and his students to face the challenging but difficult and time-consuming task of developing new measures of "welfare" that might fix those less tangible qualities that may have eluded his 1954 study.

This is the pace at which sociology develops today: slow, pedestrian, snail-like. Many seemingly obvious relations are still not pinned down, still must bear the label, "not proved: further investigation needed." But this was not Mills' pace, not his style. His passion was less for the search, more for the story. He felt the story as a novelist does, or a poet, and he relayed it to the reader in the best tradition of the pamphleteer. Perhaps for these reasons I find what I think is a deep misunderstanding of Mills in many quarters, where he is often labeled an anti-empiricist. He was, rather, an empiricist who could not wait for the science to catch up with him.

Mills' writings stimulate students all over the world to pursue his hunches and his insights, to follow his torch and his sword. Some do as Fowler did, applying the tools of empirical sociology to the study of power in social structures. Others adopt his pamphleteering techniques to expose injustices and to urge social change. The students he has inspired now and in the future to fight the good fight against injustice will be the measure of his stature as a social critic. Those who pursue the evidence and develop his thoughts in the scientific discipline will be the measure of his stature in the science of society.

NOTES:

1. "On Disbelieving Atrocities," in *The Yogi and the Commissar* (New York, 1945), pp. 88-92.
2. Op. cit. p. 89.
3. In *Small Business and Civic Welfare*, Report of the Special Committee to Study Problems of American Small Business, U.S. Senate, 79th Congress, 2d Session, C. No. 135 (Washington, 1946). Hans Gerth says Mills gathered the data and wrote the report in six weeks; "C. Wright Mills, 1916-1962," *Studies on the Left*, 2, 1962, p. 10.
4. Irving A. Fowler, *Local Industrial Structures, Economic Power, and Community Welfare: Thirty Small New York State Cities, 1930-1950*. Ph.D. thesis, Cornell University, September 1954. An article condensing his study appeared in *Social Problems*, 6, Summer, 1958, pp. 41-51, under the title "Local Industrial Structures, Economic Power and Community Welfare." It received the Helen DeRoy award of the Society for the Study of Social Problems.
5. The latest reprinting that has come to my attention is L. Broom and P. Selznick, *Sociology* (New York, Third Ed., 1963).
6. The eleven facets are repeated here. In parenthesis after each appear only one or two examples to indicate the kind of indicator Fowler used in each case:—Economic Income (e.g. average annual income per industrial wage-earner); Income Security (e.g. per cent unemployed and number of relief recipients per 1000 population); Consumer purchasing power (e.g. median rental and annual per capita retail sales); Home ownership; Housing adequacy (e.g. per cent of dwelling units reported in need of major repairs, or with central heating or with exclusive use of bath or shower); Health needs (e.g. as infant mortality; tuberculosis and pneumonia death rate); Health facilities (e.g. number of hospital beds and number of physicians per 1000); Literacy (e.g. median school years completed and per cent 16-17 year olds in school); Adequacy of educational provisions (e.g. current expenses per pupil, school tax per $1000); Political expression (e.g. voter registration and actual vote); and Municipal wealth and service (e.g. per capita tax levies, per capita costs of government and protection of persons and property). See Fowler, op. cit. pp. 68-9.

# 6

ANATOL RAPOPORT

## The Scientific Relevance of C. Wright Mills

Mention of "mathematical sociology" hardly elicits a raised eye-brow today, but when I was a student in the 1930's the idea was bold and exotic. People always asked the same question. How can an exact and "dry" science like mathematics be linked with human behavior, which is "unpredictable" or "purposeful" or "greater than the sum of its parts," to protect the human being from becoming the "object" of a dehumanized science? The positivists, operation-alists, and behaviorists—in short, those whom Mills called the Sci-entists—were lined up on one side; those whom he called the Humanists were on the other.

Most of the Scientists were empiricists, which means they were partisans of deductive mathematical theory in the behavioral sci-ences. To be sure, we were somewhat patronizing to the data col-lectors and significance test runners, whose research could pro-vide the same basis for the social sciences that experimenters did for the physical sciences. The important point was to apply the Method. The Method consisted of making Observations, drawing an Induction from the Observations, which served as a Hypothesis to be tested by Further Observations or a Controlled Experiment, which would corroborate or disconfirm a Prediction, which, if con-firmed, would lead one to make Further Deductions from the Hypothesis, to be likewise tested, or, if disconfirmed, forced one to modify the Hypothesis and to make the corresponding Predictions, and so forth and so forth.

The key to the whole process was Prediction. Everything remained all right as long as the Predictions were verified; if not, the Hypothesis was changed until they were. If no Predictions could be deduced from the Hypothesis, one was simply not using the Scientific Method.

The Humanists had a hard time arguing with this procedure. They took a dim view of prediction and sometimes pointed out that not much has yet been predicted and verified in human affairs, at least not by the Method. To this the reply came that this was because the techniques of observation and deduction were still primitive. But sometimes the Humanists blasphemed: they said that prediction was not the aim of the social sciences; that especially in sociology to understand was more important than to predict. To this the stock reply was: "If you can't Predict, how do you know you Understand?"

Now, twenty-five years later, I still believe in the twin towers of physical and behavioral sciences and that mathematics will be the mortar of the second, as it has been of the first. But I also believe that the disdain I once felt for the essay-writing sociologists and for the whole idea of "understanding" as something apart from specific prediction was no more than a symptom of immaturity.

I cannot honestly say that this change of view was brought about in me by the writings of C. Wright Mills. Rather it was this change which brought his writings into the focus of my attention. But this I will say: reading Mills has helped me reconcile my fundamental commitment to scientific method in the broadest sense with the realization that social science does not yield to scientific piety alone.

Mills' main critique seemed leveled at the trivialization of content in contemporary "scientific" sociology. In particular, he distinguished between "macroscopic" and "molecular" social inquiry. He gave as examples of macroscopic inquiry questions of this sort: "How did the Crusades come about? Are Protestantism and capitalism related? If so, how? Why is there no socialist movement in the United States?" As an example of a molecular inquiry, he gave, "Why are 40 per cent of the women who give marketing advice to their neighbors during a given week on a lower income level than those who gave it during another week?"

The reader may sense a grain of sarcasm in the example, but it seems to me that Mills endowed the question with more leverage than such projects usually have. Actually it is quite unusual for a molecular study to be directed toward answering a "why" question. The typical objective is to direct such a study toward the testing of a "hypothesis," and in the instance cited the hypothesis might well have been, "Significantly more women who give marketing advice to their neighbors during one week are on a lower income level than during another week." The result of the study would be the Acceptance or the Rejection of the Hypothesis at "a given level of significance." The question "why" would not be anywhere in sight.

Molecular studies are models of scientific objectivity in the sense that the rules laid down by the Method are scrupulously observed. Methodological faithfulness becomes the supreme criterion of excellence. Was the sample properly chosen? Were the statistical tests appropriate? There is no point in asking whether the conclusion was justified, because, as a rule, no "conclusion" is drawn. Instead we have a measure of confidence in the hypothesis or in the justification of its rejection. But the very inconclusiveness of the results bespeaks scrupulous objectivity. Human behavior is notoriously erratic. Conclusions from characteristics of samples to characteristics of populations are notoriously risky. The limits of confidence which qualify the findings are only reflections of the investigators' care not to assert anything without sufficient evidence. Is this not the way to build a science? Mills thought not.

Part of Mills' objection to the Scientists' approach to sociology was directed to the content of their studies. He considered the "knowledge" obtained in them irrelevant to the significant questions of sociology. Now the reason why so many of the "molecular" studies in sociology, the bread-and-butter research of the academic professional, are trivial is not necessarily because they deal with seemingly trivial matters. It is not possible to say what knowledge will prove important and what trivial in the long run. Mendel, counting his red, pink, and white sweet peas, must have appeared to his contemporaries as engaged in trivial research. Dubinin, the great Russian biologist, was accused by Lysenko and his cohorts of squandering government funds on trivialities when he studied genetic changes in the fruit fly brought about by the drastically changed environment of shell-blasted Voronezh; and, in addition, he was branded "callous" for paying attention to such lowly creatures while human beings were suffering privation. Galileo "amused" himself by rolling cannon balls down inclined planes; Galvani poked wires at dead frogs to see them kick. Gilbert played with magnets; Franklin with kites. Much of the greatest work in science must have seemed an atrocious waste of time to serious people.

No, it is not the "triviality"—the seeming detachment of the "molecular" problems from important human concerns—that marks so much of this approach as sterile. Rather, it is the ritualistic attitude of present-day investigators. If an investigator knows before he begins that his investigation will contain everything that he is going to ask; if he knows the entire range of alternative answers to every one of his questions; if he considers the investigation "finished" when the questions have been answered, and he feels no gnawing pains while going through the process; if he is not spurred to undertake new and *related* inquiries long before the old one is exhausted—then his "science" is probably little more than an empty shell. He has  paid too high a price for his objectivity and irreproachable methodology. As someone put it, he has polished his eye glasses until they are spotless, but he has not used them to look at anything worthwhile.

One must be careful to spell out what one means by "worthwhile" in this context. One must avoid the connotations of "practicality," for who heckles louder against "useless" research than the babbits and the bureaucrats? On the other hand, the stock defense of "useless" investigations ("the scientist should be guided by curiosity and by the spirit of free inquiry") does not fit, either. Remove discipline and selectivity from scientific endeavor, and what remains is not emancipation but a dissipation of effort, for the mediocre are always bound to outnumber the creative. Neither "practicality" demanded by men of affairs nor "uselessness" (glorified by some effetes in science) is a criterion of worth. Much of molecular research is highly "practical" in the sense that it answers questions which businessmen and the military want answered, in their preoccupation with organizing or inducing large numbers of people to do what they want them to do. On the other hand, much of this sort of research serves no other purpose than to demonstrate to a committee that a candidate for a doctor's degree has learned how to use the Method. None of these samples of "social science"' appealed to Mills. Nor do they appeal to me.

I think that the scientific relevance of an investigation is at issue. Scientifically relevant research is that which contributes to the emergence of a coherent picture of some aspect of the world. It is not easy to say what that "picture" is, not even in the case of a mature discipline like physics. But I will try my hand at it and then draw an analogy; that is, I will argue that Mills' contribution to sociology was his insistence that there is an emergent picture in that field, and that sociologists ought to be guided by it, not by extraneous matters. It will turn out that, in pointing out what those extraneous matters were, Mills himself contributed to the emergent picture.

The picture which emerged in physics toward the end of the sixteenth century, when that science really began, was a picture of the world with no purpose. If there was a God, His work was really finished on a certain Friday, after which He had nothing further to say about running the universe. The universe ran itself. Even if God had created the laws according to which it was run, He could no longer change those laws. Now it is generally believed that this picture of the physical world is constantly confirmed by experience. But this is not the whole story. For, if by "experience" we mean the accumulated evidence of controlled experiment and systematic observation, then it is strange that the picture was already firmly established before this experience had accumulated. And, if by experience we mean everyday experience, then it is not clear why the picture of physical determinism was not established much earlier, not only in the minds of physicists but also in the minds of all reasonable people.

It seems to me that a picture of the world is not primarily the result of relevant experience but the result of attitudes which guide the selection of experiences. Something which happened to Europeans in the centuries preceding the Renaissance changed their attitudes. Changes in attitude led them to pay attention to events which had been ignored and so brought about changes in their philosophical outlook. Then people went to work accumulating evidence to justify the outlook. The triumphant history of physical science is a record of fortunate selection of observations and problems. What has become established as our scientific heritage is a vast network of knowledge where each node is a nexus that holds the strands, which in turn, hold the other nodes. For all its triteness, the jigsaw puzzle metaphor well describes the scientific enterprise.

Thus the slogan "free choice of problems" is grossly misleading. No great scientist was ever "free" in the choice of his problems. He might have been free (if he was so fortunate) from outside interference, but he was by no means free of inner compulsions. He might have been spurred on by curiosity, but certainly not by idle curiosity. It was curiosity driven by a vision. It is a mistake to think that men shifted to the heliocentric view of the solar system because "facts" forced them to do so. Facts could be explained from the geocentric point of view, too. Indeed, the Church insisted that they be so explained. The shift was a real break, a change of attitude (in which, one suspects, disillusion with the Church played a part), an active choice of a new kind of hypothesis, not a revision of an old one in accordance with new "facts." (The idea that facts and hypotheses constantly interact, propelling knowledge forward, is, in itself, an attitude—a philosophy of knowledge.)

Some would have it that practical necessity was the force behind the scientific revolution. Granted that physical science emerged very largely from the problems posed by craftsmen, engineers, and navigators, it is difficult to apply the same criteria to biology and its relation to medicine. Concern with healing alone would never have brought about scientific medicine, let alone an overview of the world of life. Physicians were stuck in the metaphysical quagmire from the time of Hippocrates to the time of Semmelweis, in spite of the fact that the practical problem of healing could not have been more clearly put nor more pressing. Scientific medicine emerged only when the streams of physical, chemical, and biological knowledge merged and when two new visions of man appeared, namely, man as a physico-chemical system in homeostatic equilibrium with the environment and man as an organism interacting with other organisms.

It appears, then, that neither practical necessity nor curiosity are sufficient in the making of a science. Both, however, are necessary, and they provide the motivation when a relevant picture of some aspect of the world has emerged.

Mills urged sociologists to recognize the emergent picture. He applauded the pioneers of macroscopic sociology—Marx, Weber, Mannheim, Durkheim, Veblen—for having contributed to that picture, and he chided the Higher Statisticians, the servants of business and bureaucracy, and the compulsive conceptualizers for neglecting it. The Higher Statisticians, he rightly observed, paid all the attention to whether investigations were conducted properly, and none to what was being investigated. Those who served the manipulators, he insisted, had put on blinders and put science to bad use. The conceptualizers, in his opinion, have become entangled in their own thought processes and have lost contact with the subject matter. All three types, he suggested, behave as if they were afraid of the emergent picture. In accusing those whom he believed to be the trivializers of sociology of cowardice (he minced no words), Mills was actually propounding a sociological theory, possibly not an original one but certainly a neglected one: the sociology of knowledge.

The sociology of knowledge stems, of course, from Marx. But there is no point in tagging Mills as a Marxist. Mills valued Marx for his vision, which was of the same magnitude as the vision of Newton and of Darwin. Orthodox Marxists draw an exact parallel between Marx and Newton; they often say that Marx discovered the laws of transformation of society just as Newton discovered the laws of motion. There is a grain of truth in this, but it is obscured by the compulsion of the orthodox to take the parallel literally. The skeptic can easily demolish the analogy by challenging a Marxist to use one such law in the way Newton's laws have been used, for example in the way they were used not only to predict the discovery of Neptune but also to state its exact position, orbit, and mass. The Marxists' claim that they can predict the course of human history does not bear critical scrutiny. Their predictions are vague and full of loopholes. There is no way of coming to terms with the orthodox on such matters as the degree of specificity of the predictions to be tested, or what shall constitute a success of a prediction and what a failure. The orthodox, for example, can never ascribe a failure to their prophet.

The failure of specific theories, however, does not mean a failure of an underlying vision. A vision is not a theory. It is an illuminated attitude which confers upon the visionary an intuitive grasp of his field of inquiry, and enables him to indicate where to look for the raw material from which theories are constructed. His is an understanding prerequisite for the construction of fruitful theories.

The idea of the sociology of knowledge was, I believe, Marx's greatest contribution. It will endure long after his economic theories (sophisticated in his day but primitive in the light of contemporary knowledge) and the sociological theory which bears his trademark (the class struggle) have become historical curiosities. The sociology of knowledge is to society what the psychoanalytic conceptualization of the unconscious is to the individual. This conceptualization, too, is destined to remain as a permanent contribution, regardless of the fate of specific psychoanalytic "models" (or allegories). Both ideas contribute to the insight that man is not as free as he thinks he is. Both contain the grain of hope that man can make himself freer, if he recognizes that he is not free. ("Freedom is the recognition of necessity.") In particular, the sociology of knowledge purports to describe how the structure and the dynamics of a society determine what knowledge will be sought and how it will be interpreted. The sociologists' retreat from their proper sphere of investigation, Mills implied, was a symptom of compulsions operating in our society.

Mills' charge of trivialization applies to much of contemporary American sociology not so much because of the problems the investigators choose (it is impossible to say with assurance a priori which problems have scientific relevance) but because of their ritualistic behavior. I seem to perceive in Mills' analysis the causes of this compulsive ritualization and worship of Method; namely, the often appalling parochialism of American sociology. Here it seems that Mills emphasized the need for going outside the system in order to describe it effectively. He found that the description of power structure in America in conventional American sociology is being made from the inside (i.e. as if described by the Power Elite themselves); the description of rapid social change is written from the point of view that stability is desirable ("Professional Ideology of Social Pathologists"); the detached condemnation of ideology is made from the point of view of affluent America. In other words, the self-proclaimed detached objectivity

of the sociologists is not objectivity at all but a commitment to a
*status quo* by people who have internalized a set of values.

Is detachment, like the detachment of the physicist, then, possible in sociology? I think Mills would say no. It is possible to
escape the parochialism of American sociological ideas only by
going outside the system, but this will put one inside another
system of views. To see clearly the nature of power in American
society, you have to pit yourself against it. To see clearly the role
that American society plays on a world scale you have to put
yourself into the shoes of a Cuban or a Vietnamese peasant. The
problem of choosing problems is the problem of what we want to
talk about. Mills saw this question as intimately connected to the
question of whom we want to talk to.

Again, we are reminded of the classical Marxian views or the
emergence of consciousness through struggle. But there was nothing of the hack Marxist in Mills. He honored Marx by taking the
ideas of the sociology of knowledge seriously, not slavishly. He
applied it with true regard to the environment in which it operates.
The real fabric of American life, not a textbook case of a "capitalist
society," is the field against which he examined American institutions, culture types, and, in particular, his own profession and
its failure in his eyes. Surplus value, accumulation, or imperialism
are not responsible for the paucity of American sociology (although the structure of American economy and America's international role are, of course, important contributing sources), but
the actual social matrix which Mills described with great sharpness and detail. We know these descriptions as "true," for who
among us in academic life has not met the promoter, the scholar
or the would-be scholar turned administrator, whose life work has
become the allocation of funds and the management of personnel but who is still called a "social scientist"? Where can insights come from if research has been replaced by "projects,"
whose magnitude is determined by how efficiently they can be
administered?

Here, then, is sociology of knowledge in action. The social fabric
determines how investigations are made. How they are made determines the kind of people, with what sort of commitments, who
will make them. The totality of the investigators defines the field
of inquiry. The process is self-perpetuating.

It is easy to construe Mills' constant sniping at the Scientists of sociology as an anti-scientific position, as if he recommended arm-chair speculation in preference to the standard methods of data collection and generalization. Indeed, it is easy to take a stand defending objective data and publicly verifiable knowledge against the onslaughts of obscurantism and subjectivism. But, as I have already implied, this is not the issue. The real issue is a genuine "hard" methodological issue. I am not prepared to say that Mills' stand on this issue was entirely correct, but I feel that he had a strongly defensible position. In any case, I must take his position, as I understand it, before I evaluate it from my own point of view. (As I stated in the beginning, I belong to the class of investigators whom Mills labeled, not without derision, as the Scientists.)

It seems to me that Mills is saying that a man cannot be a good sociologist unless he is "committed"—that is, unless a certain class of problems really bothers him. These are the big macroscopic problems mentioned above. These are the problems in which Mills himself was completely involved. What is the power structure of a society? Why is the United States playing out the role of a twentieth-century Holy Alliance, dedicated to the "legitimacy" of property, just as the original Holy Alliance was dedicated to the "legitimacy" of Monarchy? What are the causes of World War III? Against this view, the standard argument of natural science method-ology is regularly invoked: namely, that you cannot be a good sociologist (or any kind of scientist) unless you are not committed.

At this level, the two positions are stated in different languages and cannot be reconciled. Suppose, however, we restate Mills' position somewhat as follows: The social scientist in his role as observer—i.e. a selector of what to observe, for all observation is selection—is an instrument. A good instrument must be sensitive to certain aspects of the social environment. This restatement does not prove Mills' thesis, but at least it makes it plausible. The social scientist becomes in this conception no different from any other creative scientist—no different, for example, from the bi-ologist who became discontented with specimen collection *per se* and began to think about the "meaning" of species differentiation, how it came about, etc. Having shifted his focus of interest, this scientist became sensitized to certain aspects of biological facts, to which the specimen collectors and taxonomists had been indifferent, and from this sensitivity the Big Idea emerged—evolution.

Seen in this way, the problem of commitment against objectivity evaporates. Perhaps the man of vision cannot be "objective" because of his commitment: he denies that all facts are created equal. But there is no getting around the necessity for selecting facts. As already pointed out, it is the selection of relevant facts which is the heart and soul of all scientific activity. Sociology is the study of man in society. The relevant facts are those which relate to the problems of Man in society. It is impossible to appreciate these problems unless one has had a direct experience with certain troubles generated by these problems.

This brings us to the other methodological aspect of Mills' position. The statement of the difference between natural and social sciences has become a cliché. The former present a picture of the world as it appears to an observer outside the system. What we think about the moon makes no difference to the moon. The latter present a picture of the world from inside the system. What men think about society may make a big difference to the society in which they live. The really anti-scientific attitude leads to the conclusion that, because of man's commitments, social science is impossible. The conventional scientific attitude leads to the conclusion that social science is possible only if the observer becomes "detached" and moves outside the system.

Mills would not agree with either of these positions. He certainly would dismiss the second position on the ground that moving completely outside the system blinds the would-be social scientist to the important problems. But for all his ranting against the Scientists, he was not, I believe, really anti-scientific. Mills' position was that the peculiarity of social science, which makes it inevitable that the world is described "from the inside" of *some* system should be accepted and turned to advantage. He believed that what we think about society will change society; therefore, we should think about it in ways which change it for the better. Again we are reminded of the Marxist view of sociology. History is determined by forces over which man has no control, so long as he is unaware of those forces. When he becomes aware of them, he can determine his future history. This is also similar to the Freudian view: man is a slave to his compulsions when their roots are repressed; exposing the roots makes man free.

This "inner view—outer view" battle has already been fought in psychology. The behaviorists in their revolt against "subjectivism" ruled out introspection as a source of psychological knowledge. Their program soon became a caricature of a science, as does any "method" which ossifies into a dogma.

In short, the strongest feature of Mills' critique of sociology is his attack against ossified method. The creative aspects of this critique reside in his suggested sociological reasons for this ossification. The "research business" has become not only an important sphere of American life but also a richly suggestive sociological symptom. Thus Mills' critique of American sociology is in itself an important, positive contribution to sociology.

It now remains for me to state the one reservation which I have to Mills' views. In a way, Mills himself was aware of the fact that the gap between the macroscopic and the molecular approaches in sociology is bridgeable. "The sociological enterprise," he wrote, "requires macroscopic researchers to imagine more technically, as well as with scope and insight; it requires technicians to go about their work with more imaginative concern for macroscopic meaning, as well as for technical ingenuity."

Now let us see what it takes to bridge the gap. Suppose we start thinking about some macroscopic problem of the sort, I assume, that Mills would rate as important. The Elite in America wield their power, at least in part, by molding public opinion. This is done largely through the mass media. But direct person-to-person contacts are probably also important. A man adopts attitudes not only from what he reads in the papers but also from what his neighbors and associates think. What is the relative importance of these two factors?

If the question is important, one must seek effective ways of answering it. And, I submit, as soon as one starts looking for these ways, one is already in the realm which the Scientists call their own. For the "commitment" part of the sociologists' job has already been served. Presumably a relevant problem has been selected, since it has a definite bearing on the structure of communication in society, on the genesis of its dominant attitudes, and so on the very fate of the society. Reliable answers to the question just asked may have bearing on questions of the following sort. What chance does a grassroots movement (e.g. Freedom Rides, the Peace

Movement, etc.) have to grow to sociologically significant size, if it has no mass media at its disposal and must rely on direct contacts only for its growth? Granted that the historical moment is of obvious importance in answering this question, certainly the character of the communication net is also of importance. Furthermore, what aspects of the communication net are most sensitive to its effectiveness? Practical leaders of mass movements have frequently been masters of organization. Their knowledge of organizational principles were, as a rule, purely intuitive. Is there a way to make such knowledge explicit, that is, scientific?

Once one gets into these problems one has landed squarely in the world of operations research, statistics, and the rest of it, the world which Mills often contended has little relevance for sociology.

In this world, however, facts are created a priori equal. If one fact looms over others, this is not because it has greater human importance but because it occupies a pivotal position in the structure of the problem. It turns out that if we are concerned with the admittedly human problem of endemic malaria, the breeding habits of the mosquito are much more important than anything we feel about the dignity of man and how it is undermined by the debilitating disease. It turns out that Pasteur's preoccupation with the fermentation of wine (which led him to study microorganisms) was more instrumental in alleviating human suffering than the saintly ministerings of Florence Nightingale. For this reason it is conceivable that the silly question about the income level of housewives advising other housewives in their marketing may lead to discoveries about how mass behavior can be profitably studied, and a methodologically powerful approach to mass behavior may yet answer questions such as, "How did the Crusades come about?" and "Why is there no socialist movement in the United States?" In principle, science is of one piece. Every aspect of it, including physical science, has a strong moral component. But also every aspect of it, including social science, has an important methodological component.

If one takes the dictum "freedom is the recognition of necessity" seriously, one must recognize necessity for what it is. It is well and good to say that, once recognized, necessity may evaporate. But methods must be developed for its recognition. One must sharpen one's tools. Much as I applaud Mills' insistence that imagination and commitment ought to be recognized as indispensable components of the sociologist's tool box, I cannnot minimize the importance of other tools whose very use is incomprehensible except to a specialist. The acquisition of relevant knowledge is not only a matter of being attuned, motivated, sensitive, and emancipated. It is also a matter of being sophisticated in evaluating the reliability of what one observes and deduces. Thus, I recognize that the Scientist and the Higher Statistician have come into sociology to stay. Even if they are alienated from sociology as a human enterprise, their services are indispensable.

Much as Mills may admire certain writings of a Tillich or a Sorokin, certain of their "insights" are sure to be incompatible with his own. It comes, then, to a showdown. Or, if those insights are not incompatible but, on the contrary, complementary, that has got to be recognized, too. Science, with its attitude of detachment, is the only mode of cognition we know which can make showdowns between incompatible views productive and which can reveal the degree of compatibility between views. Hence, logical analysis, extension of concepts, tests of hypotheses, and the rest cannot be avoided if we wish the clashes between serious thinkers to generate light as well as heat. And this means that we have to look at molecular studies, with their grubbing and their tests of significance and their deliberately imposed blindness to human issues, as necessary adjuncts of sociology, no matter how important it is for sociologists to keep the genuine sociological problems in focus.

ACKNOWLEDGMENT

I am much indebted to my colleague, William Paul Livant, for his stimulating suggestions in many conversations we have had about Mills and what his work means. Originally we were going to write this paper together, but we diverged in our emphases. Rather than keep trying to write a piece which both of us could sign without reservation, we decided that one of us should assume the responsibility of authorship. I did so with some reluctance.

# 7

ERNEST BECKER

## Mills' Social Psychology and the Great Historical Convergence on the Problem of Alienation

"...[We] must reveal the ways in which personal troubles are connected with public issues..." [1] With this declaration Mills sums up the burden of his work. At the same time he leaves himself yawningly open to his critics. The age-old problem of human troubles, as we well know, is hardly so easy to resolve. Who defines personal troubles—mass man or those who study him, the psychiatrist or the political agitator, the rhetorical liberal or the Dukhobor? The sheep is after all not an unattractive animal, yet who dares claim the right to pronounce impartial judgment on a nation of them? The dilemma is at least as old as Bentham's option for felicity, and we know the hair-splitting arguments that have raged around it.

However this may appear, Mills was on sound scientific ground: If we can put together a coherent, self-consistent, and rationally compelling theory of the causes of human ills, it will carry its own ethical imperative. In this way science and ethics become congruent. This is the Enlightenment legacy toward which sociology must still aspire. When we give a thorough-going answer to the question "What makes people act the way they act?" It will imply at the same time a criticism and a prescription.

The young Marx started on this question in his early theoretical sketch of alienation. Now, a century and a quarter later, we are beginning to uncover empirical evidence for this concept, evidence revealed by the latest theoretical work on mental illness. This is truly an almost undreamed of breakthrough, the newest glimpse of the possibility of a science of man for man. We could give vent to considerable excitement over this possibility if it did not at the same time carry a heavy apprehension. It is one thing to pry out empirical evidence that society is the true culprit for human ills, but it is another matter entirely to apply the findings of the human sciences to the service of changing society.

I. *Mills' Social Psychology.* If we had to sum up the main problem of modern social psychology, I think it would be this: We know that man is an historical actor; we also know that he is a more or less integral personality. How do we theoretically reconcile the two into one comprehensive system? If we follow the tradition of William James, John Dewey, and George Mead, we sacrifice an integral theory of personality, even while we gain an understanding of the social and historical nature of the human self. If, on the other hand, we recognize a really tight theory of personality, like Freud's, we quickly lose the view of man as a highly modifiable, historical creation. In a sense we must reconcile Marx with Freud, the tradition of Condorcet and Saint-Simon with that of Hobbes and Kant. Marx saw that "the essence of man is no abstraction inherent in each separate individual. In its reality it is the ensemble of social relations." [2] But Freud saw that man *does* act as a separate individual. This reconciliation was Mills' problem too, and it is important to see how he approached it.

Mills' option was clearly on the side of Marx, Dewey, and Mead. He saw man as "a whole entity," as an "actor in historic crises." [3] In the concluding paragraph of the social psychology book he wrote with Hans Gerth, he sums up his whole orientation, and it is worth quoting here in full:

> Man is a unique animal specie in that he is also an historical development. It is in terms of this development that he must be defined, and in terms of it no single formula will fit him. Neither his anatomy nor his psyche fix his destiny. He creates his own destiny as he responds to his experienced situation, and both his situation and his experiences of it are the com-

plicated products of the historical epoch which he enacts. That is why he does not create his destiny as an individual but as a member of society.[4]

There is little room for Freud in this vigorous appreciation of the historical nature of the self. In fact, did not Mills express his willingness to substitute Mead for Freud, even though acknowledging that they differed in important respects? [5]

But this substitution is not accomplished by mere sleight of hand. Mills had to show that Mead serves better than Freud, and in order to do this he had to attack Freud at his weakest point—his instinctual drive theory of motivation. And this he did effectively in a very early paper, a document that also serves to attest to Mills' precocious scientific stature.[6]

*The Problem of Motivation.* In this paper Mills faced the basic problem of human motivation. If man is an historical actor, a symbolic creation, then he must be pulled ahead expansively by words and images, rather than pushed forward narrowly by innate drives. At the top of the animal hierarchy, man performs on a level of his own. His conduct, then, is steered by symbols rather than driven from below. How can the forward momentum of conduct be explained? A pseudo-problem, says Mills, following Dewey. The organism is active *by definition of organism.* We do not have to explain why animals move, any more than why the universe is in motion; it is a fact we can easily accept—and, indeed, must accept. The problem for a social psychology is not to divine purpose in nature, as Freud and Ferenczi tried, but merely to describe and explain what is *peculiar* about *human* action. And for this, word-motives suffice. If the problem of action no longer resides in meeting the demands of inner drives, then it must reside in meeting the problems of external situations. Thus, Mills borrowed Peirce's and Dewey's pragmatic notion that the prime task of the moving organism is to overcome problematic situations in its field. Word-motives are supreme for man because they help the individual navigate in his social field. Motivation was thus no problem for Mills, and he used the familiar concept of role as a superordinate performance category by means of which the individual is led on. Roles tell the individual how to act for maximum self-satisfaction and facilitation of conduct. They provide prescriptions for choice in situations that present alternatives, and they guarantee public approval for the choice. Man earns, via social roles, the two things he needs most: the animal possibility of moving safely forward in his environment; and also the distinctively human need for the reflected appraisals of others, the image of himself as a creature of value in a world of evaluations.

*The Problem of Perception.* With the concept of role the problem of motivation is not resolved; it is merely shifted. It is shifted, furthermore, into a far more difficult area of theory and research, that of perception. Mills narrowed his focus down very expertly, but one senses that he felt himself on more difficult ground. After criticizing Freud's view of motivation, he says, somewhat apologetically, that his discussion is "not intended as a comprehensive statement or criticism of Freud's theory of motivation." [7] Why this strange hedging when he needs nothing less than a social psychology of historical man? Probably because Mills seems to have failed to conceptualize with needed clarity all the basic problems of a full-blown theory of personality.

But he made the requisite start. He saw that the problem of perception had to be, at the same time, the problem of personality and the problem of social role. To achieve this unity, nothing less than a fully transactional theory of perception would do, and this is what Mills used. While the most exciting empirical work on the transactional nature of perception is only now forthcoming,[8] Mills had a philosophical, theoretical tradition of long standing to fall back on. Comte, Whitehead, Dewey, Baldwin—all understood that the organism organizes, constructs a world out of its perception and action. The human organism is not born into the world ready-made; rather, it *comes into being* as it transacts with the social world around it.[9] Raw feelings must be shaped into proper emotions. Brute sensations must be organized into clear perceptions. Random impulses must become guiding purpose. Since, for the human animal, this shaping takes place in a social world, we can see the fundamental importance of a transactional theory of perception: *the very biological organism is socially formed.* The world it sees and the world it feels and moves in grows up together with the seeing, feeling, and movement.

Mills used the concept "psychic structure" to cover the feeling, sensation, and impulse that are socially converted into emotion, perception, and purpose. If the animal is thus socially fused in its basic responsiveness to the world, it is obvious that social roles penetrate literally to the core of the organism. With the concept of "psychic structure" Mills was able to maintain that man is an historical creation, even while he remains basically a biological organism. The "psychic structure" and the organism are fused into the "person" or role-player. In order to have a coherent theory of personality Mills adopted the further term "character structure" to refer to the stabilized aspect of the integration of psychic structure and social roles.[10] And he sums up his basic view of personality as follows:

> Man as a person is an historical creation, and can most readily be understood in terms of the roles which he enacts and incorporates. These roles are limited by the kind of social institutions in which he happens to be born and in which he matures into an adult. His memory, his sense of time and space, his perception, his motives, his concept of his self . . . his psychological functions are shaped and steered by the specific configuration of roles which he incorporates from his society.[11]

No doubt Mills has here brought Marx up to date, and fused perception and society. Man is not an essence from which prefashioned purpose erupts; he is a malleable locus in which social perspectives transact. But we know that, basically, Dewey provided as much in 1922 in his *Human Nature and Conduct*. And Dewey has admitted, in responding to Gordon Allport's probing appraisal of his social psychology,[12] that he failed to offer an adequate theory of personality.

*The Problem of Strain in the Human Personality.* Mills did not, however, leave his personality theory at the point which Dewey had already evolved. He had Freud, Adler, Sullivan, Horney, and Fromm to draw on for a fuller picture of the complexities of human striving. And it is precisely here, as we noted, that Mills seems less comfortable: he needs both a theory of social motivation and an adequate theory of personality. Now, an adequate theory of personality must show man pulling and straining against himself; it must reveal a man who is somehow less than fully socialized, or who is idiosyncratically socialized—which amounts to the same thing. Does this mean that man has an "unconscious"? Does it imply that there are inner stirrings in the human animal that are not amenable to socialization? Is it necessary, in other words, for the sociologist to go into the enemy camp—so to speak—in order to fill out a picture of human complexity? Mills' social psychology indeed reflects some standard borrowings from psychoanalysis, which are counterbalanced by unfinished attempts to do without these borrowings. Let us look at this cognitive embarrassment of Mills a bit more closely.

In order to get a personality theory of adequate complexity Mills had to deal with the problem of strain or fragmentation—although I prefer to use the word strain, or even, more broadly, dialectic of individual striving. There are two major poles or dimensions on which these strains or dialectics take place. Both of these poles fall under the more generic problem of perception and action; so that, by considering them, Mills was actually filling out the bare framework of the "psychic structure."

First there is *the dimension of individual action in time*. This dimension carries the basic strain in human striving that Freud conveyed so well. When Mills says that he would substitute Mead for Freud, even though they differ in important respects, I think he is acknowledging in his reservation that without Freud we could not have gained such a sharp conceptualization of the strain between early training and later adult experience. *This dimension is the primary dialectic in human action.* The child is trained for certain choices (perceptions) which he learns to handle with a sense of adequacy and well-being. When his parents approve his choices (perceptions), he earns a necessary self-esteem; when they disapprove, he feels anxiety. As he grows up, the individual is confronted with choices which cannot fall in the same clear-cut fashion into the earlier patterns of perception and action. He has to continually learn to overcome anxiety in new ways, and to earn self-esteem in new ways. The kind of early training he had, as well as the kind of opportunities which present themselves to him as an adult, will determine his flexibility in making new choices. This is a simplified way of viewing what Freud conveyed so well by the idea of "neurosis"—the fact that later adult choices will be frustrated and undermined by constricting early learning. The equanimity of the human animal is thus subverted by the carry-ing-over of old learning, of antiquities unrelated to new problems.

Now, Mills was obliged to deal with this dimension by using the old Freudian vocabulary. Thus he talked about "repression"; [13] about unconscious motives which influence our action, even though they are unverbalized; he talked in mechanical terms about "forces" which may "influence our conduct" or which may be "blocked at one outlet"; he used the term "psychic elements" that can be "latent" and "socially channeled"; and he talked about "deeper psychic levels" of character; [14] he even implied that man concealed primitive hatreds and aggressions.[15] Obviously, Mills has here failed to push on to a fully post-Freudian social psychology. True, he did talk in direct terms about society's failure to verbalize and symbolize certain areas of experience,[16] and he explained thereby some of the burden of childhood restrictions on the adult; he saw clearly the need for an uninhibited symbolic organization of experience. Understanding this, he could have chucked the Freudian baggage entirely, and adopted the fruitful existential approach to man: man's consciousness as a kind of being-in-the-world, the malleable actor in his historic situation, unencumbered by anything except the limitations of his early world view, the one imparted by the parents. A social psychology that would establish the primary relevance of the superordinate symbolic self, the priority of social role and symbolic striving, the kinds of social structure into which the individual is born—this social psychology, in sum, cannot compromise with the Freudian world view. It must understand the basic dialectic which Freud discovered—that between early training and adult experience—as a social and not a biological problem. True, there is a biological base: separation anxiety of the helpless higher-primate infant is the pivot for his early learning; but this is an anxiety in the face of the incoming world, and not of the outgoing (instinctual) one.

Next there is *the dimension of individual action in space.* This dimension reflects the basic strain between self and objects. It contains the problem of moving about in a world of things which must be labelled verbally in order to be controlled. The dilemma arises when words are not available to describe and make one critically aware of problematic situations. If we do not have the words, we are unable adequately to frame the problem. On the other hand, the dilemma can arise where we have too many words, too many vocabularies, and no behavioral order in our world. In this case, problems are manufactured where they need not exist.

Again, this is an axis of strain that derives directly from perception and learning. Mills dealt with this axis beautifully. It is here that his vocabulary of motives thesis provides rich insights, and it is here, too, that Mills makes the attempt to do without borrowings from psychoanalysis: human confusions and fragmentations, the tortuous complexity of personality, he tried to frame largely in terms of conflicting vocabularies of motive. His attempt remained unfinished, as we shall see.

A role is a vocabulary of motives suited to a performance part; it makes interpersonal action possible. What happens when there are several vocabularies for the same part? This is the dilemma that Mills underscored for man in complex, industrial society: man has lost the easy integrity of role performance that existed in simpler, more homogeneous societies. In primitive society, for example, roles are relatively integrated. On a hypothetical primitive level a woman may be associated with the motives represented, say, by the words "wife," "children," "family obligation," and so on. But society sustains her in all these identities, and the unity of her personality is assured. In modern, commercial industrial society, on the other hand, a woman's designations may be more subtle; she becomes a possibility of "romantic love," "career," "wealth," "clever children with good heredity," "winter house in Key West," "appreciation of Bach in common," ad infinitum. In itself this would not be confusing, but society does not sustain her in the unity and integrity of all these performances. Without this kind of support, social performance becomes mechanical, and the individual gets lost in the artificiality of his roles.

In addition to this, there is another kind of confusion and fragmentation in complex society, which Mills called attention to as a "segmentalization of conduct." In simpler societies the world views of the individual actors would be somewhat more homogeneous; people would tend to share similar definitions of role performances. But in modern society many contradictory perspectives can be brought to bear on the single role, depending on who is looking at the role. Thus modern man often has to adjust his vocabulary to his interlocutor, and change it each time. He might not use the same vocabulary of motives in talking about marriage, say, to his wife, as he would in talking about it to a friend—or even to his own mother. There is no consistent self-image reflected in the many perspectives, and the individual's "real self" tends to become inextricably lost in vocabularies and sub-vocabularies. Religion, business, family—all tear in different directions. Innumerable and interchangeable perspectives for self-justification undermine a firm identity.

Thus, the dialectic of individual action in space comes down to this: how sufficient and how many vocabularies of motive can the individual bring to bear on a particular situation, and what kind of self-satisfying action can be undertaken? He may be limited as well by poverty as by a plethora of word-motives. Let us then look at this problem of vocabularies of motive from another angle, which will serve at the same time to link our discussion of Mills' social psychology with some of the new directions in the theory of mental illness.

II. *The New Understanding of Mental Illness.* Mills' social psychology has been criticized for its sketchy model of the personality; [17] specifically, that Mills presented only one major descriptive construct, the self; only one mechanism, language; and only one behavioral law, a crude reward-learning theory. The whole structure was topped, as we saw, by the pivotal concept of role. Now, this very simplicity has its advantages, if it permits us to explain effectively certain behavioral phenomena. A model of personality needs to be only as complex as the problem to which it addresses itself. If we could explain schizophrenia, say, by finding a cabbage worm in the brain, as Maimonides is reputed to have done, we could happily dispense with the new family interaction models.

*Depression: A Brief Sketch of the Theory.* The phenomenon that we call depression, for example, seems to be best explained by the most Spartan model of personality functioning.[18] We seem to be able to approach it adequately as primarily a dialectic of individual action in the dimensions of space and time. For a long time psychiatrists were baffled by the two outstanding characteristics of the depressive syndrome: the sudden surrender to despair, the opting out of life; and, the unbelievably self-depreciating accusations which the depressed person brought against himself. Why should people whose lives have been normal and even exemplary suddenly give up? And why should they be so merciless in denouncing themselves, when it is obvious that they cannot possibly be as bad or as guilty as they paint themselves? The answer to these two questions, which arose as a *medical* problem only with the development of modern psychiatry, is simple—even astonishingly simple. It goes something like this: The depressed person had, like everyone else, the principal life task of keeping action moving forward in relation to those around him. He did this in the way most of us do it—by accepting to perform with ready-made vocabularies that we inherit from those others around us. The depressed person accepts to earn a reflected image of his own worth, in sum, by a more or less uncritical performance in a few tightly tailored cultural roles. Then suddenly, or gradually, a crisis develops. The crisis can take any number of forms: the individual may find himself threatened with divorce; a woman may find herself at menopause, deprived of her female role, and deprived at the same time of the only satisfying predication of her identity in a masculine world; a mother may find herself approaching old age, with the last of her children suddenly married, and herself suddenly deprived of her accustomed self-justifying action; a celibate, who has been sacrificing all rights and practice of personal decision only to earn his parents' approval, may suddenly find them dead, and, in one blow, be deprived of the only performance audience he has learned to appeal to. All of these examples have one common thread: life has suddenly been sapped of significance, and the individual does not know exactly why. He has been performing uncritically, with a limited range of vocabularies of motive, in a narrow circle of people who have significance for him. These three interlocking ingredients make up the formula for depressive breakdown: uncritical perceptions, poor vocabularies in which to frame choices, narrow range of people to whom one can appeal for his identity.

Why does action bog down into a passive surrender that we call depression? Simply because accustomed performance parts no longer serve to reflect a satisfying self-image; and, the individual does not know any other kinds of parts, or cannot begin, within the time left to his life, to undertake to learn them. What about the baffling self-accusation of guilt? This is the keystone in the new theoretical explanation of the phenomenon of depression. The self-accusation of guilt is exactly what we would expect from someone who is poor in vocabularies of motive, limited in words with which to frame the problematic situation, shallow in his critical perceptions. The guilt language, in other words, serves as the perfect justification for failure, where this failure cannot be otherwise understood. With this language the depressed individual takes cognitive command of a situation that is undermining him, and with it he also attempts to unblock his action. That is to say, if he can make himself into the most blameworthy person within his narrow circle, then he need not focus critically on it and thereby perhaps risk losing it entirely. In his surrender to his circumstances he can at least take his own fate into his hands, and work out his destiny in daily expiation. Historically the phenomenon of self-accusation of guilt as a form of positive control is not new, but in depression we see it in microcosm.

The so-called psychiatric problem of depression, then, presents itself baldly as a problem of individual stupidity. And it is best handled with the most Spartan model of personality functioning—the cognitive self, vocabularies of motive, and the need to keep action moving forward. People vary in cognitive grasp of situations, in vocabularies with which to frame these situations, and consequently in possibilities for self-satisfying action—all these aspects woven inextricably into one.

*Schizophrenia: The Need for a Complete Social Psychology.* If the simple model applies so well in the theory of depression, does it apply equally to schizophrenia? No, it will not suffice simply to tally the linguistic and perceptual repertory in order to explain this rather complex behavioral phenomenon. If depression is the microcosm of poverty in vocabularies, schizophrenia is the microcosm of the whole human condition. And in order to understand this phenomenon we have to pick up one historical current that was not elaborated in Mills' social psychology. This permits us to evaluate Mills' social psychology from still another point of view: that of phenomenology.

Actually, Mills was alive to the importance of a phenomenological approach to experience. He saw that, in order to convert impulse into purpose and to transform the primitive psychic structure into a social product, the child must come into contact with objects. He quotes Charles Sanders Peirce's observation that in order to have will we must encounter resistance—we must be able to strive against something.[19] And, in another place: "The realities of the world and the capacities of our own bodies are learned together; both come to us in terms of resistance and mastery, limitation and capacity." [20] Thus, Mills glimpses the true dialectic of organismic experience.

This rich current of thinking entered with Kant's, Fichte's, and Hegel's views on the interplay between self and objects. Hegel understood cognition as the outgoing of consciousness to an object, to which it is being attached. This simple view has far-reaching importance, for it means no less than this: that the self *needs objects in order to come into being.*[21] Meinong and Husserl kept this current of speculation alive, and elaborated on the nature of the objects with which humans can come into contact. Man operates in two modes; he possesses both thing-objects, like all other animals; and, uniquely, symbol-objects, given in full only to the symbol-using animal. Consciousness procedes to two spheres to make contact with the world, and two kinds of human powers are brought into play: active organismic powers and more passive cognitive powers. Fortunately, this line of reasoning was lifted out of the confines of philosophy and applied to human development by James Mark Baldwin.

This now much-neglected figure reckoned, at the turn of the century, with the crucial difference between kinds of objects, and the meanings they have for the individual.[22] Baldwin kept alive the full spirit of dialectical thinking, and was not reluctant to reason in terms of closely knit dualities. Thus, he was not frightened by the apparent self-body dualism, as most of us still are today, and set out frankly to describe reality as the individual experiences it, as the child constructs his sense of it. Baldwin postulated that the sense of the dualism of mind and body is something that develops as the child learns that he has an inside— a thought process—that is separate from the outer world of things. For example, there is something the child wants to control. He puts together a few memory images of how he controlled this object in the recent past, and then reaches out for the object. But suppose he finds that the object acts differently than he expected on the basis of the memory images he had put together: say, it turns out to be an unfriendly dog instead of the expected tame rabbit? In this way the child is forced to build and alter conceptual categories, refashion generalizations, and clarify specific details, to make them accord with the outer world of things. This teaches him that his memory images and thoughts are not the same as the world of hard and unpredictable things—that his "insides" (thoughts) have an existence "all their own" that may or may not permit easy control of the outer world.

Now, this self-body dualism, as we would expect, is not uniform in everyone. That is to say, some of us pay more attention to the external world, act in it more, test ourselves with the outside of our bodies. Others among us act less in the external world, shrink up more within ourselves, feed ourselves on thought and fantasy, take refuge from the demands of the outside, expand our inner life, and nourish ourselves on it. Our "self," in this case, our "sense of being," takes root more in what we feel inside, in what we think and imagine, than in what we actually do. In addressing ourselves to a different kind of opposing object, in order to come into being, *we become different kinds of organisms*. The idealistic Hegelian dialectic has now been worked out as an explanation of worldly character-types, in terms of individual preferences for ranges of objects and experience.

This is a considerable achievement. Having broached the basic dualism Baldwin went on to build up the following view of the development of the individual. The self-body dualism, he saw, was not primarily a liability for man. Far from it. By means of memory, reflection, and judgment, the individual uses the process of thought to control the external world. As an animal man alone could dependably stop the flow of experience, recombine its salient elements in his imagination, and propose new solutions to external problems. With the rise of thought as a means of control of the outer world man established his dominion over nature. The matter only becomes a liability when thought turns in upon itself, when the individual uses thought and fantasy to seek justification from within, rather than by testing himself in action. Baldwin concluded, then, that *one becomes an individual* by overcoming problems, by making successful decisions in trial-and-error action. One gains experience as he successfully combines the inner modes of thought with the outer mode of action.

What concept could serve to convey the unity of the individual —the fusion of the duality in the acting person? Baldwin, along with Dewey and W. M. Urban, borrowed a term from the Austrian psychologists—the word "funded." Baldwin used "funded" to describe the synthesis of inner and outer, the unity that is forged in successful action. As the inner thoughts meet the outer problem and help the individual to overcome it, the organism forms a coherent link with its object, and closes the gap between itself and the world. Every gap successfully closed is a satisfactory experience. Hence, in Baldwin's view, the organism "funds" experiences by overcoming the inner-outer dualism, by using the mind and body in one active, outer-directed unity. The organism then possesses a fund of experience, deposited in its very structure. Individual development takes the form of an equation: the synthesis of inner thoughts and outer acts = unity = the well-funded person = satisfactory experience = individuation.

Now, as we are finding out in the theory of schizophrenia,[23] the schizophrenic is precisely the one who lacks this unity, this funded fusion earned through outer-directed experience. He takes refuge in the world of symbol-objects, and forfeits trial-and-error experience in the external world. It was Dewey who saw very clearly the trick that nature plays on the human animal. He stressed the difference between the two kinds of experience—the experience that is lived by the flesh, and the experience that is recaptured only in hollow words.[24] Words mean little to the development of our total personality unless we connect them up with some kind of lived experience. "War is hell" means little to a munitions or missiles profiteer, who has never lived through the experience of killing, seen close friends torn apart, or children's limbs gathered up in a basket for anonymous mass burial. "War is hell" means much to one who has built the words into his system by months and years of tasting grit in a foxhole, of trembling at the sound of human breathing in the night. But man is in a peculiar position in the animal world—he can talk about things without having any actual experience of them. The fact that he can do this predisposes him to the great danger that he will cut himself off from real living in the world, from real commitment to his acts, and will take refuge in fabrications of his self in fantasy. It is this danger to which the individual we call schizophrenic has succumbed.

We can sum up this whole section, then, by adding an indispensable third dimension to the two we have already described:

*The dimension of individual action of seemingly disparate phenomenal kinds.* This is the strain between self and body; it is reflected in the difference between experience available in words, versus the experience which is funded in the total organism, the lived experience that forges a unity in the individual. Schizophrenia is the microcosm of the failure to forge this unity, the failure of the self to come into being substantially in a hard world of things. Man is basically a body, as Comte and Bergson saw, subserved by a mind, but the schizophrenic makes heroic efforts to reverse this formulation. If Mills had worked with this mind-body dialectic, he would have been able to complete what he left unfinished with his thesis of vocabularies of motivation: the plethora of role vocabularies of motivation, the profuse symbol-world that the dweller in modern complex society cannot control in any self-satisfying manner, is precisely the problem of schizophrenia. The confusion of the city-dweller that Simmel so beautifully described in *The Metropolis and Mental Life* is the schizophrenic's confusion: a profuse world of words, images, and objects, sensations which cannot be controlled, or ordered. Why not? Simply because the active organism has not developed the habit of taking a firm stance toward the external world; the individual has not learned the secure development of his initiatory powers in relation to ranges of external problems. The depressed person is, as we saw, poor in vocabularies of motive. The schizophrenic is overly rich, but this is a plenty which is unmatched by sure behavioral powers.[25]

III. *The Phenomenology of Alienation.* A complete social psychology must, then, comprise our three dimensions of individual action. It must include, indispensably, a phenomenology of object relations and organismic powers, a current of thinking that extends from Kant and Hegel to Husserl, Meinong, James, Baldwin, Bergson, and Dewey—and, more recently, Merleau-Ponty and Sartre. We know that Marx touched on this problem with his concept of alienation. But the fact that he did not develop it in full has produced two results: the continued strong appeal of his tantalizing hints and the frustration we experience when we try to put the unfinished concept to use. Mills himself was led to neglect the idea of alienation, for he acknowledged it with a casual observation about "Marx's cryptic and not too clear comments about it."[26] In dismissing a phenomenological approach to alienation, Mills recommitted Marx's error: he abandoned a necessary, thoroughgoing study of the individual subjectivity to a full-scale critique of society. Let us retrace this process, and see if we can point to the needed balance and synthesis between an individual and a social psychology.

Marx's early writings on alienation can be summed up directly and simply: they describe what we sketched above—the organism's need for objects in order fully to come into being. Self-powers grow only as they meet resistance. As Marx put it, in order *to be,* in order to have a nature, it is necessary that there be an object outside onself.[27] In other words, each organism must relate to some kind of object in order to substantiate itself in the world. This is the basic phenomenology of alienation: the failure to develop self-powers by transacting with the world of things. "But," the reader may say, "everyone has dealings with objects and develops some kind of unified self-powers." This is obviously true, but it is important to stress the words "some kind." Let us go back here to our discussion of the schizophrenic. It is becoming increasingly clear that there are marked differences in self-body unity, as Baldwin described this dualism. Organisms that are poorly "funded" tend to lack the secure unity that is forged in active experience. Self and body drift apart, so to speak. R. D. Laing's recent work on schizophrenia is so far the best theoretical handling of this drift.[28] The schizophrenic is, as we noted, someone who has been accustomed to relating to symbol-objects rather than person-objects,[29] and his executive behaviors are not surely developed—he is less individuated in the sense that Baldwin understood this process.

*Alienation as the Forfeiting of Self-Powers.* Marx, quite correctly, and from the start, put the burden of coming into being upon the active development of one's powers. For him, alienation meant, first and foremost, the overshadowing of the organism by the object. And this is exactly what we see in schizophrenia, where the individual cannot navigate securely in a threatening world of things, simply because he has failed to develop sure powers for coping with them.[30] Marx leaves no doubt about his meaning when he singles out for criticism the traditional philosopher, who is "himself an abstract form of alienated man . . . The whole *history of alienation* . . . is therefore only the *history of the production* of abstract thought, i.e., of absolute, logical, speculative thought." [31] In other words, the philosopher is, par excellence, the individual who relates to symbol-objects rather than to person-objects, for the development of his self. What exactly is Marx driving at here? Simply, that any thought that divorces one from action, and separates itself from involvement of the total individual, is alienated. Marx makes this clear: alienation exists when man " . . . *objectifies* himself by *distinction* from and in *opposition* to abstract thought, which constitutes alienation as it exists and as it has to be transcended." [32] In the language of the new theory of schizophrenia, this would read: The individual who strives to develop a sense of self merely in opposition to symbol-objects sentences himself to the danger of the loss of the real world of external things. He sentences himself to a fantasy existence divorced from and unworthy of human powers.

By living in the fantasy world of symbol-objects, and renouncing action in the external world, the individual seems forced logically to abandon his commitment to the external world. Marx, in attacking German idealism, accused the traditional philosopher of this very failing. When one abandons commitment to the external world, one attempts to justify himself in fantasy, since he can no longer do so by his acts. The groundwork for a false morality is laid, whereby the individual divorces himself from commitment to his acts. He no longer feels that he has a stake in anything he does. This kind of fantasy justification of oneself has the direst of consequences, for it leads to the renunciation of any further stake in his own active initiatory powers. In schizophrenia the splitting off of the self and the body is carried to an extreme. Not only his acts but also the body of the schizophrenic become hindering objects, which are set off against his free consciousness. Now, free consciousness floating about uncommitted to the world of real things can hardly be a desirable condition, and, again, it is this very condition that Marx struck out against. He saw that the renouncing of commitment to the consequences of one's own acts leads logically and inevitably to something more: divorce from the *community* of fellow men.

Marx described this process in terms of alienation of the producer from his product. When the producer renounces active control in the shaping of his object, his work becomes unrelated to his own powers. The objects he produces, therefore, do not confront him as his own. This means that the world of his creation is not his own world. So, says Marx, if man is estranged from his own products, from his own life activity, he is also estranged from others.[33] *Anything* that confronts him is then alien to him. He has no responsibility for the free creation of it, or involvement in it. To lose self-powers is to lose community, for schizophrenics as well as for modern industrial man. *All* objects in their field confront them as *alien* objects, *for which they are not morally responsible.* When labor is coerced, man is separated from his fellows, because he is no longer committed to the consequences of his active powers. This is the phenomenology of contemporary immorality, which extends from politics to juvenile delinquency.

It is really striking how Marx's views on alienated labor join up with our latest theoretical understanding of schizophrenia. For example, schizophrenic passivity is a direct reflex of the abrogation of one's powers in the face of the object. The object's powers are greater than those of the self. If you relate to an object under your own initiatory powers, then it becomes an object which enriches your own nature. If you lack initiatory powers over the object, it takes on a different value, for it then becomes an individuality which crowds your own nature. This is nowhere more patent than in the schizophrenic's self-effacement in a threatening world, where everything has existential priority but himself. As a result, in order for the schizophrenic to benefit from this world, he has to take part in it on its terms. Normally, if one's own powers are sufficiently involved in producing and maintaining the relationship with an object, the power of the object becomes the power of one's own nature. Indeed, one can say that the very existence of the precise object is partly a function of one's own manipulatory powers. (For example, a girl really comes to exist as a feminine sex object for the adolescent only as he learns to exercise active courtship powers in relation to her.) Hence, it seems fair to say that modern industrial man finds himself in a true schizophrenic position in relation to the objects he makes: since he has no control over the produced object, and does not bring his own creative and directive forces into play in producing it, the object does not exist on *his* terms. As a result, he must enjoy the object on *its* terms. He must show the same passivity in the face of the object that the powerless schizophrenic shows. And this modern man does—at time-clocked work, on bombastic political issues, in the profusion of fragmented college courses, in front of the television screen. Marx's views on alienation are thus confirmed by the most sophisticated thought of the human sciences: alienated man is man separated from involvement with and responsibility for the effective use of his self-powers. Durkheim, too, in his views on anomie, summed up succinctly the identical problem: "To be a person is to be an autonomous source of action." [34]

( Marx understood alienation also in a second sense, which is too familiar to need expansion: the individual skews his perceptions by orienting to objects in terms of their use-value and commodity-value. This prevents him from throwing fresh perceptions on the object. It is just this automaticity, in fact, which the best efforts of modern psychotherapy try to remedy.)

*Alienation as an Empirical Problem.* Thus, the history of the concept of alienation is now about to enter a new phase. Kant, Fichte, and Hegel had supplied a basic phenomenology for analyzing the interplay of self and objects. First Feuerbach, and then Marx, had to relocate the analysis from the ideal level to the real: alienation had to become a man-centered problem. Now, a full century later, we are beginning to show how alienation as a man-centered problem *actually occurs.* This has been a tedious and halting hundred-year development. Marx, we know, left the man-centered focus and espoused an historicism. Baldwin picked up the earlier Hegelian focus again by centering his analysis on the development of perceptions in children. George Mead and Dewey also mined this approach. Mead fashioned a suggestive self-other dialectic. Dewey developed a very provocative but unfortunately little used phenomenology of organisms versus objects in his *Experience and Nature.*[35]

But the central problem in this historic development remained: how to unite the individual-phenomenological with the social dimensions of the problem of alienation? This means uniting early ( phenomenological ) Marx with late ( social ) Marx; and, more comprehensively, uniting Mills' social psychology with his social criticism. I hope we have demonstrated that this could only be done effectively by a fully cross-disciplinary approach to human break-down. We had to have a genetic view of individual development, which stressed both behavioral and vocabulary elements of human action. In the phenomena of depression and schizophrenia we have succeeded in uniting, theoretically, a phenomenology of individual development with the personal life history and full social field. In the modern theory of mental illness the phenomenological aspects of individual action merge with the social role aspects. We have sketched out both syndromes, and it is obvious from these sketches that they can be understood basically as problems in action and perception. This understanding did not spring full blown, as we noted, nor did it come from medical psychiatry. Simmel had spoken of the dispersal of self-identity, attendant upon role-fragmention in complex, industrial, urban society; and Mills also put heavy stress on the problems of multiple role vocabularies and conflicting allegiances between the institutions of religion, family, state, and occupation.

The circle can only really be closed by providing empirical substantiation for alienation. In order to do this we had to show that alienated individuals *really break down,* as they do in the two major syndromes of modern psychiatry. And, we had to find in the causes of their breakdown the same factors at work as in the hypothetical problem of alienation.

Finally, one more clarification remains. In order to find in the early Marx the basis for a radical critique of society, we must show how individual breakdown is related to the full social field. Is mental illness due to some peculiarly alienated conditions of society? There seems to be every indication that it is. Let us briefly recapitulate the outstanding features of the two major syndromes.

First, depression is characterized by an inhibition in perception and action. The depressed person is too uncritically committed to a narrow range of objects and role-behaviors. When something occurs to undermine role-behavior that was previously satisfying, the new problematic situation becomes overwhelmingly threatening. The individual, lacking the vocabularies and perceptions with which to move ahead, bogs down in futile self-accusation and surrender.

Likewise, schizophrenia is characterized by an inhibition in the possibilities of action. A precarious self-body integration, the foundation for which is laid in childhood, leads the individual to a dangerous separation from active engagement in the real external world. Action takes place largely in fantasy, and the self that is developed lacks a firm foundation in lived experience.[36]

In both these behavioral phenomena we can see clearly that the individual needs the possibilities for self-satisfying action in a world of rich experience. When the possibilities for this action bog down, and the individual is not armed with dependable behavioral alternatives, there is either temporary or permanent surrender of self-powers. But what are the social needs? How is society responsible in terms of the roles it makes available? If man contains no essence, how is society responsible for the kind of human nature he develops? There are any number of exciting glimpses of the social burden of individual failure. We are beginning to see some striking differences in the bogging down of action: differences by social class; [37] differences by the type of society and social structure.[38] We are beginning to understand that menopausal depression is a problem in availability of alternate cultural roles; [39] that hysteria is a problem in level of awareness and communication; [40] that, more broadly, both schizophrenia and depression are problems in early training and life experience. Along with this, we are learning that the physio-chemical, reductive approach to behavioral malfunction offers comfort only to researchers seeking prestigious grants,[41] and to those who are already sick. A *preventive* attack on mental illness must focus on the total social situation: kinds of family and early training, kinds of social structure, kinds of opportunities available to the adult.

*Alienation, Illness, and Contemporary Society.* Surely, however, even the society that we call "alienated" is building for a better, healthier, more intelligent environment for its citizens? The fight for mental health, for instance, is undertaken by social workers as well as laboratory chemists. This is just the point: we are having recourse to conventional solutions. If there is anywhere that a piecemeal approach to alienation is bound to fall hopelessly short, it is in the problem of mental illness. There must be instead a full-scale critique of the institutions of contemporary society. Alienation, as we now understand it, boils down to this: Self-powers grow up and are maintained in an increasing hierarchy of actions that overcome problematic situations. The typical syndromes that we see are *failures to carry through self-satisfying action*. The basis of this failure is, in every non-organic case, a kind of stupidity—a behavioral stupidity in the face of challenge, choice, and problems. The schizophrenic simply cannot cope with the pluralistic world of uncontrolled situations and objects; the depressed person simply cannot or will not understand the elements that make up his failure; the hysteric cannot formulate an essential cognitive grasp of the frustrating situation. In other words, *people break down when they are not "doing"—when the world about them does not reflect the active involvement of their own creative powers*. It has thus taken us a century and a quarter to return, with empirical support, to Marx's concept of alienation. Mental illness is itself the strongest possible critique of the *owning society:* man is *a doing* animal, primarily, and not an *owning* one. We cannot keep people immersed in the miasma of unreason represented by mass-consumer society and expect that they will fashion for themselves that commanding view which is the basis for health. We are so fond of talking about "emotional" problems precisely because it relieves us of the need of talking about *cognitive* problems.[42] People must be given information, knowledge, and the ability to command choices in difficult situations. This is exactly what we are not giving them. We have undertaken a mass-media brainwashing on the largest scale; we will not heed the most obvious criticism of our way of life; we are clinging to our institutions with a mechanicality that is terrifying. We are stubbornly objecting that the good life is here—that all we need do is tidy up the ramshackle neighborhoods and remedy the adolescent and traffic problems. And in all this we have sacrificed the primary task in man's search for himself: the championing of the fullest development of his own, responsible initiatory powers.

Mills' social psychology, then, however unfinished it may have been in certain theoretical areas, was supremely correct in its main contention: man must be approached from above. This disclosure stares us starkly in the face and we can no longer avoid recognizing it: *To be mentally sick is to be behaviorally stupid*, to be unable to relate one's powers to the world in an effective, self-satisfying way. Mills understood this by decrying man's loss of the "commanding view," of the grasp of the "total structure" of things, a loss attendant upon the demise of community and the fragmentation of labor in complex society.[43] In talking about the need to restore to man the "unit of prime decision," Mills could equally have been referring to behavioral breakdown in the individual case of mental illness.

With his insistence on the centrality of the concept of role, Mills saw that personality is transcended by society. Furthermore, with the accent on role, Mills opted for human possibility. Man's nature, as Nietzsche saw, is that of an animal "that may promise." He is not an animal like all the rest—who are already built firmly into their world. Alienation, in other words, is ultimately related partly to what man has not yet dared. It is related to still unformulated grand designs and as yet unknown powers. To forfeit executive powers is to forfeit humanity. Nothing could be clearer or simpler.

Nor could we, as a culture, be further from realizing this simple truth. Our most ambitious gropings aim at turning our entire society into docile consumers and uncritical bi-partisan voters on really crucial issues. But we can no longer aim at mere complacency, at consecrating the smug society. When Proudhon had urged equality of wages, Marx replied that this would only mean that society would become the capitalist. Now we see fully that the historical problem of alienation from one's executive powers would still remain. Perhaps at last, with mounting evidence from the theory of mental illness, we will not be able to avoid coming to grips with our social problems. We may yet be obliged—however painfully, reluctantly, and  deviously—to opt for man over things.

NOTES:

1. C. Wright Mills, *The Causes of World War III* (New York, 1958), p. 132.
2. Karl Marx, *Theses on Feuerbach.*
3. *Character and Social Structure* (New York, 1953), p. xiv. Needless to add, all references to this work include the specific recognition of Hans Gerth's co-authorship. But since this Festschrift is for Mills, and since my essay ranges over other works as well, it seems editorially proper to confine my references to Mills alone.
4. Ibid. p. 480.

5. Ibid. p. xiv.
6. C. Wright Mills, "Situated Actions and Vocabularies of Motive," *American Sociological Review*, 5, 1940, pp. 904-13.
7. *Character and Social Structure*, op. cit. p. 120.
8. H. Cantril, A. Ames, Jr., A. H. Hastorf, and W. H. Ittelson, "Psychology and Scientific Research," *Science*, 110, 1949, Part 1, pp. 461-4; Part 2, pp. 491-7; Part 3, pp. 517-22. Hans Toch and Malcolm S. MacLean, Jr., "Perception, Communication and Educational Research: A Transactional View," *Audio-Visual Communication Review*, 10, Sept.-Oct. 1962, pp. 55-77.
9. *Character and Social Structure*, op. cit. p. 70.
10. Ibid. p. 23.
11. Ibid. p. 11.
12. Paul A. Schilpp (ed.), *The Philosophy of John Dewey* (New York, 1939), pp. 555-6.
13. *Character and Social Structure*, op. cit. p. 78.
14. Ibid. p. 120.
15. Ibid. p. 78.
16. Ibid. pp. 154-5.
17. Elliot G. Mishler, review of "Character and Social Structure," *Public Opinion Quarterly*, 18, Fall 1954, pp. 323-6.
18. For a full discussion of this theory, see E. Becker, "Toward a Comprehensive Theory of Depression," *Journal of Nervous and Mental Disease*, 135, July 1962, pp. 26-35.
19. *Character and Social Structure*, op. cit. p. 47.
20. Ibid. p. 75.
21. Cf. the discussion of alienation in Part III below.
22. James Mark Baldwin, *Thought and Things*, Vol. 1: *Functional Logic, or Genetic Theory of Knowledge* (London, 1906).
23. E. Becker, "Toward a Theory of Schizophrenia," *Archives of General Psychiatry*, 7, Sept. 1962, pp. 170-81.
24. John Dewey, *Experience and Nature* (New York, 1958), pp. 292-3.
25. For a full development of this problem see E. Becker, *The Revolution in Psychiatry: The New Understanding of Man* (New York, 1964).

Mills did not use the dimension of strain between words and organismic powers, and consequently could not deal adequately with the problem of creating a dependable self-image. Mills points out that Fromm aptly calls a person who is completely dependent on the appraisals of others—and who consequently does not have "a center in himself"—an automaton (*Character and Social Structure*, p. 85 footnote). He notes further that Fromm does not solve the problem of the "façade self" versus the "real self." Mills criticizes Fromm's idea that the "real self" is buried somewhere in the psychic structure, and offers instead a "longitudinal" view: the "genuine self" is thought by him to be buried by "later socializations." Thus, Mills says that a person with a "real self" has a self-image that is independent of continued reflected appraisals, he has a strong center that is free of ever-renewed current opinion. Mills saw quite correctly that the self cannot exist prior to development of some kind, and this is evidently the burden of his criticism of Fromm. But he somewhat begs the question that Fromm is trying to answer. Fromm, equally correctly, sees that even the earliest self cannot be merely a creation of reflected appraisals, but must be more firmly embedded in the "psychic structure." Now, if both Mills and Fromm had stressed the organic-symbolic dichotomy of experience, this problem could have been clarified. There is a difference in the kind of self-image created by exercising one's powers, and that self-image which is gained merely through reflected appraisals. The merely reflected mirror image, in all its precariousness, shows up beautifully in the schizophrenic child who is so "loving and well-behaved." He has earned his self-image only by abrogating his executive powers, and this is a self-destructive barter. A dependable, strong, centered self, then, is earned by "funding" the total organism with experiences.

26. C. Wright Mills, *The Marxists* (New York, 1962), p. 112.

27. Karl Marx, *Economic and Philosophical Manuscripts,* in Erich Fromm, *Marx's Concept of Man* (New York, 1961), p. 182.

28. R. D. Laing, *The Divided Self. A Study of Sanity and Madness* (Chicago, 1960).

29. Thomas S. Szasz, "A Contribution to the Psychology of Schizophrenia," *Archives of Neurology and Psychiatry,* 77, April 1957, pp. 420-36; and *The Myth of Mental Illness: Foundations of a Theory of Personal Conduct* (New York, 1961).

30. Simmel's view of alienation as individual powerlessness in the face of a multiplicity of objects is also a statement of the problem of schizophrenia—the problem of lack of control over a profuse world. In fact, Simmel offered a view of individuation that is identical with Baldwin's and Dewey's conception of "funding": the subject integrates himself into the world by successfully transacting with its objects, and accumulates the *contents* of his culture both within and outside his personality, in the process. This is another instance of the great historical convergence on the problem of alienation. See Rudolph H. Weingartner, *Experience and Culture, the Philosophy of Georg Simmel* (Middletown, Conn., 1962), pp. 78, 82-4.

31. Karl Marx, *Economic and Philosophical Manuscripts,* in Erich Fromm, *Marx's Concept of Man,* op. cit. pp. 174-5.

32. Ibid. p. 175.

33. Karl Marx, *Economic and Philosophical Manuscripts,* in C. Wright Mills, *Images of Man, The Classic Tradition in Sociological Thinking* (New York, 1960), p. 503.

34. Emile Durkheim, "On Anomie," reprint of various selections in C. Wright Mills, *Images of Man,* op. cit. p. 480.

35. See E. Becker, *The Revolution in Psychiatry,* op. cit.

36. I am, admittedly, overly simplifying this complex phenomenon in this

brief space, but these are the main dimensions. For a full theoretical treatment see *The Revolution in Psychiatry*, op. cit.

37. Y. A. Cohen, *Social Structure and Personality* (New York, 1961). Arthur J. Prange, Jr. and M. M. Vitols, "Cultural Aspects of the Relatively Low Incidence of Depression in Southern Negroes," *International Journal of Social Psychiatry*, 8, Spring 1962, pp. 104-12.

38. Seymour Parker, "Eskimo Psychopathology in the Context of Eskimo Personality and Culture," *American Anthropologist*, 64, Feb. 1962, pp. 76-96.

39. Arnold M. Rose, "A Social-Psychological Theory of Neurosis," in *Human Behavior and Social Process: An Interactionist Approach*, ed. A. M. Rose (Boston, 1962), pp. 537-49; Becker, "Social Science and Psychiatry: The Coming Challenge," *The Antioch Review*, Fall 1963.

40. Thomas Szasz, *The Myth of Mental Illness*, op. cit.

41. Cf. S. S. Kety, "Biochemical Theories of Schizophrenia," *Science*, 129, Part 1, May 1959, pp. 1528-32; Part 2, June 1959, pp. 1590-96.

42. Cf. the important recent adduction of controlled empirical evidence on the relationship between the degree of alienation and the level of knowledge: Melvin Seeman and John W. Evans, "Alienation and Learning in a Hospital Setting," *American Sociological Review*, 27, Dec. 1962, pp. 772-82.

43. C. Wright Mills, *The Power Elite* (New York, 1956), p. 322. See also Mills' important late paper "Culture and Politics," in *Power, Politics and People: The Collected Essays of C. Wright Mills*, edited by Irving Louis Horowitz (New York, 1963), pp. 236-46. Here Mills' social psychology demonstrates its full applicability to the problem of "behavioral stupidity" in complex society. To be a "normal Cheerful Robot" is to have more choice than the mentally ill, but to be—all the same—restricted in certain crucial perceptions and choices. The cure for stupidity on *all* points of the continuum would be to maximize personal flexibility to face historically new challenges. This would take care of "abnormal neurosis" as well as the "normal neurosis" decried by Rousseau and Nietzsche. Mills saw his task as that of providing a compelling picture of historically crucial automaticity in the present social system.

# 8

ANDREW HACKER

## Power To Do What?

There has seldom been a more perplexed group of reviewers than those asked to comment upon *The Power Elite*. The book was "important," "provocative," even "brilliant." That it ought to be read and pondered was a universal recommendation. But in the final analysis what was most troublesome was Mills' perception of American society.

The America he described was quite different from that usually perceived by students of the social scene. He had a question: Who runs the country? And he had the answer: A power elite. But the reviewers remained skeptical, for to their minds neither question nor answer was spelled out sufficiently to be convincing. They wanted detailed illustrations showing just how the power elite uses its power. Nowhere, they complained, was there an inventory or even a sampling of the elite decisions that have shaped the course of American life.

"It is far from clear what kinds of decisions the decision-makers make," one reviewer commented.[1] Another wanted to know "what the power elite does and precisely how it does it."[2] A third found it "remarkable and indeed astounding" that Mills did not "examine an array of specific cases to test his major hypothesis."[3] The general perplexity was summarized by a critic who complained: "Curiously, except in a few instances, Mills fails to specify what the big decisions are."[4]

An attempt will therefore be made here to complete a piece of business that Mills left unfinished. But before this is done it is in order to comment on the limits of elite power in American society.

America has been and continues to be one of the world's most democratic nations. Here, far more so than elsewhere, the public is allowed to participate widely in the making of social and political policy. The public is not unaware of its power, and the ordinary American tends to be rather arrogant about his right and competence to participate. The average citizen, moreover, is not a deferential person, and he looks down on rather than up to those who in other times and places might be considered his "betters." This is why, from Alexander Hamilton and Alexis de Tocqueville to the present day, the specter of the "tyranny of the majority" has haunted America. The power of the public—Mills would call it the "mass"—is real, and its manifestations are all too familiar. In the realms of public education and popular culture, in civil liberties and civil rights, and often in local government—in all of these areas majority sentiment prevails. The people think they know what they want and are in no mood to be led to greener pastures. This is why we have driver-education courses in the high schools, lowbrow comedy on television, public loyalty investigations, and de facto racial segregation.[5] These conditions persist because they have the wholehearted backing of local and national majorities. Policy-makers know that in a democracy public sentiment must be accommodated.

It should be emphasized that these conditions are not the product of elite manipulation. If the majority flexes its muscles, it is usually a spontaneous show of strength and quite independent of the urgings of the mass media or the plans made in the higher circles. Indeed, the public throws up leaders of its own choosing on issues such as these. At one juncture it will be a Wisconsin senator, at another a Mississippi governor. These personalities are outside the elite, and their power is a reflection of the power of the majority. Indeed, the elite has no real interest in or objection to democracy in the areas that have been mentioned here. The military establishment will cheerfully check the loyalty of its draftees; the large corporations are quite willing to sponsor televised trash; and the inner circle of the Executive Branch will move very slowly indeed in matters of desegregation. In short, the elite is content to let the public blow off steam on certain questions. This is acknowledged to be necessary, for democracy must have issues to squabble about. If attention is focused on fluoride in the water and progressivism in the schools, then eyes will be deflected from more important matters. For there are realms where the public cannot participate, must not participate, and ought not to want to participate.

To return to the original problem: Mills' failure to show "what kinds of decisions the decision-makers make," to "specify what the big decisions are." A reading of *The Power Elite* makes clear that the men who run America's large corporations stand at the center of the topmost circle. They, more than their military and governmental counterparts, have power that is both autonomous and unchecked. The military are still heavily controlled by the politicians, and the politicians must be responsive to the public.

The conventional view, of course, is that the businessman is far from a free agent. Any executive will wax eloquent on how he is hemmed in on all sides. He will point to a plethora of government agencies, all of which regulate his conduct. There is the Federal Trade Commission, the National Labor Relations Board, the Antitrust Division of the Justice Department, and of course the Internal Revenue Service. And then there are labor unions, further limiting his freedom of action. He has customers and suppliers, telling him what they want and what he can get; and he has stockholders clamoring for dividends, capital gains, and efficient management. And of course there is the ubiquitous public that must be satisfied at all stages, lest bankruptcy be the consequence. The question, however, is not whether businessmen feel hamstrung, for they have protested their powerlessness since they were first told to buy safety-devices for their dangerous machines. The point is whether or not these limiting factors take on much significance when weighed against the areas of unrestricted action open to the corporate elite.

It should be noted at the outset that large corporations do not go bankrupt. They can be inefficient, as the steel companies have demonstrated, and still be profitable. Their relative share of the market can rise or fall, and their rank in the industry may change slightly over the years. But mergers and reorganizations keep the

assets and production facilities intact. To be sure, the corporate
elite must make its decisions with an eye on profitability. But in the
highest circles the concern is with the expansion of the enterprise
over a period of several decades, and profits are but a means to
this end. The real issue is how autonomous these enterprises are
and what are the consequences of their decisions for society as a
whole. What, in short, can the corporate elite do with the power
it is alleged to have?

First, in prices. Despite an occasional outburst from the White
House, the corporate managers can administer prices as they see
fit.[6] They are not required to submit proposed increases to any
government agency for approval, and they may ask what the market will bear. Generally speaking, the market will pay what is
asked.

On profits, stockholders expect only a certain modest dividend,
and this is usually passed on to them without discussion.[7] Top
management maintains a minimum level of earnings by its ability
to fix prices. In addition it decides what proportion of the earnings
will go to the stockholders and what proportion is to be retained
by the company.

Wages are of course subject to collective bargaining. But this
process simply maintains the status quo. For wage increases just
about keep pace with the cost of living, and the share of a corporation's income going to wages remains about the same over the
years. Management has even more freedom in setting salaries. Here
it can determine who is to become wealthy and how great this
wealth is to be. Decisions on executive compensation, in particular,
go far toward determining aspirations for an entire society. The
purchasing power bestowed on the men at and near the top makes
for a style of life that becomes a goal for those lower in the pyramid.[8]

Enough has been said and written about organization men emphasizing that employee behavior is both scrutinized and shaped
by those in the executive suites.[9] If it is asked why so many succumb to the pressure to conform, the answer is that most Americans want to succeed in their careers and are willing to pay the
price of success. That such a high price is exacted by the corporate
elite is itself instructive, for it has not been demonstrated that the
bland and well-rounded personality results in more sales or higher

production. Rather, this outlook is what management finds congenial to its own sensibilities. More significant, the habits inculcated in work-life inevitably spill over into private life—if such it can be called. The kinds of attitudes necessary for career-success are imparted to children and pervade marriage and other social relations.

The corporate elite decides what kinds of jobs are to be made available and how many of them there are to be. This is not simply management's traditional power to hire and fire. It is also the power to decide what kind of work individuals will do for a living. The decision to automate, for example, lessened the need for blue-collar workers and created permanent underemployment for many groups in society. The earlier decision to expand the number of white-collar jobs opened new opportunities to millions of Americans, thus elevating them to new stations in life and creating not only new benefits but also new anxieties. People fill jobs; jobs are not made for people. Corporate decisions to create certain types of employment cause people to alter their lives in such ways as to qualify for those positions. Those who cannot make the changes are consigned to the human discard-heap.

Corporate managements are free to decide where they will locate their plants and offices. The decision of many companies to have their headquarters in New York, for example, has changed the face of that city. This power has also contributed, probably more than anything else, to the suburban explosion, for the burgeoning white-collar class must find a place to live. A handful of executives decide which parts of the country are to prosper and which are to stagnate. If over half the counties in the United States lost population in the 1950-60 decade, this is largely because the corporate elite was unwilling to locate facilities in areas it considered unsuitable. On the other hand, those regions it does favor experience a radical transformation. New citizens move in and old values must adjust themselves to new influences. Cities and towns, while welcoming branch plants as sources of jobs and revenue, find that what were once local decisions are now made from the outside and by outsiders.[10] Moreover, as corporations expand across the nation they turn many of their white-collar employees into transients, a rootless middle-class prepared to pick up stakes as management beckons it to new job opportunities. The nomadic life has consequences for family and personality that are not without their disturbing qualities.

Quite obviously even the most respected corporation, with the most persuasive advertising agency, cannot induce the American public to buy a white elephant. But the example of the Edsel—like President Kennedy's 1962 ultimatum on steel prices—is an exception proving the rule. For if management is sensitive to the kinds of products that consumers will be willing to purchase, it also has the power to persuade the public that it ought to own such goods. Even more autonomy surrounds decisions on methods and materials of production. What should be noted is that the number and character of possessions have a signal impact on the personality of the owner.[11] Materialism is not uniquely American, nor is the high valuation placed on material possessions entirely the result of management decisions. But the perpetuation of this system of values, with its stress on tangible possession and labor-saving devices, is due to the corporate elite's judgment about what sales are needed if rates and turnover of production are to be kept at the optimum level.

Investment is the most important area of corporate decision-making, and it governs most of the decisions mentioned up to this point. Management alone decides when to invest—in new capital equipment, in new locations, in new processes, products, and personnel. It need not receive the approval of any governmental agency, and no such agency can compel a corporation to go ahead with an investment program if it feels like retrenching. While top executives will be attuned to the public's buying expectations, it can just as well shape those expectations by announcing a buoyant expansion program. The good will of investors need not be courted, since large corporations can use their retained earnings for investment purposes. And there is increasing reliance on the huge investing institutions—insurance companies, pension funds, banks, brokerage houses—for funds.[12] Representatives of these institutions sit on or are close to the boards of the large corporations and are really part of the corporate elite. Together they decide how and in what amounts capital will be invested over the decades to come. The power to make investment decisions is concentrated in a few hands, and it is the power to decide what kind of a nation America will be. Instead of government planning there is planning by an elite that is accountable to no outside agency. Its decisions set the order of priorities on national growth, technological innovation, and ultimately the values and behavior of human lives. Investment decisions are sweeping in their ramifications, and no one is unaffected by their consequences. Yet, this is an area where neither the public nor its government is able to participate. If the contours of the economy and society are being shaped in a hundred or so boardrooms, so far as the average citizen is concerned these decisions are in the lap of the gods.

Finally, it should be noted that the corporate elite is free to decide when the power at its disposal will not be used. It has already been noted that corporations have concluded that civil rights is not a concern of theirs, that they have made no voluntary effort to establish equal employment opportunities for all Americans. Ministers and professors may work for desegregation but executives, by far a more influential group, simply are not interested. While companies might, on their own initiative, endeavor to locate, train, and promote Negroes for positions of responsibility, such a suggestion would be looked upon as outlandish in any executive suite. Corporate management, by the same token, has decided that it bears no responsibility for upholding civil liberties, nor does it feel any obligation to stand behind employees who are attacked by self-appointed patriots. It might be proposed that corporations not only refuse to discharge employees who are unwilling to co-operate with legislative committees, but that they also make public their support for such dissenters. Needless to say, such a course of action does not occur to the corporate mind, even though such an exercise of influence would go far in the direction of defending freedoms of expression. Notwithstanding all the talk of a corporate conscience or a new dawn of corporate statesmanship, such rhetoric usually produces little more than a company contribution to the Boy Scouts or the Red Cross. On larger issues having political and moral overtones, the corporate elite remains quiescent, electing neither to lead the public when leadership is possible nor to defy the majority when that course is the only alternative.

These, then, are some of the decisions made by one segment of Mills' elite. These decisions add up to a substantial power, a power that is concentrated in a small circle of Americans who need not

account for their behavior. The decisions of the corporate elite do
not determine whether the nation is to have peace or war; but they
do decide what will be the shape of the nation in the decades
ahead. It should be clear by this time that the power of the corporate elite is not simply economic. On the contrary, its influence
reaches far into society and has a deep impact on the character and
personality of individual Americans. While additional forces are
at work, the corporation is becoming our most characteristic institution and other agencies are taking secondary positions. As the
corporation moves, so moves the nation. While predictions are
difficult, it is possible to suggest that corporate tendencies will become accelerated in the years to come, with power growing more
concentrated and individual citizens more dependent on large institutions for sustenance and direction. Yet, even as this development takes place, the power of the corporate elite will be invisible
to the unaided eye and the forms of political democracy will perpetuate the view that the public is master of its own destiny.

Mills never suggested that the corporate elite was a "conspiracy."
The top managers of the largest companies do not foregather at
periodic intervals to make their key decisions in concert. At the
same time it is clear that they know what is on one another's minds.
Whether they come together casually at their clubs or hunting
lodges, or slightly more formally at the Business Advisory Council
or the Committee for Economic Development or the Foreign Policy Association, they are definitely not isolated from each other.
Informal conversation elicits plans, hopes, and expectations. There
is a community of interest and sentiment among the elite, and this
renders any thought of a "conspiracy" both invalid and irrelevant.
Moreover the critical investment decisions bring together many
members of the elite—executives, bankers, brokers—and the agreement to expand or retrench is clearly based on consultation and
consensus. Such decisions, in addition, are made with the knowledge of what others are doing or plan to do. The lines of communication are built into the system.

Nor is there any notion that the corporate elite is a "class," any
more than the corporate world is "capitalist" in the traditional
sense. The members of the elite come from a variety of backgrounds, or at least from every stratum of the middle-class.[13] Birth

and breeding are of negligible importance, and promotion to the highest corporate circles is based on talent more than manners or connections. The conception of a "ruling class" does not apply. Those in the elite group are simply the men who sit in particular chairs at any particular time. The chairs, moreover, have the power rather than their occupants. And it is this point that deserves some elaboration.

The greater part of *The Power Elite* was a discussion of the personal characteristics, backgrounds, and morals of the men at the top. This emphasis on persons rather than positions grew stronger as the book proceeded. Mills' closing paragraph deals exclusively with the "men," the "they" who travel in the upper circles of power:

> The men of the higher circles are not representative men; their high position is not a result of moral virtue; their fabulous success is not firmly connected with meritorious ability. Those who sit in the seats of the high and the mighty are selected and formed by the means of power, the sources of wealth, the mechanics of celebrity, which prevail in their society. They are not men selected and formed by a civil service that is linked with the world of knowledge and sensibility. They are not men shaped by nationally responsible parties that debate openly and clearly the issues this nation now so unintelligently confronts. They are not men held in responsible check by a plurality of voluntary associations which connect debating publics with the pinnacles of decision. Commanders of power unequaled in human history, they have succeeded within the American system of organized irresponsibility.[14]

This, unfortunately, is a misplaced emphasis. It caused the book to be regarded as an attack on the *individuals* who preside over the corporate, military, and governmental bureaucracies. Mills, in so many words, accused these men of being not only pompous, vain, and ignorant, but also mediocre and immoral. This indictment has a great deal of truth in it. The men at the top are, as men, by no means an impressive group. Their character, however, is not at issue. For if the analysis is of power in contemporary American society, then the focus must be on the institutions rather than the individuals who staff them.

Mills gave some indication that this would be his line of approach in the opening pages of *The Power Elite*. There he pointed out that the elite are those with "access to the command of major institutions." Hope was held out that the institutions themselves would be analyzed in terms of their ability to make key decisions:

> The elite are simply those who have the most of what there is to have, which is generally held to include money, power, and prestige—as well as all the ways of life to which these lead. But the elite are not simply those who have the most, for they could not "have the most" were it not for their positions in the great institutions. F · such institutions are the necessary bases of power, of wealth, and of prestige. . . . No one, accordingly, can be truly powerful unless he has access to the command of major institutions, for it is over these institutional means of power that the truly powerful are, in the first instance, powerful.[15]

There is little point in discussing who has the power unless one explores the sources of that power. This needs to be stressed because there is strong reason to believe that the institutional structure determines the behavior of the men who hold positions in it. Put another way, it does not really matter who the officeholders are as individuals; for anyone placed in such an office would have much the same outlook and display much the same behavior.

To be sure, it is a lot easier to talk of people than positions, of individuals rather than institutions. For one thing, only the most technically-oriented reader can follow a discussion that omits personalities. Yet the really great social analysts—Marx, Weber, Veblen, Pareto—refused to be tempted in this direction. What is required, then, is an analysis of the great corporate institutions rather than the men who sit astride them.

Here are the names of a dozen of the institutions that direct the course of American society:

> General Motors Corporation
> Standard Oil Company of New Jersey
> American Telephone and Telegraph Company
> Atomic Energy Commission
> Central Intelligence Agency
> Ford Foundation
> National Education Association
> Chase Manhattan Bank

Metropolitan Life Insurance Company
Columbia Broadcasting System
*The New York Times*
Merrill, Lynch, Pierce, Fenner, and Smith

It is doubtful if even the well-informed citizen can name the president or chairman of half of these institutions. Nor should he feel any embarrassment about his ignorance. The man in one of the top chairs may have just arrived at his position last week, while the man in another may be just about to retire. Tenure is surprisingly short, and all incumbents are quite similar to those who have preceded and who will succeed them.

What is being said is that these institutions have lives and purposes of their own. No single person, not even the president or chairman, can be said to have made a critical corporate decision. If the man at the top sits at the controls, the car rides on rails he cannot move. The reason, of course, is that our corporate institutions are too large for a single individual to impress with his personality. Moreover the typical chief executive, sitting at the top for only a few years, spends much time in carrying out policies he did not himself inaugurate. His job is to organize his subordinates so that decisions will be carried out. He must, however, share the task of making those decisions, and it is hard to affix responsibility even at the top. The time has come when the institution in fact directs the man who in theory presides over it.[16]

The future holds in store a corporate America. The power that Mills attributed to the elite is a real power. The decisions the corporate elite is free to make are real decisions. Unfortunately the men at the top cannot in any meaningful way be held responsible for the actions the institutions take. Other men, in the same chairs, would behave no differently. At the same time we persist in thinking of great institutions as if they were small enterprises or voluntary associations. We assume either that they have no power or that their power is effectively nullified by countervailing forces. Corporate institutions are free to plan their future course of development, but they plan for their own purposes. The consequences are not simply profits but, more important, expansion of the corporate world into more and larger sectors of our national life. In defining their own roles and jurisdictions these institutions are oblivious to whether certain individuals are injured or neglected by the corporate thrust. At the same time they are above public control and take no responsibility for the social and psychological impact of their decisions. The situation, looked at from one vantage point, is highly rational and organized: corporate behavior is predictable and the corporate life is secure.

Viewed from a different direction a corporate America will hang on the edge of anarchy. Despite their sophisticated rhetoric and civilized demeanor, the great institutions of the nation have the power to carry the public along a road it has not consented to travel and for which there are no discernible alternatives.

NOTES:

1. Robert Bierstedt, *Political Science Quarterly*, 71, Dec. 1956, p. 607.
2. Alexander Heard, *Annals of the American Academy of Political and Social Science*, 311, May 1957, p. 170.
3. Robert Dahl, *American Political Science Review*, 52, June 1958, p. 466.
4. Daniel Bell, *American Journal of Sociology*, 64, Nov. 1958, p. 238. The "few instances," Bell points out, were all military decisions, such as dropping the atom bomb over Japan, intervening in Korea, and defending the offshore islands of Quemoy and Matsu. But these "examples" of autonomous elite decisions fail to underpin Mills' thesis. For they were, in reality, presidential decisions, and they were taken only after painstaking study of what the public reaction would be to them.
5. For an elaboration of this argument, see Andrew Hacker, "Common Men and Uncommon Men," *Nomos IV* (New York, 1962), pp. 308-33.
6. The steel industry is, of course, the outstanding example. See Gardiner C. Means, *Pricing Policy and the Public Interest* (New York, 1962).
7. The actual role of the presumed "owners" of American industry is laid bare in Joseph Livingston's *The American Stockholder* (Philadelphia, 1958).
8. In a *New Yorker* advertisement aimed at recruiting advertisers for its own columns, a newspaper widely circulated in executive circles proclaimed: "What the *Wall Street Journal* reader learns to favor, others everywhere will yearn to possess."
9. The better-known are: William H. Whyte, Jr., *The Organization Man* (New York, 1956); Vance Packard, *The Pyramid Climbers* (New York, 1962); and Martin Gross, *The Brain Watchers* (New York, 1962).
10. The question of changing power relations in local communities is just beginning to be studied. For a brief analysis, see Roland J. Pellegrin and Charles H. Coates, "Absentee-Owned Corporations and Community

Power Structure," *American Journal of Sociology*, 61, March 1956, pp. 413-19. Mills himself did an important study in this area during World War II: "Small Business and Civic Welfare," Report of the Smaller War Plants Corporation to the Special Committee to Study Problems of American Small Business, Senate Document No. 135, 79th Congress, Second Session (Washington, 1946).

11. The best work on new consumption patterns and what they mean has been done by David Riesman. See his essays in *Individualism Reconsidered* (Glencoe, 1954).

12. See A. A. Berle's two books, *The Twentieth Century Capitalist Revolution* (New York, 1954) and *Power Without Property* (New York, 1959).

13. For a study of the backgrounds of the presidents of America's 100 largest corporations, see Andrew Hacker, "The Elected and the Anointed," *American Political Science Review*, 55, Sept. 1961, pp. 539-49.

14. C. Wright Mills, *The Power Elite* (New York, 1956), p. 361.

15. Ibid. p. 9.

16. John K. Galbraith has written: "Organization replaces individual authority; no individual is powerful enough to do much damage. Were it otherwise, the stock market would pay close attention to retirements, deaths, and replacements in the executive ranks of large corporations. In fact it ignores such details in tacit recognition that the organization is independent of any individual." *The Affluent Society* (Boston, 1958), p. 102. A former president of Du Pont, Crawford Greenewalt, says much the same thing: "The more effective an executive, the more his own identity and personality blend into the background of his organization." *The Uncommon Man* (New York, 1959), p. 72.

# 9

KENNETH WINETROUT

## Mills and the Intellectual Default

The world of multiplicity, acceleration, discontinuity, which Henry Adams foresaw in his autobiography, is with us. This sort of world, with its confusions and intricacies, would seem to be the very kind which would place heavy demands on him we call the intellectual. Further, it would seem that such a world would offer an inviting prospect for the intellectual. The present situation suggests, however, that the world is not looking to the intellectual; nor is the intellectual particularly looking at the world. We have, as it were, a mutual withdrawal.

C. Wright Mills in his books and teaching has tried manfully to understand this withdrawal and at the same time to bring about a juncture of the intellectual and the world. This is an underlying theme in each of his books. Mills looks at the world and sees a mass society without hope, plan, or rebellion; a society of little men who never talk back, never take a stand. He sees a power elite characterized by mindless immorality and organized irresponsibility; a world moving toward World War III. When he turns to the intellectual, he sees a series of unfortunate developments: a methodological failure, a refusal to formulate an ideology, a retreat from political involvement, and a loss of nerve.

Mills' description of the function of the intellectual seems commensurate with the fearful situation he himself finds in the world at large. He would have him serve as, he believes, the classical

147

sociologist did in the past: to state "the main drift of modern society"; "to make sense of what is happening in the world and to gauge what may be going to happen in the near future." It has to do with the kind of questions a man asks and how he goes about answering them.[1] The intellectual confronts "the situations of all men everywhere . . . he is capable of transcending drift." [2] He has the capacity to "shift from one perspective to another, and in the process to build up an adequate view of total life and of its components." [3] An intellectual pushes "people a bit closer to the experience of being full citizens." [4] His duty is "to confront complications," "to sort out insistent issues in such a way as to open them up for the work of reason," to "respond to events." [5] With so broad an assignment to the scholar and perhaps an unduly pessimistic view of the world, Mills understandably finds the intellectual deficient.

To many a fellow sociologist, a serious shortcoming in Mills would be the lack of a coherent theoretical framework, his disinclination to apply statistics in support of his hypotheses. Mills declares that we have become a "white-collar" culture, and then grounds this assertion largely in a few descriptive chapters bolstered by his personal convictions. His accusation that a power elite has taken over the United States is treated much the same way. By and large, Mills' method is that of concerned protest. He does not develop any technique for measuring conformity, deviation, or authoritarianism. As a result many would consider him a failure as a methodologist.

However, one of Mills' definite contributions is his criticism of the methods of those who have made a reputation as originators of methodologies. His condemnation of two weaknesses in contemporary sociology is the heart of *The Sociological Imagination*. While his attack is centered on members of his own discipline, it applies to a high percentage of functioning intellectuals whatever may be their special area.

Mills engages in a running battle with those at one end of the continuum who are all theory and those at the other end who are all statistical fact. He calls the first Grand Theory:

> The basic cause of grand theory is the initial choice of a level
> of thinking so general that its practitioners cannot logically get

> down to observation. They never, as grand theorists, get down
> from the higher generalities to problems in their historical and
> structural contexts. This absence of a firm sense of genuine
> problems, in turn, makes for the unreality so noticeable in their
> pages. One resulting characteristic is a seemingly arbitrary and
> certainly endless elaboration of distinctions, which neither en-
> large our understanding nor make our experience more sensi-
> ble. This in turn is revealed as a partially organized abdication
> of the effort to describe and explain human conduct and society
> plainly.[6]

It ends up as an "arid game of Concepts" rather than a clear and
orderly description of problems which could help us solve them.[7]
Mills selects Talcott Parsons as the representative grand theorist.

> In *The Social System* Parsons has not been able to get down to
> the work of social science because he is possessed by the idea
> that the one model of social order he has constructed is some
> kind of universal model; because, in fact, he has fetishized his
> Concepts. What is "systematic" about this particular grand
> theory is the way it outruns any specific and empirical prob-
> lem. . . . Its problem, its course, and its solutions are grandly
> theoretical.[8]

Mills recognizes the need for theory, but theory is "only a formal
moment." One departs from theory to work on specific issues. The
grand theorist does not take this step. He suffers from a "formalist
withdrawal," and what should have been only "a pause seems to
have become permanent." [9]

If grand theory is all theory, then abstracted empiricism is all
statistic. One aspect of the scholar's work monopolizes his enterprise and other aspects are ignored. In abstracted empiricism, we
encounter the "methodological inhibition." Only that which lends
itself to statistical manipulation is worthy of study, and is in fact
studied. Under these circumstances, what is left are the problems which survive "the fine little mill of the Statistical Ritual."
These ritualists are men whose "most cherished professional self-
image is that of the natural scientist." [10] Method determines the
area of study. "The thinness of the results is matched only by the
elaboration of the methods used and the care employed." [11]

We wind up with fact-fetishism, with a "social science of the narrow focus, the trivial detail, the abstracted almighty unimportant fact." [12] I confess I despair when I turn to some of the scholarly journals and find their pages dominated by formulae and tables and, perhaps, in the conclusion there may be something, somewhat less than, in William James' expression, that peppercorn of knowledge. I readily grant that we need some of this refinement in procedure, but there is the danger that methodological tools may replace sociological problems.

In both cases, Mills finds an abdication, a lack of "firm connection with substantive problems." The grand theorists escape from real problems "by a cloudy obscurantism" and the empiricist by a "formal and empty ingenuity." [13]

Perhaps the trouble starts in the cradle of the intellectual, namely, the graduate school. Whatever may be the strengths of the graduate school, it encourages a number of trends inimical to the work of the intellectual as seen by Mills. There is an over-emphasis on specialization; technicians are prepared for tiny niches. Specialization re-enforces another trend: the superstitious respect for disciplinary boundaries. "... it is usually considered poor taste, inside the academies, to write a book outside one's field. The professionalization of knowledge has thus narrowed the grasp of the individual." [14] It is easier and safer "to restrict oneself to smaller problems as part of a tacit conspiracy of the mediocre." [15] All of this seems quite out of touch with what is actually happening, with what needs to be done. "Intellectually, the central fact of today is an increasing fluidity of boundary lines; conceptions move with increasing ease from one discipline to another." [16]

But the academic world has ever been prepared to defy reality if it so decides. As a result of specialization and this protective attitude toward boundaries, college work readily lends itself to bureaucratization. "Bureaucracy increasingly sets the conditions of intellectual life and controls the major market for its product." [17] In 1951, Mills finds the graduate school organized as a feudal system where "the student trades his loyalty to one professor for protection against other professors." [18]

Eight years later, things have changed a bit as Mills sees it. The professor is no longer lord at the top but is now himself vassal to a new lord known as the client. This client could be a foundation, the military, the Department of Agriculture, or an industry. Mills speaks of a shift of scholarly responsibility from the public to the client. The habit is "large-scale bureaucratic research into small-scale problems." [19] The goal in this atmosphere is to develop a "gadget" which can be marketed successfully: an interview technique, a test, which can be sold to a client.[20]

To meet the new needs, there arose a new breed, "academic entrepreneurs"—men who could organize a group of academic technicians into a team, could oversee work-flow, write directives, and have a consultant budget of $100,000 to keep things going. As Mills puts it, one could now become a university executive without becoming a dean; and when someone has something to sell, one may sell out.

If Mills finds the intellectual dedicated to grand theory and the statistical ritual, more and more a technician member of an administrative team affiliated to a client, then it can come as no surprise that he finds the present-day intellectual in ideological retreat. The methodological concentration is matched by ideological neglect.

An ideology, in the broad sense, a political philosophy, has four aspects: a position which guides attacks on other ideologies, conditions speeches; an articulation of ideals; agencies of action; and a theory of man, society, and history. It runs a full gamut from theory to action, from past to future.[21]

Mills issues two warnings: ideology is playing an increasingly important role in making history; [22] and "the end of ideology is an ideology—the ideology of an ending—the ending of political reflection as a public fact," a "refusal to work out an explicit political philosophy." [23]

Three primary qualities condition this ideological failure in the United States: the conservative mood, the liberal rhetoric, and an inadequate understanding of Marx. Mills would be less disturbed if mid-century Americans had come up with something akin to classic conservatism: "traditionalism become self-conscious and elaborated, argumentative and rationalized" with a belief in a natural aristocracy.[24] But this did not happen. "Neither Burke nor Locke is the source of such ideology as the American elite have found truly congenial. Their ideological source is Horatio Alger." [25] When Alger seems a trifle too unsophisticated, they can turn to Russell Kirk and his fellow neo-conservatives with their reliance on Providence.

The United States is "a conservative country without any conservative ideology." [26] We are engaged in an ideological war without any clear notion of an ideology; what we have instead is the conservative mood.

> . . . an irresponsible style of pretentious smugness. Curiously enough, for a conservative mood, it is not a snobbery linked with nostalgia, but, on the contrary, with what is just one-step-ahead-of-the-very-latest-thing, which is to say that it is a snobbery based not on tradition but on fashion and fad. Those involved are not thinking for a nation, or even about a nation; they are thinking of and for themselves. In self-selected coteries, they confirm one another's mood, which thus becomes snobbishly closed—and quite out of the main stream of the practice of decision and the reality of power. One may thus suppose, quite correctly, that the conservative mood is a playful little fashion toyed with in a period of material prosperity by a few comfortable writers. Certainly it is not a serious effort to work out a coherent view of the world in which we live and the demands we might make upon it as political men—conservative, liberal or radical. [27]

The best the conservative can do is offer the shadow stuff of a conservative mood; and turning to the liberal, we get not an ideology but the "liberal rhetoric." Liberalism has been stretched verbally until there is no common core of meaning, banalized into softness, formalized into administrative routine. "The New Deal left no liberal organization to carry on any liberal program." [28] The defenders of civil liberties get so busy defending civil liberties that there is neither time nor energy left over to use these liberties. We have "the intellectual and political collapse of American liberalism." [29]

In *The Marxists*, Mills continues to hammer away at this theme. Liberalism is certainly not its former self: "as an ideology, and on a world wide scale, liberalism now becomes conservative. In its terms, liberals justify capitalist democracy, seated primarily in the richer nations of Western Europe and North America, and in Japan and Australia." [30] Today it is useful primarily as a defense of the *status quo* rather "than as a creed for deliberate historical change." [31]

Liberalism is a mannerism characterized by "ideological double talk," a "redtape of an ideology," provincial, strong on ideals but weak on means and agencies, irrelevant to key happenings, and in the process of being by-passed by history.

> Used by virtually all interests, classes, parties, it lacks political, moral, and intellectual clarity; this very lack of clarity is exploited by all interests. In this situation, as has often been noted, professional liberals, politicians and intellectuals make a fetish of indecision, which they call open-mindedness; of the absence of moral criteria, which they call tolerance; and of the formality—and hence political irrelevance—of the criteria, which they call speaking broadly.[32]

Radicalism is dead, says Mills; and who will deny it? We are left, then, with the conservative mood and the liberal rhetoric which make for public mindlessness and organized irresponsibility. In *The Power Elite* we read:

> The combination of the liberal rhetoric and the conservative mood, in fact, has obfuscated hard issues and made possible historical development without benefit of idea. The prevalence of this mood and this rhetoric means that thought, in any wide meaning of the term, has become largely irrelevant to such politics as have been visible, and in postwar America mind has been divorced from reality.[33]

> Intellectuals accept without scrutiny official definitions of world reality. Some of the best of them allow themselves to be trapped by the politics of anti-Stalinism, which has been a main passageway from the political thirties to the intellectual default of our apolitical time. They live and work in a benumbing society without living and working in protest and tension with its moral and cultural insensibilities. They use the liberal rhetoric to cover up the conservative defaults. . . .

> Smug conservatives, tired liberals and disillusioned radicals have carried on a kind of discourse in which issues are blurred and potential debate muted, the sickness of complacency prevails and reasoning collapses into reasonableness. Not liberalism as a political philosophy, but the liberal rhetoric is the common denominator of this approved style. Its sophistication is of tone rather than of ideas.[34]

*The Marxists* is an effort to counteract the ideological indifference to Marx. In the fearful mood of the cold war Marx becomes identified with Russian, and thus achieves an out-of-bounds status. Both Mills and Erich Fromm [35] try to show that Marx represents a good deal more than the ideas of Russian Communism. Mills declares that Marx is Western, for he represents the foremost intellectual drama of our time; that we cannot understand the history of any major nation without understanding Marx.

> To come to grips with Marxism, whether that of the young Marx or of yesterday's Moscow slogan, forces us to confront: (1) every public issue of the modern world; (2) every great problem of social studies; (3) every moral trouble encountered by men of sensibility today. Moreover, when we try to observe and to think within the Marxist point of view, we are bound to see these issues, problems and troubles as inherently connected. We are forced to adopt an over-all view of the world, and of ourselves in relation to it.[36]

Marx gave us "the very categories dealt with by virtually all significant social thinkers of our immediate past." [37]

We could possibly tolerate our ideological neglect of Marx in an era of extreme isolationism. With Africa, Asia, and Latin America on the move, we become grievously incapacitated to know what is going on and how to participate in events because of this indifference. Whatever may have been the military disaster in Cuba, there is an equivalent ideological disaster.

> No matter what you may think of it, no matter what I think of it—Cuba's voice is a voice that must be heard in the United States of America. Yet it has not been heard. It must now be heard because the United States is too powerful, its responsibilities to the world and to itself are too great, for its people not to be able to listen to every voice of the hungry world. . . . If we do not listen, let us realize that other powerful nations are listening—certainly the Russians . . . perhaps it is not too late for us to listen—and to act.[38]

It is this same ignorance that makes us inept in our relationship with the underdeveloped nations. "There is no comprehensive plan, no systematic idea, no general program for the economic development of India, Latin America, the Middle East, Africa, South-east Asia." Mills feels that American capitalism is not an exportable item in today's world. We have been given to spotty grants usually under some military guise. When we do not see profit or military advantage, we tend to withdraw aid.[39]

Mills exhorts us to study Marxism, to study the present "as history," as a corrective for our ideological retreat. We are warned periodically that empty rice bowls cry for rice not democracy. It may be that an "over-developed" nation cries for surplus subsidies not ideology.

Lacking an ideology, receiving comfort from the conservative mood and ambivalence from the liberal rhetoric, our intellectual is a political failure; which is to say, he is not effective in the use of power. This may be seen at three different levels: the masses, the leaders, and war.

The intellectual has failed the masses in education. William Whyte, David Reisman, and Mills are in essential agreement that schooling has become more and more the escalator to carry one up the ladder of economic and social success. Mills views our society as a power structure with unity and concentration at the top and at the bottom drift, fragmentation, and inaction. In such a structure education should rightfully concern itself with politics. We have had a shift from political education to economic, and this constitutes a loss of power.

> The prime task of education, as it came widely to be understood in this country, was political: to make the citizen more knowledgeable and thus better able to think and to judge of public affairs. In time, the function of education shifted from the political to the economic: to train people for better-paying jobs and thus to get ahead ... In large part education has become merely vocational; in so far as its political task is concerned, in many schools, that has been reduced to routine training of nationalist loyalties.[40]

The task of liberal education is "to help produce the disciplined and informed mind which cannot be overwhelmed," [41] to help man "understand his own experience and gauge his own fate ... by locating himself in his period." [42] We need to grasp the meaning of the intersection of biography and history. This education has not done. We have been unable to transfer personal problems into public issues. The question we should address to education is "what kind of a product do its administrators expect to turn out?

And for what kind of society?" The answer in the nineteenth century was the good citizen in a democratic society. In our day, the answer is "the successful man in a society of specialists with secure jobs." [43]

Our often expressed confidence in universal education for the whole man or even some part of him may be sadly misplaced. It may lead "to technological idiocy and national provinciality— rather than to informed and independent intelligence." [44] Instead of lifting the level of culture, we merely banalize what culture we have. We have education by the politically timid of those who will likely remain politically timid. This becomes a political failure, a power failure, at the level of the masses.

The intellectual of our day is a busy-body: he is too occupied. On the one hand he is active in "powerless grouplets" talking over the technicalities of the new criticism whatever the new criticism may be at the moment. On the other hand, he can join the "hired myth-makers and hack apologists" of Hollywood and Madison Avenue. On campus, he can be the paid consultant. As Irving Howe has remarked, for once the carrots are real.

We have a culture where it literally pays to think likewise rather than otherwise, as Carl Becker once advised. The able scholar becomes a hired co-worker rather than an outside critic. Hence there is "no opposition to the divorce of knowledge from power," "no opposition to public mindlessness." [45] Public relations become central, and "public relations are something you hire." [46]

It is, however, above all in relation to the prospect of war that the intellectual suffers his most dismal default; here we see his capitulation, his political failure most vividly. As a scientist, he may become part of a "science machine geared to the war machine." [47] As a mathematician, he may become a game-theorist with Herman Kahn and others. He now engages in the pleasantries of estimating the number dead in a nuclear war and the time-table of restoring normal air travel and supermarket service. Kahn is a realist and extends his realism to the point of 120,000,000 dead. With that number vaporized it will take us an even century to stage our comeback to normalcy. This kind of forecast has led Robert Oppenheimer to observe, "What are we to think of a civilization which has not been able to talk about killing almost everybody except in prudential and game-theoretic terms." [48]

We are left with "crackpot realism" and a "military metaphysics." War is the solution, the only one indeed. War is inevitable; we must prepare for it. The peace side is simply not heard. Silence is self-enforced or officially enforced. There has been "a series of cumulative defaults." Ideas which do not go along with this hard line realism are considered "utopian, naïve, impractical, unrealistic." [49] "Very many scientists, very many preachers, very many intellectuals are in default." Ministers become "theological tranquilizers," and religion as a social and moral force "has become a dependent variable. It does not originate; it reacts. It does not denounce; it adapts." [50]

Mills says he does not believe intellectuals will save the world, but he sees nothing wrong in their trying to save the world, and by this he means the avoidance of war. In the climate of the current realism and metaphysics, Mills has an unequivocal answer to the intellectual who asks, what should we do? "We ought to act as political intellectuals," we should "awake and unite with intellectuals everywhere." [51]

To the above failures, we add the final one, the failure of nerve. For some years—the practice is dying out just now—the social observers referred to college students as "the silent generation." Professors in a petulant mood of obvious displeasure complained: we just cannot get a rise out of them. I suspect that in large part the college student is silent because his somewhat older tutor is silent on pivotal issues. There are lone voices, to be sure, on the campus. They are heard, but no one takes them seriously, except deans who think maybe they should be dismissed. Things may be improving a little, but Jacob, Eddy, and Sanford [52] leave one rather short of rejoicing.

In fact the improvement is so slight that Mills' comments on commitment remain most relevant. Those who exhibit "the curious passion for the mannerism of the non-committed" are still with us. Many social scientists "conform to the prevailing fear of any passionate commitment. *This,* and not 'scientific objectivity,' is what is really wanted by such men when they complain about 'making value judgments.'" [53] This fear is largely self-imposed.

> Yet the deepest problem of freedom for teachers is not the occasional ousting of a professor, but a vague fear—sometimes

called "discretion" and "good judgment"—which leads to self-intimidation and finally becomes so habitual that the scholar is unaware of it. The real restraints are not so much external prohibitions as manipulative control of the insurgent by the agreements of academic gentlemen.[54]

Objectivity, discretion, and alienation—these become intellectual poses. Mills makes much of alienation. He speaks of it as the cause of our "immediate intellectual malaise," "a major theme" in the contemporary world.[55] The alienated man feels powerless. He sees history as either drift or conspiracy.[56] He may become the cheerful robot. But this very outsidedness of the alienated state is a precise advantage. "The alienation that intellectuals enjoy and suffer" offers them a chance "to formulate radical views and higher standards." But alienation is "often a whining little slogan of escape; it ought to be seized opportunity." [57]

The exploration of alternatives is the purpose of historical study.

> We study history to discern the alternatives within which human reason and human freedom can now make history.... Freedom is not merely the chance to do as one pleases; neither is it merely the opportunity to choose between set alternatives. Freedom is, first of all, the chance to formulate the available choices, to argue over them—and then, the opportunity to choose. This is why freedom cannot exist without an enlarged role of reason in human affairs ... The future of human affairs is not merely some set of variables to be predicted. The future is what is to be decided—within the limits, to be sure, of historical possibility. But this possibility is not fixed; in our time the limits seem very broad indeed.[58]

In the writings of C. Wright Mills we encounter the basic theme: the intellectual is in a state of serious default. He withdraws from pivotal events by means of his methodology. His escape can come respectfully through theorizing so grandly that irrelevance results; through statistical ritualizing which produces the almighty unimportant fact; by specialization which leaves him indifferent to the total scene; with a bureaucratization which is client-centered instead of public-centered.

The intellectual also suffers from an ideological retrenchment. The conservative gives a mood; the liberal, a rhetoric; and there is a refusal to come to grips with Marxism. The intellectual, lacking an ideology, eventuates as a political failure; he does not exert an influence at all commensurate with his ability. As educator, he fails to bring the masses into participation on the big decisions. As counselor, he fails to condition the decisions of the power elite. As a moralist, he fails to expose the metaphysics of the military. There is, too, the failure of nerve; he has not uttered the emphatic "no"; his is the mannerism of the non-committed.

Mills' great goal is to work against this mutual withdrawal: world from intellectual, intellectual from world. Does he succeed? My answer is a qualified "yes," or a hesitant "no" that approximates a mild "yes." His books have a circulation and an attention quite in excess of that given to any other working sociologist, Riesman being perhaps the only one to surpass him; and we should remember that *The Lonely Crowd* is multi-authored and *Faces in the Crowd* a research team product. Mills claims the admiration and loyalty of his students. He works at the big themes, the large questions.

Still his supporting observational work is scarcely equal to his large themes. He goes beyond his own evidence, if not beyond his own passion. Yes, there is a new class, but it is not so all-embracing and homogeneous as Mills would have us believe in the *White Collar*. There is a coming together of a new elite, but there are substantial cracks in it which he ignores. One cannot help wondering if much of *Listen, Yankee* is not fabrication performed to bolster an honest conviction. Too often he seems to write with the haste of a journalist trying to meet a deadline.

Mills is a sociologist in a hurry; he is an intellectual in anger. He is not our conventional academician. He advises the aspiring scholar, "To overcome the academic *Prose* you have first to overcome the academic *Pose*." [59] Mills is the book-length pamphleteer. We are scarcely lacking in men who run their material through statistical, historical, and linguistic analysis. Works from scholars of these dispositions have their place; and so do *Listen, Yankee* and *The Causes of World War Three* have their place. As Rousseau's *Emile* and Thoreau's *Essay on Civil Disobedience* show, haste and anger are not necessarily inimical.

I so accept, whatever simplifications and exaggerations may be present, Mills' account of the intellectual default, that I welcome and applaud his harsh angry books. When we begin to sense the cumulative effect of the trends Mills describes along with the cumulative default of the intellectual, then we realize our need for a Mills to jar us out of our pleasant complacency or our flabby petulance. A book is not to be judged solely on its accuracy; we must also judge it on its ability to make us take a fresh look at our situation.[60]

In our present-day world it is not enough to be scholarly; one must also be concerned and angry enough to shout. It is not enough to understand the world; one must also seek to change it. If we add the courage to shout to the effort to understand and change, then C. Wright Mills is one of the first among us.

NOTES:

1. C. Wright Mills, *Images of Man* (New York, 1960), pp. 2-3.
2. C. Wright Mills, *The Causes of World War Three* (New York, 1960), p. 144.
3. C. Wright Mills, *The Sociological Imagination* (New York, 1959), p. 211.
4. C. Wright Mills, *The Marxists* (New York, 1962), p. 9.
5. *The Causes of World War Three,* p. 22.
6. *The Sociological Imagination,* p. 33.
7. Ibid. p. 34.
8. Ibid. p. 48.
9. Ibid. p. 48.
10. Ibid. p. 56.
11. Ibid. p. 52.
12. *The Marxists,* p. 10.
13. *The Sociological Imagination,* p. 75.
14. C. Wright Mills, *White Collar* (New York, 1951), p. 131.
15. *Images of Man,* p. 5.
16. *The Sociological Imagination,* p. 139.
17. *White Collar,* p. 149.
18. Ibid. p. 130.
19. *The Sociological Imagination,* p. 104.
20. Ibid. p. 106.
21. *The Marxists,* pp. 12-13, 28.
22. Ibid. p. 473.
23. *The Causes of World War Three,* p. 147.
24. C. Wright Mills, *The Power Elite* (New York, 1956), p. 326.
25. Ibid. p. 329.
26. Ibid. p. 335.
27. Ibid. p. 337.

28. Ibid. p. 334.
29. Ibid. p. 332.
30. *The Marxists*, p. 19.
31. Ibid. p. 29.
32. Ibid. p. 20.
33. *The Power Elite*, p. 337.
34. *The Causes of World War Three*, pp. 145-6.
35. Erich Fromm, *Marx's Concept of Man* (New York, 1961).
36. *The Marxists*, pp. 30-31.
37. Ibid. p. 34.
38. C. Wright Mills, *Listen, Yankee* (New York, 1960), pp. 7-8.
39. *The Causes of World War Three*, p. 81.
40. *The Power Elite*, pp. 317-18.
41. Ibid. p. 319.
42. *The Sociological Imagination*, p. 5.
43. *White Collar*, p. 266.
44. *The Sociological Imagination*, p. 168.
45. *The Power Elite*, p. 338.
46. Ibid. p. 330.
47. *The Causes of World War Three*, p. 175.
48. Robert Oppenheimer, as quoted in William G. Carleton, "World Crisis and the Eroding of American Democracy," *Antioch Review*, 22, Spring, 1962, p. 8.
49. *The Causes of World War Three*, p. 113.
50. Ibid. p. 166.
51. Ibid. pp. 155, 164.
52. P. E. Jacob, *Changing Values in College* (New York, 1957); E. E. Eddy, *The College Influence on Student Character* (Washington, D.C., 1959); and Nevitt Sanford (ed.), *The American College* (New York, 1962).
53. *The Sociological Imagination*, p. 79.
54. *White Collar*, p. 151.
55. *The Sociological Imagination*, p. 171.
56. *The Power Elite*, p. 27.
57. *The Causes of World War Three*, p. 159.
58. The Sociological Imagination, p. 174.
59. Ibid. p. 219.
60. See Horowitz, "An Introduction to C. Wright Mills," in Irving L. Horowitz (ed.), *Power, Politics and People* (New York, 1963), pp. 2-3. "Mills' reputation does not rest upon any single essay or book. Whether he is right or wrong on the causes of World War III, or on the merits of Castro's Cuba may be subject to debate. But what is not open to debate is the need for social scientists to address themselves to the great agonies and issues of our age. This Mills did more conscientiously than any of his peers ... Mills' feat consisted in combining empiricism and prescriptivism; describing the world of human relations and also presenting solutions (albeit partial solutions) to the worst infections of the American social structure."

# 10

FRED H. BLUM

## C. Wright Mills:
## Social Conscience and Social Values

All great social scientists have been passionate men. C. Wright Mills was a man of passionate commitment to the values he cherished most: truth, reason, and freedom. He was concerned with these values in their totality, as living realities which manifest themselves in the realm of existence as well as in the realm of ideas. His passion was ultimately a passionate concern for man, for the human condition in the mid-twentieth century. And the three values which guided all his work are but the manifestations of one ultimate value: the development of true persons forming a true public.

Such a passion combined with a depth of intellectual penetration places Mills in the main stream of the classical tradition in the social sciences. Marx, Weber, and Veblen are some of the relevant names which first come to mind in this connection. Mills' work is marked by his encounter with these men. Like them he was deeply concerned with the destiny of man in modern industrial society and with the role of the social scientist in such a society. Like Weber in particular, Mills was passionately dedicated to objectivity as part of the problem of truth. Unlike the *epigoni* of his time, for whom truth and objectivity were a limited problem of methodology, Mills grasped this problem in its totality, as a problem of true and false consciousness. The question of true and false consciousness is indeed a total problem which demands an understanding of the nature of man, the nature of society, and their interrelationship. It is at this level that all classic thinkers have posed the problem of objectivity which, in the social sciences, has been the focal point of the problem of values.

The theme of this paper demands, therefore, a perspective on the whole work of C. Wright Mills. Only within such a framework can we meet the problem of values as Mills saw them. Indeed, an examination of the problem of objectivity as understood by him necessarily opens a perspective on his whole work.

At the very beginning of his work, Mills was concerned with the problem of objectivity in the social sciences. In a series of articles dealing with "Language, Logic, and Culture," [1] "The Methodological Consequences of the Sociology of Knowledge," [2] and "The Professional Ideology of Social Pathologists," [3] he examined the fundamental epistemological and logical questions which arise in sociology. He saw clearly that the question of objectivity and truth necessitated a social theory of perception and an understanding of the role of categories and their social and cultural determinants. "Verificatory models upon which the models of truthfulness rest are forms drawn from existent inquiries and have no meaning apart from inquiries. . . . " [4] This fundamental position led him to a position already taken by Max Weber: namely, that the problem of values could be adequately understood only if we realize that all "existent inquiries"—that is, all inquiries in sociology—arise because of, and are concerned with, specific problems.

From his first discussions of sociology of knowledge to his last writings on the nature of social science, Mills insisted that all social science revolved around problems. "For the classic social scientists," he said, "neither method nor theory is an autonomous domain; methods are methods for some range of problems; theories are theories of some range of phenomena. . . . The working social scientist must always keep uppermost a full sense of the problem at hand." [5] Once this basic fact of the orientation of *all* social sciences towards certain problems is recognized, it follows that values permeate all of social science. "To formulate any problem requires that we state the values involved and the threat to those values." [6]

It also follows that the meaning and significance of observable events and phenomena differ according to the way the problem is posed by the investigating scientist. It is in this sense that we must understand two statements of Mills, the first from his early writing, the second written later: "Focus on 'facts' takes no cognizance of the normative structure within which they lie" [7] and "Social research of any kind is advanced by ideas; it is only disciplined by fact." [8] We could paraphrase this by saying: events or phenomena become meaningful facts at the very moment when they enter into the realm of values. Hence "facts" and "values" always exist within the same universe of discourse and of meaning. Facts without values are meaningless. Values without facts are mere abstractions. Observable events and phenomena are facts which become humanly significant and meaningful only by entering into the total context of human consciousness.

At a time when values are shared by a community and unchallenged, this fundamental epistemological problem does not cause any difficulties for the social scientist. Indeed, it does not even demand his attention. But we live at a time of deep upheaval in which traditional values are challenged from within and from without. Such a time is inevitably a time of confusion. Mills saw clearly that this very confusion is an important reason why "the epistemological models of philosophers of natural science have such appeal as they do." [9] He saw equally clearly how crippling and inhibiting such an appeal is: "To limit, in the name of 'natural science,' the problems upon which we shall work seems to me a curious timidity." [10] It is indeed a curious timidity reflecting a deeply rooted anxiety.

Mills did not share such anxiety. He had the courage to recognize "the tyranny of concepts" and the "fetishism of method and technique" [11] and to accept the role of an "intellectual craftsman" who masters "method" and "theory" but is not mastered by them. In taking such a position he restored a measure of true objectivity to the social sciences. Instead of reducing the concept of objectivity to certain methodological postulates quite unrelated to the nature of the object-matter with which the social scientist deals, Mills had the courage to take a fresh look at this object-matter and ask himself what demands it makes on the social scientist of today. He called for an imagination which combined facts and ideas creatively and which demanded both involvement with and distance from the object of investigation.

Since all social scientists are human, they are part of, and hence related to, the object-matter which they investigate. As scientists they should be in a dual relationship to their object-matter. They are involved with it—otherwise they would not bother to ask questions about society. At the same time they must be able to see society at a distance and must have respect for the integrity of their object-matter. Such respect is an essential attribute of any concept of objectivity in the social sciences.

C. Wright Mills bothered the conscience of so many of his colleagues because he insisted—to use his own words—"that the king is without cloth," that the social scientists who work within the traditional academically respectable framework (particularly those who espouse the "bureaucratic ethos") are not properly clothed for the task at hand. They have neither enough vision nor enough distance from their object of research to discern its true or "proper" attributes.[12] The impact of Mills' work shocked them profoundly because they were so unaware of their peculiarly time-bound way of posing their problems, so unconscious of the whole structure of values which guided their work. Imbued by the "classic ethos" Mills exposed the spuriousness of their claims to objectivity.[13]

Mills, it should be noted, was painstakingly objective and exacting in his actual method of working. Even those who read his comments on "intellectual craftsmanship" can scarcely imagine how avidly he collected facts and how laboriously and diligently he worked. His notes quite literally amassed, and for each project they were sorted in special hand-made beehive-like file shelves. When thoroughly worked through, these facts were interpreted and condensed and became the substance of what he wrote.[14]

It is not always apparent from his writing how much his statements and conclusions were soaked with facts. Five sentences in his *Power Elite,* for example, were based on intensive research of economic data which took several weeks and which few economists have ever seen. The extent of his preparatory research is often obscured because Mills wrote well. He did not confuse science or depth with incomprehensibility. Mills abhorred the scientific jargon of his time.[15] He abhorred it because he knew so well how little knowledge that was significant and humanly relevant was left once the jargon was "translated into English." [16]

History will judge our generation of social scientists according to the extent to which they deal with significant problems. C. Wright Mills chose key problems of the mid-twentieth century.[17] Being concerned with the totality of the human situation, he dealt with them wholistically—as a "world encounter." [18] This way "of posing the problem" is decisive for an understanding of the values and of the basic categories which guided his work. The basic categories of Mills' work are "order and change—that is, . . . social structure and history." [19] The fundamental questions which arise in connection with such an approach are man's picture of "reality as a whole" and "the true outline of human destiny." [20] Mills himself has given us the leitmotif of his work in these words: "The passion to define the reality of the human condition in an adequate way and to make our definitions public—that is the guideline to our work as a whole." [21]

The first task of a sociologist who devotes himself to such a task is to unmask the false consciousness of his time. Mills struggled against this false consciousness wherever he met it. An important theme of *White Collar* is to show "how the individual often becomes falsely conscious and blinded." [22] He passionately rejected "official definitions of world reality," [23] and he indicted religion in America for having become "part of the false consciousness of the world and of the self." [24] He objected, in particular, to "nationalist definitions and ideologies" which serve as a "mask behind which elite irresponsibility and incompetence are hidden." [25]

The false consciousness which Mills unmasked is rooted in the structure of a mass society which is dominated by markets and by machines. It destroys the unity of human existence and creates men who each day "sell little pieces of themselves in order to try to buy them back each night and week end with the coin of 'fun.'" [26] The mass society is responsible for the "cheerful robot, the technological idiot, the crackpot realist." [27] It creates the "science machine." "Estranged from community and society in a context of distrust and manipulation; alienated from work and, on the personality market, from self; expropriated of individual rationality, and politically apathetic—these are the new little people, the unwilling vanguard of modern society" [28]—such is Mills' characterization of the world of white-collar workers. The world of the blue collar is not basically different. Both worlds are part of an economy which is "most efficiently wasteful." [29]

The mass society destroys both person and community, and, by undermining a true public, it threatens the very foundation of democracy. A true person acts from a "moral center" and stands for the values of truth, reason, and freedom. And a true public has an adequate picture of reality and is "morally directed." Instead of true persons forming a true public, we have "mass indifference" and "moral insensibility." [30] Hiroshima and Auschwitz, embodying the "principle of obliteration," are extreme but significant expressions of "the moral universe of the mass society." [31] Its more general and all-pervading result is "men with rationality but without reason" and an "inhuman lack of sensibilities." [32] These words sum up Mills' portrayal of the human condition, and they partly answer the question posed by Max Weber fifty years before. In speaking about the development of a capitalist, free-enterprise economy, Weber said, "Nobody knows yet who will live in this cage of the future . . . whether at the end of this tremendous development entirely new prophets will arise . . . whether there will be a great rebirth of old ideas and ideals or, if neither, mechanized petrification, embellished with a sort of convulsive self-importance. For that last stage of cultural development it might well be said . . . 'Specialists without spirit, sensualists without heart, this nullity imagines that it has attained a level of civilization never before achieved.' " [33]

Men without reason and sensibilities are also men without freedom. They are men who have no creative response and are, therefore, irresponsible. They are helpless in the face of Fate which man can overcome only through reason. They lack moral autonomy and substantive rationality. They are alienated. "The advent of the alienated man and all the themes which lie behind his advent now affect the whole of our serious intellectual life and cause our immediate intellectual malaise. It is a major theme of the human condition in the contemporary epoch and of all studies worthy of the name. I know of no idea, no theme, no problem, that is so deep in the classic tradition—and so much involved in the possible default of contemporary social science." [34]

This is Mills' formulation of the "major theme of the human condition in the contemporary epoch," which is also the basic problem around which his work has evolved. Alienation is the fundamental "threat" to the values which guided Mills' work. After having indicated that the definition of a problem requires that "we state the values involved and the threat to those values," Mills said, "For it is the felt threat to cherished values—such as those of freedom and reason—that is the necessary moral substance of all significant problems of social inquiry." [35]

In those words Mills indicated that the definition of a problem does not only imply a definition of values; it also contains a moral substance. This moral substance he proclaimed with a true "moral passion" whose absence in the world around him he felt strongly.[36] Mills was passionately concerned with "the moral identity of men" —a phrase from Emerson which he quoted [37]—with man's "moral center" or, more precisely, with man's "moral center of responsible decision." [38] It is not accidental that the epilogue to *The Power Elite* is entitled "The Higher Immorality." In the face of this higher immorality he called for a "politics of responsibility" [39] and a "publicly responsible economy." [40] And his "passion to define reality in an adequate way" implied a call for intellectual responsibility to pit itself against the false consciousness and the "irresponsible ignorance" prevailing "among men of power." [41]

We must understand Mills' involvement in many aspects of the human condition in this light. When he entered the field of politics he did not become a man of politics who forgot the proper task of the social scientist. Quite to the contrary, he was concerned to "lay bare the structure of politics and so today of the human condition as an object of human will and reason." [42] Given a concern with true and false consciousness, politics is an important problem area for the social scientist, because it is the most rationally organized expression of man's consciousness, as well as the sphere where vital decisions affecting man are consummated. "A political idea," Mills said, "is a definition of reality in terms of which decisions are formulated and acted upon by elites, accepted by masses, used in the reasoning of intellectuals." [43]

Concern with politics is, therefore, as important an aspect of Mills' concern with the human condition as a whole as is his concern with religion or the question of war and peace. When Mills

examined the sphere of religion he was again centrally concerned
to present those facts which show how organized religion affects
the human condition. When Mills spoke about the problem of war
and peace, he did so because he saw clearly that war and peace
had become "total" and hence were "of structural relevance." [44]
They were central phenomena in the human condition of our time.
And they were evidence of false consciousness. The "military
metaphysics" is as removed from "reality" as are "the capitalist
notions of industrialization" [45] which are connected with it.

Mills' concern with these issues was rooted in his dedication to
truth, reason, and freedom. It was the responsibility of the social
scientist—it was his "proper job" [46]—to counteract these trends and
to give a true image of reality. The more the actual image deviated
from an objectively true picture, the greater was Mills' concern.
He saw clearly that alienation, and the abdication of reason which
it implies, could be so severe as to manifest themselves in forms
of insanity. "We are at a curious juncture in the history of human
insanity," he wrote, "in the name of realism, men are quite mad,
and precisely what they call utopian is now the condition of human
survival." [47] He correctly analyzed decisive aspects of the moral
insensibility of our time in terms of a schizophrenic consciousness.[48] He could discern a "paranoid atmosphere of fright" in
"capitalist brinkmanship," [49] and the "abdication of any possible
role of reason, indeed of sanity, in human affairs" was a central fact
of which he was fully aware.[50]

But when Mills made such statements he did not speak as a
psychiatrist but as a sociologist. He clearly recognized the significance of personal life history for social science. He spoke about
"the orienting conception of social science as the study of biography, of history, and of the problems of their intersection within
social structure." [51] In the introduction to *White Collar*, he said,
"It is one great task of social studies today to describe the larger
economic and political situation in terms of its meaning for the
inner life and the external career of the individual." [52] But he
strongly rejected "psychologism" and "any style of empiricism"
which has made the metaphysical choice to consider the psychological reaction of individuals as "most real" and to understand
"the institutional structure of society. . . . by means of such data
about individuals." [53]

For Mills "social structure and history" remained the basic reference of all his thought. He looked at all problems in terms of "structural realities" or "structural significance," that is, in relation to the institutional structure of society.[54] This poses a final problem as to the role of the individual in this structure, particularly his role in transforming the structure of society. As we now turn to this problem we will find that it is inseparable from the question as to the ultimate source of the values which permeate Mills' work.

In addressing young social scientists, Mills gave them "the central and continuing task of understanding the structure and the drift, the shaping and the meanings, of your own period, the terrible and magnificent world of human society in the second half of the twentieth century." [55] He also told them that "in the end, it is this—the human variety—that you are always writing about." [56] This definition of the central task and of the end for which sociologists undertake this task contains the two poles of the structure of values permeating Mills' work: society and the individual. The question with which we must now deal is how the two are interrelated, particularly what role the individual plays as a passive subject and the active agent of social transformation and change.

The central function which Mills ascribes to the sociologist—to overcome the false consciousness of the time and to create a true consciousness—remains decisive for what he had to say about the role of the individual in transforming the social structure. The creation of a true consciousness is the precondition for becoming responsibly involved in the transformation of our society. Only if man acquires such a true consciousness can he act on the basis of his moral center.

The acquisition of such a consciousness, Mills conceived as a dialectic process. In this context his distinction between "personal troubles of milieu" and "public issues of social structure" is important. Mills considered this "perhaps the most fruitful distinction with which the sociological imagination works" [57] and illustrated it as follows: "When, in a city of 100,000, only one man is unemployed, that is his personal trouble, and for its relief we properly look to the character of the man, his skills, and his immediate opportunities. But when in a nation of 50 million employees, 15 million men are unemployed, that is an issue, and we may not hope to find its solution within the range of opportunities open to any one individual. The very structure of opportunities has collapsed." [58] The social scientist, by describing "the larger economic and political situation in terms of its meaning for the inner life and the external career of the individual," enables the individual to transcend his "personal troubles" and to see them in terms of "public issues." In a mass society, Mills says, men "are gripped by personal troubles which they are not able to turn into social issues." [59] But the social scientist who follows the classical tradition must make man aware of the interrelationship between personal troubles and public issues. The very concept of structure thus becomes of ethical relevance, again illustrating the intimate interrelationship between categories of thought and values imbuing a system of thought. Mills himself shows us this interrelationship in the following reference to Weber: "Weber's use of the notion of structure enabled him to transcend 'the individual's' own awareness of himself and his milieu." [60]

This transcendence eventually leads to a transformation of consciousness. Mills' holistic way of posing the problem for the social sciences and the implications of such an approach for this crucial process of transformation of consciousness are clearly indicated in the following statement: "The industrialization of academic life and the fragmentation of the problems of social science cannot result in a liberating educational role for social scientists. For what these schools of thought take apart they tend to keep apart, in very tiny pieces about which they claim to be very certain. But all they could thus be certain of are abstracted fragments, and it is precisely the job of liberal education, *and* the political role of social science, *and* its intellectual promise, to enable men to transcend such fragmented and abstracted milieux: to become aware of historical structures and of their own place within them." [61]

The individual is thus made an agent of the transformation of society by transcending "personal troubles of milieu" and becoming aware of "public issues of structure." In this dialectic interplay man is both creator and creature of society. Instead of being the center of a private universe, men must be made aware of themselves as part of the universe formed by the structure of society and thus become objectively conscious of the human condition. By acquiring a true consciousness of this structural universe, men become intellectually and politically involved and assume moral responsibility. They become active agents rather than being "spectators" at best and "idiots" at worst. If we accept the Greeks' definition of the "idiot as an altogether private man," Mills says, "then we must conclude that many citizens of many societies are indeed idiots. This—and I use the word with care—this spiritual condition —seems to me the key to much modern malaise among political intellectuals, as well as the key to much political bewilderment in modern society." [62]

It is noteworthy that Mills defines the problem under discussion as a fundamental spiritual problem. It is indeed a problem which involves the essence and the totality of a person and which stands at the convergence of the educational, political, and intellectual tasks of the sociologist. It also stands at the center of the responsibility which Mills would allot to the intellectual community of whom the sociologist is part.

In contrasting the "scientific ethos," which is the core of such a responsibility, with the "ethos of the war technology," Mills said, "We must cease being intellectual dupes of political patrioteers. This disgraceful cold war is surely a war in which we intellectuals ought at once to become conscientious objectors. To make this decision does not even require great risk or self-sacrifice. It requires only sanity and getting on with our proper job." [63] To become a conscientious objector to the false consciousness which is objectified in the present-day structure of society is an aspect of the transformation of society.

In the discussion of the ethical implications of a true consciousness thus conceived, Mills quoted the following story: "Suppose I live in a big apartment house and burglars attack me; I am allowed to defend myself and, if need be, I may even shoot, but under no circumstances may I blow up the house. It is true that to do so would be an effective defense against burglars, but the resulting evil would be much greater than any I could suffer. But what if the burglars have explosives to destroy the whole house? Then I would leave them with the responsibility for the evil, and would not contribute anything to it." [64]

Here is a truly human ethic which Mills expounded as the basis of a professional code for sociologists. He said: "As conscious members of the cultural community, scientists ought to work within their scientific tradition and refuse to become members of a Science Machine under military authority. Within the civilian Department of Science, within their profession, and before larger publics, they should publicly defend and practice science in terms of its classic, creative ethos, rather than in terms of the gadgets of the overdeveloped society or the monstrous weapons of the war machines." [65] If such a call for the restoration of the "classic creative ethos" were heeded by the scientific community, it would have far-reaching consequences. To those scientists who might object, saying, "But if I don't do it ... others will. So what's the difference?" Mills answered: "To refuse to do it is to begin the practice of a professional code, and perhaps the creation of that code as a historical force. To refuse to do it is an act affirming yourself as a moral center of responsible decision; it is an act which recognizes that you as a scientist are now a public man —whether you want to be or not; it is the act of a man who rejects 'fate,' for it reveals the resolution of one human being to take at least his own fate into his own hands." [66] Here is the picture of a man who, acting responsibly from his true moral center, overcomes the fate inherent in the social structure. Only such men can be true persons forming a true public.

Mills lived the professional code which he advocated. In him it became existential reality. He thus demonstrated to us more convincingly than any theoretical argument the possibility of becoming an active agent in transforming the social structure. He showed that men—or at least some men—are able to overcome the alienation brought about by forces operative in the mass society and to activate stronger forces rooted in their moral center.

In his existential choice he also revealed to us the ultimate value which permeated his work: the autonomy of the individual. "Above all," he advised young social scientists, "do not give up your moral and political autonomy by accepting in somebody else's terms the illiberal practicality of the bureaucratic ethos or the liberal practicality of the moral scatter." [67] In these words he admonished social scientists to be, above all, themselves.

The proclamation of this as the highest value poses problems so fundamental that they cannot be omitted and at the same time so vast that they can only be mentioned briefly here: the problem of the relative or absolute character of values. As far as invariant laws of society and history are concerned, Mills made a clear statement: "The only meaning of 'social laws' or even of 'social regularities' is such *principia media* as we may discover, or if you wish, construct, for a social structure within an historically specific era. We do not know any universal principles of social change." [68] But as far as man is concerned, Mills was more cautious. He recognized the problem of a universal nature of man,[69] but indicated that it was beyond the boundaries which the quest for objectivity sets for the social scientist.[70]

Mills' approach to this problem was determined by the "principle of historical specificity" which "holds for psychology as well as for the social sciences." He said: "Even quite intimate features of man's inner life are best formulated as problems within specific historical contexts. To realize that this is an entirely reasonable assumption, one has only to reflect for a moment upon the wide variety of men and women that is displayed in the course of human history." [71] But in referring to human variety, Mills was focusing his attention not so much on the biography of the individual man as on "social biography" and the varying social contexts of structure and public issues: "So many of the most intimate features of the person are socially patterned and even implanted. Within the broad limits of the glandular and nervous apparatus, the emotions of fear and hatred and love and rage, in all their varieties, must be understood in close and continual reference to the social biography and the social context in which they are experienced and expressed." [72]

The implications of this principle are clearly indicated in the following statement: "The idea of some 'human nature' common to man as man is a violation of the social and historical specificity that careful work in the human studies requires; at the very least, it is an abstraction that social students have not earned the right to make. Surely we ought occasionally to remember that in truth we do not know much about man, and that all the knowledge we do have does not entirely remove the element of mystery that surrounds his variety as it is revealed in history and biography. Sometimes we do want to wallow in that mystery, to feel that we are, after all, a part of it, and perhaps we should; but being men of the West, we will inevitably also study the human variety, which for us means removing the mystery from our view of it. In doing so, let us not forget what it is we are studying, how little we know of man, of history, of biography, and of the societies of which we are at once creatures and creators." [73]

Here Mills clearly acknowledged that there is something in man not exhausted by the principle of historical specificity. But as a man of the West—that is, as a man of reason—he would not define that part of human nature which may be common to all men. In the name of objectivity he demanded from the social scientist "the sacrifice of the mystery" of whatever transcends historical specificity. As a scientist he rejected, therefore, the notion of an "absolute value" or a "human universal."

But Mills knew that men had something that allowed them not merely to react to the social structure; he knew that human consciousness was not completely molded by the structure of society. His whole work was oriented toward making man an active agent in society. He recognized man as both creature and creator of society: "We are not merely upholders of standards; we are also creators of standards." [74] But he neither relied on any immanent historical necessity, nor on the manifestation of an absolute value immanent in man or transcendent in God to realize new forms and bring about the new age of truth, reason, and freedom. Instead he called for a Promethean effort to achieve the transformation of society. "The values involved in the political problem of history-making," he said, "are embodied in the Promethean ideal of its human making." [75]

With this statement Mills also defined his basic attitude toward religion. But this attitude is more complex than it may first appear. It would be ridiculous to claim Mills for any organized religion. He was an agnostic, and, when addressing the clergy, he even called himself a pagan. But he also labeled what he had to say "a sermon." Anyone who reads his "Pagan Sermon to the Christian Clergy" [76] cannot help but be impressed by Mills' intuition of what religious consciousness can mean and touched by the human sensibility and moral passion with which he indirectly reveals to us his own most intimate values. Mills spoke in the course of this sermon about the meaning of preaching (an unusual theme for a pagan!), which meant, first, "to be religiously conscious" and, second, "to serve as a moral conscience." He elaborated on this second point in these words: "you must *be yourself* in such a way that your views emanate unmistakably from you as a moral center. From that center of yourself you must speak." [77] Taking this as a criterion he challenged the assembled clergy by saying: "I am religiously illiterate and unfeeling. But truly I do not see how you can claim to be Christians and yet not speak out totally and dogmatically against the preparations and testing now under way for World War III."

A representative of the clergy said in response to Mills' pagan sermon that he felt it was truly Christian. And shortly afterwards someone answered publicly the assertion that God was dead by saying, "God is not dead because He exists partly in the writing of C. Wright Mills." [78]

Our evaluation of these statements depends upon òur definition of God, and of religion. If religion means an ultimate concern, Mills certainly was religious. His work went to the roots of man's social existence and by dealing with the totality of the human condition he also dealt with the essence of man. His ultimate concern was a spiritual one. He was involved in his life-work with his whole person. Imbued by the spirit of truth, he asserted with courage and absolute conviction the values of truth, reason, and freedom as central. Calling himself "secular, prideful, agnostic and all the rest of it," [79] he met his God as Prometheus.

We can only be moved by the work of a man who gave his whole life to preserve and to develop what is truly human in man. And we cannot help recognizing in his call for "sociological imagination" a call to find a new way, an attempt to activate the deepest in man, to free men from the false gods of the present age, and to become responsibly involved as creators of a new age to come. If such an age is to come, then it is partly because men like C. Wright Mills have shown us the dangers and risks of total annihilation of all that is human, and because they have been witnesses to the higher potentialities of the human spirit. "In the dark nights of [his] soul, in fear and trembling" Mills was "cruelly aware of [the] moral peril in this time of total war." [80] But he felt in himself the call "to redeem the day because [he] knew the times are evil," and he brought us in his sociological imagination the light of true consciousness.[81] His voice was prophetic in its passion and its depth of penetration.

NOTES:

1. "Language, Logic and Culture," in *Power, Politics and People,* edited by Irving L. Horowitz (New York, 1963), pp. 423-38.
2. "The Methodological Consequences of the Sociology of Knowledge," in *Power, Politics and People,* op. cit. pp. 453-68.
3. "The Professional Ideology of Social Pathologists," in *Power, Politics and People,* op. cit. pp. 525-52.
4. See "The Methodological Consequences of the Sociology of Knowledge," op. cit. p. 427.
5. *The Sociological Imagination* (New York, 1959), p. 121.
6. Ibid. p. 175.
7. See "The Professional Ideology of Social Pathologists," op. cit. p. 531.
8. *The Sociological Imagination,* p. 71.
9. Ibid. p. 119.
10. Ibid. p. 120.
11. Ibid. p. 224.
12. Ibid. pp. 100-18.
13. Mills insisted on self-awareness as a precondition for objectivity; see *The Sociological Imagination,* p. 21.
14. There are many references to the "classic ethos" in *The Sociological Imagination,* see also *The Causes of World War Three* (London, 1959), p. 108. This book will be referred to from now on as *The Causes.*
15. See *The Sociological Imagination,* Appendix, pp. 195-226.
16. See *The Sociological Imagination,* p. 219, footnote 8, p. 219, and pp. 25-33.
17. In his chapter on "Intellectual Craftsmanship" Mills insisted "above all ... specialization according to significant problems." *Sociological Imagination,* p. 225. There are numerous references in *The Sociological Imagination;* Mills speaks about the need "to have a genuine sense of significant problems and to be passionately concerned with solving them," (p. 141). See also ibid. pp. 90, 128, 129, 130, 134, 225.
18. *The Causes,* p. 73.
19. *The Sociological Imagination,* p. 47.
20. *The Sociological Imagination,* p. 16.
21. *The Causes,* p. 142.
22. *White Collar* (New York, 1951), p. xx.
23. *The Causes,* p. 131.
24. Ibid. p. 151.
25. Ibid. p. 86.
26. *White Collar,* p. 237.

27. *The Causes,* p. 175.

28. *White Collar,* p. xviii.

29. *The Causes,* p. 66.

30. Ibid. p. 81.

31. Ibid. p. 82.

32. Ibid. p. 77, see also *The Sociological Imagination,* p. 113, where Mills speaks about the "rationalistic and empty optimism" of abstracted empiricism.

33. *Die protestantische Ethik und der Geist des Kapitalismus* (Tübingen, 1934), p. 204, quoted from F. H. Blum, "Max Weber: the Man of Politics and the Man Dedicated to Objectivity and Rationality," *Ethics,* LXX, October 1959, p. 13.

34. *The Sociological Imagination,* p. 171.

35. Ibid. p. 175, see also pp. 129, 130-31.

36. *The Causes,* p. 132.

37. *The Sociological Imagination,* p. 37.

38. *The Causes,* pp. 156 and 170.

39. Ibid. p. 100.

40. Ibid. p. 123.

41. *The Sociological Imagination,* p. 183.

42. *The Causes,* p. 138.

43. Ibid. p. 140. It is also significant that the final chapter in his book *The Sociological Imagination* deals with politics, see pp. 177-94.

44. Ibid. p. 119.

45. Ibid. p. 74.

46. Ibid. p. 148.

47. Ibid. p. 117.

48. Ibid. p. 83.

49. Ibid. p. 63.

50. Ibid. p. 98.

51. *The Sociological Imagination,* p. 134.

52. *White Collar,* p. xx.

53. *The Sociological Imagination,* pp. 67-8.

54. See ibid. p. 154. The theme of "structure" was taken up by Mills so often that specific quotations would be too numerous. See in this context also Hans Gerth and C. Wright Mills, *Character and Social Structure, the Psychology of Social Institutions* (New York, 1953), and *The Causes,* p. 40.

55. *The Sociological Imagination,* p. 225.

56. Ibid. p. 223.

57. Ibid. p. 8.

58. Ibid. p. 9.

59. Ibid. p. 187.

60. Ibid. p. 162.

61. Ibid. footnote 1, p. 189, italics in original; see also p. 105.

62. Ibid. p. 41; see also *The Causes,* p. 81.

63. *The Causes*, p. 148.
64. Ibid. p. 169.
65. Ibid. See also *The Sociological Imagination*, p. 106.
66. Ibid. p. 170.
67. *The Sociological Imagination*, p. 226.
68. Ibid. p. 150.
69. Ibid. p. 163-4.
70. The following passage, for example, clearly implies the concept of a universal nature of man: "Man's chief danger today lies in the unruly forces of contemporary society itself, with its alienating methods of production, its enveloping techniques of political domination, its international anarchy, in a word, its pervasive transformation of the very 'nature' of man and the conditions and aims of his life." See *The Sociological Imagination*, p. 13.
71. *The Sociological Imagination*, p. 163.
72. Ibid. pp. 161-2.
73. Ibid. p. 164.
74. *The Causes*, p. 143. See also *The Sociological Imagination*, p. 117.
75. *The Sociological Imagination*, pp. 175-6. I once discussed the question of human universals and absolute values with Mills and suggested to him that his analysis of the human condition implies the concept of some universal, some absolute—something in man that is "common to man as man" and which stands in a more complex evolutionary relation to the principle of historical specificity than do those aspects of man which are clearly molded by the social structure. I suggested in particular that his concept of alienation implied such a human universal, some conception of man's "true" nature. He answered me in a joking mood: "Maybe I will come to this, after all I was brought up as a Roman Catholic."
    In the definition of values imbuing his work and in the categories of thought which result from his way of posing the problems he dealt with, Mills did not take such a step. It is true that the use of the word "proper" which is sparingly but most significantly used in regard to "the proper job" of the sociologist or of the politician and the political administrator (see *The Causes*, p. 60) implies the idea of a "self-evident" and in this sense absolute value. The "proper job" or "the properly developing society" (see *The Causes*, p. 104) corresponds to what may be called a "natural" or a "true" function. But this is quite incidental in Mills' work. The central conception of alienation is defined strictly in terms of role alienation. He speaks, for example, in terms of the "alienation" which the intellectuals enjoy and which makes it possible for them to be intellectual. (*The Causes*, p. 143.)
76. See "A Pagan Sermon to the Christian Clergy," *The Nation*, March 8, 1958, 186, pp. 199-202. Mills wrote this "sermon" in a few hours. It came directly from his own center. He made no corrections in the original manuscript.
77. Ibid. p. 201, italics mine.

78. *The Nation,* March 29, 1958, 180, Correspondence.
79. *The Nation,* March 8, 1958, op. cit. p. 202.
80. This is a paraphrase of a section of his "Pagan Sermon" as reprinted in *The Causes,* op. cit. p. 160.
81. See "A Pagan Sermon to the Christian Clergy," *The Nation,* op. cit. p. 202. Mills relates the "religious imagination" to what Christians call "the Holy Spirit."

# II

**Studies in Social Science and Social Theory**

# 11

SIDNEY M. WILLHELM

## Scientific Unaccountability and Moral Accountability

That scientists have finally "arrived" upon the contemporary American scene is an unquestioned fact. Surely such persons now possess a highly elevated status within our society. This development is so apparent that even former President Eisenhower, in his farewell address, expressed a personal alarm at the ever-increasing influence of American scientists. Yet, while we are aware ostensibly of the changing status of our scientists, we somehow overlook the significance of this transition for our democratic heritage. For in advancing scientists to new heights we unconsciously promote a scientific ideology which is basically indifferent to moral, political, economic, and social consequences. We are, in short, permitting scientists the possibility of establishing themselves as an aristocratic class.

The alarming consequences of this development rest within the very nature of aristocracies. Not only do aristocracies hold claim to prominence by seeking avenues of power mobility, but they also reject notions of responsibility. The success of any aristocracy depends upon the capacity to combine power with ideas of non-utility. The elevated aristocrat aspires to sustain his power, while, simultaneously, he perceives no necessity to validate his behavior through an ideology that commits him to others or to generalized moral principles. He insists upon detachment in order to perform activities that Lewis Mumford aptly designates as "exquisite uselessness."

The aristocratic contention is simply, "We do because we are." For instance, the traditional aristocrat calls for the preservation of nobility for the sake of nobility; the patrician poet, immersed in a sense of his own importance, pleads for poetry for poetry's sake; the businessman, inflamed by a feeling of self-righteousness, boasts of business for business' sake; the scholar, isolated from worldly affairs, insists upon knowledge for knowledge's sake. In each case, the deed serves to justify the act whereby the aristocrat seeks to perpetuate his respectability without an awareness of responsibility beyond the deed itself. Such inclinations as these display a remarkable disregard for moral accountability so essential to democratic institutions.

Yet, today we find certain scientists assuming the identical course; they ignore the social implications of scientific deeds by arguing science for science's sake. The scientific ideology furnishes a ready rationale for this aristocratic pronouncement even as scientists receive greater acclaim.

Those who advocate scientism claim that all scientific endeavor is free from moral implications, regardless of the consequences of scientific investigation. The scientist imposes on society, as did his aristocratic predecessors, an insistence that:

> The scientist *as scientist* can take little credit or responsibility either for facts he discovers—for he did not create them—or for the uses others make of his discoveries, for he generally is neither permitted nor specially fitted to make these decisions. They [i.e. decisions] are controlled by considerations of ethics, economics or politics, and therefore are shaped by the values, fears and historical circumstances of the whole society.[1]

The sort of reasoning contained in this quotation makes a mockery of moral obligation on the part of the scientist. There is the contention that science can only deal with what already exists and, therefore, scientists cannot be concerned with the inferences or resulting implications of their scientific discoveries. Consequently, to ask the nuclear physicist to justify his development of arsenals that can render our planet lifeless is to raise a moot issue;

to ask the astronaut what can be expected from space exploration is to raise a spurious question; to ask the sociological scientist the meaning of the social life he examines is to raise a vain inquiry.

This scientific perspective binds us to a half truth. While it is correct that the scientist seeks only to discover what "is" rather than desiring to voice what "should be," it is folly to overlook the fact that the scientist does expose. In the very process of uncovering facts, he lays bare data that would otherwise not be known. In short, the scientist's findings establish a negative which is then exposed to a society to produce inadvertently a picture that can profoundly alter the course of human events.

To argue from the premises of the scientific ideology that the scientists who revealed to the world the properties of hydrogen energy for the deliberate development of military weapons can in no way be held accountable compels us to ignore all the credit given to the scientists who discovered the properties of germs. Pasteur is a case in point. Why should he be granted outstanding recognition merely for the development of a process that purifies milk? After all, this is a scientific discovery that had to be made before man could protect himself from the ill effects of germs carried within now-pasteurized milk. To contend, as many of our modern scientists would have to admit, that Pasteur—as a scientist— can be given no credit for humanitarian considerations is to deny reality itself.

Through his ideology of non-involvement in the social effects of scientific research, the scientist is simply trying to free himself from social responsibility. And in doing so he creates a situation that no democratic society can afford: the luxury of an unaccountable scientific aristocracy. The scientist seeks to thrust upon our society his view of complete and personal freedom through the gimmick of aristocratic insulation. His insistence upon ethical neutrality is merely a veneer for irresponsibility by a group that will amass untold power. Like any elite that finally "arrives," the scientist wishes to camouflage the true nature of his behavior through an ideological cloak of non-responsibility which, in reality, will eventually come to mean irresponsibility.

The drift from non-responsibility toward irresponsibility seems to be the only adequate interpretation to give to the scientist's obsession with massive destruction. The boast of non-commitment grants protection to those who, in a most casual manner, speak of urban annihilation as though one contemplated the elimination of ant hills. The overproduction of military might also reveals the dissipation of non-responsibility into irresponsibility. At the moment it is estimated that there is the equivalent of ten tons of TNT in atomic-hydrogen power for each living individual—surely a sufficient sum to conduct warfare. Thus, the physicist and his co-worker, the technician, seem only too eager to conform to Veblen's reflections concerning excessive display of status symbols. The production of unwarranted weaponry via scientific channels can only serve the purpose of conspicuous self-indulgence.

To contemplate that any group acquiring control of knowledge that will definitely influence the destiny of the entire human race must somehow remain aloof from the social implications of its deeds, is simply to rely upon an unproven faith. Indeed, the very complexity of the scientist's discoveries must come to motivate him to interpret the significance his exposures contain for the course of human events. Upbraided by the insistence to comment upon the social importance of his accomplishments, the scientist cannot remain aloof. The scientist may not be in keeping with the ethical neutrality espoused by the scientific ideology when reflecting upon his own handiwork, but, nonetheless, his scientific knowledge cannot continue unchecked in the aristocratic fashion he so fervently advocates.

Thus we arrive at a most fundamental conclusion concerning the ideology of the scientific apologists: scientific objectivity is a nihilistic philosophy par excellence. The scientific ideology simply places the scientist in a moral vacuum. "Objectivity" does not permit humanitarian obligations to society; it only obligates the scientist to science itself. Nowhere in the formalized scientific ideology do we find a regard for man's cultural destiny. The indifference displayed toward ethical principles and the ideals of a society as guidance for scientific inquisition offers nothing but a nihilistic contention. The scientist merely exclaims the aristocratic axiom of previous elites: "We do because we are." He perceives no necessity, no moral obligation to expound further. Recognizing that knowledge itself involves power, can a society accept the notion that scientists be allowed to accumulate unlimited power through knowledge without a sense of social obligation? Is there any doubt but that mankind must exercise extreme caution when considering science as the final answer for the establishment of universal tranquility?

But a society need not despair. For a scientist's insistence upon ethical neutrality provides a solution for the exercising of control over scientific activities within a society: the scientist's refusal to commit himself to an ethical system above the scientific deed serves as a legitimate rationale for scrutiny by a society. But should the society fail to heed this challenge, and should the scientist refuse to question the social milieu that imposes the demand for scientific research apart from humanitarian consequences, mankind will surely be doomed. Yet, should there be excessive control exerted by non-scientists, then originality itself will be threatened; scientific endeavor will then be condemned only to those pursuits in keeping with the prevailing taste of a society. On the one hand, no society can now afford a scientific elite completely independent of responsibility and indifferent to the course of human events; on the other hand, strenuous demands for conformity to the whims of the whole society fail to provide an atmosphere for creativity.

We have, then, a situation that calls for a delicate balance. But even more important, we have a situation that must be faced to avert what will otherwise become a holocaust for mankind. For it now seems that the paramount strain in our society—perhaps for all industrial societies—does not revolve about C. P. Snow's two cultures. Basic social disruptions do not necessarily result from the lack of integration between the literary tradition and scientific knowledge as implied by Snow.[2] Instead, there is the necessity to integrate a group of powerful scientists, whose ideology shuns all notions of commitment to humane values, with the democratic ideology that requires responsibility of all persons. How is it possible for our democratic ideology to assert accountability and yet absorb scientists as men of power with an ideology that flouts commitment? How can a democratic society continue to grant power to scientists who insist upon disaffiliation from control? This is not a philosophical problem; it is a rapidly developing source of actual disruption. This is the reason why a Rand Corporation can never be legitimatized within the framework of a democracy, as it relies upon neutrality to avoid accountability while seeking unlimited influence. Too many scientists attempt to bargain for power through non-obligation. Should this trend continue, the very foundation of democratic control will be jeopardized.

The atomic test-ban talks at Geneva demonstrated the failure to integrate the non-committal scientist into a democratic ideology of responsibility. These discussions were abandoned several years ago when, apparently, the Russians and Americans disagreed over the technological capacity to detect underground nuclear explosions. United States scientists insisted that blasts could be muffled in salt formations and remain indistinguishable from a natural earthquake. Yet, the Gnome five kiloton test fired 1,200 feet below the desert near Carlsbad, New Mexico, in a rock salt formation produced shock waves to distances of 7,200 miles for detection by nearly 150 seismic stations within the United States and as far away as the Philippines, Japan, and Finland. It is reasonable to suppose that the information could vitally affect disarmament agreements. But to whom is the scientist who errs accountable under these circumstances? Can our society allow the scientist to invoke his non-committal ideology and yet assume responsibility at the disarmament table?

In the light of the scientific format, we should not be surprised by the conflict between the intellectual and the scientist. Recognizing his historical obligation to impose the very moral accountability which certain scientists seek to avoid, the intellectual insists upon his right to direct the affairs of a recalcitrant scientist. The unaffiliated scientist responds with an unwillingness to embrace the intellectual for this very reason.

We can conclude that those physical and social scientists who religiously uphold objectivity to sustain ethical neutrality toward society do so for the purpose of escaping feelings of personal guilt for the consequences of their deeds. The physical scientist desires to escape from the prospect that he must ultimately accept at least partial blame for his contribution to the development of weapons fully capable of destroying mankind; social scientists, such as sociologists and political scholars, wish to refrain from examining the real social consequences of racial discrimination, the armaments race, and, in general, the course of human affairs. Both groups of "objective" scientists insist upon studying what "is" in order to avoid the necessity of accepting responsibility for the social events immediately affected by their investigations. Apparently the "objective" scientist naïvely reasons that somehow social forces will move onward, leaving the scientist unhampered as a reciprocal gesture for the scientist's willingness to let the world pass unhampered.

NOTES:

1. Gerald Holton, "Modern Science and the Intellectual Tradition," in George B. deHuszar, *The Intellectuals: A Controversial Portrait* (New York, 1960), p. 184.
2. It is worth noting that C. P. Snow's *The Two Cultures* does not develop a single instance of harm for a society that perpetuates "two cultures." It is not the isolation of one culture from another, but rather the antagonism toward and unaccountability to one another that generates serious problems. After all, homogeneity—the establishment of "one" culture—produces difficulties of sorts for a society. Variety seems not only essential but desirable.

# 12

ERICH FROMM

## Problems of Interpreting Marx

Among the problems of interpretation of Marx in which one finds more than the usual amount of misunderstanding is a psychologistic interpretation which assumes in its crudest form that Marx's materialistic theory of history meant that man's motivation is his wish for material satisfaction, his unlimited desire to use more and to have more. Greed for possession and consumption is supposed to be, according to Marx, the driving force in man, and hence in society. It is hardly necessary to explain to anyone who knows Marx that this opinion is not only not that of Marx but its exact opposite. First of all, Marx's materialism was not the bourgeois materialism of his time, but a "historical materialism" (a term, incidentally, which Marx himself never used). Marx stressed that one cannot understand men through their ideas, but one has to understand ideas by knowing the practice of life of the men who create and believe in these ideas. "In direct contrast to German philosophy," Marx wrote, "which descends from heaven to earth, here we re-ascend from earth to heaven. That is to say, we do not set out from what men imagine, conceive, in order to arrive at man in the flesh." [1] We set out from real active men and on the basis of their real life process we demonstrate the development of ideological reflexes of these processes.

The economic factor in Marx's sense has been misconstrued to mean that a psychological factor, greed for possession, determines man's life. But for Marx, historical materialism is not at all a psychological theory; its main postulate is that the way in which man produces determines his practice of life, and that his practice of life determines his thinking and the social and political structure of his society. Economy in this context does not reflect a psychic drive but the mode of production, not a subjective psychological but an objective socio-economic factor.

Marx's analysis starts with a premise which is physiological rather than psychological; namely, man has to eat and to drink, to produce shelter and clothing; and this necessity cannot be waived. Hence he must produce things under all circumstances and he must produce them under the given circumstances of raw material, productive forces, climate, geography, etc. This implies that his psyche is more flexible than the external conditions under which he produces and also more flexible than certain demands of his body.

Contrary to the popular distortion, Marx assumed that various kinds of social structure will produce different kinds of men, with different feelings, attitudes, etc. Certain societies will produce ascetic men; others men who have little need for wealth, even though not being ascetic. It is precisely Marx's criticism of capitalism that it produces men who want to "have much" and to "use much" rather than to "be much." Socialism for Marx is the society in which man is liberated from the chains of economy, and especially from the greed to have things; socialism for Marx is the society which permits man to be fully human, to grow, to unfold, and to be free from the fetters of economy and greed because the economy has been transformed into a rational, transparent non-mystifying and human one.

In spite of the fact that Marx's ideas in this respect are clear, the misunderstandings continue. This is probably less due to any intrinsic difficulty in Marx's writings than to the circumstance that Marxists—Communists as well as reformists—have misinterpreted Marx. Instead of recognizing that Marx's socialism transcends the structure of capitalism, they have interpreted socialism as meaning state capitalism (the Communist version) or the increasing participation of the working class in the benefits of corporate capitalism (right-wing socialism). Another reason for this misinter-

pretation may also lie in the fact that Marx's ideas are in the
tradition of humanist thought, which reaches from prophetic,
Christian, classic Greek and Roman thought through Renaissance
humanism, to Spinoza and Leibniz, the Enlightenment philosophers, and Goethe. Marx lived and thought in this tradition, as did
many of his contemporaries. Today, humanism is less alive; it has
become a slogan, just like religion, and is often used even for the
purposes of the cold war by both sides. As a result, Marx's humanism is too little understood, except in some countries like Yugo-
slavia and Poland and among a number of Western Socialists and
religious and philosophical humanists.

The misunderstanding of Marx discussed above has been repeated in one of the most serious and thoughtful books published
recently, in Robert Tucker's *Philosophy and Myth in Karl Marx*,[2]
and precisely because of the excellent quality of Tucker's book I
want to discuss his interpretation.

Tucker says quite rightly that for Marx "alienated man is a man
who produces under the domination of egoistic need." But then
Tucker proceeds to say that Marx believed that "greed" (*Habsucht*)
—the fanaticism of appropriation of the world of created things,
a lust for power—dominates man. According to Tucker, Marx believed that greed, a passion much more profound than the calcu-
lating self-interest of the classical economists' "economic man,"
was a maniacal obsession of man. Tucker states that, while Marx
imputes the notion of human egoism to Anglo-French economy,
Marx thinks and writes as a German philosopher of the Hegelian
school, for whom passion is the human force in life.

Tucker was confirmed in this misinterpretation of Marx's thought
by a wrong translation of an important passage in the latter's
*Economic and Philosophical Manuscripts*. Tucker quotes Marx as
saying: "The only wheels that set political economy in motion are
*greed* and the war between the greedy—competition." But the
original text says: "Die einzigen Räder, die die National-Oeko-
nomie in Bewegung *setzt* [my emphasis], sind die Habsucht etc."
An error in translation can easily occur in a somewhat involved
text such as this; nevertheless, the original text is clear and unequivocal. The subject of the sentence is political economy, not
greed. It is political economy that sets in motion or mobilizes, as
it were, greed, not greed that sets in motion the wheels of politi-

cal economy. In other words, according to Marx, greed is one of the potentialities in man, which is mobilized and activated by a particular form of social organization, the political economy of capitalism.

I believe it all the more important to clarify this point, since both the capitalist and the Soviet systems, in practice if not by explicit statements, are based on the belief that the passion of having more is the motive power of history. Marx, on the contrary, believed that man can be saved from this greed if he lives in a society which does not mobilize it by its economic structure. The doctrine that greed is an inherent and incurable motivation in man is another version of the doctrine of original sin. Marx's theory, on the contrary, is close to Pelagius' heresy; it is a doctrine of salvation in non-theistic terms.

What has become of Marxist thought in the more than one hundred years of its existence? Here we must begin with a statement of what it was originally, which means essentially from the middle of the nineteenth century to the beginning of the First World War. The Marxist theory, as well as the socialist movement, was radical and humanistic—radical in the above-mentioned sense of going to the roots, these roots being man; humanistic in the sense that it is man who is the measure of all things, that his full unfolding must be the aim and the criterion of all social efforts. The liberation of man from the stranglehold of economic conditions which prevented his full development was the aim of all Marx's thought and efforts. Socialism in these first fifty or sixty years was, though not in theological language, the most important spiritual movement in the Western world.

What became of it? It became successful, gained power, and in this very process succumbed to its opponent—the spirit of capitalism. This development is not too surprising. Capitalism was successful beyond anything the early socialists could have visualized. Instead of leading to an ever increasing misery of the workers, capitalist society, through its technological advance and organization, brought great benefits to its workers. True enough, this happened to some extent at the expense of colonial peoples; and, furthermore, it resulted partly from the fight of the socialist parties and trade unions for a greater share in the social product. But whatever the role of these various factors may have been, the result is that the socialist workers and their leaders were more and more captivated by the spirit of capitalism and began to interpret socialism in accordance with capitalist principles. While Marxism had aimed at a humanist society transcending capitalism, a society which would have as its aim the full unfolding of the individual personality, the majority of socialists regarded socialism as a movement to improve the economic and socio-political situation within capitalism; they considered the socialization of the means of production, plus the principles of the welfare state, as sufficient criterion of a socialist society. The principles of this type of "socialism" were essentially the same as those of capitalism: maximum economic efficiency, large-scale bureaucratically organized industry, and subordination of the individual under this bureaucratic but economically efficient system.

Basically the majority of socialists in the West and in the East shared this economistic interpretation of socialism, but, according to their respective economic and political positions, they arrived at different solutions. The Western leaders began to make their peace with capitalism at the beginning of World War I. Instead of remaining faithful to their basic doctrine of peace and internationalism, the socialist leaders of both warring camps supported their governments, for the sake of freedom, they claimed, since they had the good luck to be fighting the Kaiser and the Czar respectively. When the imperial system in Germany collapsed as the result of prolonging a virtually lost war far beyond any reasonable consideration, the same leaders formed a secret alliance with the generals in order to defeat the revolution. They permitted the growth of the *Reichswehr*, and of secret and half-secret semi-military organizations which became the basis of Nazi power—and they virtually capitulated completely before the increasing strength and oppressiveness of the Nazi and nationalistic right-wing forces. The French socialist leaders followed a similar direction, which eventually led the French socialist party, under the leadership of Guy Mollet, to support the Algerian war. In England, as in the Scandinavian countries, the situation was somewhat different. In these countries the socialists won majorities, either temporarily or more or less continuously, and used their strength to build a welfare state. They brought to fruition a highly developed system of social security and particularly a social health service the beginning of which had been laid by conservatives in Europe in the nineteenth century and had been further developed in the United States under the leadership of Franklin D. Roosevelt in the 'thirties. In addition, the British Labour Party socialized some of the key industries, in the belief that such socialization of the means of production was the touchstone of true socialism. But, while these measures satisfied the economic interests of the workers, this brand of socialism ceased to be the vision of a fundamental change of the human condition. The German Social Democrats lost one election after another and sought to recoup their losses by giving up almost all radical aims. They not only abandoned their socialist aims but also accepted the principles of nationalism and rearmament to such an extent that their policy became hardly distinguishable from that of their opponents.

What happened in Russia was apparently the opposite of the Western development, and yet there are certain similarities. In contrast to the Western European countries, Russia had not yet become a fully industrialized country, despite the fact that the industry that did exist was highly developed; three quarters of the population were peasants, most of them poor. The Czarist administration was corrupt and largely incompetent, and, in addition, World War I had bled the Russian people without bringing them victory. The first revolution of 1917, led by Kerensky and others, failed mainly because of the unwillingness of its leaders to end the war; thus Lenin was confronted with the task of taking over power in a country which did not have the economic conditions necessary, according to Marx's thinking, for the building of a socialist system. Logically, Lenin put all his hopes in the outbreak of a socialist revolution in Western Europe, especially in Germany. But these hopes failed to materialize, and the Bolshevik Revolution was confronted with an insoluble task. By 1922-23 it was perfectly clear that the hope for a German revolution had completely lost its basis; at the same time Lenin became gravely ill and died in 1924. He was spared having to solve the final dilemma.

Stalin, using the names of Marx and Lenin, devoted himself in reality to building up a state-capitalism in Russia. He organized an industrial monopoly of the state led by a new managerial bureaucracy, and employed a method of centralized, bureaucratic industrialization which was also developing in Western capitalism, although less completely and drastically. Stalin used two means to transform a peasant population into one with the work discipline necessary for modern industrialism, and, furthermore, to induce the population to accept the sacrifices in consumption necessary for the rapid accumulation of capital to be used for the construction of basic industries. One was force and terror, which was extended, because of his own mad suspiciousness and unlimited desire for personal power, far beyond what would have been necessary for his economic aims, and, indeed, in many ways weakened his economic and military position. The other means, the incentive of increased income for more work, was the same one used by capitalism. In fact, any capitalistic manager convinced that the "profit motive" is the only efficient motivation for progress would be delighted with the Russian system, especially if he is opposed to the interference of trade unions in the managerial function.

By the time of Stalin's death, the Soviet Union had built a sufficient basis for increased consumption; it had also trained its population sufficiently in industrial work discipline to end the reign of terror and to bring about the construction of a police state, where expression of opinions critical of the system is not permitted and where there is little political activity. This system, however, has ended the average citizen's fear of being arrested in the early-morning hours for expressing critical thoughts or because he had been denounced by a personal enemy.

The degradation of Stalin, which was completed at the Congress of the Communist Party in the fall of 1961, and the new program of the Communist Party accepted by the same Congress are the final steps in the transition from the Stalinist phase to the Khrushchevist phase in the Soviet Union. This phase can be characterized as consisting of various elements: economically, a completely centralized state capitalism, bringing the monopolistic principle of contemporary industrialism to its final development; socially, a welfare state which takes care of the basic social and economic needs of the whole population; politically, a police state which restricts freedom of opinion and political activity, yet which has a considerable amount of legalism, protecting the citizens from arbitrary police measures. The citizen knows what he can do and what he cannot do, and, provided he moves within these limits, he need not be afraid. Culturally and psychologically the Khrushchevist system proclaims a Calvinistic work ethic, and a strict morality centered on fatherland, work, family, and duty—a morality closer to the ideas of Pétain or Salazar than to those of Marx. The Soviet Union today is a conservative "have" state, more reactionary in many ways than the "capitalist" states, more progressive in one essential point—namely, that private corporate interests cannot interfere with the general political and economic plans of the government.

The Soviet system still uses revolutionary and socialist ideas voiced by Marx, Engels, and Lenin as ideologies which give a sense of meaning to the masses. Yet, they have lost effectiveness. The situation can be compared with that of the West, where the Christian idea is still used mainly ideologically, that is, without an effective basis in the hearts and actions of most of the people who profess these ideas.

The foregoing description of the socialist movement ends on the tragic note of stating its failure. However, while this statement is correct as far as the established great bureaucracies are concerned, it does not take into account more hopeful aspects.

Socialism has not been destroyed by its enemies, nor by its "representatives," right or left. All over the world there are small groups of radical socialist humanists who express and revise Marxist socialism, and who try to contribute to the growth of a socialist humanism which is as different from Soviet communism as it is from capitalism. These voices which express the spirit of Marx are still weak and isolated; yet they exist, and they give rise to the hope that, if mankind will avoid the supreme madness of nuclear war, a new international socialist movement will realize the principles and promises of Western and Eastern humanism.

NOTES:

1. *The German Ideology,* ed. G. R. Pascal (New York, 1939), p. 14.
2. *Philosophy and Myth in Karl Marx* (Cambridge, England, 1961), pp. 137-8.

# 13

**ALVIN W. GOULDNER**

## Anti-Minotaur:
## The Myth of a Value-Free Sociology

This is an account of a myth created by and about a magnificent minotaur named Max—Max Weber, to be exact; his myth was that social science should and could be value-free. The lair of this minotaur, although reached only by a labyrinthian logic and visited only by a few who never return, is still regarded by many sociologists as a holy place. In particular, as sociologists grow older they seem impelled to make a pilgrimage to it and to pay their respects to the problem of the relations between values and social science.

Considering the perils of the visit, their motives are somewhat perplexing. Perhaps their quest is the first sign of professional senility; perhaps it is the last sigh of youthful yearnings. And perhaps a concern with the value problem is just a way of trying to take back something that was, in youthful enthusiasm, given too hastily.

In any event, the myth of a value-free sociology has been a conquering one. Today, all the powers of sociology, from Parsons to Lundberg, have entered into a tacit alliance to bind us to the dogma that "Thou shalt not commit a value judgment," especially as sociologists. Where is the introductory textbook, where the lecture course on principles, that does not affirm or imply this rule?

In the end we cannot disprove the existence of minotaurs, who, after all, are thought to be sacred precisely because, being half-man and half-bull, they are so unlikely. The thing to see is that a belief in them is not so much untrue as it is absurd. Like Berkeley's argument for solipsism, Weber's brief for a value-free sociology is a tight one and, some say, logically unassailable; yet, it too is absurd. Both arguments appeal to reason but ignore experience.

I do not here wish to enter into an examination of the *logical* arguments involved, not because I regard them as incontrovertible but because I find them less interesting to me as a sociologist. Instead what I will do is to view the belief in a value-free sociology in the same manner that sociologists examine any element in the ideology of any group. This means that we will look upon the sociologist just as we would any other occupation, be it the taxicab driver, the nurse, the coal miner, or the physician. In short, I will look at the belief in a value-free sociology as part of the ideology of a working group and from the standpoint of the sociology of occupations.

The image of a value-free sociology is more than a neat intellectual theorem demanded as a sacrifice to reason; it is, also, a felt conception of a role and a set of more or less shared sentiments as to how sociologists should live. We may be sure that it became this not simply because it is true or logically elegant but, also, because it is somehow useful to those who believe in it. Applauding the dancer for her grace is often the audience's way of concealing its lust.

That we are in the presence of a group myth, rather than a carefully formulated and well-validated belief appropriate to scientists, may be discerned if we ask, just what is it that is believed by those holding sociology to be a value-free discipline? Does the belief in a value-free sociology mean that, in point of fact, sociology is a discipline actually free of values and that it successfully excludes all non-scientific assumptions in selecting, studying, and reporting on a problem? Or does it mean that sociology should do so? Clearly, the first is untrue, and I know of no one who even holds it possible for sociologists to exclude completely their non-scientific beliefs from their scientific work; and if this is so, on what grounds can this impossible task be morally incumbent on sociologists?

Does the belief in a value-free sociology mean that sociologists cannot, do not, or should not make value judgments concerning things outside their sphere of technical competence? But what has technical competence to do with the making of value judgments? If technical competence does provide a warrant for making value judgments, then there is nothing to prohibit sociologists from making them within the area of their expertise. If, on the contrary, technical competence provides no warrant for making value judgments, then, at least, sociologists are as free to do so as anyone else; their value judgments are at least as good as anyone else's, say, a twelve-year-old child's. And, if technical competence provides no warrant for making value judgments, then what does?

I fear that there are many sociologists today who, in conceiving social science to be value-free, mean widely different things, that many hold these beliefs dogmatically without having examined seriously the grounds upon which they are credible, and that some few affirm a value-free sociology ritualistically without having any clear idea of what it might mean. Weber's own views on the relation between values and social science are scarcely identical with some held today. While Weber saw grave hazards in the sociologist's expression of value judgments, he also held that these might be voiced if caution was exercised to distinguish them from statements of fact. If Weber insisted on the need to maintain scientific objectivity, he also warned that this was altogether different from moral indifference.

Not only was the cautious expression of value judgments deemed permissible by Weber, but, he emphasized, these were positively mandatory under certain circumstances. Although Weber inveighed against the professorial "cult of personality," we might also remember that he was not against all value-imbued cults and that he himself worshipped at the shrine of individual responsibility. A familiarity with Weber's work on these points would only be embarrassing to many who today affirm a value-free sociology in his name.

What to Weber was an agonizing expression of a highly personal faith, intensely felt and painstakingly argued, has today become a hollow catechism, a password, and a good excuse for no longer thinking seriously. It has become increasingly the trivial token of professional respectability, the caste mark of the decorous; it has become the gentleman's promise that boats will not be rocked. Rather than showing Weber's work the respect that it deserves, by carefully re-evaluating it in the light of our own generation's experience, we reflexively reiterate it even as we distort it to our own purposes. Ignorance of the gods is no excuse; but it can be convenient. For if the worshipper never visits the altar of his god, then he can never learn whether the fire still burns there or whether the priests, grown fat, are simply sifting the ashes.

The needs which the value-free conception of social science serves are both personal and institutional. Briefly, my contention will be that one of the main institutional forces facilitating the survival and spread of the value-free myth was its usefulness in maintaining both the cohesion and the autonomy of the modern university, in general, and the newer social science disciplines, in particular. There is little difficulty, at any rate, in demonstrating that these were among the motives originally inducing Max Weber to formulate the conception of a value-free sociology.

This issue might be opened at a seemingly peripheral and petty point: namely, when Weber abruptly mentions the problem of competition among professors for students. Weber notes that professors who do express a value-stand are more likely to attract students than those who do not and are, therefore, likely to have undue career advantages. In effect, this is a complaint against a kind of unfair competition by professors who pander to student interests. Weber's hope seems to have been that the value-free principle would serve as a kind of "Fair Trades Act" to restrain such competition.

This suggests that one of the latent functions of the value-free doctrine is to bring peace to the academic house, by reducing competition for students, and, in turn, it directs us to some of the institutional peculiarities of German universities in Weber's time. Unlike the situation in the American university, career advancement in the German university was then felt to depend too largely on the professor's popularity as a teacher; indeed, at the lower ranks, the instructor's income was directly dependent on student enrollment. As a result, the competition for students was particularly keen, and it was felt that the system penalized good scholars and researchers in favor of attractive teaching. In contrast, of course, the American system has been commonly accused of overstressing scholarly publication, and the typical complaint is that good teaching goes unrewarded and that you must "publish or perish." In the context of the German academic system, Weber was raising no trivial point when he intimated that the value-free doctrine would reduce academic competition. He was linking the doctrine to guild problems and anchoring this lofty question to academicians' earthy interests.

Weber also opposed the use of the lecture hall as an arena of value affirmation by arguing that it subjects the student to a pressure he is unable to evaluate or resist adequately. Given the comparatively exalted position of the professor in German society, and given the one-sided communication inherent in the lecture hall, Weber did have a point. His fears were, perhaps, all the more justified, if we accept a view of the German "national character" as being authoritarian—in Nietzsche's terms a combination of arrogance and servility. But these considerations do not hold with anything like equal cogency in more democratic cultures such as our own. For here, not only are professors held in more modest esteem, but the specific ideology of education itself stresses the desirability of student initiative and participation, and there is more of a systematic solicitation of the student's "own" views in small "discussion" sections. There is little student servility to complement and encourage occasional professorial arrogance.

When Weber condemned the lecture hall as a forum for value-affirmation he had in mind most particularly the expression of political values. The point of Weber's polemic is not directed against all values with equal sharpness. It was not the expression of aesthetic or even religious values that Weber sees as most objectionable in the university, but, primarily, those of politics. His promotion of the value-free doctrine may, then, be seen not so much as an effort to amoralize as to depoliticalize the university and to remove it from the political struggle. The political conflicts then echoing in the German university did not entail comparatively narrow differences, such as those now between Democrats and Republicans in the United States. Weber's proposal of the value-free doctrine was, in part, an effort to establish a *modus vivendi* among academicians whose political commitments were often intensely felt and in violent opposition.

Under these historical conditions, the value-free doctrine was a proposal for an academic truce. It said, in effect, if we all keep quiet about our political views, then we may all be able to get on with our work. But if the value-free principle was suitable in Weber's

Germany because it served to restrain political passions, is it equally useful in America today, where not only is there pitiable little difference in politics but men often have no politics at all? Perhaps the need of the American university today, as of American society more generally, is for more commitment to politics and for more diversity of political views. It would seem that now the national need is to take the lid off, not to screw it on more tightly.

Given the historically unique conditions of nuclear warfare, where the issue would not be decided in a long-drawn-out war requiring the sustained cohesion of mass populations, national consensus is no longer, I believe, as important a condition of national survival as it once was. But if we no longer require the same degree of unanimity to fight a war, we do require a greater ferment of ideas and a radiating growth of political seriousness and variety within which alone we may find a way to prevent war. Important contributions to this have been made and may further be made by members of the academic community, perhaps especially by its social science sector. The question arises, however, whether this group's political intelligence can ever be adequately mobilized for these purposes so long as it remains tranquilized by the value-free doctrine.

Throughout his work, Weber's strategy is to safeguard the integrity and freedom of action of both the state, as the instrument of German national policy, and of the university, as the embodiment of a larger Western tradition of rationalism. He feared that the expression of political value judgments in the university would provoke the state into censoring the university and would imperil its autonomy. Indeed, Weber argues that professors are not entitled to freedom from state control in matters of values, since these do not rest on their specialized qualifications.

This view will seem curious only to those regarding Weber as a liberal in the Anglo-American sense: that is, as one who wishes to delimit the state's powers on behalf of the individual's liberties. Actually, however, Weber aimed not at curtailing but at strengthening the powers of the German state and making it a more effective instrument of German nationalism. It would seem, however, that an argument contrary to the one he advances is at least as consistent; namely, that professors are, like all others, entitled and perhaps obligated to express their values. In other words, professors have a right to profess. Rather than being made the objects of special suspicion and special control by the state, they are no less (and no more) entitled than others to the trust and protection of the state.

In a *Realpolitik* vein, Weber acknowledges that the most basic national questions cannot ordinarily be discussed with full freedom in government universities. Since the discussion there cannot be completely free and all-sided, he apparently concludes that it is fitting there should be no discussion at all, rather than risk partisanship. But this is too pious by far. Even Socrates never insisted that all views must be at hand before the dialogue could begin. Here again, one might as reasonably argue to the contrary, that one limitation of freedom is no excuse for another. Granting the reality of efforts to inhibit unpopular views in the university, it seems odd to prescribe self-suppression as a way of avoiding external suppression. Suicide does not seem a reasonable way to avoid being murdered. It appears, however, that Weber was so intent on safeguarding the autonomy of the university and the autonomy of politics that he was willing to pay almost any price to do so, even if this led the university to detach itself from one of the basic intellectual traditions of the West—the dialectical exploration of the fundamental purposes of human life.

In so far as the value-free doctrine is a mode of ensuring professional autonomy, it does not, as such, entail an interest peculiar to the social sciences. In this regard, as a substantial body of research in the sociology of occupations indicates, social scientists are kin to plumbers, house painters, or librarians. Most, if not all, occupations seek to elude control by outsiders and manifest a drive to maintain exclusive control over their practitioners.

Without doubt the value-free principle did enhance the autonomy of sociology; it was one way in which our discipline pried itself loose—in some modest measure—from the clutch of its society, in Europe freer from political party influence, in the United States freer of ministerial influence. In both places, the value-free doctrine gave sociology a larger area of autonomy in which it could steadily pursue basic problems rather than journalistically react to passing events, and it gained more freedom to pursue questions uninteresting either to the respectable or to the rebellious. It made sociology freer—as Comte had wanted it to be—to pursue all its own theoretical implications. The value-free principle did, I think, contribute to the intellectual growth and emancipation of our enterprise.

There was another kind of freedom which the value-free doctrine also allowed; it enhanced a freedom from moral compulsiveness and permitted a partial escape from the parochial prescriptions of the sociologist's local or native culture. Above all, effective internalization of the value-free principle has always encouraged at least a temporary suspension of the moralizing reflexes built into the sociologist by his own society. From one perspective, this of course has its dangers—a disorienting normlessness and moral indifference. From another standpoint, however, the value-free principle might also have provided a moral as well as an intellectual opportunity. In so far as moral reactions are only suspended and not aborted, and in so far as this is done in the service of knowledge and intellectual discipline, then, in effect, the value-free principle strengthened Reason (or Ego) against the compulsive demands of a merely traditional morality. To this degree, the value-free discipline provided a foundation for the development of more reliable knowledge about men and, also, established a breathing space within which moral reactions could be less mechanical and in which morality could be reinvigorated.

The value-free doctrine thus had a paradoxical potentiality: it might enable men to make better value judgments rather than none at all. It could encourage a habit of mind that might help men in discriminating between their punitive drives and their ethical sentiments. Moralistic reflexes suspended, it was now more possible to sift conscience with the rod of reason and to cultivate moral judgments that expressed a man's total character as an adult person; he need not now live quite so much by his past parental programing but in terms of his more mature present.

The value-free doctrine could have meant an opportunity for a more authentic morality. It could and sometimes did aid men in transcending the morality of their "tribe" by opening themselves to the diverse moralities of unfamiliar groups and by seeing themselves and others from the standpoint of a wider range of significant cultures.

Doubtless there were some who did use the opportunity thus presented; but there were also many who used the value-free postulate as an excuse for pursuing their private impulses to the neglect of their public responsibilities and who, far from becoming more morally sensitive, became morally jaded. In so far as the value-free doctrine failed to realize its potentialities, it did so because its deepest impulses were—as we shall note later—dualistic; it invited men to stress the separation and not the mutual connectedness of facts and values; it had the vice of its virtues. In short, the conception of a value-free sociology has had diverse consequences, not all of them useful or flattering to the social sciences.

On the negative side, it may be noted that the value-free doctrine is useful both to those who want to escape from the world and to those who want to escape into it. It is useful to those young, or not so young men, who live off sociology rather than for it, and who think of sociology as a way of getting ahead in the world by providing them with neutral techniques that may be sold on the open market to any buyer. The belief that it is not the business of a sociologist to make value judgments is taken, by some, to mean that the market on which they can vend their skills is unlimited. From such a standpoint, there is no reason why one cannot sell his knowledge to spread a disease just as freely as he can to fight it. Indeed, some sociologists have had no hesitation about doing market research designed to sell more cigarettes, although well aware of the implication of recent cancer research. In brief, the value-free doctrine of social science was sometimes used to justify the sale of one's talents to the highest bidder and is, far from new, a contemporary version of the most ancient sophistry.

In still other cases, the image of a value-free sociology is the armor of the alienated sociologist's self. Although C. Wright Mills may be right in saying this is the Age of Sociology, not a few sociologists, Mills included, have felt estranged and isolated from their society. They feel impotent to contribute usefully to the solution of its deepening problems, and, even when they can, they fear that the terms of such an involvement require them to submit to a commercial debasement or a narrow partisanship, rather than contributing to a truly public interest.

Many sociologists feel themselves cut off from the larger community of liberal intellectuals, in whose satire they see themselves as ridiculous caricatures. Estranged from the larger world, they cannot escape in fantasies of posthumous medals and by living huddled behind self-barricaded intellectual ghettoes. Self-doubt finds its anodyne in the image of a value-free sociology because this transforms their alienation into an intellectual principle; it evokes the soothing illusion, among some sociologists, that their exclusion from the larger society is a self-imposed duty rather than an externally imposed constraint.

Once committed to the premise of a value-free sociology, such sociologists are bound to a policy which can only alienate them further from the surrounding world. Social science can never be fully accepted in a society, or by a part of it, without paying its way; this means it must manifest both its relevance and concern for the contemporary human predicament. Unless the value-relevance of sociological inquiry is made plainly evident, unless there are at least some bridges between it and larger human hopes and purposes, it must inevitably be scorned by laymen as pretentious word-mongering. But the manner in which some sociologists conceive the value-free doctrine disposes them to ignore current human problems and to huddle together like old men seeking mutual warmth. "This is not our job," they say, "and if it were we would not know enough to do it. Go away, come back when we're grown up," say these old men. The issue, however, is not whether we know enough; the real questions are whether we have the courage to say and use what we do know and whether anyone knows more.

There is one point which those who desert the world and those who abandon themselves to it have in common. Neither group can adopt an openly critical stance toward society. Those who abandon themselves to the world are accomplices; they may feel no critical impulses. Those who desert it, while they do feel such impulses, are either lacking in any talent for aggression, or have often turned it inward into noisy but essentially safe university politics or professional polemics. In adopting a conception of themselves as "value-free" scientists, they may no longer find a target in society for their critical impulses. Since they no longer feel free to criticize society, which always requires a measure of courage, they now turn to the cannibalistic criticism of sociology itself and begin to eat themselves up with "methodological" criticisms.

One latent meaning of the image of a value-free sociology

emerges: "Thou shalt not commit a critical or negative value judgment—especially of one's own society." Like a neurotic symptom,
this aspect of the value-free image is rooted in a conflict; it grows
out of an effort to compromise between conflicting drives: On the
one side, it reflects a conflict between the desire to criticize social
institutions, which since Socrates has been the legacy of intellectuals, and the fear of reprisals if one does criticize, which is also a
very old and human concern. On the other side, this aspect of the
value-free image reflects a conflict between the fear of being
critical and the fear of being regarded as unmanly or lacking in
integrity, if uncritical.

The doctrine of a value-free sociology resolves these conflicts
by making it seem that those who refrain from social criticism are
acting solely on behalf of a higher professional good rather than
on their private interests. In refraining from social criticism, both
the timorous and the venal may now claim the protection of a high
professional principle and, in so doing, can continue to hold themselves in decent regard.

Should social scientists affirm or critically explore values, they
would of necessity come up against powerful institutions which
deem the statement or protection of public values as their special
business. Should social scientists seem to compete in this business,
they can run afoul of powerful forces and can anticipate efforts at
external curbs and controls. In saying this, however, we have to be
careful lest we needlessly exacerbate academic timorousness. Actually, my own first-hand impressions of many situations where
sociologists serve as consultants indicate that, once the clients come
to know them, they are often quite prepared to have sociologists
suggest (not dictate) policy and to have them express their own
values. Nor does this always derive from the expectation that sociologists will see things their way and share their values. Indeed,
it is precisely the expected difference in perspectives that is occasionally desired in seeking consultation. I find it difficult not to
sympathize with businessmen who jeer at sociologists when they
suddenly become more devoted to business values than the businessmen themselves.

Clearly all this does not mean that people will tolerate disagree-
ment on basic values with social scientists more equably than they
will with anyone else. Surely there is no reason why the prin-

ciples governing social interaction should be miraculously suspended just because one of the parties to a social relation is a social scientist. The dangers of public resentment are real, but they are only normal. They are not inconsistent with the possibility that laymen may be perfectly ready to allow social scientists as much (or as little) freedom of value expression as they would anyone else. And what more could any social scientist want?

The value-free image of social science is not consciously held for expedience's sake; it is not contrived deliberately as a hedge against public displeasure. It could not function as a face-saving device if it were. What seems more likely is that it entails something in the nature of a tacit bargain: in return for a measure of autonomy and social support, many social scientists have surrendered their critical impulses. This was not usually a callous "sell-out" but a slow process of mutual accommodation; both parties suddenly found themselves betrothed without a formal ceremony.

Nor am I saying that the critical posture is dead in American sociology; it is just badly sagging. Anyone who has followed the work of Seymour Lipset, Dennis Wrong, Leo Lowenthal, Bennett Berger, Bernard Rosenberg, Lewis Coser, Maurice Stein, C. Wright Mills, Arthur Vidich, Philip Rieff, Anselm Strauss, David Riesman, Alfred McClung Lee, Ernest Van den Haag, and of others, would know better. These men still regard themselves as "intellectuals" no less than sociologists: their work is deeply linked to this larger tradition from which sociology itself has evolved. By no means have all sociologists rejected the legacy of the intellectual, namely, the right to be critical of tradition. This ancient heritage still remains embedded in the underground culture of sociology; and it comprises the enshadowed part of the occupational selves of many sociologists, even if not publicly acknowledged.

In contrast with and partly in polemic against this older tradition, however, the dominant drift of American sociology today is compulsively bent upon transforming itself into a "profession." (Strangely enough, many of these same sociologists see nothing contradictory in insisting that their discipline is still young and immature.) This clash between the older heritage of the critical intellectual and the modern claims of the value-free professional finds many expressions. One of these occurred at the sociologists' national meetings in Chicago in 1958. At this time, the convention in a session of the whole was considering Talcott Parsons' paper on "Sociology as a Profession." After long and involved discussion, E. C. Hughes, then of the University of Chicago, rose from the floor and brought a warm response by insisting that we were not a professional but, rather, a learned society. It was at this same meeting that the American Sociological Society rechristened itself the American Sociological Association, lest its former initials evoke public reactions discrepant with the dignity of a profession.

Another indication of the continuing clash between the critical intellectual and the value-free professional is to be found in the phoenix-like emergence of Young Turk movements, such as the Society for the Psychological Study of Social Issues, which arose in response to the depression of 1929. When it was felt by Alfred McClung Lee and others that these Turks were no longer so young, they founded the Society for the Study of Social Problems. Both these organizations remain ongoing concerns, each characteristically interested in value-related work, and each something of a stitch in the side of its respective parent group, the American Psychological Association and the American Sociological Association.

Another case in point can be found in the recent studies of medicine conducted by men trained at Columbia or Harvard on the one hand and those trained at the University of Chicago on the other hand. The former seem more respectful of the medical establishment than the Chicagoans; they more readily regard it in terms of its own claims, they are more prone to view it as a noble profession. Chicagoans, however, tend to be uneasy about the very idea of a "profession" as a tool for study, and seem to believe instead that the notion of an "occupation" provides more basic guidelines for study. They argue that occupations as diverse as the nun and the prostitute, or the plumber and the physician, reveal instructive sociological similarities. The Chicago group seem more likely to take a secular view of medicine, for they see it as an occupation much like any other and are more inclined to investigate the seamier side of medical practice. Differences in the two groups can be seen even in the titles they have chosen for their medical studies. Harvard and Columbia have soberly called two of their most important works "The Student-Physician" and "Experiment

Perilous," while the Chicagoans have irreverently labeled their own recent study of medical students the "Boys in White."

One of the most interesting expressions of resistance to the newer, value-free style of "professional" sociology is the fascination with the *demi-monde* shown by several former members of the Chicago group. For them orientation to the underworld has become the equivalent of the proletarian identifications felt by some intellectuals during the 1930's. For not only do they study it, but in a way they speak on its behalf, affirming the authenticity of its style of life. Two of the leading exponents of this style are Howard S. Becker and Erving Goffman.

As a case in point, Goffman's subtle study, "Cooling the Mark Out," takes its point of departure from an examination of the strategy of the confidence rackets. In the Con Game, Goffman points out, after the victim, the "mark," has been taken, one of the con men remains behind "to cool the mark out," seeking to persuade him to accept his loss of face rather than go to the police. Goffman then uses this stratagem as a model to explore a great variety of legitimate groups and roles—the restaurant hostess who cools out the impatient customer, the psychoanalyst who cools out those who have lost in love. The point is insinuated that the whole world may be seen as one of marks and operators, and that, in the final analysis, we are all marks to be cooled out by the clergy, the operator left behind for the job. This, it would seem, is a metaphysics of the underworld, in which conventional society is seen from the standpoint of a group outside of its own respectable social structures.

This group of Chicagoans finds itself at home in the world of hip, Norman Mailer, drug addicts, jazz musicians, cab drivers, prostitutes, night people, drifters, grifters, and skidders: the "cool world." This stream of work cannot be fully appreciated in terms of the categories conventionally employed in sociological analysis. It has also to be seen from the viewpoint of the literary critic as a style or genre and, in particular, as a species of naturalistic romanticism, a term which I do not in the least intend opprobriously. That is, it prefers the offbeat to the familiar, the vivid ethnographic detail to the dull taxonomy, the sensuously expressive to dry analysis, naturalistic observation to formal questionnaires, the standpoint of the hip outsider to the square insider.

It may of course be asked, "Is it any the less sentimentally romantic to regard medical research on incurable patients as an 'Experiment Perilous'?" Possibly not. But it is at least much more decorous than seeing it as a process of "Cooling the Mark Out." That, I suspect, is nearer the bone. The one thing that "classicists," whether sociological or literary, can never abide is a lack of decorum, even if the performance is in other respects brilliant. In sociology, objections to a lack of decorum as such are not made and, instead, often take the form of criticizing methodological deficiencies or moralistic proclivities. And, in truth, this Chicago group does betray persistent moral concerns, as evidenced, for example, by their readiness to focus on the degrading impact of the mental hospital on its inmates, or on the legal straitjacket in which the drug addict is confined.

The pathology characteristic of the classicist is too well known to require much comment: theirs is the danger of ritualism, in which conformity to the formal canons of the craft is pursued compulsively to the point where it warps work, emptying it of insight, significant truth, and intellectually viable substance. Of the classicist degenerating into neo-classicism we might say with Roy Campbell, "They use the snaffle and the curb, all right, but where's the bloody horse?"

For its part, romantic social criticism is vulnerable from two directions. The usual occupational hazard of the romantic is, of course, excess of the emotions or of the imagination. Such excess stems not only from the personalities indigenous to those whom romanticism attracts but, just as much, from the bitter attack upon them by the neo-classicist and from their resultant polemic. Again, and perhaps more importantly, this romantic standpoint is vulnerable to the crasser temptations of its own talent-earned success. Indeed, they have now learned to mute their language to the point where they can communicate profitably with their stockbrokers. Perhaps the time will come when they will no longer have to pretend to be respectable and when they will, instead, have to work at seeming cool. But that time is not yet. Whatever the outcome, they have shown us still another facet of the resistance to the emergence of a value-free professionalism in sociology, and they have given us still another evidence of the intellectual vitality of a critical stance.

Despite the vigor of this and other groups, however, I believe that they are primarily secondary currents whose very visibility is heightened because they are moving across the main ebb. The dominant drift in American sociology is toward professionalization, the growth of technical specialists, toward the diffusion of the value-free outlook to the point where it becomes less of an intellectual doctrine and more of a blanketing mood. American sociology is in the process of accommodating itself.

In its main outlines, such efforts at accommodation are far from new. For the doctrine of a value-free sociology is a modern extension of the medieval conflict between faith and reason. It grows out of, and still dwells in, the tendency prevalent since the thirteenth century to erect compartments between the two as a way of keeping the peace between them. One of the culminations of this tendency in the Middle Ages is to be found in the work of the Arabian philosopher, Ibn Rochd, better known as Averroes. Averroes had believed that absolute truth was to be found not in revelation but in philosophy, which for him meant Aristotle. He felt that revelation, faith, and the work of the theologians was a kind of footman's philosophy, necessary for those devoid of intellectual discipline and useful as a way of civilizing them.

Seeing theology as containing a measure of truth, albeit one inferior to that of philosophy and, being a prudent man, Averroes recommended that philosophers and theologians ought each to mind his own business and, in particular, that the philosophers, being intellectually superior, should show *noblesse oblige* to the theologians. He suggested that philosophers should keep their truth to themselves and write technical books which did not disturb or confuse simpler minds.

His disciples, the Latin or Christian Averroists, particularly at the University of Paris, accentuated this prudential side of their master's work; their strategy of safety was to define themselves as specialists, as technical philosophers. Their only job, said they, was to teach philosophy and to show the conclusions that flowed from it. These conclusions were logically "necessary," but, when at variance with the truths of revelation, it was not their job to reconcile them, said the philosophers. From this developed the so-called Doctrine of the Twofold Truth—the truths of philosophy which were formally necessary and the divine truths of revelation. If there were

contradictions between the two, the philosophers merely reaf-
firmed their belief in revelation, and let it go at that. This sometimes took a cynical form as, for example, in John of Jaudan's
comment about a matter of faith, "I do believe that is true; but I
cannot prove it. Good luck to those who can!" They thus built a
watertight compartment between philosophy and faith, a separation which St. Thomas Aquinas continued and yet sought to
transcend. To St. Thomas, knowing and believing are distinct
processes, each having its own separate and legitimate function and
therefore not to be invaded by the other. In this view, there were
two main classes of truths, both of which, however, derived from
Divine Revelation. There were truths obtainable by natural reason
alone, and there were truths of revelation, genuine articles of faith
which elude the grasp of reason and which were susceptible
neither to proof nor disproof by reason.

With the development of modern science varying efforts to accommodate it to religion continued. They often took the form of
some kind of separatist doctrine in which each is assigned a different function and each is chastened to acknowledge the authority
of the other in its own sphere. Weber's doctrine of a value-free
sociology, which creates a gulf between science and values, is in
this tradition; it may be regarded as a Protestant version of the
Thomistic effort at harmonizing their relations.

The core of Weber's outlook rested on a dualism between, on
the one hand, reason or rationality, especially as embodied in
bureaucracy and science, and, on the other hand, more elemental
emotional forces, partly encompassed in his notion of Charisma.
He regards each of these forces as inimical to the other. He himself
is ambivalent to each of them; he views each as both dangerous
and necessary.

On the one side, Weber is deeply concerned to protect the
citadel of modern reason, the university, and fiercely opposes the
professorial "cult of personality" which was the academic expression of the charismatic claim. This in turn disposes him to project
an image of the university which is essentially bureaucratic, as a
faceless group of specialists, each sovereign in his own cell and all
sworn to foresake their individuality. He nonetheless hates bureaucracy precisely because it submerges individuality and de-
humanizes men, and thus he is led to deny that he intended to

bureaucratize the university in pleading for the doctrine of a value-free social science. (Yet while this was doubtless not his intention, his two-pronged polemic against the cult of academic personality and in favor of the value-free doctrine does seem to drive him toward such a bureaucratic conception of the university.)

If Weber is concerned to protect even the bureaucratic dwelling-places of rationality, he also seeks to confine bureaucracy and to circumscribe the area of its influence. In particular, he wishes to protect the highest reaches of statecraft from degenerating into a lifeless routine; he seeks to preserve politics as a realm in which there can be an expression of personal will, of serious moral commitment, a realm where greatness was possible to those who dared, persevered, and suffered, a realm so powerful that it could overturn the institutional order to preserve it. He wants to safeguard high politics as an arena of human autonomy, of pure value choices at its finest.

Yet Weber also fears for the safety of rationality in the modern world. He knows that there are powerful forces abroad which continue to threaten rationality, that there are still untamed things in men which he, more than most, had had to face. Not unlike Freud, Weber was both afraid of and drawn to these unbridled forces, the passionate Dionysian part of men. While he believed that they were being slowly subdued by an onmarching rationalization, he continued to fear that they could yet erupt and cleave modern institutional life. Although fearing these irrational forces, he also felt their disappearance from the modern world to be a "disenchantment," for he believed that they contained springs of vitality and power indispensable to human existence.

Weber is a man caught between two electrodes and torn by the current passing between them; he fears both but is unable to let go of either. He attempts to solve this dilemma by a strategy of segregation, which excludes charismatic irrationality from certain modern institutions, such as the university, but admits it into and, indeed, exalts its manifestations in the inward personal life of individuals. He wanted certain of the role structures of modern society to be rational; but he also wanted the role-players to be passionate and willful. He wanted the play to be written by a classicist and to be acted by romanticists. Unusual man, he wanted the best of both worlds. Yet whatever the judgment of his intellect, his sentiments are not poised midway between them, but tend toward one of the two sides.

Weber's involvement appears when we ask if science cannot be the basis of value judgments, what then was to be their basis? To answer this, we must go beyond Weber's formal doctrine of a value-free sociology to his own personal profession of belief. Weber certainly did not hold that personal values should derive from the existent culture, or from ancient tradition, nor again from formal ethical systems which he felt to be empty and lifeless. Unless men were to become inhuman robots, life, he insisted, must be guided by consciously made decisions. If men are to have dignity, they must choose their own fate.

To Weber as a man, only those values are authentic which stem from conscious decision, from a consultation of the inner conscience and a willful commitment to its dictates. From his personal standpoint, it is not really true that all values are equally worthy. Those consciously held by men are more worthy than those which are merely traditional and unthinkingly repeated. Those values that men feel deeply about and passionately long to realize are better than those which are merely intellectually appealing and do not engage their entire being.

In short, Weber, too, was seeking a solution to the competing claims of reason and faith. His solution takes the form of attempting to guard the autonomy of both spheres but, most especially I believe, the domain of conscience and faith. He wants a way in which reason and faith can cohabit platonically but not as full partners. The two orders are separate but unequal. For in Weber, reason only consults conscience and perhaps even cross-examines it. But conscience has the last word, and passion and will the last deed. Here Weber stands as half-Lutheran, half-Nietzschian.

If Weber thrusts powerfully at traditionalism, he nonetheless wages his main campaign against science and reason and for confining their influence. To Weber, even reason must submit when conscience declares, Here I stand; I can do no other! Weber saw as authentic only those values that rest on the charismatic core of the self and on its claims to intuitive certainty. Weber, too, was a seeker after certainty, the certainty that is more apt to come from the arrogance of individual conscience. For while much may be truly said of the arrogance of reason, reason always seeks reasons and is ready to sit down and talk about them.

To Weber as a Protestant, the individual's conscience is akin to the voice of revelation. He would have been dismayed at the implications of considering it as the echo of parental remonstrations. To him, individual conscience was transcendental, while reason and science were only instrumental. Science is the servant of values and of personal conscience, which, like the heart, has reasons of its own. From Weber's standpoint, science and reason could only supply the means; the ends were to be dictated by values which, even if inscrutable, were to have the final voice.

I have therefore come to believe that the value-free doctrine is, from Weber's standpoint, basically an effort to compromise two of the deepest traditions of Western thought, reason and faith, but that his arbitration seeks above all to safeguard the romantic residue in modern man. I have personal reservations not because I doubt the worth of safeguarding this romantic component, but, rather, because I disagree with the strategy of segregation which Weber advances. I believe that, in the end, this segregation warps reason by tinging it with sadism and leaves feeling smugly sure only of itself and bereft of a sense of common humanity.

The problem of a value-free sociology has its most poignant implications for the social scientist in his role as educator. If sociologists ought not express their personal values in the academic setting, how then are students to be safeguarded against the unwitting influence of these values which shape the sociologist's selection of problems, his preferences for certain hypotheses or conceptual schemes, and his neglect of others? For these are unavoidable and, in this sense, there is and can be no value-free sociology. The only choice is between an expression of one's values, as open and honest as it can be, this side of the psychoanalytical couch, and a vain ritual of moral neutrality which, because it invites men to ignore the vulnerability of reason to bias, leaves it at the mercy of irrationality.

If truth is the vital thing, as Weber is reputed to have said on his deathbed, then it must be all the truth we have to give, as best we know it, being painfully aware and making our students aware, that even as we offer it we may be engaged in unwitting concealment rather than revelation. If we would teach students how science is made, really made rather than as publicly reported, we cannot fail to expose them to the whole scientist by whom it is made, with all his gifts and blindnesses, with all his methods and his values as well. To do otherwise is to usher in an era of spiritless technicians who will be no less lacking in understanding than they are in passion, and who will be useful only because they can be used.

In the end, even these dull tools will build, through patient persistence and cumulation, a technology of social science strong enough to cripple us. Far as we are from a sociological atomic bomb, we already live in a world of the systematic brainwashing of prisoners of war and of housewives with their advertising-exacerbated compulsions; and the social science technology of tomorrow can hardly fail to be more powerful than today's.

It would seem that social science's affinity for modeling itself after physical science might lead to instruction in matters other than research alone. Before Hiroshima, physicists also talked of a value-free science; they, too, vowed to make no value judgments. Today many of them are not so sure. If today we concern ourselves exclusively with the technical proficiency of our students and reject all responsibility for their moral sense, or lack of it, then we may someday be compelled to accept responsibility for having trained a generation willing to serve in a future Auschwitz. Granted that science always has inherent in it both constructive and destructive potentialities, it does not follow that we should encourage our students to be oblivious to the difference. Nor does this in any degree detract from the indispensable norms of scientific objectivity; it merely insists that these differ radically from moral indifference.

I have suggested that, at its deepest roots, the myth of a value-free sociology was Weber's way of trying to adjudicate the tensions between two vital Western traditions: between reason and faith, between knowledge and feeling, between classicism and romanticism, between the head and the heart. Like Freud, Weber never really believed in an enduring peace or in a final resolution of this conflict. What he did was to seek a truce through the segregation of the contenders, by allowing each to dominate in different spheres of life. Although Weber's efforts at a personal synthesis bring him nearer to St. Thomas, many of his would-be followers today tend to be nearer to the Latin Averroists, with their doctrine of the twofold truth, and their conception of themselves as narrow technicians who reject responsibility for the cultural and moral consequences of their work. It is precisely because of the deeply dualistic implications of the current doctrine of a value-free sociology that I felt its most appropriate symbol to be the man-beast, the cleft creature, the minotaur.[1]

NOTES:

1. Presidential address delivered at the annual meeting of the Society for the Study of Social Problems (August 28, 1961), and originally published in *Social Problems*, 9, No. 3, Winter 1962. It is reprinted here, with slight alteration, with the permission of the author.

# 14

ABRAHAM EDEL

## Social Science and Value:
## A Study in Interrelations

When the intellectual history of contemporary soc..l science comes to be written, one of its major themes will be the relation of social science to value. It will be a story of mutual isolation, affecting theory and practice alike, with losses to both the social sciences and the philosophy of value. C. Wright Mills was one of the powerful voices in American social theory of recent decades raised against this isolation. He focused clearly on the value potential of social science, and on the value consequences of its different styles of work. If he saw this as the politics of sociology, it was not in the debunking spirit of the older unmasking of ideologies. Rather, he tried to make social scientists self-conscious about the major ways in which their work did affect the solution of critical human problems, so that they could face responsibly the choices which they were often avoiding.

The practical understanding that Mills called for requires a more systematic co-operation of social science and philosophy on the very question of this relation of science and value. This is itself no simple problem, and an understanding of its complex structure is a necessary step in its systematic practical solution. Here, I should like to explore the interrelations of social science and value, and make a start on analyzing the entry-points, if we may so call them, where value issues enter into social science, and where social science assumptions enter into value theory.

Since three central concepts are involved in our inquiry—value, science, entry—some initial refinement and consideration of present use is desirable.

Value is a high-powered concept, and in modern thought has shown a considerable tendency to become an imperialistic category. In philosophy, it was set up as a genus for a whole host of species, covering religious feeling as well as economic utility, and beauty as well as obligation. The guiding hope was that the study of generic problems of identification, measurement, and validation of "values" would yield important widely applicable results. It is still an open question whether the whole development of general value theory in contemporary philosophy should not be regarded as a blind alley, in spite of some theoretically liberating effects it produced. In any case, it diluted the concept of value so completely that what remains is the general idea of a pro-or-con attitude. Recent social science, however, has not gone so far. It has tended to retain in the concept of value an element of judgment or discrimination, so that having a value often means in its studies not merely desiring something, but also thinking it or holding it in some way as desirable. Such conceptual history is not our present concern, but it conveys an important lesson for one who would study the entry of values into science. There is no existent discipline, philosophic or scientific, which validates the concept of value *en bloc*, or as more than a tag. There is no advance guarantee that as one type of value is relevant or irrelevant to science, so another type will be, or that any generalizations from one sample of value will hold for another sample from some other corner of the field. I would thus suggest that at the outset some formally distinct aspects be sorted out, that we differentiate at least a specific concept of purpose, a general concept of pro-attitude, a judgmental concept of worthwhile, and a prescriptive concept of obligation.

Science in the present day is likely to go in a number of different directions. Our concern with social science does not bind us too strictly, for boundary questions are themselves highly moot in the field. We can cross without passport into a large segment of psychology (even beyond what is labeled "social" psychology) and into a great deal of history, and we are not surprised—for example, when reading political science or sociology—to find ourselves occasionally in social philosophy. As to the meaning of "science," it sometimes is as broad as "systematic knowledge," sometimes it is limited to the "experimental"; sometimes it means invoking scientific method, sometimes scientific results, sometimes just the scientific temper. Discussions of value and science may have in mind pure science, applied science, or sometimes even the scientist operating on the social scene. All these distinctions are easy enough to make when required; it is only when we forget them that there is a tendency to overgeneralize from what is concluded in one sense of "science" to what holds for "science in general."

To speak of the entry of value assumptions into science, or conversely of scientific assumptions into value theory, calls attention to the form of results we may anticipate, or rather the task of differentiating types of relations. Some values are smuggled into science, and the best thing to do when we uncover them is immediately to deport them. Others, however, may have been around a long time, and claim either prescriptive or native-born (not to speak of natural) rights. Here we may want to let them stay, but delimit carefully what influence they may or may not have: they may, for example, permissibly motivate budgetary support for science, but not dictate the questions of basic research. On the other hand, some value-attitudes—the virtue of impartiality, for example —are ushered into the inner sanctum of science and kept constantly at work. Certainly, then, two categories of entry will be external purpose and internal influence. But there is a third which may prove even more ingrained. Let us speak of it as a value parameter. What this kind of entry would be, if it actually exists, may be seen by analogy. The sense intended is the same in which a theory of society is seen to involve a specific picture of the nature of man. We would then say that a social theory has a human-nature parameter. The question would not be whether it can be eliminated, since some theory of human nature is unavoidable; rather, it would be a choice of which picture to accept, or at least the realization that unsettled questions of social theory are in some definite part a function of unsettled questions in the theory of human nature. Now whether there are value parameters in this sense in social science is a question for inquiry. If there are, the kinds of values that occupy such a position would be unavoidable or non-eliminable. But whether or not there are, this type of concept is required. For there is not only the question of possible value parameters in social science, but also the comparable question of social science parameters in value theory.

No doubt further conceptual refinements will be needed as research progresses. For a start, we should not be less refined than our four concepts of value (purpose, pro-attitude, worthwhile, obligation), our multiple meanings of science (at least the distinction of pure, applied, and social action), and our three modes of entry (external purpose, internal influence, and value parameter, and comparable converse concepts for entry of science into value) will allow us to be so.

What kind of research questions can be raised about the entry of values into pure science? Unless we simply plunge blindly, we would first need a sketch of the scientific process as it takes place typically in social science, so that we can map the sensitive entry-points for values. Such a sketch would differentiate at least the following aspects: determination of the basic aim of the science, establishment of field boundaries, modes of identifying phenomena in the field, problem selection, problem formulation, concept formation, hypothesis selection, verification procedures, theory development, and concepts of adequacy in results. It would be too grim a task at this point to push on into each of these in the hunt for values to be assessed. Let us rather start from the different modes of entry, and take illustrations, where relevant, from these many aspects.

First, then, as to the role of external purposes. This has been amply studied in theories of ideology. It is easier to spot a class distortion of economics or a racialist use of the IQ than to ferret out a subtle limitation of hypotheses through the use of a deeply hidden value-carrying model. But even in spotting ideology there is considerable complexity. What exactly are we criticizing a thesis for, when we label it ideological in the derogatory sense of that term?

On the face of it, it seems simple enough. A view is enunciated as a scientific thesis—say, a doctrine of racial superiority in the early twentieth-century imperialistic era, or the wage-fund theory in nineteenth-century economics, or the identification of business success with evolutionary leadership in Spencerian or Sumnerian sociology. It is then found to operate in such a way as to enhance the economic interest and power position of a particular social group. What more is needed to warrant the attribute of an unmasked ideology, as intruding external purpose?

Actually, a whole host of differentiated requirements are called for. First, as to the view itself, what is its truth property? It may be classified as sheer nonsense, or as logically possible but actually false, as largely false though partly true, or finally even as wholly true. (Quite literally, in a given period, true theses in physics and chemistry may, by their discovery, enhance the economic interest and power position of a particular social group that controls productive resources.) Second, as to the way in which the view is held. It may be held on presumed (though incorrect) evidential grounds, or on "projective" grounds expressing unconscious demands, whether the thesis be true or false (Freud illustrates this by the belief of alchemists in the transmutability of metals), or for conscious advancement of the external purposes. Third, as to the locus of the ideological activity. The external purpose may operate directly in the act of discovery, or in the perpetuation of the thesis after discovery, or in influencing the direction of further scientific inquiry, or in the social application of the thesis. Fourth, as to the consequences of the ideological activity in the ongoing life of science and social activity. The external purpose may operate directly or indirectly (by limiting inquiry or by turning promising minds from a given path), deliberately or through unintended consequences, outside the science in applied areas or by standardizing presuppositions of the scientific pattern of inquiry (by affecting the philosophy of science so that certain models are given a privileged position). Fifth, as to the relation of the factors. Relations of truth-status of theses, purposes of holders, consequences of action, may be logical or psychological or historical. They are likely to be logical—in the three examples cited above, the truth would be logically compatible with an ethical demand for supreme sacrifice by the "superior" group rather than a demand for special privileges. But all sorts of combinations of psychological and socio-historical relations may be found.

What combination of these, and no doubt of other factors, shall be dubbed with the title of ideology is not our present concern. It is more important to realize the vast program of conceptual refinement and social science research required to map the entry patterns of external purposes. But it would be a mistake to think of them wholly in malevolent terms. Dire needs may prompt scientific research and hopes of practical solution stimulate hypotheses. Depressions have quickened theories of the role of consumer spending in maintaining economic stability. Desires to win elections have by no means been absent from the rise of political sociology. Studies of workers' morale grew to prominence in an atmosphere of apprehension about the rise of trade unions and a fear of their taking a class-struggle attitude. Institutional demands in education and in war developed intelligence testing; manpower demands and wide skill demands may militate against ideological theories of the fixed IQ. Large-scale organization has stimulated the study of bureaucratic structures; though sometimes prompted by the fear of socialism, it has also raised problems that socialist countries find it necessary to face as a result of their own experience.

At the present time there has been a kind of consolidation of external purposes in relation to pure social science, a growing conviction that, on the whole, research in social life is practical. Thus external purposes are standardized in general support of *basic research*. Analytic caution is still required to a high degree to spot the operation of purposes within the scientific processes. In fact, the general acceptance of basic research may tend to obscure these purposes by making all decisions of direction in inquiry seem intra-scientific. But quite obviously today, to take the most glaring examples, there is incomparably more research on the social aspects of waging war than of advancing peace, and on the techniques of control and command rather than on the techniques of liberty and self-realization. Since the problems investigated tend to limit the kind of work done, the hypotheses suggested, questions asked, and models proposed, the impact of external purposes by this route is a strong one. There can, however, be no question of removing human purposes, of "neutralization" at this point. It is rather a question of agreeing on broad human purposes to guide interests in inquiry. This would help unify a variety of already recognized aims: greater facilities for freedom of research, conscious specification of guiding purposes rather than subterranean channels of their operation, greater place to the goal of truth as against ignoring social sore spots or existing patterns of economy or power. And of course there is also the question of facing realistically the human costs involved in moving from understanding to application. These are all familiar social issues.

We turn from external purposes operating on pure social science to internal influence. It is worth noting initially that the very discovery of the operation of external purposes can itself have internal consequences—especially on verification procedures. The more one establishes a check-list of the kinds of purpose that have given a special turn to scientific work, the more one clarifies the operational concept of a "reliable observer"—just as the comparable discovery of color-blindness or different reaction-speed or influence of drugs or alcohol affects the concept of a reliable observer in other fields. Thus the realization that there are class attitudes has consequences for sampling techniques, for interview procedures, for assumptions about differential goal strivings, and so on. It is in the accumulation of a knowledge of specific biases, and thus of specific techniques for penetrating and avoiding them, rather than in some philosopher's stone to test for bias in general, that the contemporary theory of ideology can make its contribution to scientific rationality.

We may omit here the internal operation of general values, in the sense of obligations and pro-attitudes not peculiar to social science—regard for truth, objectivity and impartiality, clarity, systematic power, and so forth—in brief, the methodological virtues of all scientific endeavor. On the whole, the internal value influences in social science seem most apparent in special pro-or-con attitudes which affect such aspects as concept-formation and basic theoretical schemata. Take the use of the central concept of power in political sciences, often advanced to do the same kind of job there as the concept of energy does in physics. Clearly, its centrality comes from the existence of power structures in contemporary institutions, as well as the prevalence of power struggles in both individual and international relations. It would take a long historical inquiry to see how and why older purpose-concepts were driven out from a central role. We cannot assume it was for scientific reasons alone. Since political science has not flourished or made notable discoveries under the reign of the power concept, its use can be seen rather as imposing or expressing a dominance-submission pattern than as exhibiting the fruitfulness of a meaningful scientific construct. Here the science simply reflects the attitude rather than brings an understanding of it. Consider, for example, what would happen if political science were construed as the science of decision systems in all areas of life—small-group decision, national decision, global decision. The science would stretch out in different directions from those in which it now moves, would focus on different additional phenomena, and would weave altered affiliations. This, too, would be a very limited central category, no doubt reflecting the need of decision and the growth of institutional mechanisms of decision in modern times. But it would cast the sciences in a quite altered pattern.

To illustrate internal influence in basic theoretical frameworks, we may point to functionalist theory. By positing the existence of a more or less stable system in relation to which the functions of specific social forms are to be interpreted, a pro-attitude to stability is embedded in the scientific quest. Specific purposes of adherence to or rejection of the *status quo* may be winnowed out by warning against the conservative and the radical capture of functionalist concepts. But the value tone may still remain. The social scientist, who complains at this point that, after all, the business of science is the discovery of order, is missing the deeper philosophical issue. Is the order to be discovered within the social system, or in the historical panorama within which social systems rise and undergo basic transformation? How often is the very expression "social system" used with the presupposition that there must be equilibrium characteristics in all social organizations so that history and evolution can be ignored? When Aristotle identified wisdom with the knowledge of causes, and thus with the contemplation of order—as he said, there is no science of the accidental —he assumed an eternal or fixed basic order. Perhaps today we should rather say with Robert Bridges, in his *The Testament of Beauty,* "Our stability is but balance, and wisdom lies in the masterful administration of the unforeseen." Whether the central stress falls on knowing what to expect, or having a large enough armory of expectations to deal with the unexpected, is a question of basic philosophical orientation to order and disorder. The value-tone in any specific use of the order concept seems quite clear in the history of social science.*

Whether such values as pro-attitudes in concept formation and in general schemata may be eliminated once they are tracked down is not an all-embracing question. Certainly some can, but others may turn out on deeper exploration to lead to value parameters in the sense defined above. Let us continue the political science illustration to trace the outcome. There is no reason why, having come to suspect that the power stress in contemporary political science is a value-structuring of social life in terms of an acceptance of dominance-submission relations, a political scientist may not try to correct for it by greater attention to interpreting governing from below—that is, from a wider view of the aims and purposes of men in terms of which they on the whole accept governmental structures. How far would he be removing embedded values? If he proposed the decision orientation suggested as an alternative for the field, he would probably be embodying a general democratic value attitude—human beings working out cultural devices to embody their decisions. If he began to study political phenomena in terms of the whole structure of a society, with its given cultural history, in the light of its patterning of human goals, he might very well be led to question the traditional boundaries of the field which is his science. Now in the physical sciences it has already been established that the boundaries of a field are a function of the results already achieved in the sciences, and may be shifted as new results emerge. Social science boundaries have frequently embodied value attitudes. How much of the traditional separation of political science from economics has reflected the separateness of governmental institutions from business institutions in the last few centuries of Western history? In so far as the boundaries of the sciences are a function of the institutional structure, all "laws" discovered in each field as separate might hold only for limited given historical conditions. But what is more, the maintenance of these conditions in a given epoch may embody the policies of a given economic sys-

---

* Interestingly enough, Mills at one point in *The Sociological Imagination*, p. 117, attacks the very ideal of prediction in social science as substituting for responsible choice. Perhaps this could be taken care of by specifying the form of prediction to be: "Under such-and-such conditions, an event of the class X will happen, unless some action of the class Y is taken."

tem, such as the state keeping its hands off business in traditional laissez-faire capitalism. Hence the insistence on political science being developed separately from economics would embody a pro-attitude to such economic policies.

Critical consideration of the foundations of social science will have to decide whether selection of field boundaries and basic field concepts unavoidably embodies one or another basic value attitude to the continuation or alteration of basic institutional structures. If this is so, we would have at this point a value parameter in the inner structure of our science. Whether it is so in this particular example would require much more formal and factual analysis to determine. It might be suggested that the value parameter could be removed by treating all social sciences as one science, and being attentive to changing structures, rather than by favoring or assuming a specific stability of structures. But it may be that such a change itself could be construed as a specific interpretation ( or "value" in the neutral mathematical sense) for the parameter in question.

We cannot here pursue all the many general aspects of the scientific enterprise in which comparable studies would have to be made. Certainly the innumerable controversies in the history of social science methodology suggest sensitive spots where value parameters might be located. For example, the issue of whether social science is "ideographic" (painting portraits of individual wholes) or "nomothetic" (finding laws) has embodied a sizable component of value attitudes to the creativity of men as against his being "submerged" in a natural world. Issues of verification modes, such as behavioral versus phenomenological, or public observability versus private empathy, often rest on some interpretation of the self as social or as isolated, and an element of value-patterning of the self, rather than simply discovering its inherent nature. Similarly, whether to use a framework of individual behavior, some specially construed sense of "action," interpersonal transactions, or qualities of group relations as fundamental "units" contains more often than not a battle of a social against an individual perspective, with all the controversies about individualism that have accumulated in the past three centuries.

Now it is quite possible in principle to argue that these many questions, which tend to divide social scientists into theoretical "schools" and to send them off at times into quite different directions of inquiry, with different initial selection of phenomena analyzed in different ways (though perhaps all in the nature of scientific jobs), will in the long run admit of resolution in generally accepted scientific value terms of "fruitfulness." Just as teleological physical science gave way to a causal schema, so, for example, reductionist social formulations in terms of individual properties may run their course when it is found that they lead scientists to "psychologize" social phenomena and to be unable to explain or predict men's social reactions; formulations in terms of group properties and group structures may then prove scientifically unavoidable. Or again, present operationalist rigidity, which embodies a high pro-attitude to communicability and a fear of obscurantism, may find that to be fruitful it must relax and embrace some modicum of responsible phenomenological inspection, or risk remaining scientifically barren; phenomenological inspection meanwhile may shed its matrix of resistance to the scientific study of man as continuous with the order of nature.

Such theses of long-range convergence may themselves be seen as pro-attitudes toward the unity of science. At present, such methodological values are surrogates for long-range theories about how social science can most fruitfully develop. Whether their value character will diminish and their predictive character come to the front, it is probably too early to judge. In the physical sciences this happened to some extent, but not wholly. In ancient times, differences of schools embodies not only value differences but those of methodological direction. Ancient medical writings bear witness not only to the general conflict of functionalists and atomists, with their different feelings about the order of the universe, but also to their specifically different hypotheses in explaining the workings of individual organs in the body (e.g. how the heart works, or how urea gathers in the kidneys). Long-range solution of specific differences did not remove all value components; rather, they were standardized. The residual values were incorporated as built-in aims in the very meaning of "science"—systems for prediction rather than simple contemplation of eternal necessities; or again, into modes of verification—the sensory as yielding stable agreement, rather than emotional reaction as productive of divergence. The sciences of man today, resembling ancient physical

science in their conflict of schools, may be destined to a similar outcome—that is, standardized "values" for basic value parameters
rather than complete elimination of values. But more complex
solutions are of course logically possible. Meanwhile, research can
proceed in two directions. One is to render explicit the value parameters in existent theoretical structures; the other is the speculative
reconstruction of theoretical structures with minimal, standardized
value parameters, including possibly even conjectural attempts at
their complete elimination.

Questions of value in applied social science, beyond those raised
for pure social science, stem from the very notion of application.
Does this notion involve a reference to additional values, and if so,
what are they?

Some applied sciences, such as medicine, spell out specific value
in their very definition—the science of curing or maintaining health.
Others, like engineering, seem to embody a minimal idea of control in a given medium, whether that control be utilized for construction or destruction. Which path should a definition of an
applied science follow? Or should it refer in general terms to satisfying human needs or solving practical problems?

This last straddling procedure will not bear up under analysis.
Such concepts as needs or practical problems are by this time
clearly seen to embody specific value considerations. To say that
men need something is to say that the something is a necessary condition for their survival, growth, progress, satisfaction, or aim-
fulfillment. To say something is a practical problem is similarly to
point to specific hindrances or dangers and so to specific goals or
values. After all, if to solve a practical problem meant simply to
make the problem disappear, all human problems could be solved
in a great thermonuclear bang.

To limit the additional value in the notion of an applied science
to the aim of control has some advantage, but it is likely to prove
misleading. The advantage is that it shows the double potential—
for good or ill—in any body of knowledge that furnishes skills. It
thus compels one to state explicitly and separately the values
sought. Along these lines, medicine would have to be redefined as
the applied science of body-state control; it would then be a separate value judgment to use medicine for healing rather than for

mass-extermination and debilitation, as indeed the Nazis used it. However, this policy in defining an applied science is probably misleading in suggesting the value neutrality of an applied science as such, at least as an historical matter. The Nazi use of medical skill for extermination has seemed to most men an outrageous violation of the "nature" of medicine. And even the apparent neutrality of engineering stems not so much from any inherently value-free character of the discipline as from the fact that it has historically been associated with opposing values; its destructive use stems from its role in war. To be on one side or another in a conflict is not to be on neither side. (Even mercenaries do not belie this; they are neutral to sides, but not to their pay, their lives, their comforts.) To strip the notion of application, therefore, to the minimal idea of control does not conform to preponderant usage, nor to analytic necessities. In fact it is a normative proposal for extending the presumed value-free character of science into the domain of application, and so to fashion a certain image of the scientist and limit his responsibilities as scientist. In the light of the confusion that reigns in this area at present, clarity can best be achieved by recognizing that any limited skill *per se* can be used in opposing ways, and by insisting that any actual applied science which has grown up as an enterprise of men in the pursuit of goals should specify the goals it has embodied, so that any controversy about their desirability will admit of an explicit socio-moral reckoning.

Once the value base of applied science has been made clear in this fashion, another feature emerges about the relation of applied to pure science, which may have special relevance to social science. There is not a one to one relation, so that every pure science has its unique applied science as correlate. Engineering draws on a whole range of sciences. Space engineering is the most recent and clearest illustration of the way in which biology, psychology, and social science tie in with the physical sciences in determining feasibility of accomplishment. The same holds for medicine, drawing on everything from physics to entymology and psychology. Is not the same thing true today for, say, developmental economics?

If the unity in an applied science is a problem-unity crystallized by human goals, the relation between the applied science and the pure sciences on which it draws becomes a closer one to the extent to which these problems and their embedded goals in fact play a role in setting questions, encouraging theoretical development, offering guiding models, and so forth. It may even be that at the present stage of development of pure social science, it could prosper more with a goal or problem inner unity. For example, could not economics today advantageously be considered as the science of avoiding depressions and generating a high productive level throughout the globe, politics as the science of social control productive of the greatest human freedom, sociology as the analysis of society to find the points of control for removing obvious evils (crime, delinquency, discrimination, etc.) and advancing obvious good, cultural anthropology as the science of achieving one world without a loss of all divergent cultural values, linguistics as the science of maximum effective and aesthetic communication, and so forth? Something like this, I take it, was at the root of Robert Lynd's approach in *Knowledge for What?* I am not sure about the answer. It may be that a goal reorientation of the social sciences might tend to disparage descriptive content and systematic relationships and risk a narrow pragmatism. But on the other hand, nothing could be narrower than the traditional disowning of values by the social sciences in modern times. The issue is not one to be settled in terms of external purposes. It is a question for the social scientists themselves to decide how to carry on their work to achieve the widest descriptive, historical, and theoretical results. That a value reorientation is a possible path, however, indicates that there is no inherent barrier to a constitutive role for values, in the nature of a social science.

It is not unusual in the present social conflicts for a social scientist to engage in social action, in his own words, "as a citizen." That is, he draws a fine line between the neutrality of his discipline and the possession of certain values on his part as a citizen or a person. The analysis of this troubled question is helped by separating the different kinds of value judgments the social scientist may be called upon to make as a scientist.

The most obvious commitment he has as a scientist is of course to the dominant value of truth inherent in his enterprise. This means that if he speaks out on a question of his discipline he is committed to stating what he knows as a scientist. Of course, the obligation to speak out is a separate strand, and occasionally some philosophers have lauded a silent devotion to truth. But it is likely that the general obligation of the scientist to speak out where the truth is socially important stems from the wider obligation of the intellectual in modern society, which in its turn could be subject to a comparable analysis.

A second obligation is to maintain the conditions of his scientific enterprise. If he is committed to the pursuit and extension of truth, he is committed to maintaining and extending the conditions requisite for scientific work. Most social scientists would accept this obligation as scientists. But in doing so they are not merely accepting a platitude but opening an area for social science research. For the social conditions relevant to the scientific pursuit of truth are not discerned a priori but issues for social science evidence. Hence quite correctly, a social scientist can oppose McCarthyite guilt by association and restrictive military secrecy in science, not just as a citizen, but as a scientist, if the evidence is clear enough that these are conditions which hinder scientific development.

A third sphere is making judgments about what is good for a man, or worthwhile, on the basis of the contributions of the scientist's area of inquiry. It is clear that many segments of social science furnish such judgments, or at least kindred judgments about human evils. Psychologists on the effects of repeated frustration and breakdown, sociologists on the existence and conditions of social disorganization and anomie, economists on the danger of unemployment and the destruction of economic resources, anthropologists on the loss of a sense of dignity in exploitative cultural contact, need no outside sanction—beyond perhaps a formal explication of the terms "good" and "evil"—to make such value judgments as scientists. Sometimes they are hindered in such judgments by a failure to make conceptual distinctions in ethical terms. To judge something good if men could achieve it is one thing; to say that we ought at a given time to devote given resources to achieving it rather than some alternative realizable good, or that we ought to pursue it when it will involve some given cost or sacrifice, may be quite another thing. The judgments about what is good or worthwhile are not irrelevant to the scientist as scientist, although there may be differences about the precise obligations; for the latter involves scaling problems among competing goods as well as judgments of means.

But, fourth, there may be judgments of social obligation which a scientist could make as scientist, if the scaling and means components become clear. Here the emphasis on the modern scene often falls on the co-operation of different scientific disciplines in concerted social action. For the one science may supplement the gaps of knowledge which prevent another from turning judgments of good into either conditional or highly probable obligations. In such contexts there is not, then, an inherent barrier to obligation judgments, but simply a limitation of knowledge or sometimes a difference in comparative values which further investigation may diminish. The scientist as scientist may thus find himself able to state contingent or hypothetical obligations—for example, "if such-and-such a country wants peace, it ought to abandon such-and-such attitudes." Sometimes the if-clause drops away by common consent. Contemporary social scientists argue about the comparative social advantage of socialist and private enterprise in developing underdeveloped countries. But where is the social scientist who will sponsor the preservation of feudalism in Egypt or Iran or Saudi Arabia? This rejection is not just a value judgment about the intrinsic worth of the feudal way of life; it embodies a scientific thesis that whatever sets of values contemporary men may hold as basic, feudalism if perpetuated will thwart them.

Finally, there may be limiting points at which knowledge is insufficient, or conflict in purposes too great. Even here it may be rather as a scientist offering an informed guess or a plausible hypothesis or as a trained thinker clarifying alternatives, than as an ordinary citizen, that the scientist engages in social action.

In this domain, again, there need not be an all or nothing attitude. The gap between values that social scientists commonly agree on and the dominating policies of practical politics in our society is often so great that there is the most pressing need for the independent effort of the scientist in social action.

Research into ways in which social science enters value theory is doubly difficult, because it has been attacked from both sides. For a long time the social scientists insisted values were not their business while the value theorists were busy widening the gap by arguing for the philosophical irrelevance of scientific-factual materials. Together they have gathered a formidable array of slogans:
Science tells you the means but not the end.

Science tells you the cause of your choice but not whether it is the right choice.

Science may help you map the pattern of your past choices, but cannot tell you whether to choose to adhere to the pattern of the past.

Science fashions beliefs, not attitudes.

You can't get the "ought" from the "is."

You can't get the "desirable" from the "desired."

You can't get the "prescriptive" from the "descriptive."

You can't get the "imperative" from the "indicative."

And so on, with considerable ingenuity in saying the same thing in different ways.

The philosophical arguments for maintaining the gap pose the issue of the relation of science and value in a deductive model: how to deduce value conclusions from scientific premises. What is thus demonstrated by the arguments is really not that science and value have no relation but that such a model oversimplifies their relation to the point of irrelevance, that the relations are much more varyingly and complexly patterned. At the same time, a sociological analysis can readily discern that a grim battle is being fought. It appears to be a strange alliance between two quite disparate forces. One is the general resistance to those changes in traditional values which the growth of scientific knowledge might suggest. The other is the determination to keep value judgment open as a continuing human process with a major measure of autonomy. In this respect it constitutes a modern resistance to the bureaucratization of men's choice of their lives, whether the bureaucracy be religious or political or scientific. It is thus a recall to responsible choice.

The path of solution I have suggested for ethical theory in other writings,[1] is to distinguish four methodologies or enterprises—analytic, descriptive, causal-explanatory, evaluative. Carried on as an activity, each enterprise is distinct from the others, having its own aims and forms of results. But this does not mean that they are dealing with distinct materials nor that the results of one may not promote the carrying out of another. Each in itself has unlimited scope. Analysis may go after the concepts of science as well as those of value. Description may focus on the activity of men having a purpose, or making moral choices, or reflecting in ethical theorizing, just as it may focus on men moving or behaving. Causal explanation may be sought for any of these processes, although different philosophical outlooks may have different hopes concerning the outcome. Similarly, evaluation is a human enterprise appropriate to any field: it has but to render explicit the criteria and standards that are being invoked in the particular value process. On the whole, in scientific activity the descriptive and causal-explanatory aspects have stood out more prominently; in philosophical activity the analytic and evaluative. But each has some portion of the other two as well, at least in the background. The division here may be historically grounded, having no ultimate rationality once the relation of the enterprises is carefully worked out.

As to the mutual help of the enterprises, this in turn is a subject for careful study. It is by now commonplace that the extension of description into new areas forces the analytic construction of new concepts (as, for example, the minute study of abnormal behavior prompted concepts of repression and the unconscious; or the extended study of differences in group behavior prompted the development of the concept of culture). Causal explanation similarly extends the range of phenomena under investigation. Cumulative scientific activity along all these lines restructures the field for investigation; new and more subtle questions are asked, new meanings found, new values fashioned or discerned.

It follows that the entry of social science into value requires the same type of extended and differentiated analysis as the entry of value into science demanded of us. In a full study we would have to distinguish value theory, specific value judgments, and applications of value judgment in conduct, just as we distinguished pure science, applied science, and social action. Instead, let us deal briefly with having purposes and pro-or-con attitudes on the one hand, and distinctively moral judgments of worthwhile (good) or obligation on the other.

In the case of having purposes and having pro-or-con attitudes, the descriptive and explanatory scientific task coincides with a large part of social science itself. Such values are part of the very content of the psychological and social sciences. Anthropological mapping of cultures and patterns, sociological value study, and psychological attitude and personality study, are concentrated in great measure on this field. Similarly they may study how changes take place in the existent value system of persons or groups, the conditions and theory of their transformation, whether from internal pressures or external encounters. In all this investigation we see the external role of science in value.

At what points do we find science passing into an internal influence in having purposes or pro-*and*-con attitudes? This can mean at what points do we find the knowledge gained about human purposes and attitudes affecting or altering human purposes and attitudes. This again is clearly a research problem for social science, especially for the sociology of science (pure and applied) and the psychology of knowledge. There is no simple key to it; it cannot be settled by a philosophical formula or by deduction from a historical theory of determinants or a psychological theory of consciousness—though they are relevant. It requires careful distinction of types of purposes and attitudes, and special research for different types. Or again, the internal influence of science in this area may refer to the way scientific knowledge affects our ideas of purposes and attitudes. This leads to the third type of entry, through the existence of social science parameters in this segment of value theory.

The role of social science parameters in having purposes and pro-or-con attitudes can best be grasped by focusing on the very concepts of having a purpose and holding an attitude. Are these simply lines of direction in action and feeling? Or consolidated habits of reaction? Or deeper impulses and drives fashioned into an organization under specific familial and social relations? Or manifestations of a developed self with stabilized boundaries and internal dynamic patterns? And so on, for different approaches in the theory of psychological and social determinants of human action. Our problem here is not to settle what is not yet settled in these inquiries, but to recognize the sense in which the very understanding of human purpose and human attitude embodies within its social science answers to social science questions. For a scientifically oriented outlook it seems clearly established by this day that human purpose and human attitudes are thoroughly socio-cultural phenomena. The attempt to pinpoint the social science parameters is simply the struggle to make one's factual presuppositions in this domain of value theory explicit and responsible.

So far we have dealt only with the purpose and attitude subdomain of value. The more critical questions arise in the distinctively moral sphere where the focus is on judging good (worthwhile) and bad, or on assessing obligation. Here again, having reassured ourselves that no attack is intended on the enterprise of evaluation or the activity of responsible moral choice, we have to differentiate the types of scientific entry. The external role of science is granted in the slogans by surrendering the sphere of means to science while retaining ends for ethics. Even this surrender is over-hasty; means problems are permeated with evaluation which should also be rendered explicit.

The internal influence of science in morals is seen most dramatically in the effects of causal knowledge on evaluations, especially in the growth of psychological knowledge. Formally, one might be tempted to say that the influence has its impact not on the value but on the relation of the men to the value in the given situation. It is their "holding" of the value which is scrutinized, and its relation to other values that they hold which proves to have a sizable component of factual "cement." Men may come to realize that their punishing or disciplining others contains a large component of aggressivity; the result, within the pattern of other accepted values, may be a humanization in the values assigned to judicial decision or discipline of the young. The technique of developing insight in the individual therapy situation is a model of the internal influence of science on value. Comparably in socio-cultural patterns the understanding of functional relations may affect the evaluation of institutions and social practices.

The social science parameters in moral choice and ethical theory also emerge in careful inquiry. One may expect that there will be some carry-over from the subdomain of purposes and attitudes, but this raises the ethical theory question of how far ethical concepts of goodness and obligation are to be understood in terms of complexes of attitudes, purposes, feelings. For example, can the ethical notion of an "ideal" be analyzed as a mode of functioning of major human purposes in the search for a form of organization that will advance the movement of men toward a solution of specific human problems and at the same time enlist deep feelings over a long time-span? We need not minimize the conflict that is to be found in ethical theory over such problems of meaning-analysis. In the long run, I think it can be settled only by analyses that take their point of departure in ethical theory, that map its phases fully and pinpoint its processes, and that precisely where alternative solutions or proposals take different form as one assumes different results in the psychological and social sciences.[2]

In general, a scientifically oriented approach, mindful of the lessons of an evolutionary social theory about man and his works, will see the moral and ethical subdomains of value as an emergent level in the development and functioning of man. Such an emergence by no means rules out phenomenological qualities of a specifically moral sort in the field of awareness, nor unique conceptual constructs. It affirms, however, that this moral level arises, expresses, and functions with respect to the range of human needs and purposes, and that the meaning of these concepts is to be found in their systematic relations to purposes, attitudes, feelings (and complexes of these) in the wider value domain. Thus scientific study (psychological, cultural, social, and historical) of purpose, striving, and aspiration, means and ends in their interrelations, of pleasure and pain, sympathy, love, guilt and shame, of human development in familial and social milieu, and a whole host of human actions and reactions, including intelligence and creativity, throws light on the moral and ethical domain. Men can thus achieve a fuller understanding of their existent morality and of their own ethical reflection in guiding and reconstructing it.

A social science that sees its value-bearings, and a value theory that sees its scientific linkage, need no longer seem a dream in the present state of man's development. It can instead become a powerful instrument in human growth.

NOTES:

1. Especially in my book *Method in Ethical Theory* (New York, 1963). Various phases of the problem of the relation of science and ethics are dealt with in: *Ethical Judgment: The Use of Science in Ethics* (Glencoe, 1955); *Anthropology and Ethics,* written in collaboration with Professor May Edel (Springfield, Ill., 1959); and *Science and the Structure of Ethics* (Chicago, 1961).

2. For an investigation along these lines, see my *Science and the Structure of Ethics,* op. cit. Part III.

# 15

MARVIN B. SCOTT

## The Social Sources of Alienation

As a key concept in the social sciences, alienation refers to various mental states, often identified by such terms as "powerlessness," "meaninglessness," "anomie," and so on. Recent advances in sociological theory permit us to indicate systematically the social conditions linked with these states. A simple though exhaustive typology of the social sources of alienation is here presented. To illustrate the typology, examples of alienation are drawn from the writings of classical and contemporary social theorists.

The alienated man goes by many names. He is the stranger, the free floater, the outsider. He is the underground man in a Dostoevski novel; the man underground in a New York subway—alone in a lonely crowd.

Despite its chameleon character, the notion of alienation, as Robert Nisbet remarks, "has reached an extraordinary degree of importance. It has become nearly as prevalent as the doctrine of enlightened self-interest was two generations ago. It is more than a hypothesis, it is a perspective." [1] Like Nisbet, Robert Merton observes that, although much is said about alienation, the concept has been given little systematic attention.[2] This essay is a step in that direction.

I do not intend to delve into the inner workings of the psyche; rather my perspective is distinctively sociological—that is, I am concerned with the social conditions that bring about these mental states. Before launching into a discussion of these social conditions it is first necessary to lay bare the theoretical framework that informs my approach to the study of alienation.

By action is meant any behavior to which the individual attaches a meaning.[3] Behavior can be meaningful only if governed by rules, that is, shared understandings. In addition, rules presuppose a social setting. These points can be illustrated by voting behavior. An individual, asked why he cast his ballot, might respond: "I voted for the Democratic Party because I think it is the best way to preserve freedom in this country." The behavior is socially meaningful because the individual has some idea of the concept of preservation of freedom. The application of a rule presupposes a social context. The voter, for instance, must live in a society with specific political institutions (e.g. Congress). Moreover, he must perceive the relation of his vote to what these institutions will later do. Finally, he is aware of the techniques of voting, such as marking ballots and dropping them into boxes. This example illustrates all the components of meaningful behavior. First, there is some ultimate goal, which we can call a value, that the individual is striving for; e.g. political freedom. Second, there is a notion of the proper means of obtaining that value; e.g. the two-party system. This component of meaningful action will be called norms, i.e. the rules and regulations by which the values are obtained. Third, there is an agent, or organization of agents, who perform the action; e.g. the voter. We can speak of this component as the role or organization of roles. Finally, there are the means by which the agent can perform his role; e.g. ballot boxes, voting booths, etc. This component we label situational facilities. In sum, all socially meaningful behavior consists of values, norms, organization of roles, and situational facilities.

Another example may clarify the meaning of these terms. The ultimate goal, or value, of members of feudal society was salvation. The means through which salvation was to be obtained—i.e. the institutional norms—was the Catholic Church. The organization of roles involved the hierarchy of the priesthood, the situational facilities included prayer, the liturgy, and so on.

From the viewpoint of the individual what is implied by values, norms, roles, and facilities? With respect to values an individual is committed or not committed. One is committed to salvation or not: there are no shades of gray. Whereas a person is committed to a value, it makes little sense to speak of commitment to a norm. Rather, one conforms to norms. Thus, in ordinary usage, we say a person is committed to the value of salvation and conforms to the regulations of the Church in the attainment of that value.

At the level of the individual's role, the appropriate behavior is neither commitment nor conformity but responsibility. Thus in ordinary language we say that an individual is responsible in his role whenever his role performance fulfills our expectations. We speak of the individual's confidence in his control (or prediction) of situational facilities. For instance, in our religious example we might say that the individual has confidence in the efficacy of prayer.

From a sociological point of view, then, the sources of alienation are to be found in the lack of a) commitment to values, b) conformity to norms, c) responsibility in roles, and d) control of facilities. Consistent with this perspective, one may speak of alienation from values, norms, roles, and facilities. Thus when Marx discusses the worker's alienation from his machine (facilities, in our terminology), he is indicating both a social cause and psychological consequence.

The psychological states of alienation, or so-called variants of alienation—e.g. powerlessness, meaninglessness, isolation, etc.—do not correspond to any single source. Between the source and the variant falls the shadow of indeterminacy. Otherwise viewed, there is no one to one correspondence between a source (alienation from facilities) and a variant (powerlessness). An analogous case can be drawn from the field of collective behavior. As a variant of collective behavior, a millenarian movement is often viewed as having its source in status deprivation. The difficulty is that many other types of collective behavior can result from status deprivation, such as crazes, booms, and revolutions. In like manner, alienation from facilities may lead to powerlessness, meaninglessness, or any number of variants.

Under the following headings of alienation from facilities, roles, etc., the examples I use are merely illustrative of how the social sources may be articulated into patterns of alienation. Whenever possible, I have pointed out the psychological mechanisms—e.g. relative deprivation—that relate the individual to the social structure. Finally, I will emphasize the theoretical and empirical convergences of the work of classical and contemporary sociologists.

Alienation from facilities may be traced to the distinction society has made between the sacred and the profane. Among the ancient Hebrews, for instance, holiness aroused fear. "The increasing craving for holiness," writes the Hebrew scholar Pedersen, "caused a growing isolation of the temple at Jerusalem. . . . Yahweh sanctified the house when Solomon built it. In early times this meant that the people must not approach it because its power was too great." [4] Just as the ancient Hebrews were alienated from the facilities of worship, so, too, according to Marx, were men under capitalism alienated from the facilities of production.

The crippling effect of this type of alienation produces a type of anxiety that modern existentialists call "existential anxiety." [5] Daniel Bell has recognized the nexus between Marx's concept of alienation and the one advanced by existentialist thinkers. "With the decline in religious belief went a decline in the power of belief in eternal life," Bell writes: "In its place arose the stark prospect that death meant the total annihilation of self." [6] Work, he adds, staved off these fears. "Although religion declined, the significance of work was that it could still mobilize emotional energies into creative challenges." However, because of man's alienation from the workplace he is left with a sense of the absurdity of existence.

Most sociologists, less concerned with the implications of Marx's notion of alienation for existentialist philosophy, have raised this question: Is industrialization demoralizing for the worker? For the most part the answer has been "yes." In *Automobile Workers and the American Dream*, Eli Chinoy notes the alienative consequences of the absence of control of the rhythm of production. "Its coerced rhythm, the inability to pause at will for a moment's rest, and the need for undeviating attention to simple routines make it work to be avoided if possible and to escape from if necessary." [7]

It is the ability to control production that explains why certain workers—otherwise objectively deprived—are not dissatisfied. Gouldner, for instance, found that miners in a gypsum plant showed greater work motivation than surface workers, although they were deprived as compared to the latter in pay and status. Unlike the surface workers, the miners "were not 'alienated' from their machines; that is, they had an unusually high degree of control over their machines' operation." [8]

Gouldner, Chinoy, and others have thus verified Marx's claim that the worker suffers psychologically because of his separation from the means of production. It is Weber's achievement, however, to have emphasized that the worker's separation from the means of production (facilities) is but a single case of a general societal trend.[9] Soldiers, for instance, are separated from the means of violence. Such separation leads to a sense of powerlessness, graphically described by George Orwell:

> A soldier sprawls in a muddy trench, with the machine-gun bullets crackling a foot or two overhead, and whiles his intolerable boredom away by reading an American gangster story. And what is it that makes that story so exciting? Precisely the fact that people are shooting at each other with machine-guns!

The reason why imaginary bullets are more thrilling than real ones "is that in real life one is usually a passive victim, whereas in the adventure story one can think of oneself as being the centre of events." [10] Clearly, alienation from facilities may lead to a sense of powerlessness. Indicators of powerlessness can be found in songs and common expressions. Pre-Nazi German workers, for instance, used to sing: "We are like marbles rolled against the wall," and Americans in Korea during the war were often heard to say (of their misfortune), "that's the way the marbles roll." Both are expressions of man's sense of powerlessness and separation from social processes he does not understand.

The concept of role is commonly defined as "a set of expectations oriented toward people who occupy a certain 'position' in a social system or group." [11] But what role shall one choose when discussing a person's lack of responsibility? To clarify what is here meant by alienation from role I shall limit my discussion to the "primary status-carrying role." That is, the role which is primarily responsible for a person's status in the community. For the male this is generally his occupational role; for the female her role as wife-

mother.[12] Of course, a person may not be responsible for his role
for a variety of reasons, such as mental illness, failure to understand what is expected of him, and so on. But he is alienated
from his role only when he fails to identify with it.

Why would a person fail to identify with his role? Why the lack
of responsibility? Some theorists would argue that the lack of responsibility to one's role is simply a question of the worker's frustration. Indeed Lewis Feuer has gone so far as to identify alienation
with frustration. "Alienation," he writes, "lies in every direction of
human experience where basic emotional desire is frustrated . . ." [13]
Feuer, however, overlooks a contribution made by the psychologist
Maslow, who points out that "perhaps frustration as a single concept is less useful than the two concepts which cut across it, (1)
deprivation, and (2) threat to personality." [14] In itself, though, deprivation does not produce frustration. Stouffer, for instance, reports that military police were less likely to ask for transfers than
members of other branches of the army, though they were more,
objectively speaking, deprived—they received very few promo-
tions.[15] Undoubtedly, the military policemen desired more promo-
tions, but they remained loyal and responsible to their roles; that
is, they did not have the sense of being alienated from their position. The concept that explains this anomaly is "relative deprivation." In simplest terms this means that a person does not experience his deprivation as frustration if he feels others in his group
are also deprived.

"Relative deprivation" also accounts for the alienation women
experience today in their roles of wife-mother. Women today, asserts Clara Thompson, find marriage and motherhood unacceptable
roles, and they are being driven out of their homes by restless-
ness.[16] Talcott Parsons concurs that ambivalence to the role of wife-
mother is widespread. The girl, he writes, grows up to discover she
is dependent "on the favor—even 'whim'—of a man, that she must
compete for masculine favor and cannot stand on her own feet."
Herein lies the source of much of her "insecurity" and "high level
of anxiety." Without using the term "relative deprivation," Parsons
clearly suggests that the root of the problem is the girl's identification with a masculine culture, stressing independence and self-
assertiveness, which serves as her reference group.[17] In other
words, compared to the prerogatives of the male, the female feels

relatively deprived. From this framework Parsons explains the girl's lack of identification with the role of wife-mother "and the role of being a woman in any other fundamental respect."

Another example of alienation from role is discussed by Gouldner [18] in terms of the conflict between manifest and latent roles. An individual's manifest role (or "social security") is the one regarded as consensually relevant in a given context; a latent role is one deemed irrelevant or illegitimate in a given context. As his point of reference, Gouldner is concerned with members of formal organizations whose manifest roles are in conflict with their latent roles. The manifest role of an individual, for instance, may be one of researcher. In accord with this role, other members of the organization come to expect the researcher to exhibit specific behavior, such as the pursuit of research problems dictated by the organization; the researcher, however, may have as part of his latent role certain professional commitments which dictate different standards of research procedure. Now if these professional standards, dictated by the latent role, are in conflict with the organizational standards, then we may speak of the researcher as being alienated from his role. That is, he is forced to pursue an activity with which he does not identify.

The social condition characterized by too little conformity to norms is often described as anomie. From the viewpoint of the individual this means he distrusts the motives of those around him. He regards others as determined to use him for their own ends. In short, he lives in a "context of mutual distrust." To describe this condition Merton uses the term pseudo-Gemeinschaft.[19] Pseudo-Gemeinschaft—the glad-hand, the non-involved intimacy—is the conceptual bridge between anomie and the gallery of alienated "rogues," made up of the other-directed man, the organization man, and so on. And as Mills points out, pseudo-Gemeinschaft has become institutionalized in our society as part of the grand salesroom where the business of life is conducted.[20]

Like the other forms of alienation already discussed, pseudo-Gemeinschaft has religious roots. The mixture of Gesellschaft relations in a Gemeinschaft context is met with the horror accorded to the profaning of the sacred. Parsons, in his note on Gemeinschaft-Gesellschaft, comments that Gemeinschaft relations "constitute particular modes of expressing more fundamental and permanent attitudes. This means ipso facto that they take on a symbolic significance in addition to their intrinsic significance. There can be no doubt of the enormous importance of this fact in social life. Sentiments cluster about such acts. They acquire a meaning for those who perform them." In a Gesellschaft relation the individual rationally pursues his own self-interest. According to Parsons our horror of prostitution is the mixture of Gesellschaft motives in a Gemeinschaft context.

> In our society not all extramarital sexual relations count as prostitution. We specifically distinguish from it those which occur in a context of friendship. No matter how severely the latter may be condemned in our mores they are never treated in the same way as prostitution. This is because friendship is also a Gemeinschaft type of relationship.[21]

Prostitution, once a religious activity, is the archetypical form of pseudo-Gemeinschaft. It explains in part what we mean when we say that people in service occupations, where pseudo-Gemeinschaft is institutionalized, are prostituting themselves. A salesman like Willy Loman cannot have integrity: he is detached from the object he sells and can have little pride in his role. He must personalize himself with the buyer—i.e. "prostitute" himself—and, if he ceases to find approval, he comes to the end of a career of self-deception and dies the death of a salesman.

When Merton undertook an empirical study of anomie, he regarded it as the breakdown of reciprocal trust. To explain the fact that $39 million worth of bond pledges were traceable to a single broadcast marathon of Kate Smith, Merton emphasized the symbolic values embodied in the figure of Smith herself. Smith was perceived as sincerity incarnate. This belief occurred in a "context of distrust": that is, a society that tends to exploit human relationships and produces a sense of alienation which, according to Merton, actively demands reassurance. Smith, then, had the symbolic significance of sincerity. Merton's informants contrasted her integrity "with the pretenses, deceptions and dissembling which they observe in their daily experience."

> On every side they feel themselves as the object of manipulation. They see themselves as the target for ingenious methods

of control, through advertising which cajoles, promises, terror-
izes ... through cumulatively subtle methods of salesmanship
which may stimulate values common to both salesman and
client for private and self-interested motives. In place of a
sense of Gemeinschaft—a genuine community of values—there
intrudes pseudo-Gemeinschaft—the feigning of personal concern with the other fellow in order to manipulate him the
better.[22]

The climate of reciprocal distrust occurs in a society where human relations are instrumentalized and where insecurity and uncertainty prevail as a result of the absence of regulating codes.
"Society is experienced as an arena for rival frauds," declares Merton. "There is little belief in the disinterestedness of human conduct."

Mutual distrust, according to Finestone, reaches a high pitch of
intensity in the lower-class Negro subculture. Drawing on his study
of the Negro subculture in Chicago's "Black Belt," Finestone found
that the drug addict in this culture constituted an ideal type. The
addict achieved his goals by relying "on persuasion and on a reper-
toire of manipulative techniques." The "cat," as he calls himself, is
skeptical about all motives. Thus his alienation is similar to the
type characterized by Kate Smith's audience. He has a "complete
skepticism as to other persons' motives ... his world seemed to
preclude any relationship which was not part of a 'scheme' or did
not lend itself to an 'angle'." [23]

Like the other dimensions of alienation, this one, too, finds its
prototype in religion. In fact Abram, according to John Schaar, is
the universal symbol of alienated man. "Separated from his family,
his nation, and his national religion, he wanders without a home
in soil, society, or faith. He is the nomad unable to love and belong." In return for his total estrangement, Schaar continues "he
gains a new identity, which is symbolized by the change of his
name to Abraham." [24]

Unless one can in some way obtain a new identity, madness must
follow. To illustrate what I mean I will draw upon the lives of two
figures, one historical, the other fictional.

In the autumn of 1862, John Stuart Mill posed to himself this
question: "Suppose that all your objects in life were realized; that

all the changes in institutions and opinions which you are looking forward to, could be completely effected at this very instant: would this be a great joy and happiness to you? . . . And an irrepressible self-consciousness distinctly answered, 'No!' At this my heart sank within me: the whole foundation on which my life was constructed fell down . . ." [25]

The fictional character who illustrates this extreme form of alienation is Arthur Miller's salesman, Willy Loman. Loman, like a biblical outcast, first arrives on the scene carrying the two battered, black sample cases which are his cross. He is the symbol of the wanderer Abram, no longer enamored of the values of society (the American Dream). Gone are his pride, his youth—indeed, he no longer has even himself to sell. Willy Loman is thus a study of an alienated man—a man pursuing a way of life which he can no longer identify with and "in the end, when he is discarded because his personality credit has been exhausted, he must destroy himself." [26]

As social types, Mills and Loman are "outcasts." The outcast suffers from a variant of alienation perhaps best termed "extreme isolation." By extreme isolation I mean, following Kahler, "not just a devaluation of specific values, nor a mere invalidation of a world of values; it is a dwindling of the faculty of valuation altogether; it is a devaluation of valuation as such." [27]

Sociological literature offers very few accounts of "extreme isolation" of an entire community. Among the best accounts are those of Bettelheim and Lowenthal. According to Lowenthal, the Nazis' method of terror produced the type of alienation I have in mind here. Lowenthal writes:

> Terror accomplishes its work of dehumanization, through the total integration of the population into collectivities, then depriving them of the psychological means of direct community in spite of—or rather because of—the tremendous communications apparatus to which they are exposed. The individual under terrorist conditions is never alone and always alone. He becomes numb and rigid not only in relation to his neighbor but also in relation to himself; fear robs him of the power of spontaneous emotional or mental reaction. Thinking becomes a stupid crime; it endangers his life.[28]

In his recollections of life in a Nazi concentration camp, Bettelheim confirms Lowenthal's analysis. Under the impact of a long period of disorientation—"extreme situation" in Bettelheim's phrase —the individual develops a state of detachment in which he feels "as if what happened did not really happen." [29]

But can such extreme situations as described by Lowenthal and Bettelheim come to characterize a whole society? Weber recognized at least the possibility of this state of affairs in his discussion of the process of secularization of the "rationalization of life." As magical elements are lost, the question of the meaning of things and events in the world is raised. "Rationalization of these discrete meanings into a coherent system," asserted Weber, "an inclusive interpretation of the world as a whole and man's place in it, is an imminent need of the intellect once the question of meaning is raised." He argued that once rationalization is carried to a certain point there follows a break with tradition.[30] Weber also noted the relation between man's search to make sense of life, the mergence of a prophet and the compulsive conformity that often follows. Add to this the element of terror—and the prophet may be a prison guard! The conformity that follows is described by Bettelheim:

> A prisoner had reached the final stage of adjustment to the camp situation when he had changed his personality so as to accept as his own the values of the Gestapo . . . old prisoners who seemed to have a tendency to identify themselves with the Gestapo did so not only in respect to aggressive behavior. They would try to arrogate to themselves old pieces of Gestapo uniforms . . . This identification with their torturers went so far as copying their leisure-time activities. One of the games played by the guards was to find out who could stand to be hit the longest without uttering a complaint. This game was copied by the old prisoners, as though they had not been hit often enough without need to repeat this experience as a game.[31]

In Fromm's judgment Western society has virtually reached a state of affairs such as described by Bettelheim. "Our culture is perhaps the first completely secularized culture in human history," rendering man powerless and life meaningless.[32] Fromm's analysis, if not applicable to Western society at large, is certainy descriptive of Hilltown, a community described by Homans:

Because Hilltown still has a name, geographical boundaries, and people who live within the boundaries, we assume that it is still a community and therefore judge that it is rotten. It would be wiser to see that it is no longer, except in the most trivial sense, a community at all.

Homans points to technical change, economic expansion, and warfare as the agencies responsible for "breaking up social units without putting anything in their place ... In the old society, man was linked to man; in the new agglomeration—it cannot be called a society—he is alone ..." [33] Central to Homans' argument is the importance of the small group in saving the individual from feelings of alienation. Thus alienation from values seems to occur in those situations where the small group has been destroyed; that is, where individuals have been atomized.

In a much quoted article, Melvin Seeman [34] has identified five variants of alienation: powerlessness, meaninglessness, normlessness, isolation, and self-estrangement. One major shortcoming in Seeman's work has been pointed out by Feuer, who notes that "a multitude of alienated persons would be dissatisfied equally with conditions of power-possession, meaningfulness, norm-orientedness, involvement, and self-acknowledgement." Take, for instance, meaninglessness. Contrary to Seeman, Feuer writes, "a great deal of contemporary thought finds a state of alienation precisely in those ideologies which profess to predict with high confidence the outcome of people's behavior." That is, many intellectuals "find themselves alienated in a world of social determinism; they wish for a world in which the degree of social predictability would be low." Further, Seeman regards the intellectual as suffering from "isolation," and points to his alienation from popular culture as an indicator of such isolation. But as Feuer remarks, artists are proud of their individual loneliness; their problem today is that they can no longer have "a pride in isolation" because of their large-scale acceptance in contemporary society.[35]

A more serious shortcoming of Seeman's typology is that his five variants of alienation are an *ad hoc* listing. Why five? Perhaps one could locate fifty, if all the synonyms for alienation—affectlessness, aloneness, dehumanization, etc.—were to have their nuances ex-plicated. Because of his *ad hoc* listing, Seeman fails to state any relation between the five variants. It is perhaps in this regard that the scheme developed here has its greatest potential theoretical power; for the components of action have a certain logic to them: values, norms, roles, and facilities stand in a hierarchy. For example, increasing cleavage results in society as facilities, roles, and so on come under attack. For instance, in the earlier example of voting behavior, persons may dispute about voting facilities, the location of polls, long or short ballot, etc., without affecting the definition of who the voting agents are. Conflicts may arise, however, as to who should be allowed to vote. But even such conflict does not necessarily impair normative institutions such as the two-party system. More serious cleavage would follow if these institutions came under attack, but it would not necessarily affect the value of political freedom. Following the same logic one could generate, on the basis of our discussion, the proposition: As we move up the hierarchy of the components of action, alienation is increasingly disruptive to the stability of a society. Seeman's scheme is devoid of such proposition-generating potential.

In sum, then, a typology must be more than an *ad hoc* listing of concepts, however sharp their reflection of reality. It is the blend of logical closure and empirical correspondence that seems to me to be the *sine qua non* of scientific theory. And it is toward that end that this essay has been directed.

## NOTES:

1. Robert A. Nisbet, *The Quest for Community* (New York, 1953), p. 15.
2. Robert K. Merton, *Social Theory and Social Structure* (Glencoe, 1957), p. 269.
3. This section leans heavily on the theoretical framework advanced by Neil J. Smelser. See his *Theory of Collective Behaviour* (London, 1962), esp. Chapter 2.
4. Cited in Dorothy Emmet, *Function, Purpose and Powers* (London, 1958), p. 219.
5. See F. H. Heinemann, *Existentialism and the Modern Predicament* (New York, 1958), p. 12, for an attempt to link Marx to the existentialist movement.
6. Daniel Bell, *The End of Ideology* (Glencoe, 1960), p. 262.
7. Eli Chinoy, *Automobile Workers and the American Dream* (Garden City, N. Y., 1955), p. 71.

8. Alvin W. Gouldner, *Patterns of Industrial Bureaucracy* (Glencoe, 1954), pp. 140-41.
9. Hans Gerth and C. W. Mills (eds.), *From Max Weber* (New York, 1946), p. 50.
10. George Orwell, "Raffles and Miss Blandish," in *Mass Culture*, edited by H. Rosenberg and D. White (Glencoe, 1959), p. 159.
11. A. W. Gouldner, "Cosmopolitans and Locals: Toward an Analysis of Latent Social Roles," *Administrative Science Quarterly*, 2, 1957, p. 282.
12. Talcott Parsons, "Age and Sex in the Social Structure in the United States," in *Personality in Nature, Society and Culture*, edited by C. Kluckhohn, *et al.* (New York, 1953), pp. 368 ff.
13. Lewis Feuer, "What is Alienation," *New Politics*, Spring 1962, p. 132.
14. Abraham H. Maslow, "Deprivation, Threat, and Frustration," *Psych. Review*, 48, July 1941, esp. pp. 364-6.
15. Cited by Merton, op. cit. p. 240.
16. Clara Thompson, "The Role of Women in This Culture," in P. Mullahy (ed.), *A Study of Interpersonal Relations* (New York, 1949), pp. 153 ff.
17. Talcott Parsons, "Certain Primary Sources and Patterns of Aggression in the Social Structure of the Western World," in Mullahy, op. cit. pp. 280-81.
18. Gouldner, "Cosmopolitans and Locals," op. cit. pp. 284 ff.
19. Robert K. Merton, *Mass Persuasion* (New York, 1946).
20. C. W. Mills, *White Collar* (New York, 1956), Chapter 8.
21. Talcott Parsons, *The Structure of Social Action* (Glencoe, 1949), p. 692.
22. Merton, *Mass Persuasion*, op. cit. p. 142.
23. Harold Finestone, "Cats, Kicks, and Color," in M. Stein, *et al.* (eds.), *Identity and Anxiety* (Glencoe, 1960), p. 436.
24. John Schaar, *Escape from Authority* (New York, 1961), p. 174.
25. *Autobiography of John Stuart Mill* (New York, 1960), p. 94.
26. Cesar Grana, "Productiveness, Social Efficiency and Intellectual Gloom." Unpublished paper, University of California, Berkeley, 1961.
27. Erich Kahler, *The Tower and the Abyss* (New York, 1957), p. 203.
28. Leo Lowenthal, "Terror's Atomization of Man," *Commentary*, Jan. 1946, pp. 1-9.
29. Bruno Bettelheim, "Individual and Mass Behavior in Extreme Situations," *Journal of Abnormal and Social Psychology*, 1943. Reprinted in part in R. H. Turner and L. M. Killian, *Collective Behavior* (Englewood Cliffs, N. J., 1957), pp. 48-51.
30. Parsons, *The Structure of Social Action*, op. cit. pp. 565-7.
31. Turner and Killian, op. cit. pp. 48-9.
32. Erich Fromm, *The Sane Society* (New York, 1955), p. 176.
33. George C. Homans, *The Human Group* (New York, 1950), pp. 367, 456.
34. Seeman, op. cit.
35. Feuer, op. cit. pp. 128 ff.

# 16

EPHRAIM HAROLD MIZRUCHI

## Alienation and Anomie:
## Theoretical and Empirical Perspectives*

One of Mills' major concerns was the utilization of the classical approach of nineteenth-century sociology in the process of gaining insight into twentieth-century social problems. This interest is manifested in a number of his works, but that this remained a major focal point in his thought is reflected in one of his last publications. *Images of Man: The Classical Tradition in Sociological Thinking* [1] is an effort to view twentieth-century man through a classical looking-glass as reflected in the writings of Marx, Durkheim, Weber, Mannheim, and the early Walter Lippmann, to name only a few.

The high valuation which Mills awarded the representatives of this approach is reflected in his stance that,

> ... the important thing about the classic sociologists is that even when they have turned out to be quite wrong and inadequate ... even then, by their work and by the way in which they did it they reveal much about the nature of society, and their ideas remain directly relevant to our work today ... In general, our immediate generation of social scientists is still living off their ideas. [2]

* Parts of this essay are adapted from Ephraim Harold Mizruchi, *Success and Opportunity: A Study of Anomie* (New York: Free Press of Glencoe, 1964). By permission of the publisher.

253

Looking at Mills and his diverse sociological interests, we see a social scientist who was clearly appreciative of efforts to wed the classical tradition with its brilliant insights and hypotheses and contemporary empirical methods. What sets Mills apart from others who found this process to their taste was his concern with the ultimate utilization of the understandings derived therefrom, as well as the process of selecting socially meaningful problems with which to deal.

The current essay, dealing with Durkheim's *anomie* and Marx's *alienation*, demonstrates that Mills' faith in the utility of the classical tradition was not unwarranted.

Marx's concept of alienation was most clearly formulated in his *Economic and Philosophic Manuscripts of 1844*. Unlike Hegel and Feuerbach, whom he derided for their metaphysical philosophies, Marx approaches alienation within a specific institutional context—the economy. Marx held that four types of alienation emerged directly from the work situation: (1) alienation from the process of work; (2) alienation from the products of work; (3) alienation of the worker from himself; and (4) alienation of the worker from others.

Marx's concern, at this stage of his career, was with the impact of the Industrial Revolution on man. Like the existentialist philosophers who were his contemporaries, such as Kierkegaard, he was concerned with the complexities of achieving a meaningful, productive experience for the individual in modern society. It was toward man's subjective reaction to an objective societal condition that Marx's early efforts were directed.

Durkheim was also deeply concerned with the outcome of the Industrial Revolution. From his perspective the disruptive processes created strains in man's relationships with others and his aspirations for himself. Noting that suicide rates increased both in times of poverty and prosperity, Durkheim introduced the concept of anomie to modern sociology. Primarily interested in the effects of anomie during times of economic prosperity, he stressed that aspect which had reference to the striving for unattainable goals. Under conditions of relative stability social mobility is somewhat limited and man strives for limited but genuine goals. Under unstable conditions, however, these limits are removed: "The limits are unknown between the possible and the impossible, what is just and what is unjust, legitimate claims and hopes and those which are immoderate. Consequently there is no restraint upon aspirations . . . With increased prosperity desires increase." [3]

Thus, unlike Marx's concept of alienation, which referred to man's feeling of estrangement from work, its products, self, and others, Durkheim's concept was directed to a condition of the social system in which the rules of the group no longer provide limits to man's impulses.

During the past three decades Robert K. Merton's rendering of anomie has had a decisive effect on contemporary sociology. Stressing Durkheim's suggestion that the deregulation of goals is not the only condition of anomie, Merton focuses on the deregulation of means. To Merton, concerned primarily with the causal nexus surrounding deviant behavior, anomie is a result of the disjunction between socially mandated goals and the structurally available means for the attainment of these goals. More specifically, the great emphasis placed on "success" in American society and the lack of corresponding emphasis placed on legitimate means for its attainment lead to a "demoralization" of the means. [4]

Furthermore, since there is unequal access to the remaining legitimate channels for the attainment of success goals, there will be unequal utilization of illegitimate means. In short, the less access to legitimate channels the greater the deviant behavior in the form of crime, delinquency, prostitution, and the like. Thus Merton's theory has been widely used to explain what are presumably higher crime and delinquency rates in the relatively lower classes as compared with higher classes. What is interesting in this context, among other things, is that, although Merton presumably takes his cue from Durkheim, for whom the greatest impact of social change affects the more affluent classes, his theory suggests that the less affluent classes suffer most from these processes. Thus it is in those classes in which Marx identified the process of alienation that Merton expects the greatest effects of anomie.

In order to throw light on the Merton hypothesis, the writer undertook an elaborate research project in a small city in upper New York State. By the use of interviews with 618 respondents in 1958 and with 227 in 1960 he gained some insight into aspects of anomie as formulated by both Durkheim and Merton. Among the findings was that, although there was a generally greater tendency for lower-class respondents to obtain high scores on Srole's Anomie scale, when multivariate analysis was utilized, it was those in the relatively higher classes who were significantly more frustrated when they felt that their opportunities were circumscribed as compared with those in the lower classes. The same relationship held for employment status. Thus it was not the lower classes who felt the greatest impact of limited opportunity but the middle classes.

An examination of the nature of the values associated with success held by the various classes will clarify these observations. By and large, the middle classes seek more nebulous and more difficult to attain goals associated with achievements, while the lower classes focus on rewards.[5] In short, our data suggest that the middle classes suffer most from what we have termed the "Myth of Infinite Elevation," the notion that there is no end to what one can reasonably expect to attain.

In this altogether too brief summary of some of our data, it seems clear that it is the nature of the differential definitions of success and its consequences which appear to be most meaningful in terms of the classical tradition. For the nature of work is integrally bound up with the kinds of goals to which the lower classes aspire and the peculiar condition of the middle classes seems to encourage unrealistic aspirations.

The analysis which we have presented here suggests that contemporary American society is suffering from the combined effects of both alienation and anomie. Let us look at these processes in several contexts.

The concern with rewards for performance rather than worthy accomplishment on the job, or success as contrasted with achievement, on the part of our numerically largest segment of the population makes it clear that work is not seen as an end in itself, a condition predicted by Marx. The emphasis on rewards as contrasted with achievement strongly suggests alienation from work in the relatively lower classes.

Marx, it will be recalled, held that work in industrial societies tended to give rise to two types of alienation in the occupational sphere. Alienation from the process of work itself represents one type. The second was alienation from the products of one's work.

There is mounting evidence derived from a great deal of sociological research which supports Marx's speculative hypotheses. One excellent example of alienation from the process of work itself is reflected in an interesting study by the industrial sociologist Donald F. Roy.

While observing in a factory, Roy held a piecework job on the assembly-line. Roy's observations suggest that mental self-manipulation appears to be characteristic of the assembly-line work process: "Making out on piecework could be a stimulating game only as long as the job represented a real challenge to the operator, only as long as the element of uncertainty was present in the activity's outcome." [6] In short, this work typically involved no challenge.

The many studies of work-group control of rate of output on the assembly line, including, for example, the Roethlisberger and Dickson study,[7] suggests that much of the activity which characterizes factory work is inherently alienative, since work satisfaction is not an inherent outcome of the work process in these contexts. In addition to the process of work itself, there is little opportunity for today's factory worker to enjoy personal attachment to those objects which he has created. The assembly-line method has homogenized the products of the worker's efforts to conform to the needs of a standardized industrial system. Parts made in Toledo, Ohio, must meet precise measures in order to fit other units which are assembled in a Detroit automobile plant.

One of our informants in the community in which interviews were made took the researcher on a tour of the factory in which the former has worked for almost two decades. Currently a parts inspector, this man has worked on the line from the beginning of his career. In describing the work and in showing the writer the parts which were made in the plant, he seemed to be taking personal pride in the items produced and in the way things were done. But the very handling of the parts, the throwing and dropping and casualness with which they were treated, suggested that there is little opportunity for identification with the material results of one's efforts in this type of work.

In an essay, "The Myth of the Happy Worker," Harvey Swados also addresses himself to the attitudes which workers have toward their work and its products:

The worker's attitude toward his work is generally compounded by hatred, shame and resignation. . . . They know that there is a difference between working with your back and working with your behind. (I do not make the distinction between hand-work and brain-work, since we are all learning that white-collar work is becoming less and less brain-work.) They know that they work harder than the middle-class for less money. . . . Nor is it simply . . . status-hunger that makes a man hate work that is mindless, endless, stupefying, sweaty, filthy, noisy, exhausting, insecure in its prospects, and practically without hope of advancement.

The plain truth is that factory work is degrading. It is degrading to any man who ever dreams of doing something worthwhile with his life; and it is about time we faced the fact. *The more a man is exposed to middle-class values, the more sophisticated he becomes and the more production-line work is degrading to him.*[8]

Swados' observations, made during his periodic employment as a factory worker, provide us with more than a description of alienation from the process of work. In the italicized statement it appears that both alienation and anomie are intertwined as factors in the relationship between aspirations associated with the larger society—presumably middle-class consumption values—and the work situation. This is consistent with my position that the two processes are bound up with each other. Furthermore, there is the suggestion that one's self-esteem is bound up with work which alludes to alienation from self and others.

Swados also offers some instructive comments with respect to alienation from the product, in this case, the automobile:

On the one hand it is admired and desired as a symbol of freedom, almost a substitute for freedom, not because the worker participated in making it, but because our whole culture is dedicated to the proposition that the automobile is both necessary and beautiful. On the other hand it is hated and despised—so much that if your new car smells bad it may be due to a banana peel crammed down its gullet and sealed up thereafter, so much so that if your dealer can't locate the rattle in your new car you might ask him to open the welds on one of those tail fins and vacuum out the nuts and bolts thrown in by workers sabotaging their own product.[9]

We could well ask, given these circumstances in the working-class occupational sphere, whether we would expect to find an interest in excellence on the job or achievement values. My reply is that one would hardly expect this kind of orientation to work. As was noted earlier, emphasis on rewards is characteristic of working-class respondents in my sample. Achievement goals must be attained in other types of occupations, primarily those associated with the relatively higher classes. Similarly, emphasis on excellence is more likely to be associated with occupations reflecting emphasis on worthy accomplishments than those which stress rewards. Excellence, as a mode of performing, we would hold tends to be integrally bound up with occupations which reflect achievement rather than success values.

But what of the middle-class white-collar employee? Is his work challenging and gratifying? While we have suggested earlier that there is a greater tendency to view going ahead in achievement terms in the relatively higher classes, this does not necessarily imply that the vast majority of workers in these classes are actually engaged in more meaningful work that those in the lower classes.

Swados has mentioned that "white collar work is becoming less and less brain-work." Standardization and automation are making robots of the middle-class worker as well. Even in teaching, educational television threatens to make more of an automaton of our teachers than the bureaucratic organization of formal education has already accomplished. In the white-collar spheres, as in industry, personal gratification as a result of work as an end in itself and also as a result of the products of one's efforts is a feeling enjoyed by the few rather than the many.

This process was already in evidence during the Lynds' second study of Middletown during the middle 1930's:

> It is important to note the strains which current cultural demands for dominance and aggression create in the individual personality. The pursuit of "success," particularly in the business world where the males of the culture struggle, involves the acceptance of a heavy burden of disciplines and constraints. Most people, as a result, spend most of their time doing things in which they are not particularly interested, at a tempo which is not their own but dictated by the system. As Lawrence K. Frank has pointed out, to be "businesslike" means in our pres-

ent culture to be "impersonal." This is but one of the false faces that the culture forces men to wear. Everywhere one is confronted by the demand that one be "on time," act "like a man," hide one's emotions, talk and appear "successful," be "energetic," "sure of oneself," and so on indefinitely through the stereotypes of being "regular." Along with this channeling of individual bent and temperament that the "success pattern" imposes upon many businessmen must be noted in the case of the workingman the major constraints of inactivity due to recurrent unemployment and to being "bottom dog" in a culture which habitually stresses and glorifies the traits and possessions of its "top dogs." [10]

Galbraith, too, has suggested that even achievement may no longer be a worthy goal among higher level employees:

> The rise of the public relations industry, which draws its clientele overwhelmingly from among business executives, shows that business achievement is no longer of itself a source of acclaim. At a minimum the achievement must be advertised. But the first task of the public relations man, on taking over a business client, is to "re-engineer" his image to include something besides the production of goods. His subject must be a statesman, a patron of education, or a civic force. Increasingly some artistic or intellectual facet must be found. A businessman who reads *Business Week* is lost to fame. One who reads Proust is marked for greatness.[11]

What we are suggesting here is that: first, the conception of success values may be a reflection of the nature of the work process; second, of the material level of living which a given group aspires to or has attained; and, third, changes are occurring in all spheres of work. As work becomes more instrumentalized, and current tendencies seem to be in this direction, gratification as a result of the work process will diminish. Indications are that the Protestant Ethic with its emphasis upon work as an end in itself is on the decline as a normative system.[12] If this is indeed occurring, then one of the most important sources for meaningful activity and direction in American society is threatened with extinction.

The problem must next be confronted in functional terms. Since one of the important requirements in a social system is a system of motivation which will encourage group participants to perform those jobs necessary for the maintenance of organized group life, American society itself may be threatened by the process of increasing instrumentalization.

The problem of motivation leads us to a speculative hypothesis. We suggested above that the middle classes are provided with an already existing avenue for attaining alternate achievement goals. The alternative to which we are referring is formal social participation which affords recognition for the active member of the organized group. It is in the nature of social processes that norms, for example, may emerge as a result of activities which are associated with processes having little to do with the objectives of these acts. We would hypothesize that, while in the lower classes criminal norms have, in the least, been reinforced as a result of aspirational strains, in the middle classes a set of counter-norms has emerged which has a tendency to limit the emphasis upon achievement goals in the occupational sphere. As William H. Whyte, Jr., has shown, there is a growing tendency for the suburban middle classes to place greater emphasis upon security than on hard work, a major pattern in the quest to attain occupational goals, and an almost intense pattern of participation in formal associations. If there has been a diminishing emphasis upon individualism, as both Whyte and David Riesman have held, then this, in part at least, may be viewed against the background of both general affluence and the emergence of a set of norms which have resulted from reactions to the strains associated with circumscribed opportunities and intense competition in the occupational sphere. Whyte has suggested that aspirations have indeed changed although his explanation for the change is at variance with our own:

> The young men speak of "the plateau." If they were to find this haven they would prove that the Social Ethic is personally fulfilling. For the goal of the plateau is in complete consonance with it; one's ambition is not a personal thing that craves achievement for achievement's sake or an ego that demands self-expression. It is an ambition directed outward to the satisfaction of making others happy. Competitive struggle loses its meaning; in the harmonious organization one has most of the material rewards necessary for the good life, and none of the gnawing pains of the old kind of striving.[13]

In short, there is a more limited effort to forge ahead in the occupational sphere, since achievement goals can be attained with much less hazard in other spheres of American life and the material rewards are accumulated, at least for this segment of the population, without a great deal of competitive effort.

Although this hypothesis is highly speculative, it is consistent with our explanation for lower-class anomie as compared with middle-class anomie above. We held earlier that certain processes, such as education, must be pursued as ends in themselves in order to provide optimum performance on the part of the individual. More important, however, we noted that institutional processes are characterized by end-valuation rather than means-valuation. Society cannot afford to have certain processes come about as a result of chance factors alone. Thus, certain patterns come to be perceived as worthy of one's efforts. Of these patterns some become mandatory and are incorporated into the institutional system.

Now, if work comes to mean little more than a means to a livelihood, then it might well be that the functional prerequisites may not be fulfilled in a manner which will, in the very least, maintain the American social system. In short, if the will to work is threatened, the social system is likewise threatened.

And what of man the individual? What will be the sources of personal gratification for him? The constant proliferation of new hobbies and do-it-yourself programs suggests that these could become the primary source of gratification for man in this society. Many of us are already deluged with the problem of excessive leisure time, and the mass culture lamentors have been quick to point out the leisurely are being misled. Emphasis appears to be directed to the novel and superficial rather than to *haute culture*. Indeed, Durkheim was not unaware of similar processes accompanying anomie during periods of excessive prosperity. As he pointed out in *Suicide*, "A thirst arises for novelties, unfamiliar pleasures, nameless sensations, all of which lose their savor once known." [14]

Leisure time activities as they are currently constituted, it would seem, are not likely to emerge as meaningful alternatives to work. Although it is hazardous to generalize too broadly, there seem to be few situations in American life in which unrealistic expectations do not constitute a problem. Daniel Boorstin, an historian, has suggested this in somewhat dramatic terms in a recent book, *The Image*.[15] Characterizing Americans in terms similar to those of Kluckhohn in *Mirror For Man*,[16] Boorstin describes us as engaged in efforts to "fill our void":

> We [Americans] expect too much of the world. Our expectations are extravagant in the precise dictionary sense of the word—"going beyond the limits of reason or moderation." They are excessive.
>
> When we pick up our newspaper at breakfast, we expect—we even demand—that it bring us momentous events since the night before. We turn on the car radio as we drive to work and expect "news" to have occurred since the morning newspaper went to press. Returning in the evening, we expect our house not only to shelter us, to keep us warm in winter and cool in summer, but to relax us, to dignify us, to encompass us with soft music and interesting hobbies, to be a playground, a theatre and a bar. We expect our two week vacation to be romantic, exotic, cheap and effortless. We expect a faraway atmosphere if we go to a nearby place; and we expect everything to be relaxing, sanitary, and Americanized if we go to a faraway place. We expect new heroes every season, a literary masterpiece every month, a dramatic spectacular every week, a rare sensation every night. We expect everybody to feel free to disagree, yet we expect everybody to be loyal, not to rock the boat or take the Fifth Amendment. We expect everybody to believe deeply in his religion, yet not to think less of others for not believing. We expect our nation to be strong and great and vast and varied and prepared for every challenge; yet we expect our "national purpose" to be clear and simple, something that gives direction to the lives of nearly two hundred million people and yet can be bought in a paperback at the corner drugstore for a dollar.
>
> We expect anything and everything. We expect the contradicting and the impossible. We expect compact cars which are spacious; luxurious cars which are economical. We expect to be rich and charitable, powerful and merciful, active and reflective, kind and competitive. We expect to be inspired by mediocre appeals for "excellence," to be made literate by illiterate appeals for literacy. We expect to eat and stay thin, to be constantly on the move and ever more neighborly, to go

to a "church of our choice" and yet feel its guiding power
over us, to revere God and to be God.
Never have people been more the masters of their environment. Yet never has a people felt more deceived and disap-
pointed. For never has a people expected so much more than
the world could offer.[17]

The problems associated with the marked tendency toward instrumentalization of work seem to be symptoms of more fundamental conditions in which the very social fabric, that is, the
normative system, is threatened with annihilation. Indeed, this is
the import of the pleas being made by Erich Fromm,[18] Hannah
Arendt,[19] and Erich Kahler,[20] to name only a few. But some writers
do not see this in what is simply a foreboding aspect. William
Kornhauser in his *The Politics of Mass Society* concludes his interesting study with the suggestion that the process of mass society
carries with itself not only the possibility of social alienation but
"enhanced opportunities for the creation of new forms of association. . . . Modern industry destroys the conditions for a new society
of small enterprises, but it also provides the condition of abundance which frees people to seek now ways of life." [21]
"Abundance" is, however, a major source of difficulty for contemporary American society. If there is any one factor stressed by
Durkheim which can be isolated as a major source of malintegra-
tion, it is abundance. It is doubtful whether Durkheim could have
envisaged a society in which middle-class families could reasonably expect to own two automobiles, as many television sets and
untold numbers of radios. Nor is it likely that he could have
imagined how extravagant expectations could become. Boorstin's
comments  could apply only to a society of abundance and prosperity, and this is, indeed, the type of condition with which Durkheim was most concerned.
Thus our more general observations, following Durkheim's lead,
suggests that contemporary American society is in a paradoxical
situation. Having achieved a very high level of material prosperity
it is in danger of attaining also a condition of social and cultural
poverty. In a suggestive study—although one not systematic by
contemporary social scientific standards—entitled *Troublemakers:
Youth in an Affluent Society,* T. R. Fyvel makes some observations
which are interesting when juxtaposed to Kornhauser's statement.

... the rise of delinquency has to be seen as one among many similar symptoms of the growing social unbalance in the affluent society.

Looking at the development in Britain of the last ten years, one can distinguish something which seems like a built-in conflict in this society—a conflict between, on one side, a growing sense of widening opportunities, of expansion, and opposed to it, an alarming drive towards purposelessness.

... the affluent society holds out tremendous possibilities of a freer life for the ordinary man. [But there is also] undeniable evidence that a fairly large section of British youth felt frustrated, angry, bored and adrift without firm moral guidance.[22]

Fyvel points out that this condition characterized not only the youthful in British society but adults as well, and, similarly, not only the British but American, Russian, and other European societies suffered from the same condition.

A very recent report by the Council of Europe has provided similar data. Twelve member countries were requested to report on juvenile delinquency, and all noted increases in non-utilitarian acts of theft and violence. Most noteworthy is that these phenomena appear much less often in the underdeveloped areas.

Fyvel's conclusions and the observations cited in the above report are compatible with our own. Increased opportunities can, if not recognized and anticipated, have undesirable consequences. And it is to the study of these factors that sociological research must now turn. Too many of the problems of deviant behavior and social pathology have been cast in the mold of poverty conditions. The time is ripe for studies of the concomitants of prosperity.

We Americans have always assumed that unfettered social mobility is necessarily a desirable condition for all. During times of prosperity, mobility not only becomes more attainable but also forces itself upon the multitude. Few see the high cost which is paid in the form of striving toward unrealizable goals and the consequences in personal demoralization and despair. Increased opportunity for success has its counterpart in increased opportunity for failure. If a social system is to maintain itself, it must provide a balance between societal needs, individual aspirations, and the possibility of achievement. American society has not solved this problem, and, indeed, it has not even seemed willing to entertain the possibility that such a problem does exist.

The fundamental question, then, becomes one of assessing the American Dream. Should it be tempered with cautionary folk wisdom or should we ignore the heavy toll which its pursuit extracts? What would be the consequences for American society of a system of motivation directed by the oft-heard injunction attributed to Confucius, "He who makes his bed close to the ground does not have far to fall"?

On the other hand there is little chance that the ideology can persist in the face of the realities of life. Ultimately some economic setback will occur, some limitations will be felt. What will the consequences be? Since our own data suggest that it is the middle classes who suffer most from circumscribed aspirations, and since they have been in the vanguard of revolutions from both right and left, we may well be sitting atop a potential powder keg. In short, disillusionment and despair provide a fertile base for extreme political movements and it is clear that it is not in short supply in contemporary American society.

Will America wait and watch and speculate or will a new set of goals emerge?

NOTES:

1. C. Wright Mills, *Images of Man: The Classical Tradition in Sociological Thinking* (New York, 1960).
2. Ibid. pp. 3-4.
3. Emile Durkheim, *Suicide* (New York, 1950), pp. 252-3.
4. Robert K. Merton, *Social Theory and Social Structure* (New York, Rev. Ed., 1957), p. 138.
5. Robin M. Williams, Jr., *American Society* (New York, Rev. Ed., 1960), p. 419.
6. Donald F. Roy, "Work Satisfaction and Social Reward in Quota Achievement," *American Sociological Review*, 19, Oct. 1953, p. 511.
7. Fritz Roethlisberger and W. J. Dickson, *Management and the Worker* (Cambridge, 1939).
8. In Maurice Stein, Arthur Vidich, and David M. White (eds.) *Identity and Anxiety* (New York, 1960), pp. 199-200 (Italics ours).
9. Ibid. p. 204.
10. Robert H. and Helen M. Lynd, *Middletown in Transition* (New York, 1937), p. 427.

11. John K. Galbraith, *The Affluent Society* (Boston, 1958), p. 194.
12. William H. Whyte, Jr., *The Organization Man* (New York, 1957).
13. Ibid. p. 173. Cf. also p. 317.
14. Op. cit. p. 256.
15. Daniel Boorstin, *The Image* (New York, 1961).
16. Clyde Kluckhohn, *Mirror for Man* (New York, 1949).
17. Boorstin, op. cit. pp. 3-4. Cf. also pp. 5-6.
18. Erich Fromm, *The Sane Society* (New York, 1955).
19. Hannah Arendt, *The Human Condition* (Chicago, 1958).
20. Erich Kahler, *The Tower and the Abyss* (New York, 1957).
21. William Kornhauser, *The Politics of Mass Society* (New York, 1956),
     p. 237. Cf. also, Winston White, *Beyond Conformity* (New York, 1962).
22. T. R. Fyvel, *Troublemakers: Rebellious Youth in an Affluent Society*
     (New York, 1962), pp. 311-12.

# 17

STEPHEN W. ROUSSEAS
AND JAMES FARGANIS

## American Politics and the End of Ideology

In a loose collection of essays written over a ten-year period, Daniel Bell [1] hails the end of ideology. In a similar potpourri of previously published essays, Seymour Martin Lipset [2] joins Bell in the apotheosis of a non-committed scientism, or what amounts to a pragmatism leached of all its passion for meaningful social reform. This growing litany in the United States, on the European Continent, and in England, in praise of the *status quo* continues to remain, in its own image, inherently liberal. It is convinced that democracy today has solved all the major problems of industrial society, and that those which do remain are of a second-order magnitude involving merely technical adjustments within a now prevailing *consensus gentium*. If modern liberalism has thus been recast into a less critical mold, it is because of its conviction that modern democracy *is* the good society. Lipset makes this very clear in the epilogue to his book. "Democracy," he writes, "is not only or even primarily a means through which different groups can attain their ends or seek the good society; *it is the good society itself in operation*." [3]

More explicitly, we are told by Lipset that within the Western democracies "serious intellectual conflicts among groups representing different values have declined sharply"; that "the ideological issues dividing left and right [have] been reduced to a little more or a little less government ownership and economic planning"; and that it readily makes little difference "which political party controls the domestic policies of individual nations." All this, according to Lipset, "reflects the fact that the fundamental political problems of the industrial revolution have been solved: the workers have achieved industrial and political citizenship; the conservatives have accepted the welfare state; and the democratic left has recognized that an increase in over-all state power carries with it more dangers to freedom than solutions for economic problems." [4]

In this milieu intellectuals functioning as critics of society have become disaffected, according to Lipset, because "domestic politics, even liberal or socialist politics, can no longer serve as the arena for serious criticism from the left." [5] Disorganized, at a loss for a cause, and unable to fulfill their self-image, the liberal intellectuals "have turned from a basic concern with political and economic systems to criticism of other sections of the basic culture of society, particularly of elements which cannot be dealt with politically." [6] Or, in Bell: "Some of the younger intellectuals have found an outlet in science or university pursuits, but often at the expense of narrowing their talent into mere technique." [7]

The full import of the Bell and Lipset thesis can be derived principally from Bell's misinterpretation of Max Weber: a misinterpretation which leads him to consider Machiavelli and Weber in the same light, and to quote them at the head of the two key chapters of his study.[8] In keeping with his own interpretation of Weber, Bell distinguishes between the normative "ought" and the empirical "is" of politics and the "ineluctable tension" between the two. Ethics is concerned with justice, whereas concrete politics involves "a power struggle between organized groups to determine the allocation of privilege." [9] Concrete politics, in other words, is not concerned with the realization of an ideal, but, following Lord Acton, with the reaping of particular advantages within the limits of a given ethic—an ethic which sets out clearly the rules of the game governing the political jockeying for position and privilege. Thus, modern, mature democracies representing the end of ideology have, in effect, separated ethics from politics; and ideology, in so far as it continues to exist as a force in modern society, is nothing more than a cynical propaganda cover for the specific self-interest of competing groups. Modern politics, therefore, becomes amenable to analysis in terms of the mixed strategies of game theory (though neither Bell nor Lipset, surprisingly, have done so). The game is to be played, however, according to the generally accepted constitutional limits of a Weberian "ethic of responsibility." It implies, above all, the flat rejection of the radical commitment required by an "ethic of conscience" which "creates 'true believers' who burn with pure, unquenchable flame and can accept no compromise with faith." The ethic of responsibility is, in sum, "the pragmatic view which seeks reconciliation as its goal." [10] Modern liberals, willing as they are to accept their progress piecemeal and within the rules of the game are, therefore, to be distinguished from genuine ideologues who are seemingly unaware that the good society has already been achieved.

The basic distinction between the modern liberal and the ideologue revolves around the notion of commitment. If the ideologue, in Bell's terms, is committed to the consequences of ideas and is governed by passion, then, in contradistinction, the non-ideological liberal is uncommitted and free of any chiliastic vision of the transforming moment. The ideologue seeks political success, according to Bell, by organizing and arousing the masses into a social movement, and the function of ideology, therefore, is to fuse the energies of the great unwashed and ignite their passions into a mighty river of fire. But in order to do so, ideology must "simplify ideas, establish a claim to truth, and, in the union of the two, demand a commitment to action." [11]

The end of ideology is therefore linked to its inability nowadays to arouse the masses. And this inability, as we have seen, is the direct consequence of modern society's having solved the basic problems of industrial society. In this kind of society there is no room for ideologues who, standing on the upper rungs of the faith ladder, have become politically destabilizing factors. They are, if anything, a direct threat to the continuation of the good society. The modern politician *qua* politician is the man who understands how to manipulate and how to operate in a Machiavellian world which divorces ethics from politics. Modern democracy becomes, in this view, transformed into a system of technique *sans telos*. And democratic politics is reduced to a constellation of self-seeking pressure groups peaceably engaged in a power struggle to determine the allocation of privilege and particular advantage. Compromise and evolution are to be the means for achieving, in the context of this struggle, the few second-order social goals which continue to remain in an otherwise near perfect society. It is in this limited sense that the end of ideology clings desperately to its self-imposed label of enlightened, non-ideological, non-committed liberalism. And the *status quo* it defends in the name of democracy is a fundamental one—the already achieved good society.

All this, by Bell, is carefully nailed onto Max Weber's door. Had Bell, instead, opened the door and looked inside, he would have found that Weber's primary concern was the fusion of the "ethic of responsibility" and "the ethic of absolute ends." Contrary to Bell's facile interpretation, Weber was in no sense advocating a politics without passion. Passion without responsibility and politics without commitment were equally unacceptable to Weber. "Passion," "a feeling of responsibility," and a "sense of proportion" were for Weber the three pre-eminent qualities which were decisive for the politician. For Weber, the problem was the forging of "a warm passion and a cool sense of proportion . . . in one and the same soul." [12] In so far as the politician plays the game of politics without any sense of purpose, his actions are without meaning. In Weber's words, "The mere 'power politician' may get strong effects, but actually his work leads nowhere and is senseless."

In Weber, the "ethic of responsibility" and the "ethic of ultimate ends" were not to be regarded, as Bell seems to have done, as absolute contrasts. They were, instead, to be thought of as supplements reinforcing each other within the mind of the true politician, who was to act as the agent of social progress. In failing to take into account the consequences of his actions, and in refusing to admit the condition of human frailty, the chiliast was irresponsible and ineffective. But equally vacuous, in Weber's opinion, was the politician who sought to enhance his own power without any vision in mind. "Certainly all historical experience," wrote Weber, "confirms the truth—that man would not have attained the possible unless time and again he had reached out for the impossible."

Despite Bell's misinterpretation of Weber, there can be little doubt that his arguments and those of Lipset on the decline, if not the end, of ideology as an operative force in the Western world are based largely on fact. But whether or not this represents a desirable state of affairs is quite another matter. The favorable interpretation given to this development by Bell and Lipset has been generally accepted, if not applauded, by most observers. Yet, there seems to be a great deal of potential confusion over the meaning of "ideology" and "ideological thought" if care is not taken to use these terms consistently. The most exhaustive analysis of the concept appears in Karl Mannheim's well-known *Ideology and Utopia.*[13] In Mannheim, ideology is taken to mean the ideas and thought-patterns of the interest-bound ruling groups which explain, justify, and rationalize the *status quo*, while utopia is the intellectual stimulus provided by the oppressed groups who challenge the established order and seek to transform it into the good society. When Bell and Lipset speak of the "end of ideology," what they mean is the "end of utopian thought," for they are both clearly referring to the decline of socialist or Marxian ideas within the context of an affluent Western society. Lipset, however, pushes his argument further (and more explicitly than Bell) when he declares, contrary to the judgment of the most profound minds of Western political thought, that democracy "is the good society itself in operation." The classical distinction between "nature" and "convention" is thus obliterated, and the traditional role of the intellectual as social critic is no longer logically possible. For if "what ought to be" already is, then the intellectual has no other function than to describe and to celebrate the arrival of a Lipsetian utopia. Yet much of the intellectual output of today in film, on the stage, and in art reveals a profound discontent with things as they are. Lipset and Bell recognize this intellectual alienation but conclude that it is not political. It is only by narrowly defining politics as concerned with "voting behavior" or with "welfare measures" that they can come to such a conclusion. But if the traditional idea of political philosophy is maintained, there is yet some small contribution that intellectuals can make, which will be something other than a justification, tacit or overt, for whatever is.

"Liberals such as Lipset," writes one political scientist, "are proud of the progress which has been made in the Western world, but it is curious that they never acknowledge the fact that we have gotten as far as we have precisely because of the ideologies which stirred men to action." And if the end of ideology is, in fact, the case, "then we have the best explanation of why we in the West are standing still." [14]

But the most bitterly forceful comments have come from another source. C. Wright Mills and Bell and Lipset have been each other's severest critics,[15] and Mills, defining the end of ideology as "an intellectual celebration of apathy" which has collapsed reasoning into reasonableness, attacks the emphasis of Bell and Lipset on strictly factual analysis:

> The disclosure of fact . . . is the rule. The facts are duly weighed, carefully balanced, always hedged. Their power to outrage, their power truly to enlighten in a political way, their power to aid decision, even their power to clarify some situation—all that is blunted and destroyed.[16]

Facts, of course, do not in themselves have the power to outrage, enlighten, or clarify. And perhaps, for this reason, Mills' argument is in need of some elaboration. An empiricist, devoid of any "passion," is no more capable of describing the world as it is than is an ideologue who views the world around him solely through the lens of his ideological *Weltanschauung*. The hope, or the belief, that the end of the ideological caste of mind will permit us to view the world uncolored by value judgments is nothing but the delusion of an unsophisticated positivism; which is, in essence, a flight from moral responsibility. For facts are themselves the product of viewing "reality" through theoretical preconceptions which, in turn, are conditioned by the problems confronting us. And the theoretical precepts which determine the relevant facts of a particular view of "reality" are not themselves entirely value free. Social theories, in short, are the result of our concern with specific problems. And social problems are concerned with ethical goals. Social theorists, furthermore, differ in their value judgments and thus differ in their theoretical constructions of "reality." They differ, that is, in the problems they see, or, what amounts to the same thing, they see a given problem in different ways. Consequently, they differ as to the facts relevant to a given problem. There is, in other words, a selectivity of facts in the analysis of social problems. Some facts included in one approach are excluded in another; and even those held in common may, and usually do, differ in the weight given to them and in their theoretical and causal interrelations.

All this raises the following possibilities: that the theory of verification in the social sciences is of a different order from that found in the other sciences; that the moral preconceptions of social theorists unavoidably determine the shape of their theories, the classification systems they employ, and their concepts and hypotheses; and that objective criteria of relevance for the evaluation of competing constructions of social reality, therefore, may not exist. Perhaps the best we can hope for is some form of objective relativism. But however that may be, it is clear that those who would suggest that sociological analysis is a pure science objectively concerned with pure "facts" are indulging in an ideological positivism uniquely their own; a *wertlos* [17] positivism which amounts to nothing more than an unthinking apologia for whatever is. And their value judgments, because of their implicit subconsciousness, are all the more inflexible and rigid. Their pronouncements, moreover, do not admit of compromise and take on an *ex cathedra* quality found only in those who believe they have somehow secured *the* truth—or *the* good society.

Along these lines, C. Wright Mills would agree that the end of ideology makes a fetish of empiricism and entails an ideology of its own—and ideology of political complacency for the justification of things as they are, and the celebration of modern society as a going concern. Utopian thought, or left-wing criticism, according to Mills, is concerned with a "structural criticism" of the institutions of society and with the formulation of programs for reform and fundamental change. It need not entail an apocalyptic or dogmatic vision. The choice is not between the wild-eyed fanatic and the cool, uncommitted pragmatist who is willing to take his progress piecemeal, if at all. Ideology need not be, as Bell tends to, equated with chiliastic fanaticism. Its major function is to apply intelligence—the fusion of passion and critical reason—to the problems of the modern world. And intelligence can never lie down with itself in a passionate embrace of self-love. It must be concerned with the human condition and its betterment in an always imperfect world. Its justification for being is, in a word, progress.

Whether or not it is true that progress in the past has been exclusively the result of ideological conflict, it is nevertheless true that progress, as distinct from mere change, can be defined meaningfully only in terms of some "vision." For progress, as Santayana has observed, "is relative to an ideal which reflection creates." And it is here that, perhaps, the most serious criticism of the end of ideology can be made.

The modern politician is viewed, appreciatively by Bell and Lipset, as a non-committed individual drenched in the art of compromise. The ideologue, on the other hand, is committed to some pattern of institutional change which, in terms of his values, becomes transformed into social progress. It is irrelevant whether one agrees with the vision of a particular ideology. The important point is that freedom, in the philosophical sense, and a social commitment which transcends the *status quo* are interrelated and interdependent.

Rejecting the notion of man tied to a merciless fate which robs him of his future, we are left to regard him free and immersed in the process of becoming. Man is, in other words, a potential, and his willingness or ability to seize life by the throat, as it were, and force it to serve his needs, is a measure of his freedom. Freedom, in short, excludes a complacency which rests on past or present achievements, or which nurtures the illusion of having already achieved the best of all possible worlds where progress, in any meaningful sense is, by definition, no longer possible. If man, living as he does in a grossly imperfect world, is not uniquely determined by his past and is nothing but a potential in terms of his impending future, then the act of commitment is a prior requirement for the realization of his freedom and thus his future. And if modern democracy is predicated on the end of ideology, that is, on the end of commitment, then it negates itself and becomes the very denial of freedom. If it has any commitment at all, it is the false commitment to itself—to the narcissistic approval of itself as it is in all its sparkling perfection—with the net result that it has retreated from the problems of the world about it, spending its time, as it does, idly admiring its reflection in the looking glass, and only now and then showing some concern over the occasional pimple which erupts to mar its beauty temporarily.

Another objection to the end of ideology lies in its inability to make the fundamental distinction between what it considers to be the good society and a social theory which has become obsolete as a result of the changing values and problems of succeeding generations. Confusing the two and still obsessed and blinded by the liberal orientation of the 1930's, it looks at the current situation and proudly declares that the problems of the Great Depression have been, by and large, satisfactorily resolved.

Bell's book was accurately subtitled "On the Exhaustion of Political Ideas in the Fifties." Indeed, we have been, and continue to be, faced with a bankruptcy of political ideas at a time when certain critical developments have been taking place in the United States —developments for which the end of ideology is in large measure responsible. On the international front there is the tendency to apply a splintering empiricism to our international problems, and on the domestic front there is our inability to cope with, let alone admit, the economic malaise that has seized the American economy since the end of the Korean war.

Concerning international matters, Hans J. Morgenthau writes of our "surrendering piecemeal to the facts of foreign policy ... of thinking and acting as though there were nothing else to foreign policy but this [or that] particular set of empirical facts" concerning this or that foreign policy problem.[18] The latter-day pragmatists, in Morgenthau's opinion, are basically anti-theoretical, antiutopian empiricists who pride themselves on having "no illusions about the facts as they are nor any grand design for changing them." Indeed, their crowning achievement, in their own view, is their "courage to look the facts in the face and ... deal with each issue on its own terms." Underlying their entire approach is their profound belief that "the problems of the social world [will] yield to a series of piecemeal empirical attacks, unencumbered by preconceived notions and comprehensive planning." As a result our foreign policy lacks an overall cohesiveness and has degenerated into a series of unrelated operations not always consistent with each other, and often far removed from the realities of the situation which the facts, of their own accord, are supposed to make clear. Thus, according to Morgenthau, in trying to escape the Scylla of utopianism we are foundering on the Charybdis of empiricism. In the name of "facts" we are reduced to approaching the major problems of our existence as though they were mere matters of technical manipulation. What is obviously needed is an ideology to interpret the "facts" of a social situation and to suggest meaningful solutions in terms of a particular reading of these self-same "facts." [19]

In a similar vein, other end-of-ideology advocates deny that there is anything substantively wrong with the American economy. It is their unwillingness to engage in any form of structural criticism, and their tendency to look upon those who do as vestigial appendages of modern democratic society that compels them to regard the existing tools as adequate for the correction of what they consider to be a temporary and fleeting imbalance. They deny the necessity for any structural reorganization of society and insist that it is all a matter of mere technical adjustment within the existing canons of responsibility. This ability of the end-of-ideology approach to blur understanding and lead to inaction is magnified out of all sensible proportions by the internal economic problems of the United States since 1953.

Since the end of World War II the American economy has continued to experience alternating periods of expansion and contraction. The postwar boom of 1946-48 involved a huge spending spree by households and business firms for long-denied consumers' and producers' durable goods. And the liquid assets accumulated by both groups during the war provided the means for financing the boom. The 1948-49 recession which followed was quickly reversed by the outbreak of the Korean War, and with the cessation of hostilities in Korea the American economy dipped into the trough of 1953-54. These two initial postwar booms are easily understood. What is not so easy to understand is the grossly inadequate performance of the economy since the end of the Korean War.

Since 1953, the number of quarters from trough to cyclical peak has steadily declined. And while these post-Korean recoveries have become progressively abortive and of shorter duration, the rate of unemployment has virtually doubled as we have moved from one cyclical peak to another—from 2.7 per cent of the civilian labor force during the second quarter peak of 1953 to 5.2 per cent for the latest cyclical peak in the second quarter of 1960. It is not surprising, therefore, that in our successive peaks of economic activity both the average duration of unemployment and the amount of long-term unemployment have increased to alarming proportions. A corollary to this rise of chronic unemployment is the slowing down of the annual growth rate (computed on a peak to peak basis) from 4.8 per cent for the period 1948-53, to 2.5 per cent for 1953-60—a drop well below the long term historical rate (1890-1959) of 3.2 per cent.

An alternate method of illustrating the seriousness as well as the magnitude of the problem currently facing us is to compute the difference between what the economy could have produced at a given point in time, assuming a full employment use of its resources, and what it actually did produce. This can be done by adopting the technique of the President's Council of Economic Advisers. Assuming a long-term potential growth rate of 3.5 per cent (comprised roughly of a 1.5 per cent increase in the labor force and a 2 per cent increase in the productivity of labor) and an unemployment rate of roughly 4 per cent (assumed, on the basis of mid-1955, to be compatible with relative price-level stability), the gap between potential and actual output amounted to approximately $34 billion for the third quarter of 1962 on an annual basis and in constant 1954 dollars. If we accept the late President's call for a growth rate of 4.5 per cent, the gap increases to $70 billion. And if we set a 2.5 per cent unemployment rate as our definition of full employment, then, at the increased growth rate of 4.5 per cent, the gap jumps to over $100 billion of output lost irretrievably.

It seems reasonable to conclude on the face of this evidence that the American economy is suffering from a non-cyclical slack of chronic proportions—despite an arms race which pumps into the economy an average of $50 billion a year. To argue that in spite of these developments things are not as bad as they were in the 1930's is to commit the error of judging and comparing business cycles solely in terms of their statistical differences, rather than in terms of the potential consequences which would follow from a protracted failure to maintain an adequate growth rate. Undue emphasis on non-ideological, "factual" analysis and their statistical comparisons breeds an unthinking empiricism which ignores the context of the data and hence their meaning. It becomes unhistorical and short-sighted. Though there is a difference between being blind and being short-sighted, in the history of things the two are indistinguishable.

Stripped to its essentials the crisis facing the United States in the 1960's involves two gaps—the internal gap between the actual and potential output of the American economy, and the external gap between the growth rates of the United States, the Common Market, and the Soviet Union. The closing of the internal gap and the narrowing of the external gap is of paramount importance if the United States is to survive as a major power. It should be made clear, however, that the closing of the internal gap does not necessarily imply a closing of the external gap. A closing of the internal gap would require a significantly larger increase in the short-term growth rate than we have been experiencing in the last decade. But once closed the economy would then proceed along its now inadequate long-term growth rate of 3.2 per cent. It is, therefore, of critical importance that, aside from the internal policies needed to close the internal gap, as measured by the Council of Economic Advisers, additional measures need to be undertaken to increase the long-term rate of economic growth; which would then require a still larger increase in the short-term rate.

On either count, and more so in conjunction, the critical factor in the American economy is the role of government. The major obstacles to a solution are the Congress of the United States, the absence of leadership in the Executive branch of government, and, in general, the built-in perversities of our political system. What is desperately needed is a radical change in the American public's assessment of the role of government in a democratically oriented society. If we are to meet the joint problem of the two gaps, long-range planning on a governmental level becomes imperative and the present division between the private and public sectors of the economy must be looked upon as unrealistic. We must not engage, as has the Council of Economic Advisers, in historical extrapolations from the past which supposedly show that nothing has changed and that our old tools are as good as new. Nor does this necessarily imply the adoption of socialist planning. It is rather a question of what changes are needed, at the minimum, to make the capitalist system viable in a power world. The internal gap, for example, may be a structural rather than merely a technical problem in cyclical instability. If so, then the indirect Keynesian controls of monetary and fiscal policy may no longer be fully adequate. For one thing, it must be kept in mind that business cycles and wars induce, however subtly, irreversible changes in the underlying institutional structure of a modern society. And our theoretical constructions of reality, if they are to have any meaning at all, must absorb these changes over time. In so far as existing social theories do not take these structural developments into account, they become obsolete and hence invalidated.

One of the problems of the postwar period has been the emergence of inflationary depressions attributable to the relative mildness of our periodic recessions and to the emergence of oligopolistic concentrations of market power in both community and factor markets. With the economic pressures thus emanating from the supply side, more so than from the demand side, serious doubt has been cast on the ability of monetary and fiscal policy to achieve a full employment use of our resources, even at an inadequate long-term growth rate based on a 4 per cent unemployment rate. And it is a bit ludicrous to suppose that, by riding things out with inadequate policies derived from inadequate theories, it is only the timetable and not the path of an economy which will be affected. It may be that no changes exist, under these circumstances, which would make capitalism, as we know it, viable. But it is at least incumbent upon us to determine if this is so and not slide into a doctrinal rigidity which would assure its defeat. The problem facing us may not be a purely technical one. We need to determine this. If our traditional tools are found to be inadequate, then what will be needed is a drastic re-evaluation of our institutional framework and the value premises upon which it is based.

It is time that the graduate departments of our major universities become more than just places where competent technicians are trained. Rather than making what Mills called "structural criticism" their business, they have enthroned a false scientism, made a fetish of an objectivity which, of necessity, must also be false, and have in the process become centers for radiating the end-of-ideology approach to social problems. In essence, they have become the great defenders of the American Establishment.

Though the intellectuals in our universities have rationalized and made the end of ideology respectable, they have done so *ex post facto;* they were preceded by the politicians who, without being conscious that their actions had a name, practiced it nevertheless. The politicians have long become, to use Max Weber's terminology, scientists without vision and sensualists without heart, but at least they have had the saving grace, unlike the intellectuals, of not rationalizing their intellectual bankruptcy into the good society.

It has been agreed that Bell's and Lipset's account of the end of ideology in the West is, in large part, accurate. There is, nevertheless, a judgment to be made apart from the accuracy of their account. Bell and Lipset regard the end of ideology as good. Our point here is that it must be judged contextually, and that under the present conditions it borders on the disastrous. This can be illustrated by comparing the two supreme technicians of American politics—Franklin D. Roosevelt and John F. Kennedy.

Early in his campaign of 1960 Kennedy assumed the mantle, sceptre, and orb of Franklin Delano Roosevelt. He presented himself to the electorate in Roosevelt's image and proclaimed the New Frontier. Sounding very much like a committed ideologue with a vision, he vowed to get America moving again. That the New Frontier, unlike the New Deal, bogged down in a series of debilitating political compromises in no way destroys the basic validity of President Kennedy's self-identification with Roosevelt. Both are supreme examples of the non-committed, non-ideological politician acting strictly out of political expediency. Both placed the highest value on political success at the polls and regarded such success as the *sine qua non* of their existence. And neither had any fixed, or well-defined vision of the good society. Any social interests they upheld were not so much out of conviction as out of their inherent political value at the polls. Yet, though they are similar in all these and other respects, the consequences of their common and purely political approach to politics are not the same. The 1960's are, obviously, not the 1930's. And it is in the context of each of these two periods of crisis that the end of ideology common to both Roosevelt and Kennedy must be judged.

The crisis of the 1930's gave rise, through the New Dealers, to a new wave of hope, and to the conviction that by social engineering, things could be put aright. The flood of social legislation in the early days of the New Deal was an extraordinary attempt to bring about the needed institutional changes. This passion for pragmatic social experimentation was deeply rooted in the belief that human nature was highly, if not infinitely plastic. It was, in other words, basically optimistic and full of hope in a time of crisis. It was an age of critical thought, of regeneration, of faith in man's power to change the institutional complex within which he lived. It engaged, unstintingly, in a fundamental criticism of man and the institutional melange within which he had entrapped himself. Society, in short, was to be reconstructed in the image and in the interests of the so-called common man. But there was no overall blueprint. It was an empirical approach to democracy.

If there was no ideological cohesion, there was at least general agreement that something had to be done and a clear understanding of the problem in personal terms. The ugly tear in the social fabric of a once prosperous society was readily understood by the man in the street. It was a part of his everyday experience and affected or was a direct and frightening threat to his continued well-being. And it was on this stage that the end of ideology entered in the form of President Roosevelt.

Being a non-ideologue, Roosevelt responded to the political pressures of his time. This supreme politician could wet his finger and hold it up to the prevailing winds. When he found the winds blowing steadily, in gale force, in one particular direction, it was not difficult for him to determine the conditions of political success and thus to bring an enormous pressure to bear on the Congress in support of his program. The political coloration and social innovations of the New Deal were largely the result of political expediency in a country where political success counts for all. The tune of the New Deal was played by ear, and the end of ideology in the guise of a charismatic president served to make the vast power of the presidency responsive to the public will.

The current crisis is not immediately understandable in direct, personal terms by the ubiquitous man-in-the-street. The threat of nuclear annihilation numbs his sense of credulity and is so vast as to be beyond his conceptual capacity. The problem of disarmament is also much too complicated to be fully comprehended by him, except in the perversely myopic sense of realizing that his economic welfare is somehow tied to the continuance of the arms race. Despite the poor performance of the economy since 1953 and the growth of unemployment, the affluent society continues to maintain its image unimpaired. There are no breadlines, as in the 1930's, and the economic problem has not yet pierced the individual's consciousness, since, for most people, it is not yet a direct threat. And if one major aspect of the economic problem is the long-run power threat implied by the disparate rates of economic growth between the United States and the Soviet Union, then surely this is the most remote of his immediate concerns. Furthermore, foreign policy has become so caught up in the ideology of the Cold War that the common man can only react to it emotionally, and unthinkingly approve the vast expenditures needed for a senseless and suicidal arms race. In short, the problems of the 1960's are much too abstract for the limited social vision of the common man.

It is in this totally different context that a non-ideological man like President Kennedy had to operate. It is not the kind of crisis which confronts the individual with understandable, let alone meaningful, problems to which he can respond politically. So when President Kennedy wet his finger and held it up to the political winds, he found them blowing simultaneously in all directions. As a non-ideologue he had no commitment, with the result that he was found standing squarely in the center, surrounded on all sides by advisers who were similarly uncommitted. Democratic politics has thus degenerated into a conforming consensus around the middle. This does not mean, of course, that nothing at all was done. In both foreign and domestic policy the President moved first in one direction, felt the situation out and then, according to his political sensibilities, moved in another. He excelled in practicing a pragmatism that has become wishy-washy; an "ideology of caginess" that became internally inconsistent and directionless. There was no coherence; no well-thought-out sense of purpose in foreign policy, as Hans Morgenthau has pointed out, and this was even more obvious with respect to domestic policy. Above all, and unlike the 1930's, there was no general consensus in the body politic to which the President could respond, out of sheer political expediency, in a clear and consistent manner. In short, there was no limiting frame of reference within which to innovate, and, lacking one of his own, he floundered, compromised, and tried to be all things to all men. Leadership in these circumstances requires vision as well as technique. President Kennedy failed to provide the needed leadership precisely because he had no clear picture of what ought to be done. Indeed, like Lipset, he rationalized the emptiness of modern society and declared that it is the good society and that all the problems which do remain are purely technical.

Two talks by the late President more than amply demonstrate just how deeply "committed" he was to the Bell and Lipset thesis. In his remarks before the Economic Conference held in Washington on May 21, 1962, the President distinguished between myth and reality in these words:

> I would like also to say a word about the difference between myth and reality. Most of us are conditioned for many years to have a political viewpoint, Republican or Democrat—liberal, conservative, moderate. The fact of matter is that most of the problems, or at least many of them that we now face, are technical problems, are administrative problems. They are very sophisticated judgments which do not lend themselves to the great sort of "passionate movements" which have stirred this country so often in the past. Now they deal with questions which are beyond the comprehension of most men.

A month later, at his 1962 commencement address at Yale University, Kennedy further elaborated on this theme.

> Today ... the central domestic problems of our time are more subtle and less simple. They do not relate to basic clashes of philosophy and ideology, but to ways and means of reaching common goals—to research for sophisticated solutions to complex and obstinate issues.
>
> What is at stake in our economic decisions today is not some grand warfare of rival ideologies which will sweep the country with passion but the practical management of a modern economy. What we need are not labels and cliches but more basic discussion of the sophisticated and technical questions involved in keeping a great economic machinery moving ahead.
>
> ... political labels and ideological approaches are irrelevant to the solutions.
>
> ... the problems of ... the Sixties as opposed to the kinds of problems we faced in the Thirties demand subtle challenges for which technical answers—not political answers—must be provided.

Thus, the art of compromise and technical manipulation is all that remains. The problems usually associated with an ethic of conscience are no longer with us. The faith ladder has been stripped of its rungs, and we are all standing on the hard ground of objective fact.

Bell and Lipset are of one mind. Whereas the old ideologies of the West have become exhausted by the march of Western progress, new ideologies have arisen in Asia and Africa—the ideologies, according to Bell, of industrialization, modernization, Pan-Arabism, color, and nationalism. The new ideologies, unlike the old, are not being fashioned by the intellectuals along universal or humanistic lines. Rather, they are instrumentally parochial and employed by political leaders who have created them for purposes of rapid development and national power. And the disoriented Western liberals have desperately embraced the new ideology of economic development to "wash away the memory of old disillusionments." [20] In this sense, Lipset believes there is "still a real need for political analysis, ideology, and controversy, within the world community, if not within the Western democracies," and the Western ideologue, stripped of issues, must now focus his attention on this new area. Though ideology and passion are no longer necessary in the affluent democracies of the West, they are very much needed in the less affluent countries of the world. In the underdeveloped countries, we should encourage the radical and socialist politicians because, according to Lipset, "only parties which promise to improve the situation of the masses through widespread reform . . . can hope to compete with the communists." [21] Therefore, the disaffected liberals of the West, the unreconstructed intellectuals, the trade union leaders (at least those who are still liberal), and the socialists have a positive role to play—abroad; where their "irresponsible and demagogic" visions and their psychological or pathological need to criticize can be put to good use in developing free political and economic institutions.

In time, if we are successful, the underdeveloped countries will become developed and as they, too, solve all their pressing political, social, and economic problems, ideologies will wither on the vines. Then peace will break out in an enlarged West and international relations and disputes will, like purely internal problems, be governed by an international ethic of responsibility. The Soviet Union, in the process, will, like some execrable disease, have been effectively quarantined and left to dissolve in its own juices. Or, if the rapid industrialization of the Soviet Union were also to result in a decline of dogma, there would then be an end to ideology throughout the world, and peace, in the absence of commitment, would descend, like a dove which would forever roost in the parliaments of man.

Lipset and Bell are, in effect, arguing that the nations of the world are all racing toward a static state of equilibrium; only some countries have had a head start. A few have already achieved the good society. Others are fast approaching it. And still others, the underdeveloped countries, have only just begun their ascent. In time, all will have arrived, but until such time it will be the responsibility of those already at the pinnacle to reach down and help the others up. In all this, it would seem, dynamic change is a transitory phenomenon, and all of human history, in all its turmoil and in all its travail, has been moving, inexorably, toward this supreme goal of universal peace. At bottom, what Bell and Lipset are giving us is a philosophy of history—if not of the past, then certainly of the future.

The argument is incredible. Indeed, it is more than that. It is the Marxian dialectic brought to a halt in the final synthesis of the modern, non-ideological, democratic welfare state shimmering in the radiance of a non-committed scientism. It has, furthermore, one element in common with most other philosophies of history—it celebrates the present. The present becomes the touchstone for measuring the past and the future. Bell and Lipset have stood Hegel on his head once more. Instead of the better being the critic of the good, the good, in Bell and Lipset, insures that the better will not come into existence.[22]

The end of ideology of Bell and Lipset is nothing more than the ideology of the *status quo*. It can be so described in the sense that if the good society has already been achieved, then, by definition, the need for structural criticism no longer exists. And American political thought, in so far as it shares the convictions of Bell and Lipset, is fast approaching the end of its ideological line. The danger is that this end-of-ideology approach to social problems will promote an ideological brittleness and intransigience which will effectively rule out any criticism of any of the basic presuppositions concerning the righteousness of its cause. For the worship of "scientism" tends to convert "facts" into revealed truths which, by their nature, brook no challenge and refuse to be negotiated.

As for the underdeveloped countries, the ideology of the *status quo* in this country, despite the admirable exhortations of Bell and Lipset, has consistently supported reactionary regimes in these underdeveloped areas and has resisted, or sought to modify in most cases, the pressures for fundamental change. The ideology of the East, on the other hand, poses with some measure of success as the champion of downtrodden peoples and as the vehicle of change. In this sense it has shown itself to be more viable and more willing to adapt itself to the pragmatics of the situation. At any rate it does not present itself in the ludicrous light of proposing to export its unwanted and socially useless ideologues to the underdeveloped countries.

As an epilogue to Bell, if it is true, as he argues, that the New Left in Britain "has passion but little definition of the future," it is also true that in the liberalism of the United States even the passion has been leached out. Liberalism in this country is dead and the end of ideology is its legacy.

NOTES:

1. *The End of Ideology: On the Exhaustion of Political Ideas in the Fifties* (New York, Rev. Ed., 1961).
2. *Political Man* (New York, 1960).
3. Ibid. p. 403, italics supplied. In response to criticisms of *Political Man*, Lipset has somewhat modified this statement and has sought to restate his liberalism ("My View From Our Left," *Columbia University Forum*, Fall 1962). "Democracy," now, "is not simply a means to the end of the good society, it is itself the only society in which social tendencies which press man to exploit man may be restrained." This rather negative approach to democracy and the good society is further confirmed by his statement that his espousal of democracy "rests on the assumption that only a politically democratic society can reduce the pressures—endemic in social systems—to increase the punitive and discriminatory effects of stratification." For it is the democratic freedom of the underprivileged classes to organize which gives rise to an effective and levelling "counter-power" operating within the rules-of-the-game of institutionalized conflict. The similarity of this to John K. Galbraith's theory of "countervailing power" is obvious, and is subject to the same

limitations. Lipset's ideal is the non-ideological welfare state toward which, he believes, the United States is moving.

4. *Political Man*, pp. 403-6. In addition Lipset cites, with apparent approval, a comment made to him by the editor of a leading Swedish newspaper: "Politics is now boring. The only issues are whether the metal workers should get a nickel more an hour, the price of milk should be raised, or old-age pensions extended." Similarly in Bell we have: "In the Western world ... there is today a rough consensus among intellectuals on political issues: the acceptance of the Welfare State; the desirability of decentralized power; a system of mixed economy and of political pluralism ... [And] the workers whose grievances were once the driving energy for social change, are more satisfied with the society than the intellectuals" (pp. 397-9).

For other views reflecting the end of ideology the following recent works should be consulted: John Strachey, *Contemporary Capitalism* (New York, 1956); C. A. R. Grossland, *The Future of Socialism* (New York, 1957); John K. Galbraith, *American Capitalism* (Boston, Rev. Ed., 1956), and *The Affluent Society* (Boston, 1958); Henry Wallich, *The Cost of Freedom* (New York, 1960); and the debate going on in England between the neo-revisionists and the fundamentalists in the pages of *Encounter, New Left Review*, and the *New Statesman*, particularly during 1960-61. Limitations of space preclude any examination of these various approaches. With the exception of the English "fundamentalists," they all reflect the view, in greater or lesser degree, that the major problems of industrial society have been solved and that the remaining problems are basically technical and easily within our grasp. Perhaps the most unabashed statement of this position is to be found in Arthur Schlesinger, Jr., "Where Does the Liberal Go From Here?" *New York Times Magazine*, August 4, 1957.

5. *Political Man*, p. 408.

6. Ibid. p. 409.

7. *The End of Ideology*, p. 399.

8. Ibid. Chap. 12, and "The End of Ideology in the West: An Epilogue." The quotations used by Bell are: "He who seeks the salvation of souls, his own as well as others, should not seek it along the avenue of politics" (Weber); and "Men commit the error of not knowing when to limit their hopes" (Machiavelli).

9. Ibid. p. 279.

10. Ibid. pp. 279-80.

11. Ibid. p. 396.

12. For Weber's position and the quotations used, see Hans H. Gerth and C. Wright Mills (eds.), *From Max Weber* (New York, 1946), pp. 115-16, 127-8.

13. *Ideology and Utopia* (New York, 1955).

14. Andrew Hacker, in an otherwise favorable review of Lipset's book (*Commentary*, June 1961). A further criticism made by Hacker con-

cerns the limitations of a purely empirical approach to the problems of modern society. If the myths of the left-wing ideology have in fact declined, this does not necessarily imply that we have matured, politically, in the sense of being willing not only to face, but to live with the facts. In the words of Hacker: "Lipset hopes to supplant myth with fact. Empiricism, like it or not, forces one to concentrate on things as they are or as they have been. A description of how things *might be* were we to embark on changing the social order is bound to be speculative, not factual. . . . The visions of ideologues, then, coupled, with their mythologies about the world of reality, should be evaluated not on empirical but on strategic grounds."

15. For an incredibly nasty reference to the late C. Wright Mills, see Seymour M. Lipset and Neil Smelser, "Change and Controversy in Recent American Sociology," *British Journal of Sociology,* March 1961, reprinted by the Institute of Industrial Relations, Reprint No. 164, Berkeley, 1961, pp. 50-51.

16. "Letter to the New Left," *New Left Review,* Sept.-Oct. 1960.

17. Max Weber distinguishes between science as being *wertfrei* and *wertlos.* *Wertfrei* is defined as being free from prevailing passion and prejudice; free, that is, to create its own values. *Wertlos,* on the other hand, is applied to the falsely objective or "scientistic" approach to social problems.

18. "The Perils of Political Empiricism," *Commentary,* July 1962.

19. Hans Morgenthau denies the existence of unalloyed facts as follows: "Facts have no social meaning in themselves. It is the significance we attribute to certain facts of our sensory experience—in terms of our hopes and fears, our memories, inventions, and expectations—that creates them as social facts. The social world itself, then, is but an artifact of man's mind, the reflection of his thoughts and the creation of his actions. Every social act (and even our awareness of empirical data as social facts) presupposes a theory of society, however unacknowledged, inchoate, and fragmentary. It is not given to us to choose between a social philosophy and an unconditional surrender to the facts as they are. Rather we must choose between a philosophy consistent with itself and founded on experience which can serve as a guide to understanding and an instrument for successful actions, and an implicit and untested philosophy which is likely to blur understanding and mislead action."

20. *The End of Ideology,* pp. 397-8.

21. *Political Man,* p. 416.

22. On this, see Irving Louis Horowitz, "Another View from Our Left," *New Politics,* Winter 1963; and the discussion on Horowitz' critique, "Two Views from the Left," Joseph Clark and Elwin Powell, *New Politics,* Spring 1963.

# 18

**S. M. MILLER**

## Poverty, Race, and Politics*

A few short years ago, little attention was devoted to poverty and the poor. It was widely assumed that poverty was rapidly declining in the "Affluent Society" and that comparatively few were touched by it. Indeed, it appeared that to think about the poor was to reveal that one was caught in a repetition-compulsion, unable to overcome the trauma of the 1930's despite the advent of prosperity and well-being. The great improvement in levels of living was presumed to have all but eliminated the vestiges of poverty except among a "hard core."

More recently a spate of books has upset this complacent picture of the United States. Michael Harrington has feelingly portrayed the strain of poverty; Lampman, Kolko, Morgan, and Keyserling have revealed its extent. The "income curtain" which has separated the American haves from the have-nots has been drawn back, and

* I have had the benefit of comments from a great number of people: Martin Rein, Warren Haggstrom, Louis Kriesberg, Philip Norris, Hy Kornbluh, Seymour Bellin, Helen Icken, Arthur Pearl, Bernard Goldstein, Walter Goldstein, Ben Seligman, Irving L. Horowitz, Melvin Weiss, Irving Howe, Herbert Gans, and Martin Fleisher. I am particularly indebted to Frank Riessman and Patricia Sexton. A grant from the Louis M. Rabinowitz Foundation aided work on this chapter. To have taken advantage of all of their comments would have required writing a book — which is precisely what I hope to do. None of the aforementioned is responsible for the present formulations.

we can no longer assume that poverty affects few, is dwindling, and is far less destructive than the poverty of old. Nor do current trends furnish much optimism. Herman Miller has shown that the income of the poor generally, and of Negroes in particular, is not increasing relative to that of the better-off. World War II stimulated a great economic change in the United States, which aided low-income groups.[1] But, since 1944, the income gap between the poor and the better-off has not been closing.[2]

Income inequality seems to be increasing rather than decreasing. Vast technological change (subsumed under the loose term "automation") is further reducing employment opportunities for the displaced and for low-educated youth. Coupled with limited economic growth, the effects are to prevent new jobs from emerging and to increase or maintain unemployment, especially of the disadvantaged — the young, the old, and the minority groups.

Poverty, then, is an American problem, but it has not as yet reached its full stature as a political problem. Whether poverty fully becomes the issue that it should will to a large extent depend on what the poor do. They will need allies from other groups if they are to be effective. But they are the likely "movers and shakers." The purpose of this essay is to set out the possibilities of political awareness and action among the poor. Since the obstacles to action are well-known, the effort is to stress these possibilities.

How many people are poor in the United States depends on how poverty is defined. It is difficult to define a "poverty line"; Lampman, for example, employs $2500 for a family of four as his base, while Keyserling uses $4000 family income without reference to size of family. Estimates of poverty vary as a result. The minimal estimate appears to be about 16 per cent of the total population, while the maximal estimate is about 25 per cent. Interpretation of the more detailed breakdown of the data has often been confused because the incidence of poverty within a given population—for example, over 65, non-white—has not always been recognized as different from the composition of poverty, i.e. what percentage of the poor have a given characteristic—over 65, non-white.

The emphasis in most reports on the frequency of poverty—what percentage of a given group are poor—has obscured some vital facts about poverty. Despite the great incidence of poverty among

Negroes—35 per cent of Negro adults in Detroit were reported as unemployed in 1960—most poor are white (this is also true in the South). Similarly, while a high percentage of farm people are poor, almost 50 per cent of the poor are in urban communities.

In addition the data lend themselves to two opposing interpretations with quite different implications. One interpretation stresses the "differentness" of the poor; they are "special cases" requiring special help. The other view emphasizes the similarity of the poor to other groups. Lampman,[3] for example, points out that 70 per cent of the poor have one or more of these four characteristics—over 65, non-white, in female-headed households, or in households headed by individuals with eight years of education or less. In the total United States, 50 per cent had one or more of these characteristics. His conclusion is that the poor are different, while, on the contrary, I am struck by the great overlap between the poor and the general population. His position is strengthened when only the first three characteristics are used, for then 50 per cent of the poor have one or more of these characteristics, while only 20 per cent of the total population are identifiable by these characteristics. The 50 per cent of the poor, however, who do not have any of these three characteristics are similar to 80 per cent of the general population.

One can obviously stress either the distinctiveness of the poor or their similarity to the general population. The first position suggests that the poor's economic needs are different from the rest of society; the second underlines the coincidence of interests. This essay will tend to over-stress the latter point of view in an effort to compensate for a lack of attention to this position.

The poor are probably more varied than ever before in American life. The farm poor live in areas where the economic sustenance has withered with the technological development of agriculture and its economic concentration. The small-town and small-city poor suffer from the demise of local industry, whether it be the coal mines of West Virginia or the dead, one-industry textile towns of the East. Industrial centers like Detroit and Pittsburgh suffer from high productivity and limited demand. The youthful poor possess limited or outmoded skills and inadequate educational credentials in a high-technology, certificate-demanding economy.

Farms and small-town America are large producers of the poor; the big cities are increasingly the receivers of the poor (as well as generators of the poor themselves). Many from "old America" move to the slum areas of large cities, where they join the left-over third-generation immigrant population and the other poor of the metropolis.[4]

While farm and rural areas are pushing people toward the cities, the metropolises are not prepared to accept them. There is no pull from most of the urban centers. In contrast, an urban labor force was needed in the beginning stages of Britain's industrial progress, and, as E. H. Carr argues, it was public policy to permit market forces to starve people off the land. In our case, we do not have cities needing the labor of the migrants or the older urban poor. (I do not want to paint a gilded picture of industrializing Britain, for the urban jobs provided a level of living that has been characterized as "grinding poverty.")

Poverty is sad (and in our kind of society, unforgivable) wherever it takes place, but I want to concentrate on the urban poor, particularly those in large cities. This urban poor is composed of many strands: refugees from the land and older settlers of the urban slums, Southern mountaineer whites and Southern Negroes, Puerto Ricans and Mexican-Americans.

Despite their diversity, the poor in the largest urban centers are rapidly evolving into a "colored" poor of Negroes and the Spanish-speakers (Puerto Ricans and Mexican-Americans). It is these groups who are most likely to be politicalized. It is the confluence of class and race issues which gives the poor a much greater political potential than is usually true of low-income, depressed populations. Obviously, the term "colored" describes perceptions of and attitudes toward these groups rather than biological phenomena.

I shall be referring to the poor as the "new" working class. The "old" working class, who still make up the bulk of skilled and semi-skilled union members as well as the majority of blue-collar workers, is made up of "old-settler" Protestant recruits largely from farm and rural areas and the second and third generation of the largely Catholic Eastern and Southern European migration.

Let me try to clarify how I see the relationship between the

"new" working class and the poor, for a way of classifying a population is a way of thinking about them.

The poor are frequently referred to, following the lead of sociologists, as "lower class." For a variety of reasons, I am avoiding
this designation. First, it has a negative connotation which an analytic term, at least, should avoid. Second, it is not a term that people use to designate themselves. This was sharply shown in Richard
Centers' study of social class identification, which made an important discovery by offering people four choices for their social
class (upper, middle, working, and lower) rather than three
(upper, middle, and lower); in the *Fortune* study which employed
three categories, most people, including the poor and manual
workers, put themselves in the middle class; in Centers' investigation, a slight majority of the total American population called
themselves "working class," and an overwhelming proportion of
the manual workers, including the poor, chose this term. Third,
"lower class" has been used to refer to a wide gamut of people
from relatively highly paid, fairly well-educated skilled workers to
third-generation welfare families where the head of the household
has only intermittently worked and then in low-paid, marginal jobs.[5]

I prefer to use the term "new" working class in talking of the
poor; the "old" working class largely includes those whose families
have been urban manual workers for at least a generation. This
"old" working class is mainly white, is likely to be in semi-skilled
and skilled occupations, and is more frequently employed in high-
wage construction and manufacturing industries in the main
economy than is the "new" working class. The latter is more likely
to be "colored," unskilled, in low-wage service and non-unionized
industries (e.g. hospitals) in the marginal economy of present-day
United States. These distinctions are overstated, for obviously some
Negroes work in unionized, skilled manufacturing occupations.
(The election in 1962 of the first Negro to the executive board of
the United Automobile Workers is indicative of the importance of
Negroes in the high-wage, predominantly semi-skilled and skilled
manufacturing occupations covered by the contracts of this union.)

This formulation runs into another difficulty because 35 per cent
to 50 per cent of the heads of low-income families are not in the
labor force—that is, they are not classified by Census statisticians as

currently employed or actively engaged in looking for work if they are unemployed. This is not the place to analyze labor force concepts, but I would emphasize that many of the adult poor who are outside of the labor force have worked and would work if jobs were available. The aged poor, who are a large percentage of the non-workers, are less interested in finding work than the new working class, but they continue to have many economic and political interests in common with them. The welfare poor (particularly in families headed by women) are again probably less actively interested in work than the new working class, but their reluctance should not be as casually assumed as it seems to be by many commentators today. Their long-run economic and political interests are frequently in common with those of the new working class. Moreover, when the welfare poor work, they are in the occupations which characterize the new working class. Many of the poor will be shifting back and forth between low-level unskilled work and government support; in both activities, they will have common interests in banding together to improve their conditions.

The concept of the "new" working class is more a fishing net than a hard container. Nevertheless, I prefer it to terms like "lower class," "the poor," the Lumpenproletariat, "skid rowers," and the like, because it points to economic and political issues rather than to personality deficiencies. It emphasizes some common economic issues which many low-income people face in affluent America and raises the possibility that they might move politically to do something about them. A less invidious term like "new" working class implies that low-income people are trying to get a foothold in urban industrial life. We should not ignore them by acting as though their plight were little involved in the basic economic situation of America.

Harrington has pictured the poor as passive, inert, and apathetic, lacking generally the capacity for action. I find this portrait misleading. The aged have been active in political movements—from the Townsend Plan to the fight for Medicare. Mexican-Americans have recently won political control in Crystal City, a small Texas town. In many cities, the young and adult poor have organized to protest their conditions, as recently in Chicago where women on welfare strongly demonstrated against the cessation of allowances.

I shall be concentrating on Negroes, because they are a sizable proportion of the under-65, large-city poor, and because they are the most likely group to become politicalized.

In this century a radical change has taken place in the geographic distribution of Negroes. In 1910, 89 per cent of Negroes lived in the South; in 1960, the percentage had decreased to 60 per cent. Between these years a social revolution took place, liberating Negroes from the land and introducing them to the possibilities as well as the woes of urban life. In 1960, for the first time, a major city was predominantly Negro: in Washington, D. C., the Negro population was now 55 per cent of the total population. In many Northern cities, the Negro proportion is rapidly increasing. In the Borough of Manhattan in the City of New York, Negro and Puerto Rican children are 70 per cent of the total elementary-school population; by 1980, the estimate is that 85 per cent of the elementary-school children will be Negro or Puerto Rican.

World War I was the breakthrough for the Southern Negro. During and immediately after the war, great numbers of Negroes left for the North, and in cities like New York and Chicago, Harlem and Bronzeville became Negro ghettos. In following years there was a steady if not spectacular movement of Negroes out of the South. Again, a war led to a rapid change; during and after World War II, there was, and continues to be, a rapid movement of Negroes into urban centers, both North and South. The Negro is no longer a rural resident as he primarily was for generations: soon, a majority of Negroes will be living in the North and in large cities there.

The numerical importance of Negroes in the large Northern cities was demonstrated in the Kennedy victory in 1960, which was largely attributed to the almost solid Democratic vote in many Negro districts in the populous industrial states. The increase in the number of Southern Negro voters accentuates the national role of Negroes. Legislative reapportionment, which will increase the importance of the urban vote, will make the Negro vote more effective in state elections. With the rapid concentration of Negroes in central cities, they will become increasingly a power grouping there; in New York City, it now seems to be Democratic party practice that the Borough President of Manhattan should be Negro.

A Negro mayor of a large city is a distinct possibility in the next few years.

Negroes, then, are beginning to develop a political "clout" which will give them the ability to demand and achieve services and help at both the federal and local levels. We are witnessing the extension of citizenship rights to a new group and their groping utilization of the potential effectiveness of these rights. Historically the trend in this nation has been toward the spread of citizenship rights. Formally, these rights have almost always been available to all; in practice, only to whites and more slowly to working-class whites. As the white ethnics—first the Irish, later the Jews, and still more recently the Italians (the first Italian was not elected to the U. S. Senate until shortly after World War II)—gained strength through organization and used their citizenship rights, they were able to obtain a more equitable distribution of political and economic rewards. This same process is beginning with Negroes and at a slower rate with many other members of the new working class. It promises to be the decisive political condition of the 'sixties in this country.

A large-scale politicalization of Negroes and others of the poor is a real possibility because of the interweaving of class (economic) factors with ethnic and racial issues. The intermeshing of these concerns will likely lead to political mobilization. The racial-ethnic factors cement solidarity within some of the groups of the poor. Usually, the long-term economically depressed are unlikely candidates for a dynamic political movement, but the race/ethnic dimension, as well as the economic factor, is propelling the poor, whether Negro, Mexican-American, or Puerto Rican.

Many of the leaders of the poor will probably come from the middle-class families of the racial-ethnic group, providing qualities and abilities that may not early emerge among the poor. E. Franklin Frazier's notion of a "black bourgeoisie" who in rising had cut itself off from feeling, contact, and identity with the mass of Negroes was probably overstated when he expressed it a few years ago; it undoubtedly is today. Less and less does "going up" mean "going out" of the Negro community: even those who are able to and do move out of the Negro ghetto frequently maintain ties with it and are deeply and actively concerned about the Negro poor. A generational factor is involved: the older successful Negroes are less likely to be identified with poorer Negroes and are more likely to emphasize "progress" than are the younger, middle-class Negroes. But even the older frequently are being pushed along by the dynamism and pressure of the younger and of the Negro community generally.[6]

The cohesion which comes from the racial-ethnic issues may also separate each of the poor ethnic groupings from one another, leading each to be concerned only with issues particular to it. This self-centering pressure and inter-ethnic hostility may be overcome by the large number of issues which are common to all of the poor. The high rate of unemployment among the new working class, their low wages, their inadequate housing as they suffer the bulk of the ravages (and reap only some of the benefits) of urban redevelopment, the poor schooling offered their children, the neglect of public services in their neighborhoods, the frequent callousness of the police and welfare departments, their bilking by merchants —in short, their second-class economic and political citizenship— provide the issues which may mold the new working class into a potent political force. To understand these possibilities, we must first understand the economic situation.

It is important to recognize that in the United States today we are increasingly moving into a dual economy in which the main economy is characterized by the provision of high standards of living, somewhat stable employment, and other rewards for those who are able to stay in it. On the other hand, the marginal economy is centered upon low-level service trades and occupations, peopled by individuals of low skill who are from minority groups or left-over immigrant populations and who receive relatively little of what the economy is producing, especially in regard to housing amenities. Those in the marginal economy frequently are unable to get jobs; when they do work, wages are low. (Twelve per cent of all those receiving welfare assistance in New York City, including the aged, are in families whose head is employed. The pay of these heads of households is inadequate to support their families.) Moreover, job insecurity is great and individuals are frequently unemployed for considerable periods of time. In this kind of colonial situation of a successful "white economy" and a meager "bush economy," there are wide disparities; furthermore, gains in the main economy do not rapidly trickle down to those in, what Harrington has called, the "other America."

The high profits, high productivity, and high wages of the affluent economy have limited effects on those in the marginal economy. Indeed, increasing productivity has meant that many are being squeezed out of the affluent economy, as, for example, auto workers in Detroit who have been permanently laid off despite the high production of cars. Those who can make the affluent economy— and making it depends largely upon education—do relatively well. Those who live in the marginal economy do not automatically progress with the gains of the affluent economy. This segmentation within the economy accentuates inequality.

In undeveloped societies, the rise of a middle class is expected to mitigate the extreme variation in standards of living in the society. In present-day United States the expansion of what C. Wright Mills emphasized was a new middle class is no longer reducing the size of the poor. In some ways the growing affluence of the upper and middle classes is increasing the relative deprivation of the poor.

The great decline in poverty took place during World War II. Since then, the rate of decline in the percentage who are poor has sharply slackened. There has actually been an increase since 1949 in the concentration of wealth assets owned by the upper one per cent.[7] This important finding has been ignored in the stress of Simon Kuznets' debated conclusion that the concentration of income in the hands of the upper one per cent decreased from 1919 to 1946. The end of the war and the post-war boom has meant that economic forces which reduced income inequality are no longer effective. The income advantage of the "diploma elite" over those who have only "some college," high school diplomas, or are school dropouts is increasing. The income spread between skilled workers and unskilled, which was narrowed during this century, is beginning to widen. Upper-level blue-collar workers, who were improving relative to lower-level white-collar workers, are now losing ground to them. And the lower-level white-collar occupations are falling behind the upper white-collar occupations.

The inability of our economic system in recent years to sustain

a high level of economic activity and to provide jobs for the growing labor force indicates that the optimistic hopes following the
war are no longer well based. The sputtering of our economic system has been reflected in rising unemployment and the maintenance of a large group in poverty.

In World War II the percentage of the labor force who were
unemployed was reduced drastically. The concept of "unemployables" was largely thrown out the window, and many people who
had not been able to work for a long period, and perhaps regarded
themselves as unable to perform on a job, discovered that their
abilities and effort were needed.

A period of high employment demand is a situation in which
poverty is rapidly reduced because of the functioning of the economic market. When the economy is not geared to this level of
production and activity, many people are thrown on the unemployment scrap-heap. They face long periods of unemployment and
frequently find themselves described as, and after a while may believe themselves to be, "unemployable." A conclusion to draw
from this is that we need sustained economic growth, high production, and high employment in order to solve many of the problems of the unemployed and the poor today in America.

We must, however, recognize that today's problems are increasingly complicated by the increasing skill requirements of our complex industrial machinery. High economic growth does not automatically assure jobs for people who are unskilled. It does not
guarantee that any kind of labor will be employed in a rising economic market. And some of the poor, especially the aged, are unlikely to work regardless of the demand for labor. All this is true,
but it should still be recognized that a high level of employment
will increase opportunities for the poor. It may be that high production will not draw people into those industries requiring high
skill, but it may provide increased demand in service and other
industries which do not require high labor skills.

Moreover, we should not take the nature of the demand for certain kinds of labor as a given. If it is discovered that over time
there is a scarcity of certain kinds of labor, it may well turn out
that industries and government can adapt technology which permits the utilization of relatively few skilled laborers and a greater

number of unskilled laborers. The results of technology can be achieved in a variety of ways, and it may eventually be that producers will have to pay more attention to the supply and quality of labor than was formerly true.

Again, a high sustained demand for labor will probably encourage many more youths to stay in school in order to obtain the kind of training which will fit them for more high-skilled jobs. In situations where jobs are scarce, where it is unsure what kind of skill will be necessary, it is unlikely that we will find many youths taking the risk of preparing themselves for the unknown. Willingness to be an adventurer grows when confidence in the outcome appears somewhat realistic. With rapid technological change and low economic growth, the value of further training is frequently problematic.

The economic binding of the various groups of the poor is their common need for decent employment and decent social services. The achievement of these goals requires political action, for economic issues are political issues today. The economic choice before us is obvious: either we have a sustained, widespread economic growth or we will have to have a shift in the distribution of income. A sustained economic growth will mean what it has meant before—that the groups which were disadvantaged will be able to get more of the goods of society; rising levels of production and employment will draw into the labor force large numbers of people presently unemployed and those classified as "unemployables." [8] If, however, the economy fails to grow at an adequate level, and if its growth does not lead to a widespread distribution of the benefits, then it will become increasingly necessary to have a redistribution of income.

In our country, the redistribution of income takes place to a large extent in transfer payments of welfare and social assistance. In an economy that is expanding with a great growth in the level of national income, it becomes relatively easy to transfer some of the income to the poor by collecting taxes and paying out "welfare." But with limited economic activity transfer payments become a heavier burden. Thus, "heating up" the economy reduces the numbers who require direct transfer aid and makes transfer payments relatively smaller as the total national product expands.

While special services and supports may have to be built around high-level economic activity, the core is a strong economy.

I suspect that the meaning of the Newburgh incident [9] is that communities which are economically declining will not easily suffer a high level of taxation in order to maintain the poor. (I recognize that the facts of Newburgh were other than what was contended by the city manager; I refer to the symbolic character of the series of events connected with Newburgh.) Newburgh, I fear, reflects the wave of the future: the unwillingness of a local community to maintain its poor. Newburgh-type crises will increase as many communities find themselves increasingly disadvantaged economically and facing the need of aiding a large percentage of the poor. There will be a further increase in the tendency to move toward state and national levels in order to sustain the poor. At the same time localities will fight to try to reduce the number of poor who are supported by welfare.

We face the situation where we are unwilling to a large extent to support those who suffer from economic development and change. As Joseph Schumpeter pointed out a generation ago, the price of economic progress is social dislocation. A society which is oriented toward justice and equity is willing to pay this price. It aids those who are disadvantaged by the growth of an economy, which is improving the conditions of a large but still limited number of people. Our society is undergoing economic change but limited economic growth. The consequence is that many communities are not improving at all and the problems of many communities are worsening. In such a society, it is likely that there will be increased outcries against the sustenance of the poor. Social services, therefore, are increasingly political issues, frequently arousing the new working class to action.

We are beginning to get the thoughtful, analytical, and detailed appraisal of our social services that Titmuss and his students have provided in England. One consequence is the beginning of an improvement in services. The following is not a comprehensive listing of current problems in our social services:

1. The inadequacy of existing services and faults is disturbing—

whether in terms of allowances, the provision of emerging and long-term shelter, or the availability of decent housing. Private agencies have been relied on to an extent unknown in any other contemporary society.

2.   It is a crazy hodgepodge of private and public services with very little co-ordination among them. "Hard-to-reach" clients are frequently the product of "hard-to-reach" agencies; "multi-problem families" may be a reflection of "single-purpose agencies."

3.   Many agencies, despite their avowed goals, have not been primarily oriented to the poor. As Cloward has indicated, the private agencies have sought a new clientele in the middle class.

4.   The orientation of much of social service is remedial and policing rather than preventive. By and large and until recently, welfare departments did not attempt to increase the employment possibilities of their clientele. They frequently performed a police function with the poor. Our concern with the morality of welfare and the danger of people receiving it who are not legally eligible for it has made welfare a substitute policing system for low-income areas. In order to provide checks on the poor, the welfare worker becomes an investigator as she (or, less frequently, he) is called in New York City; her purpose is to check periodically on the behavior of those who are receiving "alms" from the government. This essentially becomes a police function, as little legitimate initiative can be undertaken by the poor person unless it is approved by the welfare investigators. Consequently, the poor, thought of as being ignorant, illiterate, and unimaginative, have developed a variety of ways of coping with the welfare worker; evasion is frequent as recipients become "welfare-wise." And so we have a typical situation of a great deal of police and control efforts on one side and a considerable amount of matching efforts at evasion on the other. A stalemate is frequently reached with repugnance on the part of the authorities and lack of respect on the part of the recipients.

5.   Routinization and bureaucratization characterize many services, private as well as public. The emphasis on the fiscal and moral side of social services has led to welfare workers devoting a great percentage of time to filling out forms to determine which budget—federal, state, or local—should be charged for the ex-

penses of individual clients. Little individualized attention is given
to those who, to some extent, perform the function of serving as
the clientele of the social agencies.

6. The personnel of many agencies are frequently not adequate
for dealing with the problems of the poor. The more highly trained
often are oriented to a psychoanalytic framework which has not
been shaped for the specific problems of the poor. The less trained
frequently do not see themselves (or are not permitted to see
themselves) as more than clerks and bookkeepers.

7. A private government with limited checks has developed in
many communities. Private agencies, soliciting funds on a mass
basis from the community, are substitutes for public action. These
agencies, run as they are by self-perpetuating boards of the Community Chests, United Funds, and the like, tend to be undemocratic and unrepresentative of those low-income areas in which
they operate. The "tax base" of these agencies is regressive in as
much as those at the lower end of the income scale tend to contribute a greater percentage of their income to community fund-
raising drives than do those with higher incomes.

The maintenance of a private government of charity means that
the community as a whole and particularly the new working class
have limited effect upon the decisions which are made, especially
the distribution of funds. Increasingly, Community Chest funds go
to agencies which are not primarily oriented to the poor, even
though many contributors to the fund believe this is the purpose of
their contribution.

Moreover, the agencies frequently operate in the form of colonial administrators to the "natives" living in the poor areas of the
large cities. "Natives" are scarely brought into the operation; they
have little part in making the basic decisions and this is true even
when, for practical reasons, a few of the more acceptable "colored
natives" are brought into the lower levels of administration or are
sprinkled through the board of directors.

Strongly put, the main impact of social agencies is to provide
enough services to keep the "natives" from becoming too dis-
tressed by events they see around them; they "cool out" the mark.

Social services—their financing, their control and distribution—
must become recognized as the political problems they are, for

fundamental questions of who gets what, and how this is determined, are involved.

8. There has been comparatively little attention to helping
communities of the poor to move to self-action and self-help. This
is a crucial limitation of the existing orientation of most social agencies which are more concerned with using established community
organizations than with building social and political action among
the people who live in an area.

The concrete political results are the crucial aspects of social
action. But the process of social action is also important. The experience of poverty, especially if prolonged, does not make one
confident of the capacities or experiences that develop them. Emphasis on chance and luck—rather than one's own steering as determining fate—grows under these circumstances. Frequently,
among those who see no way out, a feeling prevails of being an
object acted upon, rather than a subject directing and channeling
forces. Welfare assistance in its present form tends to encourage
dependence, withdrawal, diffused hostility, indifference, and ennui.

In the course of pressing for the extension of citizenship rights
where individuals feel that they have a role and a right to demand
things and are organizing to do so, the new working class may see
itself more as actors. Members of the new working class will increasingly not look to others to produce change for them but will
demand and act themselves for change and improvement in their
conditions. It is this kind of political mobilization that will be increasingly changing the self-image and the psychology of the new
working class toward feelings of control and power.

Shying away from the political implications and dangers of trying to move Negro and other new working-class communities into
action, most social agencies have failed to strike at some of the real
things that will produce pervasive change among the poor in metropolitan America today. What we must look for increasingly is
not just the extension of social services, but the kind of situations in
which the poor will tend to try to do something about their own
plight. Saul Alinsky, Preston Willcox, and others have shown that
such action is possible among the poor.

There is increasing talk about developing indigenous leadership in the areas of poverty in the large city. Undoubtedly this is an important move. Perhaps, as Ben Zimmerman has pointed out, the thing that can be done most effectively by outsiders—non-colored, non-poor—coming into the impoverished areas is to try to develop the kinds of issues, crises, and situations that permit, encourage, and engender the emergence of indigenous leadership. The aim should not be to select those who on the basis of friendship connections or personality have the capabilities of being leaders. Rather, the aim is to help produce the kinds of situations which temper individuals and develop leadership capacities, as well as clarifying the directions toward which the residents of the community want to move.

The situation is not, of course, an easy one. In many communities of the new working class the likelihood of directed, concerted action toward political or any other kind of goals is extremely unlikely. These are communities which have a power vacuum in that they have very little internal dynamics of control and no real momentum. There are other communities of the poor which are controlled largely by the police to the extent that one can talk about power and control in these areas. These areas are ones in which a counter-movement may be most likely to happen. Finally, there seem to be areas in which local control is possible and even to a limited degree already existing.

The first neighborhood, the power-vacuum type of community, is probably most frequently found in those areas which serve as ports of entry of migrants to the city. Obviously, these would not be areas in which one could have much hope of a real drastic change in the outlook of people. But there are other areas of the new working class where there would be much more chance of movement. Sometimes in the areas which have organized rackets, the chances of an organized political movement may be strong. In other communities, where there is considerable crime but with limited organization in and around crime, then concerted political action may have a much smaller possibility.

The important thing to recognize is that, as Richard Brotman notes, one should not over-generalize about the communities of the new working class. There are some which have remote possibilities of movement but others may have considerably greater chances. The "gripes" of low-income neighborhoods — whether about unemployment, the conduct of the welfare department, the regulations of public housing, or the behavior of the police—are political issues and will emerge as such if the new working class is politicalized. We cannot recount here the incidents of action and mobilization among Negroes and others of the new working class but the growing number of such cases underlines the possibilities.

One difficulty of organization for social action is that the initial issues have to be local and immediate, directly affecting the new working class. But many of the problems facing the new working class cannot be resolved at local levels; they need national action for effective policies and programs. Linking local actions to broader national concerns and building an orientation to the national political scene is one of the most difficult and important tasks facing social actionists.

These remarks do not suggest that a powerful movement now exists in the Negro and other new working-class communities. Rather, it is my contention that there is a potential for political mobilization. Whether this potential is realized will depend to a large extent on what labor unions do. For, if unions fail to be concerned about the new working class, the likelihood is that economic issues will not bind together the various groupings of the poor against cross-cutting ethnic and racial ties.

Of great importance, especially for Negroes, would be the opening up of the craft occupations and unionization of the low-paid, unorganized service industries. The trends in the labor force seem to be clear: we are developing a new working class which is largely "colored." At the present time, this new working class is largely outside of the unions, which have not been effectively organizing old industry or new industries. Indeed in many unions, particularly those of a craft nature, there has been an exceeding reluctance to accept Negroes into membership. We are consequently moving into a situation where we have, to a large extent, a white union movement which is declining in terms of its coverage of the labor force, and the emergence of a new "colored" labor force which is highly exploited economically and is outside of the unions and the main economic structure of the United States.

If there is no concerted effort to bring Negroes into unions, whether in terms of organizing new industries which are pres-

ently unorganized or opening up existing industries and unions to
Negroes and other minority groups, the result may well be the
demise of unions as a strong force in the United States with a moral
base in the representation of the underrepresented. A move toward
the new unskilled minority worker would have important implications for unions. It would propel them to examine new issues in
American political life by providing a broad class base for unions.
This base is now lacking: increasing income-differentiation is ad-
vantaging those union members who are well paid, while the low-
paid improve their conditions at a slower pace. Problems of
poverty, urban redevelopment, discrimination, political representation—all issues central to the problems of the new working class
today in American society—will again come to the political fore if
unions move toward this group.

Effective work with the new working class may require the development of new practices on the part of unions. The effort to
organize Negro and other minority group members of the labor
force into unions may require intensive work in many communities
to overcome a generalized distrust of unions. This has occurred because of discrimination and corruption in the unions with which
the new working class has had some contact.

Once in unions, it may be important to have closer relations between their unions and their communities than is common. If I
may draw an example from a union beyond the pale, the St. Louis
local of the Teamsters directed by Harold Gibbons, later to become Hoffa's right-hand man, tried the innovation of having community stewards as well as shop stewards. The community stewards
served to help members living in neighborhoods to organize with
others to do something about their problems. For example, rat in-
festation in certain areas was a great problem, and community
stewards organized to exert pressure on City Hall to provide services to reduce the danger. Other unions have had community involvement in a variety of ways, but the community emphasis has
to be deepened and broadened. The rank-and-file members have
to be brought into increasing importance in both the community
and union. The useful activities of the community services division
of the AFL-CIO are limited because the emphasis is to a considerable extent on securing representation on Community Chests
and the like.

Many members of the new working class may become staunch, active, and useful union members. Many Negroes and other minority individuals are already effective union members. If their numbers grow and they feel accepted, the talented individuals who have not been educated into high-level occupations, as is increasingly happening among the old working class and their offspring, could serve as a reservoir of talent. If the unions do not move in the direction of reaching out toward the new working class, the likelihood is of a further attrition and atrophy of what has been a dynamic and significant force in American economic and political life. The more far-sighted leaders and staff of unions have rightly emphasized the importance of organizing the non-union and rapidly growing white-collar workers, especially professional and technical workers. If this movement were begun and effective (the reluctance of labor leaders to organize white-collar workers is pronounced and may be due to their fear of this kind of well-educated union member as well as to jurisdictional problems), it might have a dynamic for unions in increasing membership and providing new kinds of people for union leadership. But I believe that the organization of the new working class would have a greater dynamic. Not only are they probably easier to organize than professionals and technicians, but their problems, concerns, and needs would force unions to address themselves further to basic issues in American life.

If Negroes do not move toward unions, the race issue will have paramount significance in Negro life and the economic or class issue will not emerge to the prominence that it should have. Joint efforts and arrangements with white groups to fight for common political and economic interests will not develop. The prominence of race would mean that, in all likelihood, various kinds of divisive forces among Negroes will grow. The deep penetration of the Black Muslim movement would undoubtedly advance. Other groups would also come to the fore, responding to the Negroes' dismay at the lack of economic advance in an expanding and high-level economy. Political strains would grow both within and outside the Negro community; the likelihood of explosive situations would undoubtedly increase. If police departments put special pressure on Negro communities in ways considered unfair by

Negroes or if the police do not limit white attacks on Negroes, violence will grow in many metropolitan slum warrens.

In short, what we can hope for is that Negroes will move together with other new and old working-class groups and with some middle-class groups, regardless of color, to fight for some common economic and political interests. The labor unions of the 1930's played this role of fighting for legislation and social action which benefited great numbers of people beyond those then in trade unions. Negroes, today, if they move together with other working-class groups to fight for common interests, can play this same role. Issues of economic growth, unemployment, income distribution, urban redevelopment, equality, education, welfare, police, and the tax system would come to the fore at both local and national levels.

To a large extent, whether or not these developments take place depends upon the behavior of social agencies, labor unions, political parties, and the national government in making direct efforts to reach out, to provide services to, and to demonstrate interest in the plight of the new working class.

The hope of the elimination of poverty rests in the movement toward political activity to instigate the deepening of economic and social rights. Poverty, like most other economic questions, is now a political issue. It is an issue of what level of economic product we will be attaining and how it gets distributed. These are all crucial political questions. The raising of the problems of poverty to the political level and the encouragement of the new working class to do something about the situations which they face are the bases of a revived liberalism in the 'sixties.

A number of social commentators have deplored the emphasis upon economic goals in their description of the plight of humanity and have stressed the necessity of raising broader social goals which transcend those of the economic. This non-political radicalism is based upon positive feeling about humanity in an unfortunately well-based dismay about the corrosion of personal and social life today. Unfortunately we can do little immediately about the latter, and, if we tend to downgrade the importance of beginning to deal with the problems of poverty, the conditions of corrosion in American life will worsen. Although poverty visits only a large slice, but not a majority, of Americans today, the political and economic efforts to eliminate it, if broadly concerned, could have ramifying effects through all levels of society. Economic stagnation might be overcome; improving the housing and communities of the poor could be effected in such ways as to beautify and increase the amenities of city living for all.

We may not have a good chance to succeed in changing America, but the linking of the new working class to those who are comparatively affluent yet also concerned with the quality of life offers our best hope in breaking the present stalemate of our society.

NOTES:

1. Robert J. Lampman, "The Low Income Population and Economic Growth," Study Paper No. 12, Joint Economic Committee of Congress, December 16, 1959, p. 12.
2. Herman Miller, "Is the Income Gap Closing? No," *New York Times Magazine*, November 11, 1962.
3. Robert J. Lampman, op. cit.
4. Cf. the rich discussion in Richard A. Cloward and Lloyd E. Ohlin, *Delinquency and Opportunity: A Theory of Delinquent Gangs* (Glencoe, 1960), pp. 193-211.
5. For a more extended analysis of the omnibus character of the term "lower class" see S. M. Miller and Frank Riessman, "The Working-Class Subculture: A New View," *Social Problems*, IX, 1961, pp. 86-97.
6. Obviously, contrasting patterns exist among Negroes and other ethnic groups of the poor. The middle-class Negro who does not want his children to have contact with low-income, educationally deficient Negro children is a frequent cited example.
7. Robert J. Lampman, *The Share of Top Wealth-Holders in National Wealth*, 1922-56, No. 74, National Bureau of Economic Research (Princeton, 1962), p. 24.
8. Even with a growth in jobs, services would have to be expanded to extend adequate aid to those who cannot work for one reason or another.

9. In Newburgh, New York, the new city manager inaugurated a campaign in 1961 to harass welfare recipients in order to drive them from the welfare rolls. Newburgh, a declining Hudson River city, had had a sizable increase in the number of its Negro residents. Welfare recipients were "mugged" at police headquarters and treated as disreputables.

# 19

REX D. HOPPER

## Cybernation, Marginality, and Revolution

In the course of years of research on the mechanisms and processes of revolutionary social change I became impressed with the
inadequacy of orthodox conceptions of revolutionary upheavals,
and with the need for a formulation that would encompass a number of hitherto apparently discrete aspects of revolutionary movements. Out of these considerations I finally developed the following
hypothesis: The emergence of a numerically significant, economically powerful, and intellectually informed marginal group is one
of the earliest indicators of impending revolution.[1]

It is no part of my present responsibility to spell out the meaning
of all the terms in this hypothesis. It is enough to remark that marginality here means that, in pre-revolutionary societies, there is
formed a group that is marginal to the structure of political power
and social prestige. The Creoles of colonial Latin America and the
*mestizos* of the Second Mexican Revolution of 1910 are classic examples. Of immediate relevance is the fact that, until recently, I
have felt that no such marginal group was likely to develop in the
United States. The ranks of organized labor seemed to be the sole
source from which "marginal people" in sufficient numbers could
have been recruited. From the Great Depression onward, however,
the leadership of the labor movement has been so completely in-

corporated into the power and prestige structure that by no stretch
of the imagination can labor be considered "marginal."

Then I read Michael's *Report on Cybernation*. This—and many
other sources in a rapidly growing literature—led me to re-examine
my position. To Michael's suggestion that the socio-psychological
effects of cybernation may well result in "a war of desperation," [2]
I would like to add the suggestion that cybernation may also work
such changes in our social structure as to develop the kind of socio-
psychological seed-bed in which revolutionary behavior typically
has been nurtured. Should this prove to be correct, we might then
be faced with yet another instance of the classical historical situation in which war is employed as a diversion to avoid the need to
confront and resolve critical internal problems. Such may happen
if we fail to come to grips with the problems that seem certain to
follow from cybernation.

Nor does the future look too bright. If there is any serious, sustained, and co-ordinated attack on the problem of assimilating the
benefits and avoiding the "evils" of cybernation, no one is aware
of it. There is, of course, much argument of the futile "Tis-so-tain't-
so" variety. What is lacking is the sort of investigation which asks,
calmly and coolly, "What goes on here?"

In any case, as between war, revolution, and the required new
ways of thinking and acting we are most likely to choose the first
two—and in that order. If for no other reason, our "leaders" will
choose war over revolution because a totally militarized economy
will offer the best prospect both of controlling and eliminating a
troublesome emerging marginal group.

What follows then is an attempt to speculate on this question:
given the technological developments currently referred to as automation or, to use Michael's coined word, cybernation, what are the
probabilities that there will emerge in the United States a numerically significant group of economically powerful and intellectually
informed people who will find themselves marginal to the structure
of political power and social prestige?

In any discussion of the possible effects of cybernation on the
social structure, it is conventional to remark that the facts are hard
to come by. But is it so much that the facts are hard to come by
or is it that they are hard to confront? Certainly, no matter how

lacking in the strict statistical sense, data are available (in both sufficient amount and rigor) which can serve as the basis for some rather shrewd projections. Moreover, the frequent attempts to shrug off those concerned with the socio-economic implications of cybernation by derisively comparing them with the Luddites of the Industrial Revolution seems wide of the mark and a convenient escape device. Efforts to rationalize the immediate and short-run disadvantages of cybernation by appeals to long-run advantages merit the invocation of Lord Keynes' reply, "In the long run, we'll all be dead." As Howard Coughlin has recently remarked, we would do well to remember that, in this revolution "Time is moving so rapidly that the short run and the long run have blended and no realistic line of demarcation exists." [3]

Those most in a position to grasp the technological significance of cybernation seem to agree that the revolution of automation is not just a replication of the Industrial Revolution. As Alice Mary Hilton puts it, ". . . the cybercultural revolution is of far greater magnitude than the revolution that extended the labor of man's muscle power with the machine. . . . The important difference between the mechanization that followed the first industrial revolution and automation is as fundamental as the difference in the human powers that are being replaced by machines. Automation is based upon machines that are replacing the power provided by man's brains. . . . There is no doubt that the changes that are being brought about by the cybercultural revolution will be of such staggering proportions as to make the changes brought about by the first industrial revolution seem minute in comparison." [4]

Donald Michael voices the same opinion: "Both optimists and pessimists often claim that automation is simply the latest stage in the evolution of technological means for removing the burdens of work. The assertion is misleading. There is a very good possibility that automation is so different in degree as to be a profound difference in kind, and that it will pose unique problems for society, challenging our basic values and the ways in which we express and enforce them." [5]

In an extraordinarily perceptive paper Gerard Piel also argues that "Fundamental changes in the social order—in man's relationship to man—are . . . in prospect and are already in process." And these changes will be vastly different from those occasioned by the

Industrial Revolution, when the biologically generated energy of human muscle was displaced by the mechanically generated energy of steam engines. This, says Piel, is an old story. "The new story is the disemployment of the human nervous system (through automation)." [6]

Finally, in the article already mentioned, Howard Coughlin amasses impressive evidence to support his contention that the "automation revolution" is working changes and creating problems totally unprecedented in man's history.

What do these changes mean when expressed in terms of what I have chosen to call "population displacement?" [7] The most obvious aspect of the immediate effects of cybernation on population will be an enormous increase in the possibility and probability of displacement through unemployment. Even this relatively well-known and traditionally expected consequence of technological advance may slip up on us, may take the form of what Michael calls a "silent conquest." Several factors may operate to produce such an "unanticipated consequence":

First, the nature of the process of cybernation is such that it will be introduced selectively by organization, industry, and locality. This being so, the effects will be felt first on the local level and will not be likely to be recognized as a national problem of serious implications for the entire society.

Second, a chief and early result of cybernation is "not to hire rather than to fire"—that is, the working force is reduced by attrition rather than by discharge. Unemployment, then, becomes a somewhat indirect consequence of cybernation by virtue of the fact that oncoming additions to the work force are not employed.

Third, further masking of the effects of cybernation will result from other factors operating at the same time. For example, conditions in our foreign trade which, significantly, are also influenced by cybernation in Europe and Russia. All this leads Michael to suggest, "By the time the adverse effects of cybernation are sufficiently noticeable to be ascribed to cybernation, the equipment will be in and operating." Once this happens, he says, it may be too late to reverse the process no matter what the extent of unemployment.

However overtly or stealthily the process may work itself out, the end result will be the same. The tremendous upsurge in productivity made possible by cybernation will be accompanied by a strikingly great decline in the number of people needed to keep the productive machinery going full-blast. When to this is added the fact that population growth will be feeding millions into the job market, the magnitude of the problem of providing employment becomes even more evident. One writer has estimated that "Altogether the United States will need 13,500,000 more jobs in the 'sixties merely to keep abreast of the expected growth in the labor force. This means an average of 25,000 new jobs each week, on top of those required to drain the reservoir of present unemployment and to replace jobs made superfluous by improved technology." An especially critical feature of this demand for new jobs is the fact that by the end of this decade 3,000,000 youngsters will be entering the job market as against 2,000,000 now.[8]

Gerard Piel has also brought the problem into sharp focus. He points out that "During the past several years, despite a steady rise in gross national product, unemployment has been rising." Commenting on the fact that unemployment now approaches 6,000,000 or nearly 10 per cent of the labor force, he insists that this figure grossly misrepresents the seriousness of the situation. Some 6,000,-000 people are employed by the armed forces, he points out, in consequence "are certainly not employed in the production and distribution of goods." He concludes that "the total of those unemployed or employed outside the civilian economy thus comes to 12,000,000, close to 20 per cent of the labor force, only 5 per cent below the unemployment peak of 1933—and this at a time when the gross national product has reached an all-time high." After reviewing actions which might mitigate the present trend toward increasing unemployment—such as an arbitrary increase in the arms budget, a similar increase in the size of the armed forces, and a decrease in the work week to 30 or even 20 hours—Piel concludes that "the evidence that full employment is no longer an attainable objective seems to be growing."[9]

Moreover, job displacement is no longer limited to blue-collar workers; it is occurring right across the board. Indeed, Alice Mary Hilton argues, "In fact, the blue-collar workers had a reprieve. For various reasons ... computing machines were applied to white-

collar automation first." [10] Coughlin supports this position with
these figures on "Unemployment of clerical and kindred workers
in the United States": [11]

> January 1957, 263,000 workers or 2.8% of total
> January 1960, 381,000 workers or 3.8% of total
> January 1961, 438,000 workers or 4.2% of total
> January 1962, 466,000 workers or 4.6% of total

Michael discusses the "employment victims of cybernation" under these headings: blue-collar adults, service industries, middle
management, overworked professionals, and untrained adolescence.
In each category the picture is substantially the same: the prospect of increasing displacement of men by machines.[12]

There is a second type of population displacement that is even
more disturbing in its implications than simple unemployment—
displacement through obsolescence. Repeatedly it is pointed out
that cybernation means that "machines are replacing the power
provided by man's brains"; or, that automation is resulting in the
"disemployment of the human nervous system." As Coughlin puts
it, "American industry [is] gearing itself to a system of productivity
which views man as obsolete and redundant. . . ." [13] What has happened in the petroleum industry and in communications illuminates
this type of displacement. Petroleum refineries and chemical process plants are so highly automated that everything is controlled
by one or two operators, who certainly can also be replaced. If
and when they are it will not be for reasons of cost but because
they slow down the operation! Piel tells of the Middle Eastern
petroleum prince who became concerned over the unemployment
incident to automation. He asked his American engineering ad-
visors if men could not be substituted for machines in the system.
The engineers re-examined the entire control system and concluded "that no team of human beings could be trained and co-
ordinated to do its work."

Similarly, the efficient operation of the modern telephone system
is possible only through the use of computers known as "line
markers." "The American Telephone and Telegraph Company estimates that, at the present rate of traffic, it would have to employ
all the women in the labor force, plus 20 per cent more, to do the
work of its line markers. The task of coordinating the output of that

many human nervous systems in a single telephone system is quite impracticable." [14] Indeed, man already gets in the way of the efficient operation of a cybernated system—and the end is not yet in sight.

There is a third type of displacement that may well turn out to be the most disruptive of all: displacement through the unwitting undermining of the basic cultural values which make sense of the human drama. It was this "displacement" which Walter Lippmann was expressing when, speaking through Aristophanes, he voiced the disillusioned belief "Whirl is King, having driven out Zeus." It was this displacement which Joseph Wood Krutch was experiencing when he wrote "There is no place for us in the natural universe." [15] It is reflected by the whole school of writers who lament man's "alienation" from himself, from others, and from the cosmos. It appears in the writings of those who bemoan the deleterious effects of mass culture. It is this displacement which is voiced by at least a very large sector of the existentialist group.

Gerard Piel offers a penetrating analysis of this sense of "cultural displacement."' The details of his fascinating argument cannot claim space in this presentation. However, a brief and inadequate summary would run something like this:

The advance of science has for many years been undermining the two pillars of our economy—property and work.

Property is no longer the primary source of economic power, and ownership no longer establishes the significant, functioning connection between people and the things they consume. The nature of property, in the sense of the thing owned, has changed from land to machines. The institution of property, in the sense of the patterns of ownership, has also been changed. In Piel's apt phrasing, property (in the old sense) was subverted by another social institution, the corporation. With the emergence of two to five corporations in control of assets and sales in all but a few realms of industrial activity, economic power has become highly concentrated in our society. But it is no longer attached to property. The power is vested in self-perpetuating managements.

Work occupies fewer hours and years in the lives of everyone. What work there is grows less like work every year, and the less the people work, the more their product grows. Modern industrial technology produces a vast material surplus of goods, many times greater than the need of the workers engaged in producing it. That surplus goes begging for consumers because Technology has subverted the social institution of work. Thus, the primary function of work in our economy is to secure not the production but the distribution of goods. The problem has become one of finding people with the means to consume the increasing abundance of goods produced by a declining number of workers.

With the subversion of the institutions of property and work we are left with the illusion that we are "working," with old habits and compulsions as supports for the social edifice. In other words, the old cultural values are no longer functional and, in such circumstances, some very basic questions become crucially relevant: If a fraction of the labor force is capable of supplying an abundance of everything the population needs and wants, then why should the rest of the population have to work for a living? If production cannot be maintained at a profit under such circumstances, then why should a profit be made? Does profit remain a useful standard of accounting in a propertyless society? Is full employment (in the usual sense of unemployment to the extent of 4 per cent of the labor force) any longer an attainable objective? Is the very concept of full employment outmoded? What takes the place of wages in a workless society?

I concur in Piel's view that these questions suggest the kind of overturn or displacement in the values of our society "which is already quaking the ground beneath our feet." He insists, and I agree, that "the virtues of hard work and profit are rooted in scarcity." They have no relevance to the economics or the sociology of abundance. Piel concludes: "Our society is probably closer to being propertyless than workless today. But the rate of technological progress is speeding up. It appears now to be moving faster than even the responsive and resilient American social order can evolve. Some of the changes may have to come in quantum jumps. For these we need economic and political leadership whose perception and judgment are not compromised in any fashion by commitments to the past." [16]

Indeed, we do need such leadership if the onrushing cybercultural revolution is not to result in unbelievably great population displacement. In Piel's felicitous words, "During the past several years, despite a steady rise in gross national product, unemploy-

ment has been rising. Each wavelet in the now well-dampened business cycle has left a larger number of workers high and dry on the
beach."

The discussion of the relation of such displacement to marginality can be relatively brief. For, if large-scale unemployment and
cultural confusion are virtually certain in the immediate future, it
is highly probable that the future also holds an enormous increase
in the number of people who will be thrown into a marginal position.

As here used, marginality refers to a group that is marginal to
the structure of political power and social prestige. Organized labor
in the United States has, until now, been so completely incorporated into the power and prestige structure that it was in no sense
marginal. It is now suggested that cybernation may well throw
both labor and other significant sectors of the population into a
marginal position. Indeed, the whole force of our earlier discussion of population displacement points up the virtual inevitability
of this outcome of cybernation. There is no need to restate the argument here. It is enough to say that, in increasing numbers and in
every sector of the labor force, people will find themselves "displaced" and "marginal" in the three respects therein discussed.
They will be marginal in that they will be unemployed, because
they are unnecessary to keep the productive machine going at full
speed. Worse still, they will be marginal in that they will be obso-
lescent, because machines can do the work better. And, worst of
all, they will be marginal in that they will be anachronistic and
alienated, because the values they have built into the very structure of their persons will not fit into the cultural scheme of a cybernated society.

Certainly, even in our relatively democratic society increasing
numbers of people and new elements in the population will be
found to be marginal to the political power structure. Michael's
discussion of what is happening to the decision-making process in
our rapidly cybernating society serves as an excellent illustration
of the trend toward political marginality. First, he points out that
both the information fed to computers and derived from them will
be "privileged information." It is a fair guess that both big business
and big government will make increasing use of computers. To

handle many of their major problems, "the data involved are so massive and the facts are so complex that only machines can handle the material fast enough to allow timely action based on understanding of the facts." But only a privileged elite will be in a position to understand and utilize this information. Most of us must resign ourselves to accepting decisions made for us by those presumed to be in the know. In such circumstances, Michael suggests, "There may be no easy way to insure that decisions based on computers will not become a threat to democratic government." It will be harder still to avoid thrusting great segments of the population into the limbo of political marginality and apathy which is surely a threat to democracy.

Again, Michael speaks of "the inevitability of ignorance" which will surely be a correlative consequence of a condition of "privileged information." Here he is arguing that it would not help much if competing political parties, other private organizations, or even the general public had free access to all such information. Most people would not be able to understand the information if it were available. Nor would they be capable of judging the relative validity of proposed policy decisions based on such information. Once again, we seem fated to put our destinies in the hands of an elite whose decisions we shall have to accept from our position on the sidelines of political activity.

Finally, Michael treats of the change in types of personnel and personalities likely to be brought about by "computerized" government and business. In both government and business "the shift has already begun toward recruiting top management from the cadre of engineering and laboratory administrators, for these are the people who understand the possibilities of and are sympathetic to computer-based thinking." It is suggested that "For reasons of personality as well as professional perspective, many operations researchers and systems analysts have great difficulty in coping with the more ambiguous and less 'logical' aspects of society. Their temperaments, training, and sympathies may not incline them to indulge the slow, ponderous, illogical, and emotional tendencies of democratic processes." In short, they tend to consider people as nuisances who get in their way. This could lead to the recruitment of authoritarian personalities for leadership in the decision-making elite of a cybernated society. Somewhat ominously, Michael concludes, "There is no necessary correlation between the desire to apply scientific logic to problems and the desire to apply democratic principles to daily, or even to professional scientific, life. ... In fact, the whole trend toward cybernation can be seen as an effort to remove the variabilities in man's on-the-job behavior and off-the-job needs, which, because of their non-statistical nature, complicate production and consumption. Somewhere along the line, the idea of the individual may be completely swallowed up in statistics. The planner and those he plans for may become divorced from one another, and the alienation of the individual from his government and individual from individual within the government may grow ever greater." [17] In the meantime, frustrating political marginality waxes as effective political participation wanes.

It is also highly likely that political marginality will be accompanied by drastic changes in the prestige system. Michael predicts: "There will be a small, almost separate, society of people in rapport with the advanced computers. These cyberneticians will have established a relationship with their machines that cannot be shared with the average man. ... Indeed, many scholars will not have the capacity to share their knowledge or feeling about this new man-machine relationship." [18]

In sum, there will be a highly trained elite in possession of the esoteric information which bestows power on those who control it. The rest of us will be expendable. As a power and prestige system it is all very reminiscent of the great slave economies of the past but with a very significant difference: slavery, too, has been cybernated, and mechanical slaves have displaced their earlier and less efficient human counterparts. Not the least of the problems of the "new elite" will be the need to decide what to do with the millions of surplus human beings who are no longer necessary to maintain them in power and in the luxury to which they have become accustomed so quickly.

One question remains to be examined: What are the probabilities that this marginal group may become the kind of socio-psychological seed-bed in which revolutionary behavior typically is nurtured? In other words, how does this group look when examined in terms of the hypothesis stated at the beginning of this discussion? Certainly it is a numerically significant group. Numerical significance is, of course, a relative condition and no attempt will be made here to give it exact meaning. In my unpublished study of the *Struggle for Independence in Latin America* it was suggested that the Creole marginal group constituted about 10 per cent of the population at the time of the revolution. Their opponents, the Gachupins who wielded power, formed about 2 per cent of the population. This obviously gave the Creole numerical significance in relation to the Gachupin power elite. It is relevant to remark in this connection that the evidence seems to support the hypothesis that a revolution is always a function of a struggle between the group in power and a challenging group located just below it in the power hierachy. Both groups are in the minority with reference to the total population and seek to use the majority or mass of the population as pawns in the conflict.

Some such situation seems to be shaping up today. If the estimates used by Piel and others are only fairly correct, a marginal group, already equal to approximately 20 to 25 per cent of the labor force, would seem to be assuming "numerical significance." Moreover, new elements are beginning to appear in the ranks of the unemployed: "The blue-collar worker and the relatively menial service worker will not be the only employment victims of cybernation . . . As cybernation moves into the areas now dominated by middle management in government and in business—and this move is already beginning—growing numbers of middle managers will find themselves displaced. . . . Middle management is the group in the society with the most intensive drive for success and status. . . . They stand to be deeply disturbed by the threat and fact of their replacement by machines. One wonders what the threat will do to the ambitions of those who will still be students and who, as followers of one of the pervasive American dreams, will have aspired to the role of middle manager 'on the way up.'" Not even teachers, doctors, lawyers, and scientists are exempt from the threat of cybernation. Examples could be multiplied of the fact that "Much of the work that now takes up the time of many professionals . . . could be done as well by machines." [19]

Meanwhile, management and labor are both characterized by an increasing centralization of power in the hands of a relatively few institutional behemoths, which are, in turn, controlled by a relatively few individuals. These giants of industry and labor are

already locked in a struggle for power which is likely to be intensified in the immediate future. In this struggle the rank and file on
both sides are rapidly being forced into a frustrating ineffectual
marginal position. In such circumstances—and in consequence of
the effort to avoid becoming mere pawns in the conflict—it is not
too difficult to imagine the consolidation of these diverse disaffected elements into the typical and numerically significant marginal group.

In the second place, this marginal group has and will for some
time retain tremendous economic power. Because of whatever set
of factors one may choose to enumerate, the United States has hit
upon an unparalleled system of mass production and mass consumption. We live in an economy of abundance and, until now,
have had the money to be "consumers of abundance." At least,
until now, we have been able so to distribute the rewards of production as to keep the system going—even though huge surpluses
piled up in full view of those without the purchasing power to
claim them. Moreover, whatever the weaknesses of the distribution system—and they are many—it is still true that blue-collar
workers, white-collar workers, middle management, and professionals have all become as accustomed to a claim to this abundance
as have the members of the financial and managerial elite. Thus,
for even the great mass of the consuming public this is not a time
for "rising expectations"; it is, rather, a time to protect and improve
upon their already-achieved "economic rights."

It seems highly probable that cybernation will threaten all this.
A situation appears to be developing in which the hitherto relatively successful distributive system is breaking down. People are
being displaced and disemployed at such a rate that the abundance
produced cannot be distributed and consumed unless it is given
away. That this is, for most people, still largely an "unanticipated"
consequence"—a "silent conquest"—of cybernation in no wise disposes of the fact. Gerald Piel and Howard Coughlin have both
summarized the situation in clear-cut terms. Piel puts it this way:

> No reasonably predictable rate of growth in the productive
> sectors of the economy seems equal to overtaking the current
> rate of technological disemployment. Every step of progress
> in automatic control reduces the capital investment as well as
> the employment per unit of output. As the cost of investment

goes down, the rate of technological progress must increase
and with it disemployment. Even an expanding economy must
employ progressively fewer workers in its productive sectors.
At some point the terminus of full investment will be reached;
even at the present level of opulence, the consumer economy
shows signs of surfeit. There is, of course, a vast untapped
market in the income groups at the bottom third of the economic pyramid. But how are their wants to be implemented
with purchasing power when that bottom third already counts
the disemployed among its members? [20]

Coughlin writes as follows:

... The problem of unemployment caused by automation cannot be separated from the overriding necessity of maintaining
broader economic growth. It is a truism to suggest that an
expanding economy can be achieved through monetary and
financial policies designed to broaden economic activity. This
is really another way of saying that there must be a higher
level of demand and the mass income necessary for essential
mass purchasing power.
... What we must begin to think about and in the most
immediate terms are socio-economic approaches in a democratically oriented industrial society.[21]

The failure to develop adequate approaches to the paradox of
an increasing supply and a decreasing capacity for demand has led
Coughlin to ask this question: "Are we approaching a point where
the unprecedented and even mounting productivity potential of
American industry will find itself without a mass market and will,
therefore, have to consider giving away free a large percentage of
its output?" Then he adds: "Why is American industry gearing
itself to a system of productivity which views man as obsolete and
redundant when his very obsolescence and redundancy excludes
him as a buyer of the output which American industry can now
create?"

A great deal depends on the answers to these questions. It must
be remembered, too, that Piel and Coughlin are writing about
projected future developments—projections which seem highly
probable. In the meantime, this group of potentially "obsolete" and
"redundant" people still perform important economic roles and
wield great economic power. It is hardly to be expected that its

membership will accept political, social, and economic marginality without resistance.

In the third place, the group we are considering surely qualifies as representative of the remaining characteristic: it is made up of "intellectually informed" people. This is an assertion that scarcely need be defended. Most of what has been said in the previous pages points up the fact that the ranks of this marginal group are not filled by unskilled labor alone. Quite the contrary. Not only are we witnessing displacement and disemployment on an unprecedented scale, we are also confronted with increasing numbers of unemployed people whose training and background give them every reason to believe they would never find themselves in economic discard. This, too, is unprecedented, save for the dark days of the Great Depression of the 1930's. We also need to remind ourselves that today's blue-collar worker is no longer an "uninformed" person. Even when measured in terms of formal education, the unskilled, semi-skilled, and skilled groups cannot be written off as an illiterate and uninformed mass of passive nonentities. Much has happened to lift the general level of information of the labor force. To this should be added the fact that the channels of information are much more adequate and open than they once were. The result is that all levels of the marginal group are aware of what is going on, alert to the threat to their economic future, and amenable to mobilization in defense of their own interests.

We are not there yet, but we are faced with the prospect of having millions of people trained for jobs which no longer exist and other millions for jobs which have been taken over by machines. We can fend off the full effects of cybernation for a time by such palliatives as unemployment insurance, retraining, a shorter work week, public works programs, "peace corps" programs, and by military expenditures to maintain the Cold War. Sooner or later, however, we shall be faced with the necessity to consider the basic question posed by cybernation and formulated by Howard Coughlin: Can we afford to have millions of educated men and women in a society which has no use for them? The facts of history suggest that the societies which thought they could afford the luxury of such a marginal group all paid for it with violent revolution.

Are we to conclude then, that the United States is faced with the prospect of violent revolution? Not necessarily. The course of human affairs is never a matter of inevitability but of probability.

It seems evident from what has been said here that, at the very least, the present and predicted effects of cybernation on our society are such as to arouse grave concern. Also, it can now be said that cybernation is working such changes in our social structure as to foster the emergence of the kind of marginal group which typically has served as the socio-psychological seed-bed in which revolutionary behavior is nurtured—a situation occurring for the first time since our own struggle for independence.

Surely the situation warrants Coughlin's prediction:

> If the price of automation is hard core unemployment, and we know from the thirties what hard core unemployment can do to character and a sense of psychic security, are we prepared to undergo such desperate individual crises in the name of— holy of holies—Progress? The Fat Boy in Pickwick Papers enjoyed himself by saying 'I wants to make your flesh creep.' Perhaps what we need today are fat boys who can break through the euphoria in which our technicians and labor statisticians live. There are no Luddites among us, nor even pro-Luddites, nor, I think, will there be any. But what I can predict is that the American worker, whether trade unionist or not, will reject the soothsaying platitudes of the 'sweet bye-and-bye' prophets who hold before us a golden future amidst a temporarily or 'short run' cruel present.[22]

That the seeds of revolutionary change have been planted is virtually beyond doubt. Just what seeds have been planted must await germination, sprouting and full bloom. And, whether they germinate at all depends upon their being nurtured by other necessary "ingredients" of revolutionary behavior which cannot claim our attention here.[23] The probabilities are great that revolutionary changes will occur. Whether they will result in a totalitarianism of the left or the right; or whether "a democratically orientated industrial society"—which would certainly also represent revolutionary changes in the present social structure—will develop remains to be seen. My own guess is that we shall move toward a militarized and cybernatized totalitarianism of the right. My fervent hope is that I am wrong and that we shall command the kind of "economic and political leadership whose perception and judgment are not compromised in any fashion by commitments to the past." Such leadership might make it possible for us to claim the benefits of both cybernation and a more democratic social structure. Such a leadership might usher in the era envisioned by Norbert Wiener in his book on *The Human Use Of Human Beings* —an era in which, for the first time, human beings would be freed to engage in "the highest-level intellectual creative work."

In any case, "The hour is very late and the choice of good and evil knocks at our door." [24]

NOTES:

1. For the theoretical context into which this hypothesis fits, see my paper on "The Revolutionary Process," *Social Forces*, March 1950.
2. Donald N. Michael, *Report on Cybernation: The Silent Conquest* (Santa Barbara, 1962), p. 46.
3. See his "What Automation Does," *New Society*, 1, May 23, 1963.
4. See her *Logic, Computing Machines and Automation* (Washington, D.C., 1963), pp. 371, 373.
5. Op. cit. p. 5.
6. "Consumers of Abundance." An Occasional Paper on the Role of the Economic Order in the Free Society (The Center for the Study of Democratic Institutions, Santa Barbara, 1961).
7. Despite the usual connotation of "displaced people" the term seems apt in the context of the present discussion. In very truth man is being displaced by machines.
8. See A. H. Raskin, "Hard-Core Unemployment: A Rising National Problem," *New York Times*, April 6, 1961, p. 18.
9. Op. cit. pp. 8-9.
10. In her personal communication dated 13 April 1963.
11. Op. cit. p. 6.
12. Op. cit. pp. 14-24.
13. Op. cit. p. 8.
14. Piel, op. cit. p. 6.
15. See Walter Lippmann, *Preface to Morals* (New York, 1929); and Joseph Wood Krutch, *The Modern Temper* (New York, 1931).
16. Op. cit. p. 10.
17. Op. cit. pp. 33-9.
18. Ibid. p. 44.
19. Michael, op. cit. pp. 18-19. For a very recent discussion of potential displacement on the professional level see the article by Louis Lasagna, M.D., on the use of computers in medicine; "Now Dr. Robot Enters the Scene," *New York Times Sunday Magazine*, June 16, 1963.

20. "The Illusion of Civil Defense," a pamphlet based on a talk at the Commonwealth Club, San Francisco, Nov. 10, 1961.
21. Op. cit. p. 8.
22. Op. cit. p. 8.
23. For a discussion of these factors see my "The Revolutionary Process," op. cit.
24. Norbert Wiener, as quoted by Alice Mary Hilton, op. cit. p. 368.

# 20

ELWIN H. POWELL

## Reform, Revolution, and Reaction: A Case of Organized Conflict

All institutions have their ultimate foundation in a shared commitment to a conceptual scheme or value system.[1] Without a minimal allegiance to its aims and rules no institution can operate; an institution is an authority structure. Power is a derivative of an institutional office, or "command post" as Mills puts it.[2] Power is a function of organization; the power of the chief flows from the allegiance of the tribe, from consensus. But when that consensus begins to dissolve—the condition of anomie—a struggle for power ensues which results in conflict. The locus and source of conflict are not in the individual but the process of institutional dislocation. As institutions lose a grip on their participants and their public, they become coercive, and coercion intensifies the antagonism of those already alienated from the system. Moreover, the condition of anomie invites exploitation—the extension of power by force. The process can be observed in the declining phase of ancient and medieval society; both personal and collective conflicts increase with the deterioration of consensus, the growth of anomie.[3]

Every functioning society is integrated by a nuclear institution; the history of the Middle Ages is the history of Catholicism, and the past 100 years of Western life can be written in terms of the transformation of the institution of capitalism. Between 1860 and

1900 the capitalist consensus reigned supreme, at least in America.[4] More than merely an economic system, capitalism was an ethos, a faith, a way of life. Capitalist theory and ideology provided the rationale for the political order as well as the organizing principle of industry; i.e. production for private profit. The capitalist was the hero of imaginative literature (the novels of William Dean Howells) and of popular culture (Horatio Alger). The virtues of hard work, thrift, and sobriety were preached and often practiced. Yet the very triumph of industrial capitalism brought in its wake a profusion of social problems—crime, pauperism, unemployment, and labor conflict—which verged on class war. Developments of the late nineteenth century followed rather closely the Marxian paradigm, for, while there may have been a minimum of class consciousness in America, there was no absence of class struggle.[5] A relentless drive for profits intensified exploitation and gave rise to riots and strikes which were suppressed by the police and military authority of the state, thus solidifying the workers into a labor movement.[6] The drive for profit produced a disastrous fluctuation of the business cycle, with periods of over-expansion and prosperity followed by bleak times of contraction and business failure. The system exhibited all the rational-irrationality of warfare. The industrialist was a "captain of industry," the workers were his unwilling troops, and his chief task was to discipline them. Initially industries fought each other, but by the late 1890's they had entered an unspoken truce and jointly fought the farmer, small business, labor, and the general public. The result was near-anarchy, a war of each against all.

There were three major responses to this "war": the conservative capitalist elite sought to perpetuate it, occasionally turning it into a national war (as in 1898 and 1917); the reformists (populists, progressives, trade-unionists) wanted to fight a limited war; the revolutionaries (anarcho-syndicalists IWW's, Socialists) sought to turn the Hobbesian war of each against all into a class war of some against others. The reform elements accepted capitalist ends but sought rules to restrict the power of monopolies and thus restore the free competition of the market place. This objective animated the "trust-busting" and regulative legislation of the period.[7] Similarly, trade unionism pursued capitalist goals of higher wages, shorter hours—the market philosophy of more for less—and rejected political objectives which would alter basic property relations.[8]

Numerically smaller but more influential than is often recognized today, the revolutionaries wanted to transform, not reform, society by building working-class solidarity as a means of abolishing the competitive profit system of capitalism. Between 1900 and 1920 the reform forces won certain battles—income and inheritance taxes, strengthening of anti-trust laws—but in the end lost the "war." In 1919 the Wilson Administration's plan to retain control over the railroad and to establish public ownership of communications was defeated, and in the same year the Supreme Court ruled that U.S. Steel did not constitute a trust. By 1921 the capitalist elite had been able to liquidate radicalism, roll back the tide of reform, and consolidate a new position of dominance—one that has not seriously been threatened since then.[9] But the capitalist elite could no longer justify itself in terms of the traditional capitalist ethic—rags to riches, every man a capitalist. Rather, it found its justification in the concept of Americanism. Americanism was implicitly identified with capitalism—the open-shop crusade of the 'twenties was known as the "American plan"—and became the accepted rationalization of capitalist power. This is not to suggest that an all-powerful elite forcibly imposed its will on a resistant public, nor that people enthusiastically embraced the new Americanism. Rather, the power of the capitalist class after World War I was so overwhelming as to deter the very thought of opposition. In 1919 the public was weary from the frustration and futility of reform and opted for the simple alternative of disengagement; it "returned to normalcy" with a vengeance (Harding was elected by the largest plurality on record). The people preferred the imagined certainties of the past to the confusing present and the problematic future.

The decisive "battles" of this "war" between the forces of reform, revolution, and reaction were fought out in the American city between 1910-20. While the outcome of the "war" is known already, a re-analysis of the campaign may throw light on the problems of conflict and conflict resolution. The present paper deals with some of the skirmishes which occurred in the city of Buffalo, where we can see in microcosm the forces which were shaking the whole urban industrial world.

The primary source of data for this study is the newspaper file. For the sociologist, concerned with the behavior of groups and collectivities, the newspaper is an indispensable source; it is as close to a living history as one is apt to find. The newspaper is not the product of a single mind but a collective creation, a daily record of the public life of the community. Newspapers, of course, reflect the ideology of their publishers, but the news is distorted more by selection than by deliberate falsification. Important events are sometimes ignored, but where there is a competing press that danger is diminished. The decade of 1910-20, before the syndicated column, radio, TV, and the national newspaper chain, was in some ways the great day of American journalism. At that time Buffalo had six dailies (as opposed to two today), thirteen major weeklies —four in German, one Polish, one Italian—and a German and a Polish daily. Of the six dailies, the *Express* is the most reliable and substantial; in its prime it was regarded as the *New York Times* of Buffalo. Politically the daily press ranged from center to far right (*The Commercial*). The Democratic papers were mildly reformist; the Republican papers were more conservative. While none of the papers were pro-labor, they differed in their hostility to unionism; *The Commercial* equated the closed shop with Bolshevism; the others were more temperate. The Catholic press was strongly anti-socialist but mildly, and occasionally, vigorously pro-labor. Little remains of the Socialist press. The *Arbeiter-Zeitung* had a long history in the community and early connections with the de Leonite Socialist Labor Party. It seemingly flourished between 1912 and 1916, when circulation increased from 2750 to 7500, but ceased publication during the war. Copies of the *Buffalo Socialist* between 1912-14 have been preserved; although the paper continued until 1919 under the name of *New Age*, no copies of it are available now. On major issues the press follows the current of opinion of the whole nation, with the Republican papers acting as the local pacesetters and the Democratic ones following suit. Generally the opinion of the *Express* became in time the opinion of Buffalo.

With a population of a half million, Buffalo had a social life and political climate in the decade of World War I that was typical of the American city of the industrial heartland, differing in detail but not in contour from Cleveland, Pittsburgh, Detroit, or Chicago.[10] Toward the close of the century the city was dominated by a capitalist elite, described by John T. Horton as "the noblemen of America," with both the trappings and the substance of power:

> ... the power of the community in commerce and industry was concentrated in the banks. The men who wielded that power thought of themselves as capitalists and referred to themselves as such with conscious pride. Their pride was justifiable. They belonged to a class that had made itself the dominant power in the country, turning by force of intelligence and character the greatest battles of the century to its advantage. This class had supplanted the Southern aristocracy and had made the United States, on the whole, submissive to its will ... In their economic affairs they were anxious lest they leave any stone unturned in their attempt to strengthen and extend [their power] ... In their political affairs these fresh and zestful capitalists were as alert and vigilant as in their economic concerns.[11]

Some index of the capitalist command of political life in Buffalo is indicated by the voting record of the city—and the vote is always only the tenth of the iceberg above the surface. Although 60 per cent of the city were blue-collar workers, with another 20 per cent in the lower white-collar ranks, Buffalo voted Republican in every national election between 1892 and 1932, except 1912 when the Taft-Roosevelt split gave a plurality to Wilson. In 1896, McKinley, the forthright spokesman of the capitalist class, defeated the great commoner Bryan by a handy 2 to 1. The rising democratic vote as the twentieth century progressed indicates the growing spirit of reform, yet the ideology of the two parties was essentially similar. Eugene Debs said in a Buffalo speech in 1908, "The Republicans want the capitalist system as it is; the Democrats want the capitalist system as it was."[12] Debs said the choice was between: "Wall Street and Taft/Or Tammany and Graft."

While Debs' own showing in 1908 was not impressive, it represented a gain over 1904, and in the next four years the Socialist vote increased fourfold both locally and nationally. In 1912 Debs drew a larger crowd (9000) in Buffalo than did any of the other candidates, and some of his more ardent supporters were actually surprised when he did not win the Presidency. Moreover, the Socialist vote was a party vote and in Buffalo Charles E. Russell, candidate for governor, ran slightly ahead of Debs (4457 to 4207).

"After the election," says one student of the subject, "there was not the usual fading of interest." [13] The party was beginning to take root in the community, and by 1913 had 17 locals, a central office, and a biweekly newspaper, and had begun construction on a socialist school and a labor lyceum.

The strength and influence of the Socialist movement cannot be assessed by the vote. Their numbers were small, but they had a revolutionary elan which gathered momentum between 1912-14, a spirit personified in Debs: "We ask no quarter, and we grant none; we ask for no compromise and become stronger with each defeat." [14] Although the local Socialists were less articulate, they were equally defiant. "A good thing about your work for the socialist movement," the *Buffalo Socialist* told its imaginary capitalist readers, "is that every time you fire a man you make him hate the system—the capitalist system—you make him class conscious." [15] To the conservative trade unionist it said: "Talk of a living wage is tommyrot. If you were not getting a living wage now, you'd be dead. The Chinese get a living wage. The socialist wants you to get all you produce, and you're entitled to it." [16] In its rhetoric, at least, the Socialist party repudiated the whole society, demanding not only better wages and working conditions but: "the emancipation of the whole people through the abolition of the profit system and the substitution of the Socialist commonwealth. . . . The main purpose of the Socialist Party is to fight the battle of labor against grasping capitalists and employers—to put human life above the sordid scramble for dollars. And its ultimate aim is to substitute a sane system of cooperative production, democratically administered, for the present planless system which enriches the idle few at the expense of the great multitude who produce all the wealth of the world." [17]

The respectable community alternatively ignored and ridiculed the Socialists, but one eminent Buffalonian wrote in *Harpers* in 1911: "Socialism is a movement of such a nature . . . as seems likely to break suddenly, someday into avalanches and floods." [18]

To alert Buffalonians 1913 must have seemed the beginning of the flood-tide. As a year of labor unrest it is comparable only to 1877, 1892, and 1919. MacTeggart's thorough study of Buffalo labor history indicates that there was an average of less than two strikes a year between 1824 and 1917. In 1913, thirteen major strikes were recorded, the most notable of which involved 1700 street railway workers and 2300 national guardsmen. The strike was initially organized by the man who was editor of the *Buffalo Socialist* (and also vice-president of the Proleterian Club).[19] Maximum wages of street-car workers amounted to 28 cents an hour for a man of nine years' service, and some employees worked as many as eighteen hours a day for $1.80. When the strike was called, the company imported 500 strike-breakers from Chicago and Philadelphia, and the local police force was increased by 250 uniformed men. Still unable to establish car service, the company pressed city officials to call out the national guard. Both the sheriff and the mayor refused, but a local judge was prevailed upon to sign the order activating the guard. No strike before had so directly affected the total population of the city. The public reaction was a mixture of alarm and delight—which did not necessarily follow class lines. The excitement was a welcome relief from the tedium of daily life. "All Buffalo flocked to Main Street in hope of excitement," wrote the *Express*.

> The crowds were as dense as appeared on election nights in the days before voting machines . . . a moving mass of people . . . one double procession of automobiles. Trucks were fitted with seats offering joy rides for ten cents . . . A trip of a patrol wagon would attract a following of easily a 1000 men and boys screaming and yelling . . . The surging crowds poured through the side streets making the night hideous with their noise.
>
> The crowd was made up largely of the idly curious out to see rather than to take part in whatever trouble occurred. Fathers and mothers regardless of their own or their children's safety brought them out in baby buggies or toted them along by hand . . . dozens of young hoodlums passed insulting remarks and acted in a way which ought to have been sufficient to drive decent people off the streets . . . The young girls were out in force also, chattering and giggling.[20]

But the next day rioting took a more serious turn; "revolver shots were exchanged between the police and the mobs . . . the police chief's car was the target of a fusillade of bullets, though no one in the machine was hit."[21] The following day, the entire 4th National Guard brigade—2300 men—policed the city, but their efforts,

said the *Express*, "were met with jeers ... Troops with fixed bay-
onets held no terrors for the disorderly elements." Finally, more in
exasperation than malice, the troops fired on the mobs; the *Express*
describes the scene:

> "Fire!" came the command. A dozen rifles cracked. The
> crowd scattered and a woman came reeling down the bank.
> There was another spit of bullets from the other side of the
> bridge, and a boy got one of them in the arm. The crowd
> thronged to the area. The soldiers followed with fixed bay-
> onets and drove the throng back to the curb. More than one
> felt the butt of a rifle against his ribs ... and one received a
> bayonet thrust in the hand." [22]

No fatalities resulted, but the firing on the crowd tilted public
opinion to the side of the strikers, after it had become apparent
that neither the police, the military, nor the strike-breakers could
operate the lines. Even the *Express* demanded that the company
cede to the strikers' demands, which had been reduced to the issue
of union recognition:

> ... a question of union recognition is a minor matter. If the
> strikers as their leaders say, are willing to go back to work
> provided the union is recognized, then the company has no
> right to deprive the city of safe transportation ... The business
> of this company is to furnish transportation, not to fight a
> sociological question.[23]

In the meantime, the Socialists had been eased out of the strike
leadership and the conservative A.F.L. element was recognized; the
situation returned to normal, without pay increases. Under the
caption, "Wicked Loss to Business," the *Express* of April 12 totaled
up the cost of the strike:

| | |
|---|---|
| Total cost of troops (paid by county) | $40,000 |
| Fares—15,000 a day | 90,000 |
| Damage to cars | 10,000 |
| 1,000 Strike-breakers at $2.50 a day | 28,800 |
| Wages | 25,000 |

During the remainder of 1913, twelve other strikes occurred—car
workers of the railroad, the street-car laborers, the store clerks, delivery drivers, teamsters, truck drivers, icemen, railway express

men, machinists, taxi-drivers, baggage helpers, plus an abortive strike of school children.[24]

The years 1913 and 1914 brought unrest and unemployment throughout the country; in Buffalo vagrancy arrests rose from 969 in 1910 to 1931 in 1914; in this period the total number of arrests increased by 50 per cent, as Table I indicates. Although it is difficult to generalize about trends in crime, Table I parallels rather

TABLE I

MALE ARRESTS IN BUFFALO, 1910-1921 *

| Year | Total Arrests | Va-grancy | Mur-der | Dis-orderly Con-duct | As-sault | Drunk-enness | Bur-glary | Grand Lar-ceny |
|------|------|------|------|------|------|------|------|------|
| 1910 | 20,130 | 969 | 7 | 3,638 | 919 | 8,960 | 299 | 398 |
| 1911 | 22,181 | 1,081 | 7 | 3,696 | 962 | 8,957 | 306 | 428 |
| 1912 | 24,532 | 1,333 | 12 | 2,911 | 1,058 | 11,330 | 334 | 469 |
| 1913 | 25,790 | 1,104 | 8 | 2,984 | 1,379 | 11,214 | 312 | 431 |
| 1914 | 30,686 | 1,931 | 5 | 2,354 | 1,502 | 13,713 | 407 | 307 |
| 1915 | 28,643 | 1,661 | 8 | 3,779 | 1,451 | 10,772 | 358 | 450 |
| 1916 | 32,586 | 1,450 | 15 | 4,028 | 1,639 | 13,910 | 280 | 443 |
| 1917 | 32,901 | 1,598 | 21 | 4,274 | 1,685 | 14,205 | 380 | 658 |
| 1918 | 33,067 | 1,196 | 25 | 4,444 | 1,523 | 13,315 | 469 | 636 |
| 1919 | 28,314 | 1,664 | 18 | 4,498 | 1,348 | 8,853 | 384 | 564 |
| 1920 | 22,214 | 1,247 | 17 | 1,160 | 1,373 | 7,334 | 331 | 670 |
| 1921 | 23,269 | 2,426 | 22 | 842 | 1,640 | 8,655 | 345 | 614 |

* Data from Annual Reports of Buffalo Police Dept. for years cited. The population of the city was 423,715 in 1910, 506,775 in 1921.

closely the pattern which Arthur Wood found for Detroit.[25] Arrests reached a high point in 1917 and 1918, but the upward climb had begun earlier.

With the outbreak of World War I, the economic picture improved almost instantaneously. "The war had been in progress only one week," writes Irma Dickman, "when Buffalo producers began making extensive preparation for a boom in the export field. ... Steel was soon operating at or above capacity and more grain passed through the port than ever before in history." [26] All of the daily papers except the *Times* (published by a Bryan-Democrat) were united in their support for loans to belligerents. "The prop-

osition is essentially simple," said the *Express*, "the question for us
to decide is whether we would rather refuse credits and go without the trade or grant credits and keep the trade. We cannot refuse credits and keep the trade." The loans were justified by the
local press because "business, not politics" was behind them. "The
question of which Europeans benefit... is of little interest to
Americans compared with the fact that it will be a great benefit to
the United States." [27] Economically the war could not have come at
a more opportune moment. Up to the time of U. S. entry (April
1917) $1,500 million had been loaned to the Allies and $27 million
to the Central Powers, which amounts were spent in the United
States. In the last year of neutrality, exports, for the country as
a whole, jumped from $2,500 million to $4,300 million. By 1916
there was "a continuous and extraordinary prosperity." [28]

From the outbreak of hostilities the press, first subtly and then
overtly, promoted the idea of U. S. intervention, but the public
was slow to respond. On August 4, 1914, the *Express* called for
increasing national strength to full war-time levels. On the other
hand the local Socialists were holding peace meetings six months
before that date, and in mid-August 1914 protested the war at an
open-air meeting, where "3,000 people listened with interest but
displayed no great enthusiasm." [29] Toward both war and peace the
public was apathetic. "It never entered into discussion," writes the
local historian Daniel Sweeny, "not even into our thoughts, that
we had need to take sides in such a conflict. The announcement
by the umpire... at the Ferry Street ball park occasioned about
the same relative interest as the telegraph dispatches from French
and Belgium battlefields." [30] The local press ignored the subject
entirely, and "the mayor's [annual] message of 1915 contained
no mention of the war or its local effects. His communication of
1916 was likewise barren of war reference." [31] The people "went
their war-listless way," says Sweeny, but:

> On November 3, 1915 Joseph Choate, former American am-
> bassador to England held a meeting at the Bankers Club in
> New York City. Every American city was invited to participate
> through its mayor.... Addressing the meeting the mayor of
> Buffalo said, 'Buffalo... is solidly in favor of the great enter-
> prise which inspires our coming together... 450,000 of us
> stoutly favor every reasonable effort looking to national pre-

paredness . . .' While neither the mayor's speech nor the occasion for it attracted any great amount of attention here at
home . . . the mayor did not delay putting the city in entire
accord with the plans of the *National Security League*.[32]

The main function of the National Security League, composed
locally of men of high status from different segments of the community, was to promote sentiment for military preparedness. The
pomp and drama of the preparedness parades and rallies delighted
the populace, but, as Sweeny reflects sadly; "the interest was
largely recreational . . . opinion was divided on the question of
whether the trouble might reasonably be expected with England or
Germany." [33] In one such demonstration the Buffalo *Courier* could
detect "the vibrant spirit of American nationalism." [34] On the other
hand the *Express* later wondered: "With all the popular enthusiasm for preparedness it is strange that membership in the local
regiments of the national guard should have fallen off to an extent
which threatens the disbandment of these organizations." [35] While
the press and powerful voices in the national elite were urging
a belligerent policy,[36] it was clearly the peace issue which elected
Wilson in 1916 by the narrowest vote of any President prior to
Kennedy. When local troops returned from Mexican border duty in
March 1917, patriotic fervor was at such a low ebb that the *News*
was moved to ask: "Are we decadent . . . indifferent to everything
save personal business pursuits?" [37]

Patriotism increased after the declaration of war but was still
insufficient to inspire much volunteering for active service, and
so conscription was undertaken. Although the Socialist party lost
some of its top leadership in the split over the war, its electoral
strength increased. In 1917 Morris Hillquit came close to winning
the mayoralty of New York City, and in Buffalo the Socialist candidate for mayor in the primary polled 14,200 as opposed to
14,400 for the Republican and 17,000 for the Democratic candidates. (The Republican won in the run-off as a result of Socialist
support.) In Rochester the Socialists won a half-dozen city and
county offices. The high vote was attributed to the anti-war sentiment.[38]

For those on the home front in Buffalo World War I meant a
maximum of prosperity with a minimum of hardship. About 20,000

residents served in the armed forces, of whom about 951 were either killed or died of disease. The war had an integrating effect: "There was no east side, south side, west side or north side—only Buffalo," says one historian, "Personal affairs were secondary. Buffalonians will never forget the stirring, inspiring, self-sacrificing days of 1917-1918." [39] Profits and wages were equally inspiring, as Table II indicates.

TABLE II

MANUFACTURING IN BUFFALO, 1909-1919 [*]

| Year | No. of Establish- ments | Average No. of Wage Earners | Value of Products | Wages |
|------|------|------|------|------|
| 1909 | 1,753 | 51,412 | 218,808,000 | 28,727,000 |
| 1914 | 2,225 | 54,416 | 247,516,000 | 34,818,000 |
| 1919 | 2,093 | 75,899 | 634,410,000 | 95,702,000 |

[*] Data from 14th *Census of U.S.: Manufacturers*, vol. VII, 1919 (Washington: Government Printing Office, 1923), p. 232.

In July 1917, the official publication of the Chamber of Commerce observed: "Gargantuan as the task of subduing the arrogant autocracy has proven to be, nevertheless it appears to be progressing satisfactorily," and it added as an afterthought, "The slogan 'business as usual' has been expanded to 'better business than usual.'" [40]

But as the year wore on there was a mounting and diffuse anxiety. "German spies and plotters," says Sweeny, "were thick in all sections of the country." [41] Even before war was declared, the Chamber of Commerce and the city council had urged the mayor to call up troops to guard the water works. The mayor refused, but he organized a volunteer police brigade "purely for the patriotic purpose of serving their city in the case of riots or uprisings . . . After daily toil in the banks, offices and in shops (says Sweeny) the police reserve patrolled the streets . . . and many meritorious arrests were made by the members." [42] There seemed to be an urgent need for those on the home front to participate more directly in the war effort. The liberty-loan campaign and the home-defense brigades partially filled this need; in addition there was spy-hunting. "Do not wait until you catch someone putting a bomb under a factory," advised *Live Wire;* "Report the man who spreads pessimistic stories . . . cries for peace or belittles our efforts to win the war. Send the names of such persons . . . to the Department of Justice . . . The fact that you made the report will not be made public. You are in contact with the enemy today, just as truly as if you faced him across No Man's Land." [43] Sweeny notes, however, that "Buffalo, happily, escaped the stain of any great amount of disloyalty among its citizens . . . German propaganda took the form of interpreting the war as a capitalist war and fought to foment resistance to the draft. That was effectively and vigorously suppressed." [44]

By an easy transmutation the "radical" replaced the "Hun" as the primary enemy. In fact, as early as September 1917 the *Live Wire* warned: "The I. W. W. is an element more dangerous to the peace and prosperity of the United States than is Germany and her allies." The category of radical initially included the IWW's and the anarchists, but later were added all those who opposed the war—including pacifists and conscientious objectors. Locally the IWW had no organization, and apparently the Socialists were too numerous to molest, though technically they were liable for arrest under the Espionage Act. However, for fear of alienating the radical vote the press was almost civil in its discussions of socialism. The *Express* made an unheard-of concession: "We are all more or less socialists nowadays. Some of us call our socialism by the name of State Regulation or Municipal Ownership or Organized Benevolence. But it is socialism pure and simple as distinguished from the individualism of Herbert Spencer." [45]

1918 began calmly enough, with the sage advice from the Chamber of Commerce that "if we could attain sanity in all things, there would be no more difficulties." [46] But when peace broke out, hysteria rose. On November 14, 1918, the *Express* carried a banner headline: BOLSHEVISM THREATENS ALL EUROPE . . . On December 8th the headlines read: UNEMPLOYMENT GREATEST DANGER TO THE NATION NOW . . . "and it will come with attendant misery at a time when anarchistic tendencies are contagious."

Despite its opposition to the war—perhaps because of it—the Socialist party, locally and nationally, was stronger at the beginning of 1919 than at any time before or since. The number of registered Socialists in Buffalo increased from 2000 in 1916 to 5000 in 1919, and the party could muster a vote of around 15,000, between 10 and 15 per cent of the electorate. It was not the actual size but the potentiality for growth, both nationally and locally, which most disturbed the conservative elements. Socialist rallies, speeches, even party feuds, were given good press coverage, and the *Express* noted that "the party's last [1918] labor day picnic had had 10,000 in attendance." [47] Although the *Express* was mainly interested in fighting European Bolshevism, it was not happy about the domestic radical scene: "The idea that anybody could really entertain such a project as an armed insurrection to overthrow the republic of the United States—the best government on earth—impresses most Americans as so absurd as to be worth only a derisive laugh. . . . There is not going to be a revolution in the United States. There is not going to be a reign of terror. But there may be some forcible demands for those who do not like the United States to get out and stay out." [48] The demands were not long in coming.

Unrest continued throughout the year, and in September 1919 more than 365,000 steel workers struck, in what was billed as an attempt to Bolshevize the steel industry.[49] Buffalo was a steel city, and in the fall of 1919 radicalism was in the air. The Socialists held nightly street-corner meetings, as did the Minute Men, whose objective was to counteract Bolshevik propaganda, and even the Communists were able to get 400 votes in the municipal primary election.[50] Buffalo was then governed by four city commissioners and a mayor, and the election of 1919 to select three commissioners was fought on the issue of socialism. To the surprise of everyone (including the Socialists) the Socialist candidate polled the high vote of 47,000, followed by the Republican party candidate with 42,000 and an independent Republican with 39,000.[51] The election so alarmed a leading banker that he cancelled a $14,000,000 offer to buy the controlling interest in the street railway company—although the press took the election with equanimity after the initial shock wore off. The *Express* excused its own complicity in the election of a Socialist:

> The conservatives will blame the newspapers for not conducting a campaign of silence. The conservatives ought to have taken warning after the primaries, realized that Perkins [the

socialist] was a dangerous opponent, and gone vigorously to work to bring out the vote against him ... The newspapers are potent at times but not omnipotent. In fact there are well authenticated instances of candidates with every newspaper in town against them ... winning. You can't kill a man by ignoring him. But responsibility has cooled many a hot-head. May that be true of Perkins.[52]

Locally the "counter-revolution" was gathering momentum, and the concept of dangerous radicalism was expanding to include not only the anarcho-syndicalists but the Communists and Socialists— and those with "tendencies" in that direction. On November 21 the *Commercial* warned: "Outraged Patriotism to Rise Up in Righteous Wrath to Crush Foul Plot against Nation." On December 30 the headquarters of the Communist party was raided by the State Lusk Committee, and twenty men and two women were arrested. The *Express* thought:

> The raid will probably have considerable effect on the self-deceived, both those who are in the Communist party and the larger number who are on the outside looking in. Radicals for fun and particularly parlor Bolsheviks may examine a little more closely the actual location of the deadline which may not be overstepped with prudence by those who wish to retain a standing as Americans ... The arrest of local radicals conveys a warning which goes considerably beyond the limits of their party membership.[53]

Two days later, the nation-wide Palmer raid on the radicals resulted in the arrest of 136 in Buffalo. The city was not displeased with its showing, which compared favorably with 300 each for New York and Detroit, 120 each for Philadelphia and Chicago. (The poor showing of Chicago, capital of American radicalism, was due to the fact that the county sheriff, jealous of federal authorities, made a pre-emptive raid which sent the radicals into hiding.) The Justice Department issued warrants for 250 in Buffalo but only 105 were finally served.

Sociologically one of the more interesting features of the raid was the extent of citizen participation in it. "More than 200 policemen," noted the *Commercial*, "were aided by as many citizens, members of civic organizations such as the Chamber of Commerce, Rotary and Kiwanis and other clubs." [54] The information for the raid was supplied:

> ... by a secret committee of citizens which has been working day and night since last spring ... Just how powerful this organization may be is shown by the fact that all of the evidence (for both the Lusk and Palmer raids) was furnished by the committee ... All the photographic copies of membership cards, which so astounded the alleged members of the Communist party ... were secured by the committee ... For the raids on Friday, 221 names were submitted to the government by the committee ... and of these 80 or 90 were finally brought in. It was brought out that the citizens committee had had paid investigators keeping track of alleged radical activities here. Members of the committee and these investigators got memberships in the Communist party and got in at meetings, securing names and other information for the raid on the branch of the Union of Russian workers here in November was secured through the citizens committee. How much money was contributed to the investigation is not known ... but $25,000 has been subscribed by Buffalo men for the purpose of investigating the local radical press. [55]

On January 5th the *Enquirer* printed a list of 125 of the citizens who took part in the raid. By tracing out the names in various source books, we found that this group was predominantly upper class. Seventy-two per cent of the names appeared in *Dau's Blue Book*, which describes itself as "a compilation of the most prominent householders." [56] The *Social Register* listed 24.8 per cent of the names; 52 per cent of those appearing in the Blue Book were listed as members of the Chamber of Commerce; 45 per cent were members of the leading men's club. The *City Directory* revealed that approximately 70 to 80 per cent of the "raiders" were officials of manufacturing corporations. Of the eight men singled out by the *Express* as the organizers of the raid and given special commendation by the federal authorities, one was a former president of the Chamber of Commerce and general production manager of a radiator manufacturing concern, two were officials of a forge company, two were stockbrokers, another in manufacturing, and one a member of the school board and the business manager of the *Commercial*. [57]

In retrospect the raids could have been an episode in the Keystone cops comedy. "One hundred automobiles were assembled in the center of the city at 4 p.m.," writes the *Enquirer*, "and started on a dash of red hunting which radiated throughout Buffalo and the surrounding towns":

> Drivers were supplied with copies of federal warrants and while the police officer watched the prisoner the organization member searched his home for radical literature and explosives. In one man's room was found a shot gun and other weapons . . . along with some 1914 Russian war bonds. In another apartment was found a picture of Leon Trotsky and some I. W. W. papers . . . in still another a picture of the local socialist lawyer . . . A detective came to the station with arms filled with alleged radical literature but the publications were all in Polish and he was unable to make any translations. . . . The jail was crowded with 205 radicals—greatest number of prisoners in years said the jailor . . . The chief of police looked them over and said: 'A fine looking bunch they are. It's too bad we can't line them up against the wall there and shoot them.' [58]

Yet the raids were deadly serious. Throughout the country some 10,000 radicals were jailed; *The Nation* called it "an unprecedented outburst of terror and terrorism." [59] While the Red Scare came to its dramatic climax between November 1919 and March 1920, it did not begin or end then.[60] Anti-radicalism became institutionalized, a kind of permanent counter-revolution built into the legal system in the form of criminal syndicalism laws, into the investigative and police apparatus of federal, state, and local governments, and into the voluntary organizations of the business class.[61] The Red Scare terminated a decade of class conflict and ushered in a time of repression and apathy.

The period of 1910-20 was a decade of conflict, the climax having germinated for thirty years. Analogous developments occurred throughout the urban world: Buffalo was only the mirror of a larger culture. Rarely has a decade of American life been so riddled with strike and dissension. Arrests for violent personal crimes in Buffalo and seemingly throughout the nation began to rise around 1906, reached a peak in 1918, and then receded to 1940.[62] The suicide rate for the nation reached its high point for the twen-

tieth century in 1913.[63] Crime and suicide are individual manifestations of a collective discord—of anomie—and signify an unconscious repudiation of existing society. In the political sphere the
"repudiation" became articulate as an organized attack on the institutions of capitalism, an incipient class war.

In the years between 1866 and 1890 the authority of capitalism
was virtually unchallenged if not unquestioned. But from the early
1890's to 1914 there was restless agitation for some kind of limitation on the power of the capitalist class. Yet, even during the epoch
of trust-busting the concentration of capital continued unabated.[64]
The public image of big business may have been soiled by ten
years of muckraking, but its power was not seriously threatened
by the reformers.

Yet by 1910 the "ruling class," or power elite, was immobilized by
the inner paralysis of the capitalist system. External and legal restraint on capitalist power could be circumvented easily enough.
But the business class was as powerless as anyone else when confronted with the business cycle. Big business had full access to
coercive powers—the police and military were available as strike-
breakers, for instance. But force could not create jobs, nor run industry, nor win elections. Coercion was useless against labor and
tended to solidify rather than destroy the union movement. The
elite could, for a time, inhibit but it could not initiate action.

Between 1912-14 the crisis of capitalism deepened. In the years
between 1902-06 the growth rate of the total economy was 7.6 per
cent, while it declined to 4.6 between 1910 and 1913, and in the latter year both the production and consumption of goods dropped
sharply.[65] Unemployment and crime increased, locally and nationally (see Table I above). Throughout the country strikes flared in
bitter violence (Paterson, Lawrence, Ludlow), and took an alarm-
ingly political coloration. The problem was deeper than a worsening of "existential conditions." Actually wages increased slightly
between 1911 and 1915, while unemployment was a customary
feature of working-class life. It was the "definition of the situation"
rather than the objective reality which had changed. Years of reform and revolutionary agitation had altered expectations. Men
no longer bore their lot as "fate," and what had once been endured
as sacrifice came to be seen as exploitation. In the 1890's economic
collapse was no real threat to established society, because there

was no formulated alternative to capitalism. By 1912 there was not only a vigorous radical movement—international in scope—with a new model for the organization of society but a significant defection of the intellectuals. "No one, unafflicted with invincible ignorance," wrote Walter Lippmann in July 1914, "desires to preserve our economic system in its existing form." The battle for us, Lippmann continued, "does not lie against crusted prejudice but against the chaos of the new freedom." [66] Two weeks later, the outbreak of World War I put an end to the chaos.

The war in Europe brought instant prosperity to America, creating an immediate and inexhaustible market for agriculture and manufacturing. For the upper class the war was not only an economic venture but an opportunity to reassert its "rightful" leadership of the community. The war opened up a sphere of action and power to compensate for the paralysis of the upper class in the realm of politics and economics.

A sizable and organized minority actively opposed the war, and the high Socialist vote in 1917 (25 per cent of the electorate in most cities) pointed to a significant anti-war sentiment.[67] The popularity of the war sprang from prosperity rather than patriotism; for the majority it was more a spectator sport than a historic mission. But the sense of drift was ended, and progressives took solace in the belief that the war was "administering the *coup de grace* to the old capitalism." [68] In actuality the war restored the old capitalism. Wilson's timid experimentations with social and economic planning were scuttled in early 1919.

By 1919 the business class was in clear if insecure ascendancy after a twenty-year retreat. But its new position of dominance had yet to be ratified by public consensus. Moreover, corporate capitalism was threatened internationally by the spread of Bolshevism and the designs of the League of Nations; domestically by the return of the pre-war chaos, unemployment, the high cost of living, the increased power of labor (resulting from war gains) and the indefinable threat of radicalism.

The fear of radicalism seemed to have had some objective basis. The electoral strength of the Socialist party had grown during the war years, and the Socialists had made headway in the labor movement.[69] Even within the conservative A.F.L. the Socialists could muster 33 to 45 per cent of the votes and several times came close to deposing Gompers. More ominous still was the 1919 steel strike, masterminded by William Z. Foster and the left Socialists who came to constitute the Communist party. Significantly, Catholic labor—at least in Buffalo—also took credit for the strike.

The specter of Bolshevism only provided the pretext for a campaign which had been underway—and underground—for several years.[70] As early as 1916-17 the IWW's were "the victims of a determined conservative campaign to stamp out radical social and economic ideas . . . a drive with all the earmarks of class war." [71] The liquidation of the IWW was accomplished by the simple expedient of the systematic removal of its leadership by imprisonment. Next to go were the left Socialists, with the imprisonment of Debs and the top leadership of the party for opposition to World War I. Next were the right-wing social democrats—the expulsion of five legally elected assemblymen from the New York legislature and of Victor Berger from Congress. To contend that the Socialist party would have been tolerated had it supported the war, or had it not, in its enthusiasm for the Russian Revolution gone too far to the left, is to misread the facts. Gompers' A.F.L. supported the war and never missed an occasion for patriotic proclamations, yet was as badly mauled as the Socialist party. According to Robert K. Murray, the A.F.L. lost one-third of its membership between 1920-23 as a direct result of the Red Scare, "a staggering loss not recouped until after the crash of 1929." [72] After labor came the liberals, who were not imprisoned but intimidated; writes Arthur M. Schlesinger, Jr., "if but few had actual indictments hanging over them, all felt a sentence suspended over their enthusiasms, their beliefs, their innermost thoughts." [73]

The Red Scare was both a source and a symbol of the restoration of capitalist power; it marked the end of the organized opposition to the corporate order. The reform movement was bankrupt before the 1919 hysteria, its social basis eroded by the decline of the "old" middle class. Progressivism was a rebellion of the local merchant class against the translocal corporation. But by 1920 even retailing was coming under corporate control through the formation of chain stores, and manufacturing was concentrated in a few giant cartels. In Buffalo between 1913 and 1919 the value of manufactured products increased threefold but the number of manufacturing establishments declined (see Table II above). The old

middle class was consigned to second place in the power structure. Although the number of wage workers increased sharply
during the war, the trade union movement was no match for organized capital. The A.F.L. had never been an opponent of capitalism and in fact prided itself on being the main bulwark
against socialism. But in 1919 big business was in no mood for
accommodation and launched its aggressive open-shop campaign
—"the American Plan"—which nullified labor's wartime gains.[74]
While the forces of reform were on the wane, the revolutionary
movement was simply obliterated in the 1920's. The Socialist vote
for Debs in 1920 was 902,000, but in 1928 Norman Thomas polled
only 268,000, and the Communist vote for Foster amounted to only
48,000.[75] The decline of the Socialist movement was due to a variety of factors: direct suppression, dissension and distrust over the
issue of patriotism, and the business prosperity of the 'twenties.
While unemployment remained high (10 to 15 per cent of the labor
force) and agriculture was depressed, the dominant minority pros-
pered and was able to suffuse the 'twenties with a mood of
optimism which contrasted sharply with the discontent of the
progressive era. Alan Valentine speaks of the year 1913 as "a preface to the Age of Anxiety as well as a postlude to the Age of Complacency." [76] The sequence could almost be reversed. The decade
of 1920's was the  most complacent on record. Both major parties
regressed to the ideological infantilism of pure *laissez faire*. Between 1900 and 1920 progressive Republicans and liberal Democrats alike advocated some form of governmental regulation of the
economic process. In the 'twenties political  leaders simply closed
their eyes to the contradictions of industrial capitalism, and thus
sowed the disastrous results reaped by the 1930's.

In 1920 corporate capitalism was unopposed but still unsup-
ported; it had power but needed a principle to legitimate its rule.
"Power is a fact," writes A. A. Berle, "but it is also a fact that the
human mind apparently cannot be wholly or permanently inhibited
from asking certain questions ... There is ... no instance in history in which any group, great or small, has not set up some theory
of the right to power." [77] In an earlier period private property was
the legitimizing principle of capitalism, but with the dominance
of the corporation property recedes into the background and "public consensus ... indefinite, completely unorganized, without trace-

able form . . . becomes the final arbiter of legitimacy." [78] The essence of the new consensus was Americanism, which was manufactured during the war and extended to make the corporate order legitimate. In the last years of the war an Americanization crusade was launched as a "constructive" anti-radical measure, designed primarily to assimiliate the immigrant.[79] But Americanism came to mean more than assimilation; it meant above all else a belief in the sanctity of the prevailing order of society. As an Americanism speaker told an immigrant audience in Buffalo: "If you have not found your share of happiness here [in America] something is wrong. Our history proves that there is nothing wrong with our institutions, so the individual must be wrong." [80] The statement is an exaggeration of the basic thesis of Americanism: the social sysstem is sound; any defects must therefore be attributed to the individual. The whole historical tendency toward secularization was beginning to be reversed in the 1920's. To describe the antithesis of secularization Howard Becker coined the term sacralization, "the process by which societies are tightened, hardened, reintegrated and restored." [81] The idea of Americanism was the sacralizing principle of the system of corporate capitalism which has dominated American society since the 1920's.

NOTES:

1. Stanley Taylor, *Conceptions of Institutions and the Theory of Knowledge* (New York, 1956).
2. C. Wright Mills, *The Power Elite* (New York, 1956), pp. 3-29.
3. M. Rostovtzeff, *The Social and Economic History of the Roman Empire* (Oxford, 1957), vol. I, pp. 495-7, is a classic interpretation of this transition from a consensual to an anomic-coercive order. See also, J. Huizinga, *The Waning of the Middle Ages* (New York, 1954); and P. A. Sorokin, *Social and Cultural Dynamics* (New York, 1937), vol. III, pp. 500-506, *et passim* for massive documentation of this thesis.
4. On the consolidation of capitalist power, see Charles A. and Mary Beard, *The Rise of American Civilization: The Industrial Era* (New York, 1927), pp. 166-210, *et passim;* Matthew Josephson, *The Robber Barons: The Great American Capitalists, 1861-1901* (New York, 1934).
5. Louis Adamic, *Dynamite: The Story of Class Violence in America* (New York, 1931); Henry David, *The Haymarket Affair: A Study of Social Revolutionary Movements in America* (New York, 1936).
6. The first real impetus for industrial, as opposed to craft, unionism came

from the use of federal troops in the railway strikes of 1877; see Robert V. Bruce, *1877: Year of Violence* (Indianapolis, 1959).

7. Richard Hofstadter, *The Age of Reform: From Bryan to FDR* (New York, 1955); Walter Lippmann, *Drift and Mastery: An Attempt to Diagnose the Current Unrest* (Englewood Cliffs, N. J., 1961). Lippmann wrote in 1914 of the Bryan-Wilson reform ideology: "competitive business takes on a halo of life . . . The pretty record of competition through the Nineteenth Century is forgotten. Suddenly all that is a glorious past which we have lost. You would think that competitive commercialism was really a generous, chivalrous, high minded stage of human culture . . . Wilson doesn't really fight the oppressions of property. He fights the evil done by large property holders to small ones."

8. "Trade Unionism is the conservative movement of our time," Frank Tannenbaum, *A Philosophy of Labor* (New York, 1951), p. 3.

9. "The New Deal did not reverse the political and economic relations of the [1866-1920] era, but it did create within the political arena, as well as in the corporate world itself, competing centers of power that challenged those of the corporate directors." Mills, op. cit. p. 272.

10. For the earlier period, see Elwin H. Powell, "The Evolution of the American City and the Emergence of Anomie: A Culture Case Study of Buffalo, New York, 1810-1910," *British Journal of Sociology*, XIII, June 1962, pp. 156-68.

11. John T. Horton, *History of Northwestern New York* (New York, 1947), p. 232.

12. *Buffalo Enquirer*, Oct 2, 1908.

13. John J. Kager, "A History of Socialism in Buffalo" (Buffalo: Unpublished M. A. Thesis, Canisus College, 1951), p. 100. Apparently Rochester followed the same pattern, J. J. Dutko, "Socialism in Rochester" (Rochester: Unpublished M. A. Thesis, University of Rochester, 1954).

14. R. E. MacTeggart, "A Labor History of Buffalo, 1846-1917" (Buffalo: Unpublished M. A. Thesis, Canisus College, 1940), p. 220.

15. *Buffalo Socialist*, Nov. 30, 1912.

16. Ibid. Nov. 9, 1912.

17. Ibid. August 9, 1913.

18. MacTeggart, op. cit. p. 222.

19. Kager, op. cit. p. 104.

20. *Buffalo Express*, April 8, 1913.

21. Ibid. April 9, 1913.

22. Ibid. April 10, 1913.

23. Ibid. April 11, 1913.

24. MacTeggart, op. cit. p. 277.

25. Arthur E. Wood, "A Study of Arrests in Detroit, 1913-19," *Journal of Criminal Law and Criminology*, XXX, May 1930-Feb. 1931, pp. 168-200.

26. Irma Dickman, "A Comparative Study of Public Opinion in the United States and Buffalo During the Neutrality Years, 1914-17" (Buffalo: Unpublished M. A. Thesis, Canisus College, 1941), p. 136.

27. *Buffalo Express,* Sept. 28, 1915.

28. Dickman, op. cit. p. 277.

29. *Buffalo Evening News,* August 16, 1914.

30. Daniel Sweeny, *History of Buffalo and Erie County, 1914-19* (Buffalo, 1919), p. 21. The author was city-clerk and ex-editor of the *Buffalo Times.*

31. Ibid. p. 23.

32. Ibid. pp. 27-8.

33. Ibid. p. 34.

34. *Buffalo Courier,* Nov. 15, 1915.

35. *Buffalo Express,* Jan. 3, 1916.

36. H. S. Foster, "How America Became Belligerent: A Quantative Study of War News, 1914-17," *American Journal of Sociology,* 40, 1934-5, pp. 464-75.

37. *Buffalo Evening News,* Mar. 14, 1917.

38. *Buffalo Express,* Oct. 17, 1917.

39. Henry W. Hill, *Municipality of Buffalo, New York: 1720-1923,* vol. III, pp. 860-83.

40. *Live Wire,* July 1917, p. 1.

41. Sweeny, op. cit. p. 56.

42. Ibid. p. 433.

43. *Live Wire,* July 1918, p. 149.

44. Sweeny, op. cit. p. 340.

45. *Buffalo Express,* Oct. 18, 1917.

46. *Live Wire,* Jan. 1918, p. 1.

47. *Buffalo Express,* Dec. 22, 1918.

48. Ibid. Jan. 3, 1919.

49. Robert K. Murray, *Red Scare: A Study in National Hysteria 1919-20* (Minneapolis, 1955), pp. 135-52.

50. Gordon S. Watkins, "Revolutionary Communism in the United States," *American Political Science Review,* XIV, Feb. 1920, pp. 14-34. On the split of the left Socialists to form the Communist Party, Theodore Draper, *The Roots of American Communism* (New York, 1957), pp. 148-64.

51. *Buffalo Express,* Nov. 5, 1919.

52. Ibid.

53. Ibid. Dec. 31, 1919.

54. *Buffalo Commercial,* Jan. 3, 1920.

55. Ibid. Jan. 6, 1920.

56. *Dau's Blue Book: Buffalo* (New York, 1920).

57. *Buffalo Express,* Jan. 3, 1920.

58. Composite quote from the *Enquirer* and the *Commercial,* Dec. 31, 1919, through Jan. 4, 1920.

59. "Editorial," *The Nation,* 110, Jan. 17, 1920.

60. William Preston, "The Ideology and Techniques of Repression, 1903-

33," in *American Radicals*, ed. Harvey Goldberg (New York, 1957), pp. 239-64.

61. Eldridge F. Dowell, *A History of Criminal Syndicalism Legislation in the United States* (Baltimore, 1939).

62. Elwin H. Powell, *Crime as a Function of Anomie: Arrests in Buffalo, 1854-1940* (Mimeograph). Between 1866 and 1876 the crime rate rose sharply but then declined to the pre-Civil War levels by 1900.

63. S. Kirson Weinberg, *Social Problems in Our Time* (Englewood Cliffs, N. J., 1960), p. 418.

64. Ferdinand Lundberg, *America's 60 Families* (New York, 1937), p. 100. "In 1900 there were 149 trusts of $4,000,000,000 capitalization; when trust busting Roosevelt breezed out of the White House, there were 10,020, with 31,000,000,000 of capitalization."

65. Lewis Corey, *The Decline of American Capitalism* (New York, 1934), p. 35.

66. Walter Lippmann, *Drift and Mastery*, p. 17. On the desertion of the intellectuals see Henry F. May, *The End of American Innocence: A Study of the First Years of Our Own Time* (New York, 1959), pp. 302-29.

67. H. G. Peterson and Gilbert C. Fite, *Opponents of the War, 1917-18* (Madison, 1957).

68. Arthur M. Schlesinger, Jr., *The Crises of the Old Order, 1919-33* (Boston, 1957), p. 39.

69. James Weinstein, "The Socialist Party: Its Roots and Strengths, 1912-1919," *Studies on the Left*, I, Winter, 1960, pp. 5-27.

70. Jack London, *The Iron Heel* (New York, 1907) is an uncanny anticipation of the capitalist counter-revolution.

71. P. F. Bissenden, *The I.W.W.: A Study of American Syndicalism* (New York, 1919). Preface to the 1956 edition, pp. x-xi.

72. Murray, op. cit. p. 269.

73. Schlesinger, op. cit. p. 44.

74. Irving Bernstein, *The Lean Years: A History of the American Worker, 1920-33* (Boston, 1960), observes: "In the mansion of the dominant business philosophy [of the 1920's] there was no room for trade unionism. Those shrewd managers who conceived the American Plan sold the idea that collective bargaining was worse than bad, it was un-American. The mood of the time stressed individualism; one got ahead by himself not by collective action. This notion permeated the outlook of the working class" (p. 88). The results were noticeable in the decline of "union membership from 5,047,800 in 1920 . . . to 3,622,000 in 1923 . . . and 3,422,600 in 1929 . . . a bare 10.2% of the labor force, . . . a marked drop from 19.4% in 1920" (p. 84). Moreover, "no prior era in the history of the Supreme Court approached the twenties in the number of statutes invalidated, most of them labor laws" (p. 242).

75. Ibid. p. 80.

76. Alan Valentine, *1913: America Between Two Worlds* (New York, 1962), p. v.

77. A. A. Berle, *Power without Property: A New Development in American Political Economy* (New York, 1959), p. 98.

78. Ibid. p. 111.

79. The New York State Lusk Committee, *Revolutionary Radicalism* (Albany, 1920). This mammoth four-volume work devotes two volumes to the analysis of revolutionary movements and the remaining two to the presentation of constructive measures to counteract radicalism through Americanization. All four volumes are equally absurd but nevertheless revealing. The anti-radical campaign attempted to correct the thinking of the radical rather than the conditions which give rise to radicalism.

80. *Buffalo Express*, Jan. 30, 1920.

81. Howard Becker, "Normative Reactions to Normlessness," *American Sociological Review*, 25, Dec. 1960, pp. 803-10.

# 21

T. B. BOTTOMORE

## The Administrative Elite*

In all complex societies high government officials form an important part of the "governing elite" or "political class"—the minority which, at any time, effectively rules a society.[1] The position of higher civil servants in modern industrial societies is especially influential, as a result of the great extension of state activities, the growing technical complexity of public administration, and the organization of the civil service as a professional career based upon educational diplomas and training. Indeed, Max Weber, whose writings on bureaucracy form the starting point for all modern discussion of the subject, asserted that "the power position of a fully developed bureaucracy is always very strong, and under normal conditions, supreme. The 'political master' finds himself in the position of the 'dilettante' in the face of the 'expert' when he confronts the trained official established as manager of the administration." This remains true, Weber suggested, whether the political master is the whole people (armed with the rights of "initiative," "referendum," and the recall of officials) or an elected parliament.[2] Weber's judgment of the magnitude of bureaucratic power was clearly influenced by his experience of bureaucracy in Germany,

* This essay is taken from a work in progress on the higher civil service in France which will be published under the title *Bureaucracy and Social Classes in France.*

357

but also by his general opposition to socialism, which he saw as the culmination of bureaucratic rule. One of the principal doctrines which he was attacking throughout his writings on this subject was that of the Marxists, who maintained that bureaucratic power was merely one aspect of the rule of the bourgeoisie in capitalist society, that it would diminish in a socialist society, and would eventually "wither away" along with the state itself. Lenin, in *The State and Revolution*, elaborated Marx's analysis of the Paris Commune in his argument that during the transition from capitalism to socialism the power of public officials would be reduced by making them elected and subject to recall at any time, and by paying them at "workmen's wages." In fact, the experiences of present-day Communist societies reveal that high officials, both in the dominant party and in the state (and the two spheres are interrelated), are able to attain a privileged position in respect of power, prestige, and real income; in other words, to become a vital part, if not the whole, of the governing elite. Nevertheless, recent events also show that bureaucratic power is not unopposed or unrestrained even there; and it cannot be inferred from these particular experiences that Weber's assertions about the connection between all forms of socialism and bureaucracy hold true.

Modern sociological studies of elites have dealt principally with the Western industrial societies, and they have emphasized particularly two features of the social hierarchy in such societies: first, the plurality of elites, and secondly, the problematic nature of the relationships between the different elites and between elites and social classes. G. D. H. Cole, for example, defined elites as "groups which emerge to positions of leadership and influence at every social level—that is to say, as leaders of classes or of other important elements in the social structure"; and he went on to observe: "Not all elites rest on a class basis, or are to be regarded as class representatives, but some do and are, and a special importance attaches, in modern societies and especially in the older societies which have been developing from aristocracy towards some form of democracy, to the relations between classes and elites and to the differences that emerge with the increasing complexities of class structure." [3] Raymond Aron has likewise drawn attention to the shifting relationships between elites and social classes, in a study of the connections between class structure and political power in which he distinguishes five elite groups which are important elements in the "political class": political leaders, government administrators, economic directors, leaders of the masses, and military chiefs.[4]

The principal attempt to show, in one society, that the major elites may be regularly associated and in agreement about the ends of policy, over a period of time, as well as being recruited mainly from a particular social class, is C. Wright Mills' study of the "power elite" in the United States.[5] Nevertheless, Mills criticizes and rejects the Marxist conception of a ruling class based upon economic interest, and he introduces many qualifications into his thesis concerning the unity of the power elite, which is finally expressed as "the often uneasy coincidence of economic, military and political power."[6] His main propositions are rather: first, that changes in technology and in social institutions have produced an unprecedented concentration of power, and have widened the gulf between elites and masses (a thesis which has many points of connection with Weber's theory of the extension of bureaucracy); and, second, that the character and policies of an elite cannot be assessed merely by looking at the social origins of its members (although this is an important fact), but must also be considered in relation to the formation of the members' outlook by their training and experience, and to the historical and institutional framework in which they act.

What is the character of this administrative elite? What is the nature and extent of its power? What significance does the mode of recruitment to this elite have in the system of power and stratification as a whole? It will help our inquiry if, before turning to empirical materials, we first consider these questions in general terms.

The character of the administrative elite may be delineated initially by comparing it with other types of elites. It differs from other social elites principally in being relatively small, well-defined, homogeneous (as a result of training and the practice of the occupation), and cohesive. Furthermore, it is directly involved in the exercise of political power, and this distinguishes it from a number of other groups which may have high social prestige. The elite of political leaders, which is even more directly concerned with power, differs from the administrative elite especially in being less easily circumscribed, and less unitary in the sense that in most modern societies there are competing or conflicting subgroups (rival political parties or factions within one major party). The intellectual elite may be still more difficult to define, and it is evidently less organized, less cohesive, and in the strict sense less powerful than most other elites. Only the military elite has many similarities with the administrative elite, but in Western societies it has ordinarily been excluded from the direct exercise of political power. When we try to go beyond such a comparative analysis to measure more directly the distinctiveness and cohesiveness of an elite, many difficulties appear. Nevertheless, it is possible to indicate some relevant conditions which are in principle measurable—control by the group over its own recruitment, the similarity of the members in respect of social and cultural background, the extent of interaction among members within and beyond the specific sphere of activity of the group, supplementary bonds, such as those of kinship between the members—and also criteria by which the solidarity of a group may be judged—the degree of similarity in members' conceptions of the group and in their evaluations of public events which concern the group, overt manifestations of *esprit de corps*, and so on. Judged in these terms the administrative elite will be shown to be a very cohesive social group.

The second question, concerning the nature and extent of the power [7] wielded by the administrative elite, leads us into some intricate problems of analysis and some difficulties of empirical verification. It is clear that the individual members of the elite may be influential in society at large in much the same way as other individuals whose occupations have high prestige. Moreover, since high officials have regular contacts with political leaders they can perhaps more easily bring their personal influence to bear upon particular decisions. But what power does the administrative elite, as a group, have in its everyday and continuing activities? It is usually argued that this power is closely circumscribed in democratic societies, where higher civil servants act under the authority of a political executive which is itself responsible to parliament and to the electorate. The officials, according to this view, execute decisions which have been made by others, in terms of interests and values which lie outside their sphere of influence. However, in practice the higher civil servants may have a good deal of autonomy, and they may have formed their own corporate view of what are "wise," or "sensible," or "practicable" policies. At the stage where a policy is being implemented they may have the power to obstruct, delay, or modify its working. Equally, at an earlier stage, when a policy is being formulated, they may have, by virtue of long experience and expert knowledge of the departments which they administer, a considerable influence upon the ideas and decisions of the minister who is nominally their chief. Their power will be all the greater where the political executive changes frequently, and where ministers have little experience of government in general or of the particular departmnts for which they are responsible. The growing technical complexity of modern government, as has been noted, also enhances the power of the permanent officials. In some cases, the policy-making powers of important officials are explicitly recognized, in the rules or conventions by which certain appointments in the public service are treated as "political appointments," and are made not by ordinary promotion but by nomination in accordance with the wishes of the political executive.

These considerations lead to further questions concerning the sources of, and the restraints upon, bureaucratic power. As we have seen, Max Weber was inclined to regard the growth of bureaucratic power in modern societies as inexorable; the various grounds for this view included the congruence of bureaucratic administration with the general rationalization of social life, the indispensability of the technically expert administrators, and the permanence and continuity of the administration in contrast with the impermanence and changeability of the political executive. Weber added that the bureaucracy was able to strengthen its position vis à vis the political executive by enveloping its activities in the strictest secrecy. In considering the possible restraints upon bureaucratic power Weber went no further than to suggest that the adherence of high officials to general legal rules in accordance with which they would execute impartially and effectively the decisions of every legitimate political ruler, and the degree of stability of the political order as a whole, might have a certain influence. It seems likely that these factors have a greater importance than Weber, in his pre-occupation with German circumstances, was prepared to recognize. One significant restraint upon the power of an administrative elite is the development, within the elite itself, of a professional ethic which upholds the ideal of the political neutrality of officials. On the other side, it is probable that the power of an administrative elite will be increased (whether deliberately, in a striving for power, or otherwise) in conditions where the legitimacy of the political regime itself is unsettled.

The development of a professional ethic in the civil service can in fact be traced in most modern societies, although there are great variations in the degree to which it is genuinely accepted and made effective. In Britain, the political neutrality of the civil service has been strongly emphasized in the professional code, and a postwar Socialist Prime Minister has expressed his confidence in its effectiveness. Lord Attlee wrote: "There were certainly some people in the Labour Party who doubted whether the civil servants would give fair play to a socialist government but all doubts disappeared with experience." [8]

The circumstances have been different in France, where the prevailing view since the early nineteenth century has been that civil servants, and particularly the higher civil servants, owed political loyalty to the regime of the day. C. Chavanon has referred to Napoleon's demand for "complete loyalty from all civil servants, and even from all who occupied equivalent positions" [9] to his own regime; and later political rulers made the same claim. The political influences within the civil service probably attained their highest point during the difficult years of the Third Republic after the Dreyfus case, but they have continued down to the present time. In a recent essay, R. Catherine claims that the "politicalization" of the civil service has proceeded rapidly again since 1945; [10] and R. Grégoire concludes a discussion of the whole question with the observation that the idea of the political neutrality of civil servants is still less generally accepted and less influential in France than in Britain. [11]

The traditional lack of confidence in the political neutrality of high officials is illustrated by an institution which has no counterpart in the British administrative system: the *cabinet ministériel*. [12] Every minister, on taking up office, appoints a personal staff of trusted collaborators who act as intermediaries between him and the permanent officials of his department. Some members of these *cabinets* are themselves higher civil servants, frequently drawn from one or another of the *grands corps* and especially from the *Conseil d'État* and the *Inspection des Finances;* others come from outside the civil service. The existence of the *cabinets,* and particularly the growth in the number of their personnel, reflects, as Grégoire has noted, the doubts that ministers feel about the loyalty and reliability of the higher permanent officials in their departments.[13]

The case of France also lends support to the proposition that the independent power of a bureaucracy is most likely to be established where the political order is unstable. In France, the insistence upon loyalty to a particular regime (and even to party governments) has encouraged the formation of political attitudes among the higher civil servants, while the instability of political regimes has led them to assume (or to be disposed to assume) an independent political role. This phenomenon has been frequently noted, and sometimes exaggerated, by observers of French politics. Thus, Karl Marx wrote in *The Eighteenth Brumaire of Louis Bonaparte* that the "enormous bureaucratic and military organization ... this appalling parasitic body which enmeshes the body of French society like a net and chokes all its pores" seemed to have made itself completely independent of civil society. More than a century later, H. Lüthy writes of the *grands corps* and especially the *Conseil d'État* and the *Inspection des Finances:* "They constitute a supreme and sovereign self-recruiting body, immune from political intervention, responsible to no-one outside their own hierarchy, a rock against which all political storms beat ineffectively and in vain; a completely closed mandarin system, even in the social choice it exercises in reproducing itself; its *esprit de corps,* the sense of belonging to a chosen elite fostered from childhood in the great boarding schools which prepare pupils for *la carrière.*" [14] An eminent French political scientist, André Siegfried, expressed a very similar view of the political role of higher civil servants, but he went further in relating it to more general theories of the "managerial revolution." He argued that "... two groups of experts are tending to assume a leading position in the state as in the economy. The elite of the administration is recruited essentially among the *Inspecteurs des finances* and the members of the *Conseil d'État;* it is a general staff which radiates everywhere. Since these administrators frequently transfer to the private sector, they are to be found in the banks and in large scale industrial and commercial enterprises. The second source is the *polytechniciens,* who form the elite of the technical departments of state, but are also increasingly the managers of large scale industry." [15]

While the preceding considerations show that the administrative elite occupies a position which may be presumed to be powerful, it is more difficult to marshal empirical evidence for the actual exercise of power in specific circumstances. This is, however, a general difficulty which bedevils most studies of power as an empirical—not simply a constitutional—phenomenon; and it is likely to be particularly acute where the group to be studied has reason to conceal as much as possible the power or influence which it wields. Nevertheless, if we are not to rest content with the view (which is at least as difficult to support) that there are no power groups in society but only an intricate web of innumerable influences and counter-influences whose outcome resembles fate—or else to accept that the relations of power are entirely inscrutable —then we must try, so far as possible, to test our assertions about power groups by an examination of actual instances in which important social issues are decided. The power of economic interest groups, and the influence (to rate it at its lowest) of pressure groups of various kinds, have been demonstrated in a number of cases;[16] and studies along similar lines might produce evidence of the exercise of power by high officials in certain situations. It has often been asserted, for instance, that the policies of the Popular Front government of Léon Blum (1936-38) were obstructed by the higher civil servants. My own investigation of this period indicates that some legislative projects may have been obstructed, notably the bill for reforming the civil service itself, which, after being approved by a large majority in the Chamber in 1936, was passed from committee to committee through the intervention of officials until it finally expired with the fall of Blum's government in 1938.

I have so far considered two social facts which may affect, in opposite senses, the power position of an administrative elite: the development of a professional code of political neutrality and the instability of the political regime. Another important element is suggested by the third question posed above, concerning the relation between the administrative elite and the class structure of society. For it may be held that the administrative elite is only one section of the dominant class in society, and that its independent power, at one extreme, and its political neutrality, at the other, are modified and curtailed by the interests and aims of the class which it represents. Weber paid little attention to this problem; and in fact he eliminated it by two arguments which are crucial in his whole account of the development of bureaucracy. The first is that bureaucracy, in the sense of rational and impersonal administration based upon technical competence and educational diplomas, proceeds along with "democratization" and the leveling of social differences, with the result that social classes cease to have great political importance; and the second, that the officials—the managers of the administration—are the most obvious successors to the owners of the means of production as the rulers of society. These arguments were later developed in Burnham's theory of the "managerial revolution," [17] and they have attracted renewed attention through the criticisms of bureaucracy in the post-Stalinist Communist societies.[18] Whatever may be the case in the last-named societies, it can scarcely be claimed that the process of social leveling has gone so far in the Western capitalist societies that elites, including the administrative elite, no longer have any connection with social classes. As H. J. Laski observed, in the absence of a democratic educational system, the effective public service will be "confined to the comfortable classes of the community"; and he added that this implied: "First, the experience upon which its members will draw is not representative of the community as a whole; and even the new facts they encounter will be envisaged in terms of that special experience. Secondly, the advice they will offer to the political executive will be fairly narrow in range, unless they contain among them what is, in any case, rare, men of great imaginative insight." [19] Lord Attlee's observation upon the relations between Socialist ministers and higher civil servants, quoted earlier, also expresses the fear of class opposition to social reforms; and his statement that such fears were groundless has to be seen in the context of the postwar situation in Britain, where the reforms undertaken by the Labour Government continued, in many respects, policies already widely accepted during the war, and where the social composition of the higher civil service had already undergone changes as a result of wartime recruitment.

The significance of the relationship between the administrative elite and the class structure has been shown in another way by historical studies. J. D. Kingsley, in a study of the British higher civil service,[20] advanced the thesis that the administrative system in Britain worked smoothly and effectively because the members of the political executive and the heads of the civil service were drawn from the same social class and thus had similar views on important issues of public policy. And in his account of how this situation had come about, he suggested that the growing strength and influence of a particular social class in economic and social life had determined the greater participation of that class in the exercise of both political and administrative power. The agitation for civil service reform in the mid-nineteenth century had the same origins and significance as the agitation for the Reform Bill of 1832. It expressed the resentments and aspirations of the industrial capitalist class. John Bright's description of the Foreign Office as "the outdoor relief department of the aristocracy," and the embittered remark of an anonymous author that no one could obtain a position under the government who lacked family influence or had been born in unlawful wedlock, manifested such class sentiments. An historical interpretation of this kind, which links changes in the composition of the administrative elite with changes in the situation of social classes, may also be helpful in understanding more recent events. In so far as the opportunities for individuals of working-class origin to enter the higher civil service have increased, the fact may be explained by the greater strength of the working class in society as a whole; and the actual extent of such opportunities in any society, measured over a period of time, may provide a useful index of the changes in its class structure.

The recruitment of elites has a special importance in the modern industrial societies, which have been developing toward a democratic form of society which comprehends not only equal political rights and competition for political power, but also greater economic and social equality, at least in the sense of equality of opportunity. It may be argued, as Weber did, that some equalization of social conditions was an important prerequisite for the growth of bureaucracy, since the recruitment of officials strictly on the basis of ability and qualifications could only be established when public office became accessible in principle to all citizens, instead of being reserved for members of a particular social stratum. In fact, the doctrine of the *carrière ouverte aux talents* was a corollary of the principles of *liberté, égalité, fraternité*. Weber went further in asserting that the spread of bureaucracy would itself bring about a further growth of equality; but, while we should recognize the influence which the ideas of ability and merit, in the context of the scientific and technical complexity of modern societies, have had in breaking down earlier social privileges, it is necessary to qualify Weber's prognosis. Recruitment to public offices by competitive examination, or on the basis of educational qualifications, only brings about a real equality of opportunity if those of equal ability have equal chances of preparing themselves for the public service by obtaining the necessary diplomas or the necessary training for the entrance examinations. In practice, therefore, the selection of individuals for the higher civil service, as well as for many other high status occupations, takes place, for the most part, at the point where individuals are selected for higher education. And the history of institutions of higher education shows that they have been largely reserved for individuals from the upper strata of society. Indeed, they have had a pre-eminent role in perpetuating class differences which could no longer be maintained by inequalities in civil and political rights.

A study of recruitment to the higher civil service will throw light upon the processes of social mobility in a society. It will show how far there is equality of opportunity in one important sphere of society, and if it covers a period of time it may reveal the extent and trend of change. A study of recruitment to a single elite group may add useful information to that obtained from general studies of social mobility in a whole population; for the latter will ordinarily present the total outcome of different kinds of mobility (between adjacent social strata as well as between social strata which are far apart), while a study of elite recruitment will reveal the amount of long-range mobility. The opportunities to rise directly from the lowest to the highest social positions have a particular importance, for they play a large part in forming the individual's judgment of the open or closed nature of the class system, and thus in determining the character and intensity of class consciousness.

The amount of mobility may also have important effects upon the administrative elite itself. If changes in the recruitment of the elite result in its members being drawn in substantial numbers from all social classes and strata, the social bonds which unite the members cannot any longer arise merely from the similarities of social origin, but are likely to be formed principally by the occupation itself and by the educational experience which leads up to it. In this case the higher civil servants may become more conscious of themselves as an occupational elite, rather than as members of a traditional social class; and this may lead, in the circumstances of a particular society, either to a strengthening of the idea of "political neutrality" (the occupation being conceived in terms of technical competence rather than in terms of power), or to a more rapid development of the administrative elite as a new power group and even, in association with other groups, as a new class. This last possibility is the theme of much recent discussion of the "rule of the experts"—the technocrats and bureaucrats—and it was, of course, the underlying concern in Weber's analysis of social trends in the modern industrial societies.

It will be seen that the three problems which I stated earlier are not tidily self-contained; they are interrelated, and moreover they ramify into more general problems of social stratification and the distribution of power in society, of the changes which have occurred in recent times in these two spheres, and of the formation of new social classes and social ideologies.

NOTES:

1. The term "governing elite" is due to V. Pareto, *The Mind and Society* (English trans. London, 1935) and *Les Systèmes socialistes* (Paris, 1902); the term "political class" to G. Mosca, *The Ruling Class* (English trans. New York, 1939). Both writers emphasized, in opposition to the Marxist notion of a ruling class based upon economic power and represented in the political sphere by various and changing groups, the idea of an "elite" comprising those individuals who actually wielded political power at a given time.

2. Max Weber, *Wirtschaft und Gesellschaft*, Chap. VI, "Bureaucracy" (English trans. in H. H. Gerth and C. Wright Mills, *From Max Weber*, London, 1947).

3. G. D. H. Cole, *Studies in Class Structure* (London, 1955).

4. Raymond Aron, "Social Structure and the Ruling Class," *British Journal of Sociology*, I, March 1950.

5. C. Wright Mills, *The Power Elite* (New York, 1956).

6. Op. cit. p. 278.

7. By "power," I shall mean throughout this essay the ability of an individual or a group to attain its end in a course of action even against the opposition of others who are involved in that course of action (see Max Weber, "Class, Status, Parties," in *Wirtschaft und Gesellschaft*); by "influence," I shall mean the ability of an individual or group to change by persuasion, on particular occasions, the course of anyone who wields power. Evidently, there may be cases in which it is difficult to discriminate precisely between "power" and "influence."

8. Clement R. Attlee, "Civil Servants, Ministers, Parliament and the Public," *The Political Quarterly*, Oct.-Dec. 1954, p. 308.

9. C. Chavanon, *Les Fonctionnaires et la fonction publique* (Paris, 1951).

10. R. Catherine, "Les fonctionnaires," in M. Duverger (ed.), *Parties politiques et classes sociales en France* (Paris, 1955).

11. R. Grégoire, *La Fonction publique* (Paris, 1954), pp. 331-5.

12. For a comprehensive account of the *cabinet ministériel*, see J. L. Suerin, "Les cabinets ministériels," *Revue du droit publique et de la science politique*, Nov.-Dec. 1956, pp. 1207-94.

13. Grégoire, op. cit. p. 333.'

14. Herbert Lüthy, *The State of France* (London, 1955).

15. André Siegfried, *De la IIIème à la IVème République* (Paris, 1957), p. 246.

16. The introduction of commercial television in Britain provides a good example: see H. H. Wilson, *Pressure Group: The Campaign for Commercial Television* (London, 1961).

17. James Burnham, *The Managerial Revolution* (London, 1943).

18. See especially, Milovan Djilas, *The New Class* (London, 1957).

19. H. J. Laski, *A Grammar of Politics* (4th ed., London, 1941), p. 399.

20. J. Donald Kingsley, *Representative Bureaucracy* (Yellow Springs, 1944).

# 22

PETER WORSLEY

## Bureaucracy and Decolonization:
## Democracy from the Top

I wish to discuss one particular type of sociological theory belonging to the genus Mills called Grand Theory; to examine, in particular, what it has to offer for the study of bureaucracy; and then, by way of a case-study, to outline an alternative approach. The label "Grand Theory" is perhaps a little unfortunate, since I for one have no objection to macro-theory and believe that Mills himself contributed very importantly to the elaboration of what he called "master theories." I prefer, therefore, to call this style of theory Universalism. It is highly fashionable today in varying forms. Handbooks of sociological theory, for example, frequently confine themselves to the elaboration of logically-interrelated fundamental concepts and analytical categories—role, status, function, institution, etc.—in insignificantly differing propositional combinations, usually within a basically static and holistic framework: time, process, dysfunction, conflict—where they are handled at all— are tucked away in a separate "theory of change." [1]

The elucidation of fundamental concepts and forms of social action is valuable, indeed essential. But sociological theory ought to go further than preoccupation with the most general. It must also concern itself with the systematization of substantive knowledge at other ranges: the classification of types and sequences of social formations is an integral part of "theory." Such categories and fundamental concepts as role, status, etc., can only be distilled, too, out of findings about societies: the limits of validity of propositions concerning the interrelationships between these categories need defining with reference to the relevant types of social situations to which they apply; the conditions need stating. Furthermore, unless these concepts are utilized in the empirical examination of societies as systems, their manipulation results in a formal sociology, of which Simmel's is the archetype. Quite as much as the crude culture-historical school with their search for "traits," Simmel builds up a set of "forms" of social action—superordination, cooperation, conflict, scale, size, etc.—which become collecting-boxes into which discrete specimens are popped: "... the state, ... a religious community, ... a band of conspirators, ... an economic association, ... an art school, ... the family." [2]

Not that formal sociology is without system; but the systematization lies in a systematization of "explanatory concepts," to use Nadel's distinction,[3] not that of an abstraction from "empirical reality." Consequently, whatever the intellectual brillance of a Simmel, we can never do more than gain illuminating "insights" from him: his theory cannot be developed. Its end is contained in its beginning; empirical data are merely "examples" of pre-established categories. Indeed, they are not even seriously required: "Facts ... illustrate ... formal and normative patterns." [4] We don't need too many facts; therefore, two or three "illustrations" are enough. Heberle significantly comments on his ignorance of much social research of his day.[5] Why do research when personal, chance experience is as good for "illustration" purposes, e.g. a fortuitous meeting on a railway train, a domestic incident, etc.; when, indeed, fictional examples would do? [6]

This approach, then, leaving aside the underlying behavioristic system, cannot provide the basis for understanding of societies as systems.[7] Implicitly, often, much contemporary sociological theory which dwells on "elemental" components of human behavior—most notably small-group interaction theory—reposes on similar foundations.

This approach produces a horrible dilemma: the more universalistic the propositions developed, the emptier they become. The more specifically culture-bound, the less they shed light on common

processes and forms. The revulsion against universalism produces
an equally sterile response — idiography.

In his very effective round-up of "small group" and community
studies, Sprott constantly acknowledges the truistic nature of findings in experimental "small-group" research: "All this is pretty
familiar in everyday life. . . . All that has so far been reported brings
out into the open matters of common experience. . . . The advantages of cooperation are . . . just what we should expect. . . . It all
seems rather familiar. . . . This is familiar enough . . . ," etc.[8] In non-
experimental situations, however, the cultural specificity of the
situation restricts the universifiability of the findings:

> It is rather absurd to compare a democratic New England
> village with its 'town' meeting, with the non-democratic Brit-
> ish village dominated for so long by the Church and the
> Gentry.[9]

On meetings:

> According to the type of meeting, whether religious or politi-
> cal, various motivations, conscious and unconscious, are ap-
> pealed to. . . . It may be aggression, it may be guilt, it may be
> sex, it may be a need for security and leadership—motivations
> and needs idiosyncratic to the individuals. But the social cli-
> mate and even fashion have to be brought into the picture
> (p. 168).

The norms of primary groups in armies "will vary from culture
to culture" (p. 174); "it may be that only the young and not those
deeply involved in crime will be influenced [by group therapy] . . ."
(p. 181).

When we move from experimental groups to "real-life" groups,
the propositions become less universalistic and more culture-bound:
in solving crossword puzzles, division of labor helps; in constructing them, it does not (p. 114). Exclusive concentration on "formal
properties of communications systems" (p. 126) does not help us
in handling "real-life" situations, where, for example, the informal
ranking of the small group is cross-cut by formal and semi-formal
ranking-orders (pp. 148 ff.). In other words, the cultural goals of
the group, the social history and personalities of its members, and
the relationships between them—the group's cultural content—is

not something to be "added in" to any analytical schema *post hoc,* but is intrinsic to it. For there is no group free of cultural content: Balesian profiles of "people discussing a chess problem look different from those of people discussing a problem about human relations." Hence the search for universal propositions is ultimately unproductive: ". . . Attempts have been made to pin down the qualities which mark out the leader, and they have all failed" (p. 152).

In reaction against such universalizing (and against parallel claims to be establishing "laws" in other positivist, functionalist, and historicist schemas), many sociologists have relapsed into what Mills called "abstracted empiricism." "Pure" empiricism, is, of course, a contradiction in terms. The large corpus of British empiricist work, running, for example, from Booth, Rowntree, and the Webbs to the Institute of Community Studies, is, in fact, pervaded throughout by meliorative and manipulative Lib-Lab assumptions.

We fluctuate between the sterile extremes of universalism, on the one hand, and idiography on the other. If I may evaluate rather than merely classify, the choice seems to lie between Useless Universalism and Idiotic Idiography.

Much of this has been a revolt against nineteenth-century evolutionism and its postulated epochs arranged in ineluctable series. The classic primitive communism-slavery-feudalism-capitalism schema was equally acceptable to the German Social-Democratic worker in Hamburg,[10] as to Protestant republican lawyer Lewis Henry Morgan in America, the former confident in the evolutionary inevitability of the revolution, the latter in "the steady material and moral improvement of mankind from crude stone implements and sexual promiscuity to the steam engine and monogamous marriage of Rochester, New York." [11] Now, the empirical findings of the anthropologists have destroyed the Golden Age of "primitive communism"; feudalism is no longer a world phenomenon; "Asiatic society" is restored; and "socialist" societies quite unlike any envisaged by Marx have emerged in the "wrong" countries.

With this confident framework gone, only "the society" remains as the unit of analysis. The liberal social scientist, haunted as he is by the memory of deterministic unilineal or Spenglerian-cycle schemas, if he does construct a typology at all, is quite unlikely to develop one within a time-framework: a typological sequence of phases of social development. Yet most writers do, in fact, operate with a hitherto unexamined sequence-framework. Despite the great disintegration, feudalism, Asiatic society, capitalism, etc., are used as part of an implicit, confused, vaguely "multilinear," schema of world development.

A reconceived epochal framework is sadly needed, if we are to avoid Universalism and Idiography. It will certainly have to eschew unilinearism and the West-European ethnocentrism of nineteenth-century schemas. Nor are the reductionist categories of the Leslie White school any more adequate.[12]

Here, I am more concerned not to delineate specific epochal sequences appropriate to cultural regions, but to affirm something quite different: that social theory has utterly failed to grapple with the outstanding feature of the last hundred years—the emergence of a world system of social relations, a new and higher level of development in human social organization. The only serious systematic intellectual treatment of this change in levels so far has been Lenin's *Imperialism*.

Today, we have a tripartite division of the world: the two blocs and the neutral world. Yet each is a world category; all are part of a world system of relationships (including hostility, of course, as a relationship), and the neutral world carries the germ of a regenerated internationalism. Underlying these divisions is the more fundamental division of the world into millionaire nations—to use Julius Nyerere's phrase—and "proletarian nations."

The following illustrative analysis, therefore, is representative of a particular type of society, the "underdeveloped," in a specific phase of its development: decolonization. It is therefore neither universalistic nor idiographic. Some features, naturally, are entirely idiosyncratic, the results of a unique history. But parallel processes are observable in countries with very different cultures and histories, and with which no direct contact has ever existed.

This kind of specificity, reposing on foundations of a conception of classes and types of society in successive development, seems to me one of the great strengths of Mills' work. The label "middle range" does not describe it, because the theory developed is adequate to the situation—it is exhaustive for the range and level of social action it deals with—but is also part of an overall system, and therefore never autonomously "complete" as much interaction theory pretends to be. Armed with this awareness, it is therefore possible for Mills to see the connections between the specific and the general, to move from the face-to-face level to the commanding heights. His sociology has a place for the typical attitudes of the salesgirls in Macy's; for the academics' illusions about power in so far as they stem from their "middle-level" structural position; and for the macroscopic encounters of the giant powers. Equipped with this kind of sociological imagination, a meaningful analysis can be built up, starting from any level, though decisive command is unambiguously located by Mills in the higher nervous centers.

In the corpus of Mills' work, *Character and Social Structure* certainly represents an elaboration of his general concepts. These are then applied to specific types and classes of society within which different group characteristics emerge. Most of his work, however, like that of Marx, deals with one specific society at a specific stage in its development: in Mills' case, late capitalism. *Character and Social Structure* represents the only general extension of his world-view to other epochs, and *Causes of World War III* a breakthrough toward an awareness of an emergent world-system. By the time of his death, however, he had not as yet turned his attention centrally to the Third World; his concentration on the Big Two, on his own society, and on Cuba's particular experience, was preoccupying enough, and perhaps distracted him from examining more closely the autonomous development of the Third World in directions not controlled by either Russia or America.

One of the few other social scientists who has not assumed the normality of "Western" or "Soviet" models, or their inevitable predominance, is Gunnar Myrdal, a Swede and an internationalist. He has drawn attention to the fact that "in a stagnant society . . . [organs for self-government and co-operation], . . . do not come into existence except as a result of state policy. . . . This process is a totally different one from . . . [that] in the Western countries." [13]

In discussing bureaucracy, I limit myself to the "decolonization" situation, and to the low-level "field" bureaucrat in that situation. I am not, therefore, discussing universal properties of bureaucratic systems, though I do also suggest some analytical categories with which specific typologies might be built up. The situation dis-

cussed, more precisely, is that of decolonization within the context
of non-revolutionary transition to independence. Revolutionary
transitions, where social order collapses and mass revolutionary
movements emerge to transform, not merely political institutions,
but all social relationships—as in China or Cuba—constitute another species of decolonization again. Here, due to the need of a
revolutionary movement to build up support and legitimacy out of
nothing, mass participation is crucial. Hence decentralization, flexibility, unity with existing organizations, proliferation of secondary
associations, popular involvement in government, all flourish under
such conditions. Centralized political and/or military machines
may certainly exist; they do not preclude the above. Such revolutions are non-bureaucratic; Cuba is the most striking case. But
clearly, the "heroic" phase—as in Russia in the immediate post-1917
years, or Communist China from Yenan to 1950/51—must, to some
degree, be followed by some serious formalization of institutions.
Some sociologists believe that such situations can only be "temporary" [14] or "deviant cases": [15] that formalization is merely the
first phase of operation of Michels' "iron law." "Whoever says
organization, says oligarchy." Here I am concerned to disinter what
there is of scientific value in such generalizations which obviously
do relate to empirically observable processes, but which are also
ideologically overburdened. To infer that formalization inherently
leads to totalitarianism or undemocratic "mass society"—the not unusual extension of this mode of thought—seems as unentailed in
the first proposition as an awareness of the centrality of conflict or
as a social process entails subscription to Social Darwinism.

I am not concerned with the bureaucratization of political revolution, however, but with those decolonization situations where
the social revolution is unaccompanied (or preceded) by a political
revolution, but is bureaucratized from the beginning.

Social collapse, mass revolutionary and/or independence movements, and subsequent radical social reconstruction do not necessarily occur together. They did in Russia in 1917, and in China in
1949. Hence those revolutions have a particularly thorough quality. But these elements are dissociable. In Eastern Europe after
1945, there was social collapse and political revolution but little
mass movement, for the Red Army was the key agent; social revolution was imposed from above. In Egypt, the political revolution

was not preceded by social disintegration; it was the work of a handful, who—unlike the conventional South American "revolution"—launched social revolution and mass participation in its wake. In contemporary West Africa, there has been no social collapse, and although mass movements usually exist, power has been handed over, not wrested in revolutionary struggle.

Under such varying conditions, the characteristics of the resulting state structure will vary appropriately. Yet in all these cases, there is one major common feature: politico-bureaucratic machines are in the saddle from the beginning, and there is no "heroic" period of Cuban-type mass participation in government. Radical social change—if initiated at all—is initiated from the top.

The experience of the *entre deux guerres* era has produced a strong fear of bureaucracy, part of a wider revulsion against holistic tendencies in social theory and social policy. Evolutionism has collapsed under the impact of the history of our times as well as anthropologists' findings. The evils of social planning and of theoretical system-building have been so caustically emphasized by Hayek, Popper, Talmon, Polanyi, and others, that one eminent writer on the negative effects of concentration of power, Bertrand Russell, has himself been forced to remind us—in ethical rather than structural terms—that absolute condemnation of organization sterilizes both thought and action:

> Love of power . . . is the desire to be able to produce intended effects. . . . If you love your neighbour, you will wish for power to make him happy. To condemn *all* love of power, therefore, is to condemn love of your neighbour.[16]

These fears of bureaucratization, for some, revolve around fear of oligarchy. For others, alienation and dehumanization—both of the bureaucrat and his client—are the major dysfunctional and undesirable implications of bureaucracy: the fragmentation of the personality, and/or conflicts entailed in the contradiction between formal and substantive rationality.

All these analyses focus upon features of bureaucracy [17] in general, sometimes conceived of merely as widespread, sometimes as "immanent" characteristics. The equation of "immanence" with inevitability is rejected by some political and other social scientists who have pointed out that Michels has not enunciated, deterministically, any "iron law" at all; he has formulated a conditional generalization about one aspect of the organization-process whose universal applicability is limited by a number of undetermined potential-variables. As Coser and Rosenberg put it: "all organizations have a tendency to develop ... oligarchical forms if this tendency is not counteracted by other forces." [18] The nature of such "other forces," including countervailing powers, then becomes a sociological problem-area.

In this paper we are concerned as to whether the principal characteristics of bureaucracy are not determined overwhelmingly by the character of the total social and political environment in which the bureaucracies exist, rather than by autonomous "immanent" characteristics.

In the contemporary situation, there are four major sets of variables: 1) whatever remains of indigenous social institutions, modified or otherwise; 2) the legacy of colonial rule, from infrastructure to ideology; 3) the new aims and powers of government and people; and 4) normative reference-groups, negative and positive, which shape these aims (e.g. bloc-membership, anti-imperialism, etc.).

Outside Afro-Asia and Eastern Europe, cases of non-revolutionary decolonization are few, certainly in America. Yet there is one striking example even in North America: this is Northern Saskatchewan, where a party and government with a markedly co-operative ethos, and a strong belief in popular participation in "devolved" government, is engaged in decolonizing the province's undeveloped north.

Here we find a powerful though skeletal bureaucracy little checked by secondary associations, but with an anti-bureaucratic and pluralistic ideology. Because of its ideology and objectives, therefore, it provides as crucial a case as Michels' analysis of the bureaucratization of a (formally) revolutionary organization. For despite this ideology, and an actual program of democratization, a profound gulf still exists between bureaucrat and citizen, and the people remain passive. Yet "oligarchy" by no means describes the power system, either. To see why requires examination of the four variables mentioned above:

1) The indigenous heritage. Very little remains of pre-white

social institutions. Northern Saskatchewan is a poor, bare region where agriculture is virtually impossible. It was and still is inhabited by a sparse population of Cree and Chipewyan Indians, formerly subsistence hunters and collectors, whose key social unit was the family, nomadic for most of the year. Society was unspecialized, segmentary, acephalous, and governed by the seasons.

2) The colonial impact. French and British fur-traders irrupted into this region in the second half of the eighteenth century, rapidly converting the Indian population into fur-producers for the markets of Europe. The marked inequality of economic and political power as between traders and Indians made the latter become sharply dependent on the former for trade goods: the relationship was not one of egalitarian symbiosis, reciprocity, or regional specialization. Politically, the Hudson Bay Company exercised *de jure* control of the region under its Charter; *de facto,* its supremacy was only established after 1821 when its major rivals were eliminated in what had amounted at times to open warfare. From then until Confederation, "the Bay" had no other economic rivals to contend with. After 1869, its power had been so effectively consolidated that new economic rivals made little headway, despite the company's loss of legal monopoly.

From 1845, however, authority had to be increasingly shared with the Roman Catholic and Anglican missions, which rapidly established recognized zones of influence. In addition to their religious activities, the missions provided educational and medical care, and often performed the functions of local government. The Indian and the Métis (person of mixed Indian-white ancestry) were thus dependent upon a dual authority of Church and company. Ethnic domination—the occupancy of nearly all positions of power, wealth, and prestige by white men—helped to consolidate the unity of the power-wielders, and override divisions within the dyarchy. This Church-company dyarchy, and the continuing mobility of the nomads, inhibited total co-ordination of institutional orders,[19] and allowed the Indians a certain autonomy and some room for maneuver vis-à-vis the dyarchs. But attempts to manipulate one set of whites against the other could only be largely ineffective.

Nationalism has never developed in the north. It was nipped in the bud by the suppression of two Métis rebellions—outside the

north in 1869/70 and 1885. There has been little social differentiation since that time; hence little vertical mobility, no indigenous
intelligentsia, no bourgeoisie, and until very recently very little
geographical mobility either. Moreover, a multi-racial society has
now developed as a result of over 200 years of white immigration
and domination.

Consequently, the Indians and Métis have never defined any
independent aims for themselves (variable 3), though they have
by no means failed to understand their position in the total social
order; nor have they identified themselves with, say, other colonial
peoples (variable 4), social movements or groups. The population
is thus singularly lacking in any active assertion of policies to improve its own situation, and particularly in institutions through
which to act, and has a lengthy tradition of dependence, due to
the economic, political, and ethnic domination of the whites, and
in particular of the two large corporate dyarchs.

The fur trade and "the Bay" remain dominant to this day in the
north, though the trade is now marginal in the over-all Canadian
economy, which is based on the agriculture and industry of the
south. The two Churches have a virtual spiritual duopoly.

In 1944, the Cooperative Commonwealth Federation, a populist
prairie-radical party with a strong social-democratic flavor, came
into power in Saskatchewan.[20] It proceeded to implement numerous welfare-state measures in the province as a whole, but also
developed a special program for the underdeveloped north. The
main foci of this latter policy were, firstly, economic: government
intervention in fur and fish marketing, either by monopoly or by
competition with private interests; the stimulation of producer,
consumer, and power co-operatives; conservation measures to protect natural resources; and encouragement of new enterprise in
commercial fishing, tourism, and mining. Secondly, government
intervention in province-wide infrastructural fields, such as air-
ways, bus-lines, insurance, etc.; thirdly, welfare programs to raise
health, educational, and living standards; fourthly, political stimulation of self-government via community councils, co-operatives,
etc., within a multi-racial framework.

These measures produced some striking successes—and some unanticipated consequences. The improvements in education, for ex-

ample, have created new problems for the formerly nomadic family which is still dependent on trapping, but which is now obliged to (and wishes to) keep its children at school. Trapping suffers; diminished income, over-trapped areas around the settlements, and increased dependence on welfare and relief payments result. A new generation of young people are leaving school with no particular motivation toward becoming trappers, and even less developed skills, yet trapping is the main employment opportunity. Post-1945 changes in fur and fish marketing, moreover, produced serious initial dislocations. And today, despite improved conservation (22,225 beaver harvested in 1959/60, compared with 4,242 in 1947/48), 90 to 95 per cent of the trappers still earn below $1000 a year.[21] In 1960 estimates of annual per capita incomes varying between $175 and $325 in different settlements contrast with a provincial average of $1245. Since the rapidly rising population, now with greatly enhanced expectations, find themselves still poor, they express their frustrations in hostility to government, stimulated, it is true, by the largely anti-C.C.F. white population. As a result, they respond weakly to the democratization program.

Today, outside four white-dominated mining and tourist centers, the overwhelmingly Indian (including Métis) population is concentrated in some dozen settlements, mainly below 1000 souls in size.

The new element in the situation is the government, which has appeared in force in the north since 1945 in the shape of specialized officials—teachers, nurses, foresters, etc.—but especially in the person of the non-specialist "Conservation Officer." Church and company remain very powerful, broadly conservative forces, but exercise nothing like the influence of the entrenched power-network described by Selznick in his TVA study, and are thus unable to form themselves into a "constituency" dominating the bureaucracy. Now, instead of dyarchy, we have a "triangle"[22] of authorities, in which the newest element—the government—is also the most powerful. This has particularly important consequences at the lowest level: in the isolated settlements, where the Conservation Officer is the lynch-pin of the government machine.

Far from being primarily occupied with specifically conservation duties, he is, in fact, the equivalent of the District Commissioner or Officer in the British Colonial Service. The "CO" here is responsible for "natural resources, community administration, tax collections, local government projects, Saskatchewan Hospital Services Plan, social welfare, and community development." [23] He is thus a multiplex, not a specialized official. His responsibilities are many and heavy. But his rewards are also considerable, not in terms of salary necessarily, but in terms of autonomy, local prestige, and power in the community. He has a great deal of power to award or cash, food, power, and prestige to withhold. His salary, moreover, and his living conditions accord with those of comparable jobs down south, and are thus very much higher than those of the depressed Indian-Métis. He is generally recruited from down south, and oriented in his long-term life perspectives toward the south. For all these reasons, he finds himself sharply marked off from the local people among whom he works. But if he finds himself alienated from them, it is certainly not due to sheer physical separation, for he is in daily, face-to-face contact with a wide variety of individuals, and, while it is true that informal "social" inter-visiting with Indians is minimal, his relationship with them is not otherwise "fragmented": he is known as a total personality. Because of the frontier situation, he has relative freedom from supervision, and is invested with considerable discretionary power. *De facto*, he can exercise even more power. He therefore has enough administrative latitude to avoid Mertonian "displacement of goals"—ritualism, working to rule, etc. To this extent, of course, he may be regarded as imperfectly bureaucratized; in the interstices of this loosely articulated bureaucratic machine, personal values flourish.

"Imperfectly-bureaucratized" he may be when measured against the Weberian ideal type, but empirically this all-purpose, isolated, self-reliant official is a representative of an important type in the emergent world. If he is not a Weberian "bureaucrat," he is nevertheless an ideal type of "official."

In Northern Saskatchewan, despite minimal barriers of social distance arising from purely physical and similar technical *ex officio* considerations, a social gulf exists between official and people. This gulf arises less from technical or other limitations inherent in office itself, than from the intrusion into the office situation of conflicts of norms, of which the most serious arise from the clash of interest-groups outside the office-situation altogether, i.e.

the total society. These conflicts of norms subject the local official to multiple conflicting pressures.[24] To analyze their pull on him, we need to stress the trinitarian nature of this local deity: at the one time a private personality; an office-holder transmitting and administering fixed policy; and an active initiator, formulator, and modifier of policy himself.

The first serious conflict of norms arises from the clash between his private values and those laid down for him by government. He may, for example, disapprove of government support for co-operatives (though most CO's, in fact, accept and internalize the validity and desirability of most major official policies). The official's personal values may also conflict with the values of the Indian community, for instance, over conceptions and standards of cleanliness, sexual morality, gambling, saving, etc. A double clash—between private values on the one hand, and official policy and Indian values on the other—is found in the common resentment on the part of CO's of having to pay family allowances to unmarried mothers. Some officers avoid doing so, or pay at lower rates than those officially prescribed.[25]

But the personal values of the official are, of course, rarely purely idiosyncratic. They are shaped by his total life experience: the totality of roles he has occupied and continues to occupy. He generally comes from a farming or urban background down south. In the settlement, because of the cultural and power cleavage, and because of his membership within this social field of an ethnic group which has traditionally been on top throughout Canadian history, the white official interacts most intensively with other whites, both on and off duty. On duty, his office involves him in exercising authority over Indians with other whites in most settlements. Off duty, he is thrown more heavily on his own nuclear family and on a very much smaller circle of white friends, than he would be down south. Unlike the south, again, where home and work are segregated spheres,[26] other whites and his own family exercise much greater pressure on him to conform to their norms, and they include the generally conservative women. They are familiar with his activities, not merely outside the work-situation but even within it. In consequence, a closed social network develops from which Indians are excluded, and the democratization program is undermined.[27]

He is a member of a local community, then, and of the white elite within that community. He is a member of a superior ethnic category. But he is also a member of a particular division of a large administrative machine. Personal interest in promotion, for example, can conflict with community development goals: promotion means leaving the community (even leaving the north altogether, for the Department is a province-wide, not a special "northern" service); it also stimulates detachment, and counteracts ideological and official drives toward "involvement." The CO, too, has normally come into the service initially in some functional capacity, usually as a conservation expert. But in recent years a changing society has thrust upon him a new multiplicity of duties for which he is untrained, and in which he is often uninterested. Finding that "community development" work—his newest task—often meets with slight response (for reasons outlined above), he is liable to slip into cynicism about official policy, and revert in his administrative style to authoritarianism or paternalism—habits officially frowned upon.[28]

Nor can certain kinds of latent administrative "strains"—such as inter-departmental rivalries, empire-building, etc.—develop in any bureaucracy, though if countervailing forces are at work, they do not inevitably assert themselves. That other types of "strain" are unique and purely idiosyncratic to particular bureaucracies and societies, is equally obvious. But the great bulk of conflicts are products of social situations that are neither culturally unique nor universal. Rather, they are characteristic of types and classes of social situation. Thus the attributes of bureaucracy under indirect rule differ profoundly from direct-rule situations. The specialized bureaucrat differs from the "multiplex"; the expatriate from the national. The official charged with meliorative or decolonizing tasks differs basically from the classical colonial officer whose duties hardly extended beyond keeping the peace and collecting the taxes.[29]

In the Saskatchewan situation, then, there are two main unanticipated sources of conflict, each having important practical consequences: the gulf between official and people, and the passivity of the latter. The first could no doubt be minimized by the Indianization of the bureaucracy, and by promoting local autonomy. Existing barriers of ethnicity imported into office could thus be removed. But an official still has to be recruited on the basis of conformity with some criteria, formal (e.g. educational) or informal (e.g. personality). Moreover, he has to exercise authority—punish, refuse, etc.—and thus court unpopularity. To this extent there is an "immanent" problem.

But overlapping, infused into the intrinsic strains of office are other tensions fed in from the outside. The white man is divided from the Indian-Métis *qua* official, but also *qua* white man. Indian officials occupying the same roles would be equally subject to the strains entailed in office. But they would import into the bureaucrat-client relationship quite different conflicts from those imported by white men occupying the same role. Their problem would not be separateness, affective neutrality, or hostility, but over-involvement. Indian managers of co-operatives have, in fact, found the duty of refusing credit to kinsmen particularly hard. The "involved" bureaucrat may suffer greater strains in resisting, or succumbing to, nepotism and partisanship than the alien official. There is no "problem-free" solution. The answer must lie in political allocation of priorities: if democratization and "participation" are the highest goals, then Indianization suggests itself; if short term functional "efficiency" within the framework of the *status quo*, then the alien official. As for passivity, its disappearance depends upon the lowering of ethnic barriers and the achievement of effective policy successes, especially those which raise living-standards.[30]

In this kind of face-to-face situation, the bureaucrat imports into his office role "extrinsic" affective and cognitive discharges from his other roles: he is not role-compartmentalized. This infusion of extra-official norms into an office situation is peculiarly entailed in the life situation of the "frontier" official. But the "pure" bureaucrat does not exist anywhere. The rational definition of duties and the concomitant value of disinterestedness of Weber's ideal type certainly form one important dimension of the total situation of the bureaucrat: they do not exhaust it.

An official is, by definition, distinguished from the public he deals with. He is recruited, too, according to defined criteria which, negatively, set him off from the "public," and, positively, link him with particular extra-official groups and milieux: a class, an educational category, an ethnic division, etc. Norms imported from this social background still affect him even in his official role.

Some differences of character between types of bureaucrat are entailed, as Parsons points out,[31] in the very division of functions by level: whether he is at strategic, co-ordination, or implemental levels—high, middle, or low—in the hierarchy of decision-making. Other differences arise from vertical divisions of function. The official occupies a particular role in one of a descending series of subsystems within a particular departmental hierarchy: this hierarchy is articulated with others at its apex to form an over-all governmental administrative machinery. There are, therefore, divisions between department and department; "field" v. "chairborne"; technical v. administrative, etc. Any one of these divisions is at the same time inherently an interest group: it is not merely a logical or functional division; it disposes of power and seeks to promote its own welfare.

All these make up the "intrinsic" social space of the office-holder. But even though these divisions, to be strict, may be distinguishable conceptually, as apparently purely "formal" distinctions, empirically they are never "pure" (except, perhaps, in the Simmelian form of inter-departmental competitive games or rituals of departmental solidarity). They are always infused with differences of content and reflect ties and divisions in the society at large. Departmental rivalries are commonly fought out in terms of policy differences. While the "policy" fights may at times be mere rationalization, genuine differences over policy do exist and do activate or exacerbate "intrinsic" functional divisions which might otherwise remain latent and inert. Since these divisions are divisions of function, and function implies policy, structural division is never "pure": it always involves cultural content.

It is true that common cultural functions, irrespective of other—even quite gross—cultural differences, will thus entail important resemblances between societies. Armies are examples of such "transcultural" institutional forms. Since men have to be trained to be ready to give up their lives on order, organizational methods and military ethoses will have much in common in all times and climes. But armies are also parts of particular socio-cultural systems: class structure, political system, reigning ideologies, etc., will all profoundly affect the kind of army, its mode of organization, even its battle style. Even these resemblances, therefore, though in a sense "trans-cultural," are not resemblances of "pure form," but profoundly culturally conditioned by parallel goals, and by differentiating cultural determinants in the rest of the social system.

An official, then in Mertonian terms, has a many-sided role-set attached to his office, and each relationship in the set affects his behavior. So far, we have principally considered those attributes determined by membership of overlapping sets in an organizational machinery.

But his role-set includes not only other officials—equals, superiors, and inferiors—within his own department or in other departments, but also members and representatives of political pressure-groups, parties, factions, etc. both within the official political framework and outside it. It also includes those interest groups in which the total society for whom these political pressure-groups speak or which they manipulate: political associations, religious bodies, and a thousand and one other pressure-groups, formal or informal, continuously functioning or intermittent. Here, then, differences in cultural goals in the society at large over the determination of policy exert pressure on the official and penetrate into the ranks of government.

All these memberships affect the bureaucrat's behavior, and each level is affected by all the others. Even at the lowest, local level, his behavior is intimately affected by quite macroscopic national and international pressures, as well as by face-to-face interactions: the one is mediated through the other. His actions will be affected, for example, by the direction of government policy; whether it aims at meliorative reform, repression, revolutionary change, a property-owning democracy, a classless society, etc. And every government today has one eye on the United Nations, and another on the major protagonists in the world struggle.

The official, then, is not adequately treated analytically by assuming the exhaustiveness of the attributes handled by Weber's ideal type. This certainly takes care of one particular set of attributes of the bureaucratic role and one particular ideology of office. Unfortunately, modern sociologists respond to Weber's creativity merely by measuring the extent to which particular "historical individuals" approximate or deviate from Weber's ideal type. They do not pay tribute to Weber by developing his theoretical insights: they merely mechanically exemplify. This universalistic approach obscures significant typological distinctions between the classes of bureaucrat deriving from differences in their position in different types of socio-cultural situations. Weber's ideal type, therefore, needs to be incorporated into a more comprehensive model which recognizes distinctions of level and division within bureaucratic organization, and the tripartite nature of the institutional norms bearing on the official: intra-departmental, intra-governmental, and intra-social. The "immanent" characteristics then recede into decent proportion, and do not hog the stage as in Michels.

Unlike universalists and idiographers, therefore, we need ideal types and models which are not exclusively concerned with postulated "immanent" processes of bureaucratization. In this analysis, we have exemplified this approach, not by pursuing the construction of a unitary Typology of Bureaucracy, but by using multiple conceptual tools to define the typological characteristics of one kind of bureaucrat: the multiplex bureaucrat at low level; face-to-face with his clients; interacting with them as a total personality; with considerable latitude and autonomy; working for "decolonization" goals (which frequently conflict with his own or other officials' technical jurisdictions, functions, training, and interests), these goals being laid down by governments with socialist-democratic values. These variables are not fortuitous congeries: they constitute a cluster of related variables built into the role of this kind of official, located as he is at a particular level in a particular type of social system within the general framework of a world system of social relations.

Today, the Conservation Officer of Saskatchewan has his counterpart in every poor country where populations unskilled in every sense are developing new expectations and aspirations; where their non-revolutionary governments nonetheless seek to promote rapid and far-reaching "development"; and where the multiplex, autonomous, alien official in the village is the man on whom so much depends. He is a major figure of our time.

NOTES:

1. See, for example, the theories—and the treatment of those theories—in Charles P. Loomis and Zona K. Loomis, *Modern Social Theories: Selected American Writers* (New York, 1961). Only Merton and—to a

lesser extent and in different ways—Becker and Sorokin (both unfashionable sociologists) break away from the functionalist conformity.

2. *The Sociology of Georg Simmel*, translated and edited by Kurt H. Wolff (Glencoe, 1950), p. 22.

3. S. F. Nadel, *The Theory of Social Structure* (London, 1957), pp. 147-9.

4. Georg Simmel, *Conflict and The Web of Group-Affiliations*, translated by Kurt H. Wolff and Reinhard Bendix (Glencoe, 1955), pp. 171-2 (my italics).

5. Rudolf Heberle, "The Sociology of Georg Simmel: The Forms of Social Interaction," in Harry Elmer Barnes (ed.), *An Introduction to the History of Sociology* (Chicago, 1949), p. 267 and p. 273, 88f. ". . . the rich sources of socio-economic surveys, dissertations and semiofficial inquiries . . ." were neglected by Simmel; the "domestic servant problem" [sic] served him for "illustrations" from the field of labor.

6. *The Sociology of Georg Simmel*, op. cit. p. 89f.

7. Simmel's views on conflict have stimulated a whole body of admirable work, notably by Gluckman and Coser. But conflict is only one "form" within the total range of forms, which, for Simmel, make up "formal" sociology, and to this must be added "general" and "philosophical" sociology.

8. W. H. Sprott, *Human Groups* (Harmondsworth, England, 1958), pp. 114, 117, 119, 135, 137.

9. Ibid. p. 87.

10. "German workingmen would sometimes reveal an uncanny familiarity with the Hawaiian and Iroquois mode of designating kin, matters not obviously connected with a proletarian revolution," R. H. Lowie, *The History of Ethnological Theory* (London, 1937), p. 54.

11. A. R. Radcliffe-Brown, *Structure and Function in Primitive Society* (London, 1952), p. 203.

12. See Marshall A. Sahlins and Elman R. Service (eds.), *Evolution and Culture* (Ann Arbor, 1960).

13. *Beyond the Welfare State: Economic Planning in the Welfare State and its International Implications* (London, 1960), p. 99.

14. See for example Ralf Dahrendorf, *Class and Class Conflict in Industrial Society* (London, 1959), p. 221.

15. S. M. Lipset, M. A. Trow, and J. S. Coleman, *Union Democracy: The International Typographical Union* (Glencoe, 1956), pp. 403-12.

16. *Power: A New Social Analysis* (London, 1960), p. 178.

17. See Merton's standard *Reader in Bureaucracy* (Glencoe, 1952), which discusses "The Structure of Bureaucracy," "The Bureaucrat," "Social Pathologies of Bureaucracy," etc. It contains, however, one attempt to delineate a generic *type* of bureaucracy, the military, in A. K. Davis' paper "Bureaucratic Patterns in the Navy Officer Corps." Here the specific cultural goals of *military* organization — battle-winning and the maintenance mechanisms required because of the intermittent nature of actual combat — are central to the analysis.

18. Lewis A. Coser and Bernard Rosenberg, *Sociological Theory: A Book of Readings* (New York, 1957), p. 433.

19. C. Wright Mills, *The Sociological Imagination* (New York, 1959), pp. 45-6, and Dahrendorf, op. cit. pp. 271-6.

20. See S. M. Lipset, *Agrarian Socialism: the Cooperative Commonwealth Federation on Saskatchewan* (Berkeley, 1950), Chapters XI and XII.

21. See Helen Buckley, *Trapping and Fishing in the Economy of Northern Saskatchewan*, Economic and Social Survey of Northern Saskatchewan, Report No. 3, Saskatoon, 1962, Chap. III; App. III. Table 1.

22. Burridge's term for the tripartite division of power between trader, missionary, and government official in New Guinea: K. O. L. Burridge, *Mambu: A Melanesian Millennium* (London, 1960).

23. Saskatchewan Government, Department of Natural Resources, *Annual Report* (Regina, 1960), p. 145.

24. See J. E. M. Kew, *Cumberland House in 1960*, Economic and Social Survey of Northern Saskatchewan, Report No. 2, Saskatoon, 1962, p. 110.

25. See Kew, op. cit. for instances of such "latitude of action" (p. 106), and resistance to higher level policy (p. 125).

26. Cf. Kew, op. cit. p. 105: "... the Conservation Officer is seldom apart from his formal role. His extensive duties and lack of anonymity make his job never-ending ...," and the other illustrations given.

27. Jean Guiart has shown for New Guinea how European rhythms of life and the pull of domestic ties ("Madame attend, qui ne veut pas etre seule") conflict with Melanesian rhythms. The European Development Officer is thus insulated at home at the time when the villagers are discussing their problems: "Développement communautaire en Nouvelle-Guinée australienne: le Tolai Cocoa Project," *Current Problems in Community Development*, 1961, No. 8, p. 148.

28. Community Development Officers in India face similar temptations. There, however, nationalist dedication, formally incorporated into training, helps counteract these tendencies. Though many CO's in Saskatchewan are "idealistic" in orientation, their level of dedication is much lower than that of the nationalist Village-Level Worker in India (see S. C. Dube, *India's Changing Villages*, Ithaca, N. Y., 1958).

29. For an excellent demonstration of the effects of differing national cultural traditions on administrative style, see Thomas Hodgkin, *Nationalism in Colonial Africa* (London, 1959).

30. For subtle analyses of "passivity" in colonial Algeria and Madagascar respectively, see Frantz Fanon, *L'An V de la Révolution Algérienne* (Paris, 1962), and O. Mannoni, *Prospero and Caliban: the Psychology of Colonization* (London, 1956).

31. Talcott Parsons, "Some Ingredients of a Formal Theory of Organization," *Structure and Process in Modern Societies* (Glencoe, 1960), pp. 59-96.

# 23

GINO GERMANI

## Social Change and Intergroup Conflicts

I

The historic process through which Latin America is now passing may be interpreted as part of a general transition from a type of social structure generically designated as "traditional" to a type of structure designated as "industrial." There are obviously a number of species of traditional society, a number of types of industrial society, and various forms of transition from the former to the latter. These various forms of industrial society and of transition are not phenomena occurring in the past and continuing at present, but appear as practical alternatives, as ideologies. As such industrial styles compete with one another on the plane of political struggle.

An analysis of tensions occurring in national regions among the many groups comprising the structure of each country necessarily has to be made with reference to this process of socio-economic change. The analysis we are going to offer is based on a specific example of such a process.[1] Basic to a discussion of inter-group tensions in Latin America, and their points of contact with the issues of social change; are the notions of *mobilization* and *integration*.

We start with the concept of an "integrated" society. By this term we mean a society in which the following circumstances occur: (a) The various portions of the normative structure, i.e. the systems and subsystems of norms, statuses, and roles, are in a state of relative reciprocal adjustment. There is a certain degree of "compatibility" between the various parts sufficient to assure the "normal" functioning of a society (there may be conflicts, but these are either foreseen and resolved within the structure itself, or else they are not so intensive as to prevent such functioning). (b) The expectations, roles, and attitudes are "internalized," corresponding to what is demanded by and foreseen by the normative structure (there is thus a degree of reciprocal compatibility and congruence between the "internalizations" of individuals). (c) The actual circumstances within which the actions of the individuals belonging to a society correspond sufficiently to the predictions, expectations, and definitions of the situations, as they arise from the normative system and the relative "internalizations." (Such circumstances do not merely result from interaction between the members of the society in question, but also from physical and environmental facts and processes, and interferences stemming in large part from other societies.) To understand this better we shall call the first aspect of integration *normative* integration, the second aspect indicated *psycho-social* integration, and the third aspect *environmental* integration.

We shall define "disintegration" as any situation in which it is not possible to observe, even minimally, a state of adjustment to one or more of the three aspects. The concept of an "integrated" society is a borderline notion which never actually occurs in reality. All real societies display a certain degree of "disintegration" or "non-integration." There will be periods in which it becomes particularly intense, or affects essential areas of human activity, and other periods in which the lack of integration, or "disintegration," remains restricted.

Every social change, defined as a transformation of the social structure, implies a certain degree of disintegration. This is due to the asynchronism in change of the various parts of the structure. This is the well-known phenomenon of the "lag" understood in broader terms than in Ogburn's original formula.[2] Only if all social parts were to vary at the same time and in the same direction would it be possible to maintain the adjustment or congruency in norms. Further, "actual" physical circumstances within which the social structure operates would also have to undergo congruent transformations. The most frequent situation is that of asynchronism, and hence the loss of adjustment on some or all of the three levels. There will be some "disintegration." It is important to note for the purpose of tension analysis, that this disintegrative process may be perceived from a number of angles: there may be conflict, both as regards the mere diagnosis of the process (meaning and orientation of change), and in the merit of values (the most desirable type of social change).

In the first place, two opposite points of view arise: (a) that of the structure *from* which the change operates, and (b) that of the structure *toward* which the change is oriented. Each of these perspectives gives rise to attitudes of acceptance or rejection of the process. Furthermore, when change is viewed from the point of view of an anticipated structure, other divergencies may arise: different diagnoses as regards the orientation of the process itself (i.e. what type of society or partial structure is going to result from the change); and different concepts concerning the structural model toward which the tendency ought to lead. These are precisely the divergent points of view which occur in the form of contrasting political ideologies.

## II

This notion of an "integrated society" (and its correlation with states of "disintegration" or "non-integration") permits us to describe the processes of mobilization and integration. These concepts refer to the situation of social groups within the overall social structure (and with reference to other groups) at times when the situations of integration, non-integration, and disintegration occur. Although the situation of a group may be analyzed from a number of aspects, we shall here limit ourselves to an examination of just one of them—participation.

When a group feels itself to be "integrated" it will function in a "normal" manner within society; *its participation will be precisely that predicted and expected in line with the normative structure.* In view of the "internalized" expectations, and as a result of environmental circumstances, the roles, expectations, and attitudes within various spheres of behavior will be made legitimate, and will be so perceived by the other groups comprising a society.

Such normality does not imply absence of conflicts. It does mean that conflicts will be those predicted and expected by the normative and psycho-social structure. Different types of social structures may be characterized by different degrees and forms of participation of the various groups in multiple spheres of human activity. In particular, in "traditional" types of society there is a considerable majority of the population whose participation is circumscribed with respect to geographic surroundings (limited to small communities); occupation (isolation in the economic sector); non-participation in decision-making (absence in political activity); and knowledge, experience, and enjoyment of the material and non-material benefits of general culture (as occurs when a considerable portion of the inhabitants is limited to the confines of their respective ethnic backgrounds).

The so-called industrial society is characterized by a high degree of mass participation in the majority of social activities. In both traditional and industrial societies, therefore, integration is characterized in differential ways. In each case role expectation and status legitimation are performed by the groups comprising them. Further, in both types of societies, "actual" environmental circumstances will be adequate and sufficient to ensure the degree of participation which is normatively and psychologically admitted, if not required.

It is important to distinguish "integrated" participation from another very different form, "non-integrated participation." The former is that which takes place under conditions of normative, psychological, and environmental integration. The second occurs in those cases in which there is no correspondence between the degree, form, and extension of the psychological and normative participation demanded, and that which actually takes place. This lack of correspondence may result in opposite tendencies: in the direction of "excess" or that of "deficiency"; of participation in relation to what is normatively and psychologically expected, and to what is effectively possible in view of existing environmental circumstances.

We have seen that all social change, to the extent that it is characterized by lags or asynchronisms, implies "disintegration" or "lack of integration," which is perceptible both from the point of view of the preceding structure and from that of the desired or anticipated structure. The process of participation implies that groups affected by the changes relinquish the level, degree, or form of integrated participation, and pass to other types of unforeseen activity in the normative and psycho-social structure of the society prior to the change. Change in participation may imply either a reduction of an increase in level and extension. In line with an example currently employed, the group finds itself "displaced" in regulation to a pre-existent structure. This displacement may be translated, according to the particular case, by withdrawal, apathy, abandonment of activities, or increased participation. Though these phenomena occur in reality, the one which is of special importance in the analysis of social transition is that of increase in participation. This process we call "mobilization." We understand by mobilization the "excess" (in degree, extent, or form) of group participation in relation to the level defined by the old society as "normal."

Obviously mobility must be distinguished from mobilization.[3] Both concepts are related to participation but whereas the former —in all of its ecological, psychological, and occupational forms— characterizes the industrial society and is precisely the *sine qua non* for integrated participation, the latter concept of mobilization has been defined as a contrary type, that of non-integrated participation. From this point of view, mobility is a recurrent process or state, proper to the industrial society; whereas mobilization is a phenomenon of transition, a non-recurrent process, which has an origin and a destination.

The process of transition is characterized by an initial disintegration of the traditional structure (in at least some of its portions). On the group level, this disintegration is revealed through the displacement of the groups with relation to the place which corresponded to them. Such displacement has at times been called "disposability," and the groups affected by this process have been called "disposable groups." When this disposability is translated into a more intensive participation than occurs in previous structures or in spheres formerly excluded, then we speak of mobilization. When changes have occurred which make it possible on the one hand to legitimate, and on the other to afford effective possibilities of achievement of the added degree of participation of the mobilized groups, then we speak of integration. There is a temporal succession, which, though very frequent, is not essential to the definition. What we have tried to elicit are different "moments" of the transition, distinguishable as units of analysis, though they may at times occur simultaneously.

In accordance with the general phenomenon of asynchronism, simultaneity very rarely occurs. In a first phase some groups find themselves placed in disposability by the partial disintegration of certain sectors of traditional society, and when they respond with added active participation in any sector not foreseen in the preceding structure, we can say that they have been mobilized. This first phase of disposability and mobilization may be followed by a second one of integration, which may, *grosso modo*, occur in different ways and which may take place simultaneously: first, *by assimilation*, through modification in the mobilized groups which acquire the necessary features for legitimization as participating groups; and second, *by social change*, modification of the structure of society which becomes transformed in the direction required so as to make participation practically suitable and normatively and psychologically legitimate.

Furthermore, both mobilization and integration do not occur in the same social group at the same time in all sectors of behavior (or in all sectors of the structure in which the group participates), but at different times. The result is that there may be coexistence of very different situations: mobilization in certain sectors of behavior, integrated participation in others, and persistence of the traditional pattern in the remainder. As regards the others, the scheme roughly simplifies the concrete processes occurring, because even within what we considered analytically as a given area of behavior (e.g. work, the family, political activity, recreation, etc.) one may have every kind of combination between "traditional" and "non-traditional" elements. This particular phenomenon, which has elsewhere been termed "the fusion effect," features many transitional situations.

This variety of possibilities is undoubtedly influenced by the causes and forms in which the "disposability" effect and mobilization occurs (when the former leads into the latter). In principle, "disposability" arises as a result of the loss of integration in some or a number of the three levels mentioned in the definition: (a) alteration in the internal correspondence between socially valid norms; (b) alteration in the correspondence between norms on the one hand and "internalized" attitudes on the other; (c) alteration between norms and attitudes on the one hand and effective possibilities of application on the other. The specific forms which these phenomena may assume are extremely varied, and although the commencement of the process may occur on any of the three levels, in the vast majority of cases, it will tend to extend to others.

In each instance there are two essential aspects which should be mentioned. In the first place there is the "disposability" which implies always that the so-called "loss of correspondence" has affected the level of attitudes; and in the second place, whatever may be the particular sector of attitudes in which the disadjustment has taken place, it will tend to extend more or less rapidly to other fields. This is the least and most generic assertion to make. It merely indicates that the groups affected must notice the change and perceive it as an alteration which makes former prescriptions inapplicable. Such alteration can be matched by forms of anomia and individual disorganization, or by attitudes which tend to build up new roles implying participation, and it is precisely this active response that we call mobilization.

It should be mentioned that within this scheme we do not necessarily assign causal priority to "objective" changes (in the narrative system or in the environmental circumstances) in relation to "subjective" ones (alterations in attitudes or internalized roles). Hence an increased level of communication of ideas may comprise one of the elements which unleashes nothing short of an "objective" alteration in the population equilibrium, economic structure, etc. It should be stressed that these are always "circular" processes in which changes on one level stimulate and facilitate changes on other levels, which may in turn react on the former. These processes can facilitate or inhibit further circulation within the social structure.

III

The three phenomena which we have endeavored to define—disposability, mobilization, and integration—may now be taken as starting points for the analysis of tensions, to the extent that these center around the fact of a sudden active participation of groups formerly characterized by their "passivity." This "awakening" is perceived (and received) in different manners by the various sectors of the population, and in their attitudes in this respect—often in violent contrast or opposition to one another—is to be sought the main and perhaps only source of tensions. This phenomenon is well known. The term "revolution of growing aspirations" refers precisely to facts of this type. The analysis thus far has been aimed at formulating the meaning of this process with a certain amount of precision, and relating it to change as a whole. Our purpose has also been to stress that this "awakening," this "revolution of aspirations," is by no means restricted to economic sectors, to a demand for a higher level of consumption. It is all of this, but much more: it is a new attitude of generalized participation which enters into conflict with pre-existing attitudes in many groups, and also with the concrete possibilities of finding relatively adequate satisfactions within concrete circumstances. Interpretation in the strict economic sense of "rising expectations" of large sectors of the population in Latin America has been and remains a source of serious misunderstanding and error, not only on the part of the dominant elites of each country but also by many foreign observers. This misunderstanding leads to appraisal of the success or failure of a movement merely on the basis of what it offers in terms of economic improvement. However, what we might term "an inexperience in participation" in other spheres (and often a mere illusion of participation) may be as effective in assuring the support of the recently mobilized groups as an expansion in consumption.

It may be asserted that inter-group tensions and conflicts depend upon two kinds of variables. The first is related to the structure of the groups, including the system of social stratification, the ethnic structure (if there is differentiation in this respect), the distribution of the population throughout an area, and the "central" or "peripheral" position occupied by various groups. This position is related to the hegemony of certain areas within the national territory. At the same time it is concerned with the distribution of power. As regards the second kind of variable, aspects of a different kind should be noted: (a) the sphere of human activity within which disposability, mobilization, and possible subsequent integration take place, (b) the rapidity of the process of change, (c) the existence of mechanisms of integration within the society, which are adequate for the groups in course of mobilization, (d) independent of the above, previous existence or otherwise of "actual" possibilities making integrated participation viable. These last two aspects also include the rapidity with which mechanisms of integration, where non-existent, may be created through the transformation of the existing structure and the social "cost" of such mechanisms. The same remarks can be made with respect to the creation of concrete circumstances permitting or rendering such participation viable. Finally, there is (e) the respective proportions of the population already mobilized, still to be mobolized, integrated, or in the course of integration, that is to say, the state of the over-all process in which the various groups comprising the population are engaged.

Latin American countries present considerable differences with respect to the aspects mentioned above, and this makes it difficult to lay down propositions of a precise nature applicable to all of them. In general terms, the causes which have produced the breakdown of the traditional pattern are well known and might be mentioned in passing. They consist of the growing penetration of the national society into considerable layers of the population which have, in one form or another, remained isolated, the breakup of local communities, disappearance of the enclosed or isolated economies and their growing incorporation into the national economy; transformation of traditional forms of work into wage labor, either by the establishment of industries or by changes in the primary, agricultural, or extractive sector, and hence disappearance of old "primary" or community forms of social relationships in the sphere of work as well as in other sectors such as the life of the community, its means of recreation; growth of means of transportation and greater accessibility of the "central" zones from the peripheral areas; universal penetration of mass means of communication; increasing educational facilities and their dissemination among larger sectors of the population; disequilibrium in population, caused by the persistent high birth rates with falling death rates. These and other phenomena disrupt the traditional order on a scale not comparable with what has occurred in past centuries. During the period of the struggle for independence, and throughout the whole of the nineteenth century and part of the present century, with but a few exceptions, modernization affected only small groups of elites, in the central areas of each country. The process of development today affects the entire population and invades the whole national territory. Furthermore, the process has acquired unprecedented velocity.

Conflicts and tensions arise as a consequence of an incongruence in the aspirations, attitudes, motivations, and corresponding behavior of each group comprising the social structure. The most evident conflicts are those between recently mobilized groups of the lower strata, and groups possessing political and economic power, inasmuch as the new-found attitudes of participation on the part of the former are not accepted as "legitimate" by the governing elites. The old elites continue to follow an orientation in line with traditional expectations. The lining up (*enfrentamiento*) of the traditional families, with their allies—the army and the Church —are presumably the classic form assumed in Latin America, and manifested in innumerable ideological forms. Of course, conflicts and tensions are far more complicated than one simple model can indicate. There are a number of aspects which make the situation far more complex:

(a) In the first place the incongruencies—and hence the conflicts —do not arise merely between groups located in different situations within the hierarchy of power, prestige, and economy, but also include others situated within the same elite.

The role of the nascent bourgeoisie and other strata of the middle class—or middle sectors, as they have been called—in facing up to groups which formerly monopolized the power is well known. In many cases, the new entrepreneurial groups, oriented toward industrialization, confront the "traditional families," whose power and vitality are based on the concentration of land tenure, or the export of raw materials. Similar conflicts are faced by the Church and the army.

The situations created by rapid change may produce all kinds of alignments, not only between various groups but also intramural conflicts. It would be a mistake to consider the army as a monolithic sector enrolled in favor of one or other solution. Quite the contrary, in a majority of countries the army is fragmented into a number of factions which to some extent reflect the cleavages existing in society (although in general terms the intervention of the army has almost always been in favor of the pre-existing order). It must not be forgotten that new motives for conflict usually become superimposed on the former struggles between factions of a purely personalistic type which characterized the early political history of most Latin American countries.

Nor would it be correct to speak of the "lower" strata as a monolithic block facing the former holders of power. The process of transformation into an industrial social structure tends to differentiate within these strata, certain sectors with special characteristics peculiar to the productive process and living standards. Also, the process of mobilization acquires different rates of progress in the various groups and this introduces an extrinsic differentiation between more modernized and less modernized sectors. To all this must be added ethnic differences which sometimes play a role in the conflicts, particularly within the "lower" strata.

Finally there are conflicts which arise to some extent outside the system of social stratification. Such is the case with the conflict between generations, which obviously becomes more acute in times of rapid change. In Latin America the high degree of political interest and involvement of university students has made them a source of leadership of great importance in movements aimed at giving revolutionary answers (though often contradictory) to the new situations created by the process of transition.

(b) In the second place, "incongruencies" do not arise only *between* groups, but also *within* them, that is, among their individual members. In such persons certain "mobilized" aspects may coexist with the persistence of traditional attitudes in others. For instance, the rural immigrant may have become transformed into an industrial worker, but his orientation toward a certain type of paternalistic or particularistic relationship which featured his former situation on the job may not have disappeared and may continue to influence his relations toward the firm or the labor union. Equivalent asynchronisms may occur between entrepreneurs, politicians, old and new governing elites, the emerging middle class, and the nascent industrial bourgeoisie.

(c) In the third place, aspirations toward participation in consumption often do not encounter adequate possibilities of satisfaction within actual existing circumstances. The prevailing degree of economic development does not make it possible to respond to the demand for a higher standard of living. At the same time the distribution of the national product is very unfavorable to the mobilized groups. The well-known "demonstration effect" affects the lower strata just as much as the middle and upper strata. It leads toward a consumption orientation which is imitative of highly developed countries, under conditions in which the productive machinery is still in a state of underdevelopment or insufficient development. There is a production of desires relative to a stage of "mass consumption" in a period in which the "take off" has not yet occurred. This demonstration effect, in the attitudes of the higher strata, implies emphasis on consumption rather than emphasis on production. Here we find an inversion of the order observed in the historic development according to the Western model ("capitalist asceticism" and "Protestant ethics" in the stage of accumulation).[4]

These asynchronisms obviously cause conflicts to the extent that they produce contrasting expectations between social groups and stimulate certain desires, without the acceptance of the corresponding costs. A typical instance of this is the phenomenon of the aspiration—of "development" or "modernization," which is not accompanied by the recognition and acceptance of many of its consequences regarding the many privileges of these same groups. Similar considerations might be made with regard to the ideological expressions adopted by movements arising among a recently mobilized lower strata. One of the characteristic features of newly emerging nations is the adoption of unrealistic and internally contradictory attitudes. An analysis of the ideologies of development of different (or even contrary) orientation might lead to the discovery of internal incoherences. This makes it possible to relate them, at least in part, to the contradictions inherent in the position of the groups sustaining them.

The integration of mobilized groups may occur by assimilation or by change in the social structure. It should be pointed out that these forms are not mutually exclusive but may be combined in various ways. Within the situation in Latin American countries the latter form is nevertheless the predominant one, in other words, through mass mobilization of large strata of the population, the very structure of society is submitted to a radical process of transformation. Whereas the general direction of the process is toward modernization, i.e. toward the introduction of some form of industrialization, there are three aspects which vary fundamentally: (a) the type of industrial society assumed as a goal by the various groups, (b) the type of industrial society which is actually possible in view of existing conditions, and (c) the gradual or violent form characteristic of the process itself.

Particularly interesting is the last mentioned aspect. It is this which defines the nature of conflicts between groups during the transition period. It is clear, however, that gradual or violent methods of introducing change are not independent of the other two. The nature of the ideologies expressed by specific groups and circumstances limit the orientation of the developmental process.

It may be said as a general rule that the faster the process of "disposability" and mobilization, the greater the proportion of the population which becomes mobilized in a given period of time. This is called the "rate" of mobilization.[5] The fewer the possibilities of channeling such mobilization through legitimate mechanisms of participation, the greater will be the tensions, and the higher the probability of violent conflicts. Other essential aspects are the respective proportions between that part of the total population of a country which is wholly mobilized and integrated into modern forms of life, the part still submerged in the traditional order, and finally the part in process of mobilization. One important element for determining the character of conflicts consists in the possibility of social process taking place in successive stages. In other words, the time and opportunity between one stage and the next sufficient to integrate that part of the population which is mobilized. This is what has occurred in many countries in the West, both with respect to political integration and in relation to other forms of participation. In this respect, three main stages may be distinguished: (a) limited participation democracy in which only a small proportion of the population (i.e. the elites and the nascent middle classes) has effective participation in political life; (b) broad participation democracy in which the majority of the population of the "central" layers achieves legitimate participation: not only the elites but also the numerically important middle classes and the urban proletariat playing a part; (c) total participation democracy in which the population of the peripheral zones is also included. In each stage there is formation of channels of participation which makes it possible to integrate that part of the population which is to be mobilized in the next stage. The equilibrium of the system

at each stage is assured by the fact that the population not yet included does not exert pressure (or at least, not a dangerous degree
of pressure) because it remains passive, and the sequence is such
that when it later becomes active there should be existing mechanisms capable of channeling participation without catastrophic
disturbances for the system (although obviously not without relatively sharp conflicts). This model has been applied (in these or
analogous terms) to the formation of the political structure of the
most advanced countries of the Western world.[6] It could undoubtedly be applied to other forms of mobilization and integration, and
especially the sequence of expansion of the technical and economic
apparatus for mass production, to aspirations for mass consumption, has followed precisely this set-up in the countries which industrialized early.

The sequence of stages mentioned above, a low rate of development combined with a marked elasticity in social structure
(shown in the disposition of the governing classes to accept the
change and the attitude on the part of the lower strata in moderating their demands), have been the essential features of this
process in the West. But the situation in Latin America is quite
different.

## IV

The wide variety of situations existing within this region makes it
impossible to go much beyond the general terms of analysis we
have provided. Resorting to the procedure—limited and imperfect
though it be—of a typology of countries, it will be possible to give
a few concrete instances of our descriptive abstract.

As a basis for classification, a number of criteria have been taken
from among those already discussed in the preceding analysis:
(a) the proportion of population mobilized, in relation to total
population ("mobilization" not as a particular form, i.e. mobilization in relation to a particular sector of behavior, but as a kind of
"average" mobilization appraised on an impressionistic basis), (b)
degrees of integration into the national society of a population already mobilized (adopting an analogous criterion of average "integration"), (c) the "weight" that may be brought to bear on the
general equilibrium of a country by the concentration of a certain

proportion and quantity of population in selective areas of a country, (d) the presence of mechanisms or agencies of integration, institutionalized within the existing social structure. This classification is admittedly impressionistic. But it might be useful for the construction of a hypothetical system adequate for a less impressionistic analysis. As presented here, the classification has no pretense of being more than illustrative.

A. *Countries in which mobilization and integration are almost complete.* The only Latin American nation which appears to approach this type is Uruguay. The supposition is that the conflicts and tensions between groups here tend to assume the "institutionalized" form characteristic of the countries of the West, within a political structure based on some form of "representative democracy."

B. *Countries in which mobilization is almost complete and integration is incomplete.* Argentina and Venezuela may be included in this category, although due to different historical causes. Argentina is the Latin American country with the most long-standing mobilization. It is also the nation which, from the social point of view, comes closest to the "developed" model as illustrated by Uruguay. It remained stable, on a basis of expanding integration and mobilization (excluding the population cluster residing in peripheral areas), for almost seventy years, from 1860-1930. But that equilibrium was based on the existence of a very high proportion of immigrant population. The foreign born participated in all "modern" activities, however they did not exercise direct political pressure. From 1930 until the present, total mobilization took place. The conflicts of the past thirty years reflect the difficulty of finding a new equilibrium on the basis of adequate integration.

The case of Venezuela is that of a country in which mobilization started belatedly and proceeded at an extremely fast pace. The conflicts in these countries tend to assume violent forms and the possibilities of maintaining a political and social structure of the "representative democracy" type are seriously threatened. Although in the case of Argentina particularly the alternative of the "national people's revolution" type on the extreme right or the extreme left [7] seems hardly viable (in view of the degree of modernization achieved), the difficulties of achieving adequate integration might

very well give rise to attempts of that kind. Even more exposed to
this resolution is Venezuela, whose structure is far less modernized
than that of Argentina.

C. *Countries of expanded mobilization and integration in a state
of equilibrium.* The special characteristic of these countries is that
the part of the population which has been "mobilized" has at least
in some respects been absorbed by corresponding integration, although at the same time there is a sector of perhaps as much as
50 per cent of the population which coexists in a state which can be
described as partially marginal to the national life. The relative
present equilibrium is achieved on the basis of the relative "inactivity" of the marginal population. The typical example of this is
Chile. Brazil and Mexico may also be included in this category,
though with many reservations. In the latter countries the equilibrium is relatively assured by the fact that the portion of the population which is mobilized and relatively integrated, though representing a smaller proportion, is concentrated in "central" areas, and
in view of the over-all size of the population does represent an absolute volume of inhabitants capable of providing the system with
a certain amount of stability. Brazil and Mexico, as a matter of fact,
display features which are considerably different from one another.
The latter has achieved its equilibrium in an unusual form of representative democracy (with virtually a sole political party), which
has been capable of integrating the population in the course of
mobilization without thus far causing major disturbances. Certain
social reforms and an adequate ideology in the form of a kind of
"national people's" revolution have so far provided the most important integrating factors. Brazil, with a social structure far closer
to the "traditional" type, is an instance of dangerous instability.

To the extent that these countries manage to maintain a certain
equilibrium between mobilization and integration the conflicts will
assume institutionalized forms, with gradual changes. However, the
existence of a substantial part of the population which is still marginal to the system entails the continuing possibility of a more or
less drastic change in the equilibrium.

D. *Countries with low integration and extensive or very rapid
mobilization.* This is the situation in the majority of the countries in
Latin America (with the exception of Costa Rica and Colombia).
Here the conflicts tend to assume violent forms and the orientation

of such conflicts drift away from that type of political and social structure which might *grosso modo* be termed "representative democracy." Almost all of them lack a prior stage of limited or broad integration, contain archaic social structures (especially as regards the systems of social stratifications), and mobilization is taking place at a fast rate, not only by displacement of the population (migration from country to town) but also by modifications occurring in the heart of the rural population itself. The more rigid the archaic elements, the more protracted has been the process of modernization. The lack of communication between traditional elites and other strata in the course of mobilization is at a maximum and the rapidity of the process leaves little opportunity for finding temporary adjustments. Although it is possible that in each country there may be factors making it possible to develop a series of transitory solutions facilitating a non-violent change and reducing the "cost," in general terms it may be said that it is in this category that the most explosive situations are to be found.

NOTES:

1. Bibliography on this subject is vast. Our approach to the matter was mentioned by the author in *Política y Sociedad en una época de transición* (Buenos Aires, 1962).

2. I.e. based on a motion of social structure which substantially differs from that which is implicit in the well-known distinction between the so-called "material" and "non-material" elements, cf. op. cit.

3. Concepts tending to interpret the behavior of the groups comprising a society, in terms of "displacement," "disposability," "mobilization," etc., are very common in the literature on the subject, but K. W. Deutsch has given a more precise definition of the concept of mobilization, utilizing it in his book *Nationalism and Social Communication* (New York, 1953), Chap. 6. He recently defined social mobilization as the process whereby the main components of the former loyalties and commitments are broken up, in the social, psychological, and political order, and people become "disposable" for the acceptance of new forms of behavior "socialization." (K. Deutsch, "Social Mobilization and Political Development," *American Political Science Review*, LV, 1961, 493-514.) The origin of the concept may be found in Karl Mannheim, *Man and Society* (New York, 1940). The idea of "disposability" used in relation to a process which is different but analogous, occurring in the European middle classes between the two world wars, was formulated by R. Aron. Furthermore the description in

different terms of this integration of the mobilized masses may be found in a number of authors. An excellent description of the process of political integration in England, in terms conceptually similar, is found in T. H. Marshall, *Citizenship and Social Class* (Cambridge, England, 1950). In this study the author has endeavored to give to the process of "disposability" (and possible mobilization) a definition sufficiently broad to cover every type of disintegrative process of the collective type, and not only that emanating from traditional structures. The intention was to find common comparative elements (and the necessary distinctions) in relation to the phenomena which gave rise to the totalitarian movements of the right and the left in Europe. A comparative analysis of fascism and peronism, more or less in these terms, may be found in Gino Germani, *La integración política de las masas y el totalitarismo* (Buenos Aires, 1956). An application to the situation in Latin America is to be found in "Démocratie représentative et classes populaires en Amérique Latine," in *Sociologie du Travail*. A definition based on a typology of social action is contained in *Política y Sociedad*, op. cit.

4. Here we have a case of the "fusion effect." The recent attitudes which stress consumption, and which have arisen in the countries of highest development, are adopted by the elites in the less developed countries, but here they often fuse with the concepts of the "seigneurial" life which predominated in the traditional society, and which, paradoxically speaking, thus obtains reinforcement originating in the most extreme models of the "modern" society.

5. K. Deutsch, in the works mentioned above, gives indications regarding the calculation of this ratio, based on macro-sociological indices.

6. Cf. G. Germani, "Démocratie représentative . . . ," op. cit. G. Germani and K. Silvert: "Politics, Social Structure and Military Intervention in Latin America," *Archives Européenes de Sociologie,* 1 and the bibliography mentioned therein.

7. In the two articles mentioned in the preceding note, the hypothesis is presented that in the transition toward structures of the industrial type one of the forms which tends to be acquired by the process, lacking a basis for progressive expansion of integrated participation as in stages taking place in the Western world, is that of some type of "national" regime or revolution. These regimes may be oriented to the extreme right or to the extreme left, and—even more probably—assume hybrid forms hard to classify according to the traditional left-right formula. The regimes of Vargas and Peron, the cases of Bolivia and (more extreme) Cuba, are instances of the various possibilities in this respect. The common denominator is that they offer some form of "legitimate participation" to the mobilized masses, although often this is an illusory form of participation.

# 24

ROBERT A. DENTLER
AND PHILLIPS CUTRIGHT

## Social Effects of Nuclear War *

Studies of the effects of nuclear war which deal primarily with the physical damage to be expected from such a conflict tend to leave us with a picture of a surviving society composed of fewer individuals with reduced physical resources but with the same basic democratic institutions and relationships that characterize our present society. We are concerned here with the *social* damage to be expected from nuclear war; with a series of major social problems, defining these generally as breakdowns in relations between the main elements of the social system (e.g. population, social organization, technology, and physical environment) so severe as to threaten the survival of the system. Many features of each element are neglected, including medical technology, communications, and the administration of justice, not because these are insignificant, but because we are better equipped professionally to assess the problems selected. Our criteria were pragmatic; namely, our competence as sociologists and those problems on which evidence could be obtained.

Two studies by the Office of Civil and Defense Mobilization (OCDM) on the effects of thermonuclear war upon civilians in the

* We are grateful for permission to publish this article which summarizes findings from a larger study by the same authors, *Hostage America: Human Aspects of a Nuclear Attack and a Program of Prevention* (copyright, © 1963 Robert A. Dentler and Phillips Cutright, Beacon Press, Boston, 1963).

United States have been released to the public. A partial text of these reports has appeared in official government documents.[1] Each of the limited attacks discussed by the OCDM assumed a strike directed both at military installations on the continental United States and at certain cities whose industries or locations near military bases would make them targets in a thermonuclear war.

The principal difference between the two studies is in the size of the attacks assumed. The 1957 study was based on a hypothetical attack of 2500 megatons, the 1959 study on one of 1500 megatons. 1500 and 2500 megatons of explosive power do not represent the actual capability of the weapons stockpiles and delivery systems of either the United States or the U.S.S.R. However, the number and size of bombs likely to be committed in an attack and the number of missiles or planes that would succeed in delivering their payload on target cannot be known. As missiles replace planes, and as the accuracy of missiles increases, the tendency might be in the direction of less megatonnage.[2]

On the other hand, as missile bases are hardened, the tendency might be toward more megatonnage. Every study of the consequences of nuclear war must begin with an assumption about the size of the attack, and the targets against which it is directed, but all such assumptions are subject to many uncertainties. It must be understood that in adopting the assumptions of the OCDM studies, we are using only one hypothetical attack pattern.

The Office of Civil and Defense Mobilization selected 71 metropolitan areas as the most likely targets in their 1959 exercise. In our re-examination of the 1959 study we used every Standard Metropolitan Area with a manufacturing labor force of 40,000 or more and all of the 53 largest areas (1950 census). This gave us a total of 70 urban areas, and inspection revealed that they are virtually identical with those chosen by the OCDM. The results of our study are not changed by our omission of a few areas included in the 1959 report.

We differ with the assumptions of the OCDM study in a few respects. We assume, first, that nuclear weapons can utterly destroy any city if the weapon is delivered and, second, that if the enemy wanted to destroy a city he could and would deliver a bomb large enough to do the job. (Unlike the OCDM study of 1959 which, for reasons unexplained in the testimony, pictured the Chicago urban area as escaping with 70 per cent of its population completely uninjured.) We assume that a thermonuclear war is a war with no holds barred. Thus it is realistic to assume that everyone within each of these 70 areas would be killed by blast, firestorms or radiation. We do not, however, include in our estimates a single person outside of these areas; nor do we include the deaths resulting from attacks on military installations located in areas remote from these cities, such as the ICBM bases in the western and midwestern states. We are concerned only with what might happen to the people of the United States if 70 of its largest urban areas were destroyed.

The purpose of our re-examination of the OCDM study is to enable us to see the deaths not only in terms of numbers, but in terms of *who* is being annihilated. Only by understanding the probable selective effect of nuclear war on our labor force can we begin to appreciate the economic problems of recuperation. Only by viewing the dead as individuals with particular skills, religious beliefs, and political outlooks can we begin to understand how such an attack would affect the present fabric of our society.

Such an attack on 70 urban areas would result in the death of 68,755,000 persons—46 per cent of all the people in the United States. Of the 74 million church members, one of every two would be killed. One of every three Protestants would be killed, two of every three Roman Catholics, and nine of every ten Jews. On the basis of recent election figures, it can also be shown that more Democrats than Republicans would be killed, and more northern than southern Democrats, affecting a change in the political balance of our two-party system.

The same attack would kill 72 per cent of all industrial and mechanical engineers; 73 per cent of the architects; 62 per cent of the physicians; 79 per cent of the foremen in the metals industry and 76 per cent of the tool and die makers. Comparing this with the overall death rate of 46 per cent, we can see that an undue proportion of the men and women with the very skills most in demand after such a disaster would perish in the attack.

What the social effects of these population changes would be, is difficult to envision. Even in World War II no nation experienced sudden population losses of this kind or of this magnitude. But whatever their nature, we must face the possibility that these effects would be serious, if not calamitous.

Social relations between persons and groups in an advanced industrial society like the United States are based upon elaborate and delicately balanced forms of interdependence, reflected in a complex division of tasks and in social standards. Even the most intimate relations between family members are affected by subtle population factors such as the size, age, and sex composition and distribution of the population within local communities.

A society maintains certain margins of reserves that allow it to survive fairly sharp changes in population and to accommodate to natural and economic disasters of a limited magnitude. When these margins are exceeded, reorganization becomes too difficult to achieve and, for an indefinite period, organization breaks down. First-line stresses ramify throughout the system. Surface disorder penetrates the deeper levels of the structure, bringing upheavals in standards and expectations and making older divisions of activity irrelevant. Even if the system somehow manages to recover a balance, the new society is both a different entity and a permanently *scarred* arrangement.

The foregoing studies do not take into consideration the possibility of civil defense protection. What would be the difference in the impact of an attack if we had built shelters and prepared for war?

In the 1959 hearings of the Joint Committee on Atomic Energy on "Biological and Environmental Effects of Nuclear War," is an article by Hugh Everett III and George E. Pugh,[3] both of whom are employed by the Weapons Systems Evaluation Division of the Institute for Defense Analysis, Washington, D.C. called "The Distribution and Effects of Fallout in Large Nuclear-Weapons Campaigns."

Everett and Pugh studied different kinds and sizes of attacks and compared their probable effects on prepared and unprepared populations. An unprepared population was assumed to have had a few hours' warning that an attack was coming. It is given emergency instructions to remain under shelter during and after the attack, but it has only improvised shelters to go to. In contrast, a prepared population has had six months of full time preparation for an attack. The effectiveness of six months of intensive activity to provide, prepare, build, and stock shelters was then calculated.

Figure 1 compares the effects of thermonuclear attacks ranging from 100 to 50,000 megatons on a prepared and on an unprepared population. Only deaths during and for the first sixty days after the attack are included. If the sick and wounded were added, the figures for each group would increase by an additional 10 to 15 per cent.

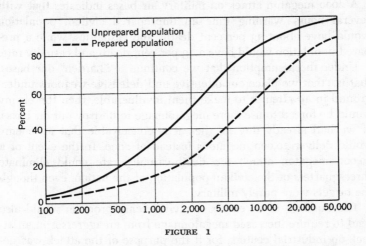

FIGURE 1

Estimated deaths in prepared and unprepared populations from nuclear attacks of various sizes, 60 days after the attack. A prepared population is assumed to have had six months of intensive work building and stocking shelters. The bombs dropped are assumed to be two-thirds fission, which produces fallout.
Source: 1959 Hearings: "Biological and Environmental Effects of Nuclear War," Fig. 9, p. 876.

Two important things are shown in this chart. A rather steady increase in the number of deaths occurs with each increase in the number of megatons dropped. And the difference in the death rate between a prepared and an unprepared population can be eliminated simply by dropping more megatons.

It would take 5000 megatons to kill about 75 per cent of the total unprepared population; about 16,000 megatons would kill 75 per cent of the prepared population. Remember that we are not talking here about the cities alone: these figures apply to the population of the nation as a whole.

An actual attack on a large scale would probably be directed at both military and industrial targets, as assumed in the mock attacks of the OCDM in 1957 and 1959. The calculations of Everett and Pugh did not take into account a mixed attack on both industrial and military targets. Their figures are based upon attacks that are *either* industrial or military, not both.

A 2000 megaton attack on military air bases indicates that with several hours' warning time an unprepared civilian population would have about 33 per cent deaths and casualties, while a prepared population would have a 13 per cent death and casualty rate.

Under the assumption that we continue to "harden" our bases, that is, that we place our offensive and defensive weapons underground in an attempt to make them invulnerable, then the enemy would be forced to use more megatonnage to destroy our air bases. If we had already dug in, then it is conceivable that an enemy would deliver 20,000 megatons instead of 2000. In the event of a 20,000 megaton attack the death-casualty rate could eliminate three-quarters of the civilian population of the nation, even though the targets were purely military.

The building of an extensive civil defense program would also tend to require increased megatonnage from an aggressor in an attack on industrial centers, for if the purpose of the attack was destruction of our industrial capacity, the labor force would have to be destroyed as well as the factories.

If 20,000 megatons were directed against a prepared population, shelters would be of no use to 74 per cent of the people. They would be dead within 60 days after such an attack. An additional 11 per cent would be casualties. This would leave 15 per cent of the people alive and in some sort of physical condition to rebuild the nation. Whether we think in terms of this 15 per cent, or of the 54 per cent survivors projected in the 2000 megaton attack, or of some other number, the end of a nuclear war would be the beginning of many problems.

There is a difference between staying alive somehow through a period of six weeks to six months, and surviving for a decade. One difference is that continued existence depends on renewed opportunity for economic and social co-operation among individuals and groups. Any society contains a handful of citizens who might be able to go it alone against great odds and a strangely hazardous environment. Some form of human or subhuman life would persist beyond even the most cataclysmic of all thermonuclear wars. As the poet Kenneth Patchen concludes in a poem entitled "O Take Heart, My Brothers": "Life is in no danger of losing the argument! —For after all . . . (As will be shown) She has only to change the subject."

But extended human survival, particularly survival at a level above that of the primitive folk community, depends for most of us on the prospects for rebuilding certain institutions, certain life-sustaining forms of social and technical organizations. The long-term existence of any human community depends on the presence of adaptive traditions that require generations for their establishment.

We know something about the minimal requirements for the survival of even the most fragmented societies. Among these, most social scientists would include health and safety standards (however high or low), population supply, and a complex of economic and political resources and regulations. There must also be institutions that motivate men or give them meaningful goals to strive toward. There are others, such as ways and means of rearing and educating the young, that we shall not consider here. But, to survive, these institutions must be built and put into sensible co-ordination, for they depend on each other just as man depends on them. Where the lives of more than random persons are at stake, health and safety, an economy, political controls, and life goals must take form—and not as independent cards in a game of chance but as features of a synchronized system.

One economic analysis, prepared for the Defense Department in the late 1950's,[4] examined the chances for recovery from an attack in which 45 per cent of the population is killed and all military and metropolitan targets are obliterated. The economists concluded that such an attack would destroy 80 per cent of the instruments, 77 per cent of the transportation equipment, 77 per cent of the electrical machinery and primary metal industries; as well as three-fourths to two-thirds of these other production systems: rubber, printing and publishing, cloth and garments, general machin-

ery, petroleum and coal. Not only would production capacity in
these industries be destroyed but equivalent proportions of all
capital goods as well.

These economists concluded that recuperation of the industrial
economy was possible in a period of from five to twenty years, *if*
a number of vital conditions could *all* be met. First, they reasoned,
the money and credit system would have to be intact and investment would have to proceed as usual. Government and corporate
credits would have to come to hand that would make new, begin-
again contracting and purchasing systems come to life. In order
of importance, the other conditions they cited were these: The
nation would need a favorable political environment—presumably
a stable, energetic government. The surviving labor force would
have to get back on the job full time as promptly as radiation conditions permitted, and the momentum of the pre-attack economy
would have to be maintained. Bottlenecks in the technical organization of production and distribution resulting from the dislocation
of population and the material ruin of the attack would have to be
overcome with speed. The surviving labor force would have to accept reduced standards of health and safety.The balance of nature
could not be destroyed by such effects as the wholesale decimation
of mammals and subsequent multiplication of insect populations,
or the death of forest cover through radiation.

The economists said their estimates depended on assuming that
government welfare programs would be cut back quite severely,
that military spending would be kept to a minimum, that bacterio-
logical and chemical warfare would not be used, and that no third
country would follow up the initial small attack.

Economic recuperation within a decade or two, according to this
analysis, requires that most or all of these conditions be met. A
single failure—say, for example, that all soft wood forestation is destroyed by low-yield radiation—and the forecast of  recovery in five
to fifteen years cannot be maintained. The conditions also must
occur at more or less one and the same time: economic momentum
depends on the prevention of production bottlenecks; energetic
governmental regulation depends on the acceptance by the surviving labor force of lowered standards of health and safety, and
so forth.

The nation must get the economy going in reasonably short order after an attack, or it may not get it going at all. The stimulation of momentum requires a usable transportation system, the swift restoration of power and communications apparatus, and provision for long-term shelter, food, and clothing for the working population. If momentum is achieved, it must be maintained across a ten-year period. Raw materials, critical inventories, stockpiled resources and equipment must be at hand. These economists concluded that food in sufficient quantities to feed the surviving populace for two to four years must be deposited in advance of any attack.

This economic analysis is perhaps a classic in view of the chain of *if-type* assumptions that must be made before the estimate of recovery is reached. The size and kind of bombs used and the altitude at which they were exploded, as well as the targets selected are all choices for the attacker, not for the agents of recuperation. Yet such assumptions as these, as well as assumptions mentioned above about human behavior and political organization are all closely linked in reaching the estimate of recovery. A change in any one of these assumptions would require an entire restudy of the hypothetical postattack situation before one could say whether or not the previous recovery estimate could be justified in the changed situation.

These economists were interested in whether we could recover economically to a point of material well-being that was something like our pre-attack existence. Suppose we are less demanding and we concern ourselves with the question of economic survival at a bare subsistence level something like that of contemporary Iran. One need not ask, after all, for the best of all possible economic worlds. Here our understanding is helped by the examples of the U.S.S.R. and Germany and their progress in recuperating from the effects of World War II. One eminent economist, Oscar Morgenstern, argues that we could not regain past levels of living, but that the experience of the Soviet Union illustrates the great resilience of industrial economies. And Herman Kahn presents the Soviet case as partial evidence that the United States could face great destruction, yet recover.

The Soviet Russian economy absorbed the shock of the German invasion and in 1945 was operating at about the same level as in 1940. By 1950, production had nearly doubled over 1945.[5] Far from experiencing the obliteration of their factories and capital, the Soviets were in relatively complete industrial operation throughout the 1940's.

How could this be? It is true that about twenty million Russians were killed during the war, or about 12 per cent of their 1940 population. But those who died were not strategic for the maintenance of the economy. The Soviets anticipated the routes that would be followed by a German *land* invasion (a kind of anticipation that is impossible in missile warfare). They relocated their industries and labor force before the main invasions occurred. In addition, most of the invasion routes ran through non-industrial rural terrain, and the German air offensive could not reach the inland industrial centers of the economy. If Russian experience documents anything, it shows how an industrial economy may be defended against a *land* and a short-range air attack.

The Allied attack on Germany extended over several years and (unlike the Nazi invasion of Russia) was directed at critical industrial sectors—with important exceptions such as the destruction of Hamburg and Dresden. Thus, several months were given over to concentration on the bearing industry, then the transport system was attacked, and then the petroleum and nitrogen refineries were destroyed. This offensive had great effects, yet sectors of the economy that were not selected continued to produce at high levels until land invasion wiped them out.

Is this an argument for the resilience of a modern economy? If our problem for comparison is a nuclear attack, it is essential to recall that the devastation of German industry took place across a two-year—not a two-day or two-week—period. It must be recalled that although Hamburg and Dresden were leveled more completely than any other cities in history except Tokyo, German civilian deaths from Allied bombings during the entire war totaled about 500,000, or less than one per cent of the German civilian population. If the German experience, for all its horror, is to be compared with a nuclear attack of similar proportions on the United States, we must assume no more than two to five million deaths. Such an attack would amount to the dropping of one ten-megaton bomb on New York City. That is a long way from 46 per cent of the nation's population dead from a 2000-megaton attack. In actual explosive power, about three megatons of bombs were dropped on Germany in the entire course of World War II.

There are other crucial differences. The German labor force was not shattered by the bombing program. The German machine tool industry was only lightly affected by direct attacks; it maintained its level of output throughout the war.[6] The final collapse of production was due to the destruction of transport routes and equipment and to the occupation.

If we go ahead with an imaginary comparison despite these differences, we are struck not with the recuperative power of the German economy but *with the time and wealth it took to rebuild in spite of many favorable conditions.* Governmental stability was achieved through the machinery of the Allied occupation. The Allies had fresh memories of the political chaos in Germany after World War I that made the rise of Hitler possible. Health and safety problems were generally resolved within one year through massive outside aid. A substantial civilian labor force was at hand, trained and properly located, and disposed to resume work. Most sectors of the economy were intact (except for postwar dismantling by the Russians in East Germany). Given these favorable circumstances, *why were three billion dollars of direct economic aid from the United States alone necessary to German economic recuperation?* In spite of massive outside assistance, economic recovery was not achieved even in West Germany until three years after World War II. No economist on record anticipates massive outside aid to the United States following a nuclear World War III. What nations would be standing by with a Marshall Plan?

If comparisons have any worth whatever (and the lack of comparable events suggests they do not), they indicate *not* that modern industrial economies are resilient, but that recuperation depends on ability to anticipate the type of attack, on what remains intact after the attack, on the extent of destruction of *people* as well as industry and capital, and on the availability of outside help.[7]

To get an inkling of some of the social and political problems involved in rebuilding, let us look briefly at the case of Hiroshima.

Hiroshima, a delta city accustomed to disastrous floods and well organized to handle crises, was not rebuilt primarily by its own citizens but by migrants from the hinterlands who surged into the ruins in the aftermath of the bombing.[8] Those who had lived through the attack suffered from extreme shock and fatigue that lingered for a year. Although American occupation authorities issued food for a year, the May Day "festivities" of 1946 took the form of hunger demonstrations and the weekend holiday was spent by most city dwellers in the search for weeds and edible barks. The mayor himself reported that a year after the attack he attempted (under an agreement with occupation authorities) to renounce the black market, but that faced with starvation he resumed private purchases. A judge committed suicide when faced with a choice between breaking the law and starvation.

Demoralization was so extreme that industrial alcohol was sold as a substitute for saki; many citizens died or went blind from drinking it. The narcotic, Hiropon, that kills the appetite and induces a torpor of well-being flourished on the black market. As late as the 1950's, Japanese sociologists reported after studying orphans of the bombing that a fear of forming attachments and producing children was very prevalent among a majority of youthful survivors.

Hiroshima's reservoirs were filled soon after the attack, but thousands of shattered pipes had to be replaced in order to build up the pressure to start the water system. For every hole the engineers plugged by day, more were dug by citizens at night to steal a drink. Gangsters organized the sale of water as a profitable racket. They fought so effectively to prevent repairs to the system that engineers had to work at night in carefully policed shifts to put the water system in order.

After the first nightmare month of locating the living and removing the dead, the struggle was resumed to keep damaged body and battered soul together. Reconstruction did not begin for five months after the attack. No gas mains operated for six months. Four months after the attack, ten buses were in operation to take more than 42,000 workers to and from points in the rubble each day. And four months after the bomb, the number of crimes reported in Hiroshima and its suburbs for one month was as high as the figure for all criminal activities throughout the entire war. Crimes of violence and theft were particularly prevalent.

Ten to twelve months after the attack, administratively undirected reconstruction efforts got underway. The city was bombed in August 1945. By early 1947, amusement districts, gambling dens, brothels, and theaters had resumed operations. Without housing aid from the government, people began to erect wooden or corrugated iron huts.

Catastrophic as it was, the attack on Hiroshima did not level the entire metropolitan area of the city. A few weeks after the explosion, the area numbered 130,000 inhabitants compared with the 390,000 who had lived there previously, if garrison troops were included. This, in short, was a miniscule attack by the standard of present-day possibilities. There is another sense in which Hiroshima, for all its unforgettable horror, is but a faint indication of future possibilities: part of the city and part of its highly skilled labor force survived. There were engineers at hand to repair the water mains. An attack on America might obliterate such urban resources. Although 120 Japanese cities were devastated by bombing and incendiary attacks, total casualties did not begin to approach what a modern thermonuclear attack would yield. *When Hiroshima began its reconstruction, there was a domestic society and an invader at hand to bring aid.*

There should be no fantasy on the question of outside help in the event of a thermonuclear war. The questions "How many people will die in the first attack?" and "How many people will survive the first two years?" pale before the question, "How will the war come to an end?" There is nothing in history to suggest that either side would cease attacking until there was nothing left with which to attack. The cost of total holocaust would be the sacrifice of help from the surviving corners of the globe where the less industrially developed nations would themselves be struggling to survive in an environment contaminated by radioactivity. Even in the event of a "limited attack," what remaining nations would be able, let alone disposed, to come to the rescue?

Survivors in the United States would face the problems of Hiroshima multiplied many times, and would have to solve them with little or no outside help. Could they do so through existing American democratic institutions?

Martial rule is the most likely form of government control to be exercised during the first year or two after a nuclear attack. It matters little whether martial law is implemented by civilian or military defense authorities; patently, some officials from each group would survive. Both have developed procedures for co-operation. We suggest that older cultural distinctions between military and civil authority would prove immaterial in any extreme crisis, just as the traditional representative functions of local, state, and federal governments would be sacrificed, however indefinitely, to the necessities of survival through authoritative control.

Depending on prevailing winds and the chance-like pattern of rainfall, certain states might survive a nuclear attack quite intact. Under the assumptions we made, North Dakota, Idaho, and Montana would survive a small attack more or less completely.* Consider the political situation, then, in terms of regulatory centers— federal, state, and local. Washington, D.C., and all pertinent centers of federal authority including military units would have been eliminated. The federal cortex of our political system and virtually all its pertinent regional extensions would be gone, as would federal communications exclusive of a fragmented civil defense radio system. National Guard units would serve under state civil defense authorities in the patches of intact society in the central northwest, and in smaller sectors of a handful of widely dispersed states. Local governmental authorities would survive in a much broader yet even more widely dispersed range of communities. In lieu of a pyramid of authorities there would exist a scatter of regional, state, and municipal enclaves, only a few of which could be expected to be in contact with more than a handful of others, for a time. Under these conditions, the stress to reconstruct a centralized political system, though deferred for a time in the face of physical problems, would be tremendous.

New goals, with new procedures for achieving them, including control over all remaining national resources, would require extreme centralization. Central authority would be limited in that the survivors would be dispersed in remote rural sectors. But for an intermediate period, responsibility for survival and reconstruction would rest with a uniquely authoritative few, a quasi-military elite, in each enclave.

Without social order men are lost; and that social order presup-

---

* However, an attack on military bases in the future might well change this picture, as a large Intercontinental Ballistic Missile base is being built in Montana and another in North Dakota.

poses law. A system of standards regulating relations between men is essential for human existence at every level, from death camp to democratic society. The novelist's notion of the modern survivor tucked away from disaster in his northern Minnesota shelter is wholly fictitious. The so-called primitive through all periods of history has clung to his laws more tenaciously, more unthinkingly, than anyone else.

For this reason, a Hobbesian choice between chaos and surrender to a central authority would eventually confront a post-attack America. Hobbes was wrong in thinking that the one thing that holds men together and makes survival possible is erection of a power able "to over-awe them all." Hobbes ignored the informal ties that bind men together. But Hobbes was wrong *only for the case of a society in balance.* In the extremes of crisis, where these ties are shattered by terror, death, and uncertainty, law and order, to exist at all, require allegiance to a strong central authority.

Extreme national crises have always placed democracies at the mercy of whatever clique acquires most efficiently the techniques of gaining power. That the United States military and civilian defense elites would constitute dispersed, competing, and eventually conflicting cliques is simple enough to demonstrate. All the resources crucial for survival would be in unprecedented short supply. We might expect co-operation and coalition of authority to develop in the North Dakota-Idaho region, where mutual assistance between rural states could be to the advantage of all parties. But surviving, isolated communities might depend on their quasi-military leadership for defense against inroads from towns suffering even more extreme shortages. The altruistic generosity that characterizes aid in time of natural disasters springs from the fact that surpluses are available to communities and states located away from the disaster area. In an extended period of extreme, relatively universal scarcity and deprivation, the altruism of emergency aid would contradict short-run group interests.

When would quasi-military rule end and democratic political reorganization begin? This would depend on reconstruction of the economic and social structure. Democratic institutions depend on political parties that come into being to mediate between community and governmental authority. Party loyalties vitally depend in turn on combinations of economic and social incentives—upon *routine* expectations within family, work, ethnic, and religious groups. In crisis, these routines would be broken up. The economic and social bases of interest groups would be dislocated. Even the pattern of two-party composition itself would be badly fragmented by a nuclear attack.

To terminate the period of martial law, individuals must have resources, including political morale, to reform voluntary associations, interest groups, and political parties. They must have access to power and influence to affect decisions of their regime. The physical security of the individual and his family, for example, must not be threatened by economic collapse. Dependence on the state must be reduced.

The survivors of a substantial nuclear attack would be strung out across the most isolated rural backwaters and backlands of the country. Our discussion of the effects of a nuclear attack on the population makes it clear that the composition of the postattack population would be so different from that of today's population that this factor alone would make for differences in the postattack society. To the interminable hazards of fallout, water and food contamination, forced relocation of families and labor assignments to individuals, therefore, must be added the obstacles of weak communications and heterogeneity. That new community, interest and party associations which would fit the new life situation could be built under these obstacles, is doubtful. Without such intermediate networks of attachment, the individual would have to choose indefinitely between the chaos of anarchy and surrender to the military or quasi-military state.

An extended period of martial law would further undermine the structures essential for the rebuilding of democracy. If the economy were to resume operations the new government would have to expand its powers and activities dramatically. This would challenge existing protections of individual freedom to dissent from government decrees or to test the constitutionality of governmental acts. Safety and health regulations, like schedules for decontamination and construction, would have to be so rigid as to place the regime in the position of dictating personal hygiene, diet, control over residence, material resources, professional services, and the movement of labor.

Although demoralizing despair might run deep, the prospect of a public reaction against the new leadership is slim. The scope of the crisis would be so grave that only the most stupid and inept exercise of authority would be likely to be attacked. Those charged with the administration of martial law would be seen as effective, and accepted as legitimate, by the surviving population. If the case of Hiroshima applies, the new regime would also tend to incorporate within itself all forms of emergent, informal leadership.*

There are powerful constraints, then, that would be set in motion by the scope of the disaster to maintain undemocratic leadership by a quasi-military elite. That the quest for democratic reconstruction might eventually assert itself also seems likely. But realization of the goal would have to await major rehabilitation of the social structure and the economy.

* Robert Jungk [8] describes vividly the emergence of an obscure young Japanese official, Shimzo Hamai, who by finding ways to provide emergency food and clothing "became overnight the most important man in Hiroshima."

NOTES:

1. Material from the 1957 study is taken from the Special Subcommittee on Radiation of the Joint Congressional Committee on Atomic Energy, "The Nature of Radioactive Fallout and Its Effect on Man" (Washington, D.C., 1957).

   Data from the 1959 OCDM study were taken from the Hearings of the Special Subcommittee on Radiation of the Joint Committee on Atomic Energy, 86th Congress, "Biological and Environmental Effects of Nuclear War" (Washington, D. C., 1959).

2. "Strategic Weapons of Nuclear War," *Nuclear Information*, July 1962, p. 10.

3. "Biological and Environmental Effects of Nuclear War," op. cit., pp. 859-81. The article is reprinted from its original source, the journal *Operations Research*, 7, March-April 1959.

4. This study by the Rand Corporation is summarized in Herman Kahn, *On Thermonuclear War* (Princeton, 1960), pp. 82-5. See also, *Report on a Study of Non-Military Defense* (Santa Monica, Calif., 1958).

5. Thomas Fitzsimmons, *et al.*, *Russian Soviet Federated Socialist Republic*, I (New Haven, 1957), pp. 65-6. Harry Schwartz, *Russia's Soviet Economy*, 2nd ed. (New York, 1954), p. 127.

6. *United States Strategic Bombing Survey: Overall Report* (European War), September 30, 1945, pp. 85-6. Data on the effect of the air offen-

sive on the German population and economy are taken from this Government report.

7. The narrowness of much American disaster research is reflected in Charles E. Fritz's "Disaster," Chapter 14 of *Contemporary Social Problems*, Robert K. Merton, *et al.*, eds. (New York, 1961). After a fine résumé of social reactions to natural disasters, Fritz cites the many mechanisms that aid in unifying and energizing groups and communities in post-disaster situations. He shows "why societies rebound so dramatically from the disruptive and destructive effects of disaster." He concludes by referring to the recuperation of West Germany, Russia, and Hiroshima, and to the Rand Study (note 4). "Disaster studies show that human societies have enormous resilience and recuperative power . . ." But such studies *also* show the conditions necessary for recuperation, very few of which occur in nuclear warfare.

8. Robert Jungk, *Children of the Ashes: The Story of a Rebirth* (New York, 1962). Our account of Hiroshima depends heavily upon this book, which is based on both first-hand social research and intensive coverage of secondary sources.

# 25

WILLIAM McCORD

## Portrait of Transitional Man

Carolina Maria de Jesus tried to raise her illegitimate children in one of the disgusting slums which disfigure São Paulo's opulence. Like many of her neighbors, she lived in a cardboard shack, earned a few cruzeiros a day collecting waste paper, and found her most succulent meals in the bones discarded by a nearby butcher. Unlike her fellow victims, Carolina wanted to write. When she composed poems or novels, she was "in a golden place, with crystal windows and silver chandeliers. My dress was finest satin and diamonds set shining in my black hair. Then I put away my book and the smells came in through the rotting walls and rats ran over my feet. My satin turned to rags and the only thing shining in my hair were lice." [1]

She kept a daily journal which tersely recorded her misery. During election campaigns, she wrote in *Child of the Dark*, the politicians condescended to visit her *favela* (slum). They distributed bread and promises, heady words and optimism. After election, they hastily retreated to the city's healthier quarters, leaving the suffering *favelados* unchanged. In her despair, she cried out, "Brazil needs to be led by a person who has known hunger. Hunger is also a teacher.... Those who govern our country are those who have money, who don't know what hunger is, or pain or poverty." [2] And again, when a kindly police officer advised her that the slum was an "unfortunate" environment for her children, she

427

exclaimed, ". . . if he knows this why doesn't he make a report and send it to the politicians? To Janio Quadros, Kubitschek and Dr. Adhemar de Barros? Now he tells me this, I a poor garbage collector. I can't even solve my own problems." [3]

Although seldom so eloquently, this plea echoes throughout the underdeveloped lands. The *favelados* of the world demand more than gestures, more than ineffective pity, more than the entrancing oratory of either corrupt "democrats" or dictators. They want action which is predicated on a deep comprehension of their most immediate, pressing needs.

The beginning of wisdom in dealing with the problems of development lies in understanding individuals such as Carolina de Jesus. Before we can intelligently examine the abstract issues of political liberty and economic change, we must divorce ourselves from our own affluent world. We must eschew, equally, the optimism which views man as infinitely adaptable, the romanticism which longs for the virtues of an unrecapturable past, and the scorn for "native" capacities which so often blinded colonial rulers. And we must give up that supposedly realistic opinion, so much in fashion today, that the *favelados* neither understand nor care about protections for individual liberty, self-government, and individualism. When transitional men have the capacity to articulate their beliefs, as did Carolina de Jesus, they often voice an inherent democratic desire which lies deep in their traditions, however easily they are forgotten by the old elite or the new tyrants.

With all of the realism at our disposal, we must try to grasp the nature of transitional man—the actual motives, and values, and social milieu of those caught midway between traditional and modern modes of life.

Too often, economic or political plans have foundered for lack of such understanding. Because its leader was a health faddist, Burma has squandered millions on yeast plants when no one wished to buy the product. Certain African factories failed to produce at capacity until the seating arrangements for workers had been changed; the managers had failed to realize that laborers, traditionally accustomed to squatting during work, could not accommodate themselves easily to the Western sitting position. Liberal, progressive political parties, such as Ghana's United Party, have gone down in defeat because of their inability to respond to the people's most basic desires or their incapacity in integrating traditional tribal symbols into their political appeals. Ambitious relocation schemes in Nigeria and Indonesia have collapsed because leaders did not recognize the degree to which peasants would cling to their land in the belief that their ancestors had made it sacred. It is evident that many (although by no means all) of the obstacles to progress in the newer nations are essentially social in nature.

Any assessment of the chance for democratic development should properly begin, therefore, with an examination of human nature as it is revealed in the emerging nations. In particular, two of the most prominent clichés about transitional man require careful consideration. These beliefs serve, sometimes innocently, as buttresses in the argument of those who desire an authoritarian solution to the problems of development. First, the almost trite opinion that a "revolution of expectations" has swept the new nations deserves re-evaluation. Exactly what are these new aspirations? Is the desire for the appurtenances of modern life so compelling, as the authoritarians argue, that men will eagerly sacrifice everything else for its achievement? Secondly, we must reflect on the argument that the traditional order—the land-tenure pattern, the religious or political systems—must be tossed into the wastebasket of history. Is traditional society so inimical to progress that it must be violently transformed? Is it correct, as one of the most brilliant analysts has concluded, that progress requires ". . . nothing short of a pervasive social transformation . . . a wholesale metamorphosis of habits, a wrenching reorientation of values concerning time, status, money, work; an unweaving and reweaving of the fabric of daily existence itself?" [4]

To answer these questions, we must look closely at village life, for it is in the village that 70 per cent of transitional men live. Yet, while political and economic battles of development may have to be fought in the village, it is in the "transitional city" where they will be initiated.

"Why should I stay in my village? It's dreary, dark, and dirty," the Egyptian youth responded, typical of high school students whom I interviewed in 1962. His father had been pathetically pleading with him to continue on the land, but to no avail, for the boy replied, "There is nothing to do in the village, no movies, no night clubs, no dancing! Anyway, the land could not support both me and my brothers."

In this lies the city's promise: the push of escaping rural poverty and the pull of excitement and luxury. The city's magnetism extends throughout the developing world to the most primitive areas. Even in rural Africa, public opinion polls show that only 8 per cent of schooled boys wish to continue in their father's farming occupation. In the more developed nations like India, the move to the cities has become a torrent.

A few statistics from India illustrate the scope of urbanization: Indian cities are growing at a steady rate of 50 per cent per decade, and some centers even outrace this pace. New Delhi, in the single decade of 1941-51, increased in size by 107 per cent. The most conservative demographers estimate that Indian cities will somehow have to absorb 140 million new immigrants before the end of the century. In a city such as Calcutta—where carts already circulate each morning to pick up the dead from the sidewalk— the extent of this growth can barely be comprehended. By A.D. 2000, unless the pattern is reversed, Calcutta's population will have expanded from 2.5 million to a possible 66 million. Some experts, noting that industrialization and urbanization have been historical bed-fellows, believe that this trend is inevitable. "To put it succinctly," sociologist Kingsley Davis, one of the most cautious of generalizers, has said, "60 per cent of its population must move from the countryside to the cities. This is a problem so formidable that few governments seem willing to face it realistically: yet, if *rapid* economic development is to be achieved, the territorial shift must also take place *rapidly*." [5]

If the ambitions and policies of developing nations are not changed, few would question the prediction that this human flood will occur (although one can legitimately quarrel with the belief that urbanization is necessary for economic growth). Regardless of the future, it seems beyond dispute that the developing nations are already heavily over-urbanized, burdened with festering cities beyond their capacity to support.

Arthur Lewis, a distinguished contributor to the dialogue of economic development, has demonstrated that in every new nation one or two towns have developed far beyond the ability of the municipality to provide houses, jobs, transportation, or schools. Part of this excessively rapid growth takes place for sheer economic reasons: new industries naturally tend to locate in areas where industry is already concentrated. Another reason lies in the tendency of some governments simply to spend more on one or two "prestige" cities and ignore others. As Lewis recalls:

> Once when I pointed out to a Prime Minister that he was proposing to spend 50% of his development program on his capital city, which had only 5% of the population, he was quite surprised. "But why not?", he asked. "Surely, when you think of England you think of London, when you think of France you think of Paris . . ." "No," I replied, "when I think of England, I think not of London, but of Manchester, and this is precisely why I oppose spending half your money beautifying the capital." [6]

However false the tinsel of these cities, their image of luxury continues to inveigle the peasant into immigration. At first, when the ex-villager enters the city, he must be overwhelmed by the glory of New Delhi's Secretariat, Mexico's Reforma Boulevard, Accra's government buildings, or by the Paris-like magnificence of Cairo along the Nile. But soon, he has to face the physical realities of city life—the *barriada,* or *favela,* or *bidonville* which are the rotten cores within the apple. Unless he has unusual training, he quickly discovers that no one wants his labor. The curious fact about the city is that its unemployment problem exceeds even that of stagnant villages. In Madras, as an illustration, only 25 per cent of the working people can engage in directly productive activity; the rest sell shoestrings, beg, sleep, find odd jobs now and then, or earn a few pennies running errands. Paradoxically, as the typical city grows and develops, greater amounts of men go out of work. As Lewis describes Kingston, Jamaica, "The more jobs you create in Kingston, the more unemployment you have in Kingston." [7] Attracted by the promise of lucrative employment, the migrant leaves his village and its system of natural social security, only to find that nothing awaits him in the city.

The first shock which cities administer to the migrant, therefore, is a tangible demonstration that he is neither wanted nor needed.*

---

* This shock is perhaps greatest for the "early-leavers," those who have received some primary education and then quit school in the anticipation of economic rewards. Bereft of specific skills, they can find no place in an urban economy. For this reason, among others, the popular policy of funneling resources into primary education must be viewed with some caution.

The new urbanite discovers in other ways, too, that he has traded his peasant heritage for a mess of pottage. Typically, his housing (if he finds any at all) is greatly inferior to that of the village. In India, to cite one case, 34 per cent of rural families live in one room, but in a city like Calcutta 79 per cent must crowd into a single chamber. Further, while only 14 per cent of Indian peasant families must somehow squeeze into a floor area of less than fifty square feet (something less than the size of an average American bathroom) the majority of urbanites (70 per cent) can find nothing better as their home. In some Indian cities, an unlucky 20 per cent must sleep in the gutters.

The city-dweller normally cannot scrape together enough food to maintain his health. Richard Meir has shown that an average subsistence budget in an Indian city—one which would provide sufficient food and clothing, but little else—requires some $250 a year. Yet, the typical city resident can earn only $60 a year. In consequence, the crude death rate in Indian cities often markedly surpasses that of villages, even though the city is more liberally supplied with medical facilities.

Objectively, then, the city migrant often discovers himself deprived of a job, housing, sufficient food, or adequate medical protection. Rather than offering salvation, the move to the city only deepens frustration.

How does the new environment affect the urbanite's character? What happens, in the city, to traditional attitudes, values, and social relationships? Exposure to a city's wiles, its contrasts, and strange experiences opens new vistas to the ex-villager. He learns that other styles of life exist, other religions, other political authorities than that of his village. Because he must, he learns to tolerate attitudes and habits which clash with his own. In some ways, this broadening of horizons is useful, for the urbanite may begin to feel sympathy for forms of behavior utterly different from his old ways. Daniel Lerner, in his extensive research on the Middle East, has nicely demonstrated the correlation between urbanization, literacy, exposure to the mass media, and empathy—the ability to put oneself in the situation of others.[8] He reports that the typical Turkish villager is at a loss to respond to such a question as: "What would you do if you were President of Turkey?" The villager cannot conceive of a situation in which he would have anything in common with such an exalted figure. The city-dweller, in contrast, can visualize the President's role and problems. He can vicariously participate in a world beyond his immediate experience. Ultimately, such empathy leads to attitudes of tolerance, so necessary for a liberal society.

Other vistas, however, are also opened to the urbanite, and these result more in jealousy than tolerance, a rage at injustice rather than a willingness to accept varied ways of life. Perhaps most significantly, the urbanite sees new levels of wealth of which he was previously only dimly aware. The villager to some degree, knows about economic inequality, of the lucky few's wealth. But the urban resident sees evidence of it at every hand. His nose is rubbed in luxury. He cannot avoid the glaring contrast between, say, the magnificent apartments which line Rio's beaches and the slums clutching its hills. Even in those countries which have striven to avoid such obvious differences, distinct inequalities still exist. The few skilled oil workers in Venezuela or the Middle East earn many times the salary of the average laborer. The schoolteacher in Ghana or Nigeria earns from five to seven times the per capita urban income. Because of the shortage of trained people, these differentials in income are built into the nature of developing economies. Often as development proceeds, the gap in income gets wider, rather than narrowing. Thus, in Mexico, despite great economic progress, one per cent of the population received 66 per cent of national income in 1955, whereas in 1940 they had taken only 34 per cent.[9]

Inevitably, the discords of inequality infect the city person with discontent. Formal public opinion polls give some signs, however inadequate, of the depth of the urbanite's alienation. Indian polls, for example, have revealed that 78 per cent of Calcutta residents believed that "a change in the present social system was necessary."[10] Similar interviews in Santiago, Chile, indicated that 89 per cent of the people demanded important social changes.[11]

This discontent can seldom be assuaged by the balm of traditional religions, for a further impact of the city is its implacable pressure toward secularization. Confronted with a society where machines have replaced the Gods, where traditional incantations have no bearing on whether people find jobs, where movie stars displace village idols, the urbanite abandons his faith in the old religion. In the Middle East, polls indicate that 50 per cent of young urban migrants give up their Islamic beliefs, and in Africa, as one anthropologist has observed, the conflict between Westernized, city values and traditional religion "results either in the abandonment of all belief, which is perhaps the most logical solution, or else in the adoption of the outer form of Western belief without any inner conviction." [12]

While losing the metaphysics which gave his life significance, the typical urban person learns that traditional modes of social intercourse are either irrelevant or harmful in the city. In trying to adjust to a commercially oriented economy, for example, the city-dweller is judged by "achievement" standards, by what he can produce, not who he is. The old village pattern where each person was automatically responsible to his neighbors and each knew his traditional role in life gives way to more individualistic criteria. Ideals of economic co-operation do not fit well with the standards of a competitive economy. The extended family system tends to disintegrate in an urban society with its new standards, higher costs, and greater mobility. Further, the traditional hierarchical relationships of the village undergo systematic attack: the chief, or brahmin, or patron loses his influence, and new authorities, frequently charismatic political figures, attempt to replace them. In every way, the urbanite becomes socially isolated. His religious, political, and familial universe crumbles in contact with the demands of an urban environment.* He stands alone and unprotected.

In response to this "culture of poverty," as Oscar Lewis has aptly termed it, the typical city person can cope with his frustration in several ways. A few can adjust themselves successfully to the city:

* Because of the simple fact that the city is a male-dominated area (more men enter the city seeking jobs than women), this isolation extends to the sexual area. As Shanti Tangri has observed on Indian cities, isolation chokes off "the traditionally accepted avenues for sex gratification, while extramarital sex . . . is severely limited. Sexual frustration is . . . very high. In addition, there are neither sufficient opportunities to participate in sports nor to attend sports spectacles, where, on weekends, like their American counterparts, they may work off their steam by yelling some team to victory." [13] It does not seem totally unlikely that this sexual isolation plays a role in the rowdy indiscipline of student groups.

they adopt the clothes and customs, learn new skills, find jobs, and shed their village background. The "adjusted elite" of civil servants, intellectuals, army officers, entrepreneurs, and some industrial workers win the city's rewards of economic and political power, but they constitute only a small minority of urbanites. C. Wright Mills' comments concerning upper-class people in large American cities apply with equal validity to the elites of underdeveloped nations: ". . . the personal solution to 'the problem of the city' is to have an apartment (with private garage under it) in the heart of the city, and one hundred miles out, a house and garden by notable architects, on a hundred acres of private land. In these two controlled environments—with a small staff at each end and a private helicopter connection—most people could solve many of the personal problems caused them by the facts of the city. But all this, however splendid, does not solve the public issues that the structural fact of the city poses." [14]

A much more common solution is that chosen by a large group of "urban villagers," people who attempt to retain peasant culture, to recreate village life while existing in a city.

A UNESCO study of Stanleyville, the Congo, illustrates the way urban villagers deal with their new situation.[15] In 1956 two-thirds of Stanleyville's Africans, who had been born in the country, had migrated to the city less than five years earlier.* Few had received any sort of education which qualified them for technical work. While earning relatively good salaries (from $17 a month for unskilled workers to $35 a month for white-collar employees), most of the city-dwellers still returned to the bush periodically, often in fulfillment of tribal obligations. Many participated in voluntary organizations (financial societies, veterans groups, new religions) created to replace tribal bonds. The majority, however, preserved many of their traditional tribal ways. Most belonged to tribal organizations, practiced traditional *rites de passage,* paid a bride price, adhered to traditional brotherhoods, and, with the usual

---

* Throughout the developing world, the adjustment of the person to the city is often facilitated by group migrations. It is not uncommon to find entire villages, or significant portions of them, moving en masse and settling together in the city. This type of migration makes easier, of course, the adjustment of the urban villager.

hospitality, welcomed indigent relatives who came to live with them in the city. They tried, in other words, to maintain traditional values while simultaneously responding to an urban culture.

The reaction of the urban villager is not a stable one, for the man who wishes to live in two worlds cannot feel at home in either. The majority of urban residents are in a transitional, anomic state, moving steadily away from peasant values. This "anomic urbanite" is a hollow man who can no longer subscribe to the old values but has found nothing to replace them. As numerous studies have remarked, profound disillusionment poisons every urban center, regardless of geographical area.[16] In São Paulo, Carolina de Jesus exclaimed, "There is no meaning to my life . . . the day is sad as my soul . . . I think that my insipid life was too long." [17] In Mexico, Oliver La Farge noted (in commenting on Oscar Lewis' profound study, *Five Families*): "The most striking things about these families are their general malaise, the rarity among them of happiness or contentment, the rarity of affection. . . . Above all, where hunger and discomfort rule, there is little spare energy for the gentler, warmer, less utilitarian emotions and little chance for active happiness. . . . These broken cultures no longer give satisfaction, no longer 'make life worth living.' " [18] And in Africa, as anthropologist Colin Turnbull has concluded about urban people, ". . . there is a common theme apparent in their attitudes and in their actions, every one of them. The theme is a sense of a lack of something in their lives. The new world they have embraced, with various feelings, leaves them with an emptiness, a void that they all recognize and all want to fill." [19]

The anomic person seeks solace in crime, alcohol, or magic. He may search for a new community, a secret society, or a new religion to replace the old order.* Or he may turn to politics in the hope that some new father figure can both provide meaning in his life and relieve his economic frustration. The anomic urban per-

---

* Social patterns in transitional cities today tend to reproduce eighteenth- and nineteenth-century European history: the urban man flocks to new salvationist religions, as the new industrial worker in London took to Methodism in droves. Thomas Hodgkin, in comparing new African churches to Methodism, has pointed out: "Both movements have offered a connection within which brotherly relations can be restored and human dignity can be rediscovered." [20]

son is remarkably amenable to authoritarian appeals, for once he has lost the comforting security of traditional order, he strives to regain his stability with frantic intensity. He who has seen the collapse of a worshipped authority wants to create a new one.

The cities become centers of modern, dynamic authoritarian movements. It is the city where the mobs rush into the streets and the demagogue's rantings find their most pulsing response. There, the "true believer" flourishes and, in consequence, the politics of irresponsibility and passion. It hardly matters what the leader says, for the anomic person responds to authoritarianism in a curiously undiscriminating fashion. In India, an urban district enthusiastically supported S. P. Mukerji, the leader of the Jan Singh, the most authoritarian of right-wing movements. When Mukerji died, the same constituency swung with equal fanaticism to the support of a Communist candidate. Politically, the anomic person simply wants someone to tell him what to do, someone who promises the sky, someone to fill the emptiness of his existence.

For the average urbanite, therefore, the city is truly the outer edge of civilization, not the utopia of his dreams. Having experienced the desperate emptiness of urban existence, many of them long for a return to the village. Indian polls, as one indication, show that 61 per cent of urban residents would prefer to go back to their villages, if economic opportunities were available.[21] This point is worth some emphasis: the urbanite who has lived in both worlds would generally choose the village.* The migrant, after all, usually succeeds only in trading a spartan rural life for the even harder ways of the city, the warmth of close personal relations for urban anonymity, the restricted authority of a village tribunal for the urban dictator's false promises of security. In the city, the transitional man loses his bread, his soul, and his freedom. An observation about urban Africans would serve well to summarize the state of impoverished urban man throughout the transitional societies: "... They are sad, because when they say that their old ways had many things to offer that western civilization has lost, they know with bitter certainty that they are right, and they

---

* Even more impressive is the fact that this particular sample was drawn from university graduates, the group presumably least likely to be attracted back to a village.

know that these are the things that have made life worth living, and living well." [22]

With the tableau of transitional cities spread before us, we are now in a better position to understand the human meaning of the "revolution in expectations." From the radio or movies, the colonial district officer or missionary, the city schoolteacher or politician, transitional men have been enthralled by a new set of ideas. Whether in the village or the city, they have begun to discard certain basic premises concerning the nature of man, society, and the physical universe.

Most important, they have come to an appreciation, however cautious, that man's own efforts can change his destiny, that progress is possible, if not probable. This new awareness leads only too often to a more profound discouragement, for progress does not come cheaply.

One might expect the discontent which bubbles within transitional men to boil into utopian aspirations, into hopes that someone will usher in a kingdom of God which will immediately end their suffering. Indeed, in the cities, authoritarian movements encourage this sentiment and draw to their ranks many who seek an all-embracing salvation. Yet, one of the most encouraging facts about developing nations is that the majority of people have not yet succumbed to utopian visions.

The aspirations of most transitional men, particularly in villages, are realistic and quite specific. Surveys in Calcutta, Tranacore-Cochin, and New Delhi have shown that the people regarded the rise in food prices and unemployment as the two most urgent problems requiring governmental attention. And in an African study, E. T. Sherwood revealed that the peasant's greatest aspiration was to have his own farm, simply "to be a free man." [23] Ninety-eight per cent of the African sample mentioned poverty and hunger as their greatest fears; 60 per cent cited the apprehension that their children might have to steal, "take to crime or commit murder" in order to live. Transitional men, in other words, have the most reasonable of aspirations: a hope that their immediate, limited economic needs can be satisfied, and a desire that their children may escape the compulsions of poverty.

In specific terms, the essential meaning of the revolution in ex-

pectations is that a vision of progress has tempted transitional
men. They will welcome change as long as it can bring a tangible
improvement in their personal economic situation.° Land of their
own, cheaper food, a job—these are the limited aspirations of the
majority.

The fact that their expectations are so reasonable, so confined to
particular goals, has major significance. Politically, it suggests that
governments which give their people only Asian Games and nationalism, nebulous visions of Pan-Africanism or social justice cannot long hold their allegiance. The people want bread not circuses
Economically, it weakens one of the major premises of planners
in both authoritarian and democratic nations: the presumption that
transitional men will sacrifice all other goods in the search for an
ever-increasing standard of material abundance. After her investigation of Indian villages, Kussum Nair concluded:

> From what I have seen and experienced ... it would seem
> that a great majority of the rural communities do not share
> in a concept of an ever-rising standard of living. The upper
> level they are prepared to strive for is limited and it is the
> floor generally that is bottomless. ... If my observation is cor-
> rect, it largely invalidates one of the principal assumptions on
> which present planning for economic development in the rural
> sector is based. For in a situation of limited and static as-
> pirations, if a man should feel that his requirements are just
> two bags of paddy per year, he works for two bags but not
> for more. If he looks up to the stars, it is only to worship them,
> not to pluck them.[25]

Thus, for those aware of the choice involved, they do not wish
to sacrifice the freedom, warmth, security, and even leisure provided by traditional life simply in a scramble for riches. Yet, is it
possible for even the best-intentioned government both to preserve the virtues of traditional order and simultaneously to create
an economy which will satisfy even the limited aspirations of
transitional men? The consensus today seems to be that even the
most minor of economic advances requires a fundamental social

---

° Even in remote Bengal villages, 62 per cent of peasants indicated their
belief that a fundamental change in the social order was necessary.[24]

transformation, a "social cost" must be paid. From the Marxist point of view, economic development ". . . implies the crude but crucial fact—often, if not always, overlooked—that development has historically always meant a far-reaching transformation of society's economic, social, and political structure. . ."[26] Equally, experts from M.I.T.'s Center for International Studies (as Keynesian a bastion of Western policies as one can find) reach similar conclusions: "The face-to-face relations and warm powerful family ties of a traditional society must give way to more impersonal systems. . . . There must be a radical shift in balance to urban life . . . the paramount requirement for the modernization of any society is that the people themselves must change."[27]

Here, we begin to enter that morass of arguments about the "social prerequisites" of progress. It is impossible to deal with the issue summarily in the space available. At this point, however, we can at least raise some questions about the sociological generalizations which underpin the position of those who advocate a politically authoritarian solution to the dilemmas of development:

1. Transitional man is not simply a newly aroused animal who will trade his heritage to anyone who promises him luxury.

2. The peasant is not just a dull clod requiring centralized direction from above. Village development need not be "an exercise in advanced animal husbandry," as one Ghanaian official described it to me. Rather, the peasant appears to be a rational man whose caution springs from experience, not "stubbornness."

Traditional peasant culture is not one which lends itself easily to the unrestrained demands of modern authoritarian governments. Although hierarchical in nature, the village has developed ancient concepts of justice, limited power, and democratic participation in government which will not die easily.

There is little reason to believe that traditional culture must inevitably be torn up by the roots for development to proceed. Obviously, there are specific social obstacles to economic growth: religious taboos in India, retrograde land-tenure patterns in Latin America and, everywhere, the pall of ignorance. But it must also be recognized that village culture can be a base for innovation. It is not the social quagmire of stagnant attitudes and customs so often portrayed.[28]

3. Rather than being a "necessary" aid to economic growth, ur-

banization in developing nations appears, at this point in history, to have worsened the masses' welfare.

While some of the generalizations of authoritarians about transitional man cannot be entertained as universally valid, they do have a single, central perception which gives weight to their position: the recognition that man in the developing nations is miserable and, most importantly, is newly aware of his misery.* To a greater or lesser degree, men of all nations have accepted the originally Western convictions that there is progress and that all men should share in it.[29] Can one really wonder, then, that authoritarianism has seduced so many transitional men, particularly among city-dwellers? The authoritarian promise of abundance and social justice inevitably appeals to those who have subscribed to the "subversive" ideals first propagated during the European Enlightenment. The authoritarian claims that no other method can as successfully overcome the economic challenge, that the human condition can be changed in no more efficacious way.

We can hope that transitional men will not succumb to this propaganda. Unfortunately, to the degree that urbanization proceeds, the likelihood that they will fall prey to the lures of dictatorship seems to increase. C. Wright Mills, in commenting on "The Big City," posed some of the alternatives: "What should be done with this wonderful monstrosity? Break it all up into scattered units, combining residence and work? Refurbish it as it stands? Or, after evacuation, dynamite it . . . ?"[30]

By whatever method, leaders in the new nations have the duty of stemming an urban flood. The instruments to accomplish this task exist: agriculture could be invigorated, small village-based

---

* The curious way in which awareness of misery can operate is poignantly illustrated in Banfeld's description of "Montegrano." He records that "Dr. Franco Gino, the health officer of the commune, says that at least 50 patients a year come to him suffering from nothing but hunger. These people present a difficult problem. Because their stomachs are shrunken they do not feel the pangs of hunger. If they were given a diet including milk, eggs, meat, together with vitamin injections, they would soon be restored to health. But then, their stomachs having returned to normal size, they would be able to feel hunger. And because there would be no possibility of their continuing the adequate diet, they would soon have to suffer the pain of returning to a state of semi-starvation. When such people come to him, Dr. Gino regretfully tells them that there is nothing he can do for them."

industry encouraged, and a planned decentralization of light industry throughout the countryside could be undertaken. Whether the "power elite" of underdeveloped nations will, in fact, have the vision, courage, and wisdom to implement such policies lies in the hands of destiny.

NOTES:

1. Carolina Maria de Jesus, *Child of the Dark* (New York, 1962), p. 11.
2. Ibid. pp. 38 and 47.
3. Ibid. p. 38.
4. Robert Heilbroner, *The Great Ascent* (New York, 1963), p. 66.
5. Kingsley Davis, "Urbanization in India," in *India's Urban Future*, ed. Roy Turner (Berkeley, Calif., 1962), p. 7.
6. Arthur Lewis, "Economic Problems of Development," in *Restless Nations*, Council on World Tensions (New York, 1962), p. 75.
7. Ibid. p. 71.
8. Daniel Lerner, *The Passing of Traditional Society* (Glencoe, 1958).
9. Oscar Lewis, "Mexico Since Cardenas," *Social Research*, Spring, 1959, p. 26.
10. *Public Opinion Surveys of the Indian Institute of Public Opinion*, I, No. 3 (Oct. 1955), 10.
11. Unpublished poll conducted by the Institute for Sociological Research, Santiago, Chile.
12. Colin Turnbull, *The Lonely African* (New York, 1962), p. 68.
13. Shanti Tangri, "Urbanization, Political Stability, and Economic Growth," in *India's Urban Future*, op. cit.
14. C. Wright Mills, "The Big City: Private Troubles and Public Issues," *Power, Politics and People*, edited by Irving L. Horowitz (New York, 1963), p. 395.
15. Nelly Kydias, *Social Implications of Industrialization and Organization in Africa South of the Sahara*, UNESCO, Tensions and Technology Series (Paris, 1956).
16. See Oscar Lewis, *Five Families* (New York, 1962); E. M. Spinley, *The Deprived and the Privileged* (London, 1953); and F. Zweig, *Labour, Life and Poverty* (London, 1949).
17. de Jesus, op. cit. p. 96.
18. Oliver La Farge, in Oscar Lewis, *Five Families*, op. cit. pp. ix, x.
19. Turnbull, op. cit. p. 42.
20. Thomas Hodgkin, *Nationalism in Colonial Africa* (New York, 1957).
21. D. N. Majundar, *Unemployment Among the University Educated* (Cambridge, Mass., 1957), pp. 33-4.
22. Turnbull, op. cit. p. 59.

23. E. T. Sherwood, quoted in *Self-Anchoring Scaling*, by F. P. Kilpatrick and Hadley Cantril, *Journal of Individual Psychology*, 16, no. 2, Nov. 1960.
24. *Public Opinion Surveys of the Indian Institute of Public Opinion*, I (Oct. 1955), 10.
25. Kussum Nair, *Blossoms in the Dust* (London, 1961), pp. 192-3.
26. Paul Baran, *The Political Economy of Growth* (New York, 1960), p. 4.
27. Max Millikan and Donald Blackmer, *The Emerging Nations* (Boston, 1961), pp. 21, 22, 23.
28. These are, of course, extremely broad and intensely controversial generalizations about peasant cultures. Lack of space prohibits their full defense. Support for these opinions can, however, be found in such writings as Frank Tannenbaum, *Ten Keys to Latin America* (New York, 1962); Turnbull, op. cit.; H. O. Davies, *Nigeria: The Prospects for Democracy* (London, 1961); M. N. Srinivas, *India's Villages* (Bombay, 1960); and P. Bauer and Basil Yamey, *The Economics of Underdeveloped Countries* (Chicago, 1957). For cogent arguments in opposition to these generalizations, see David McClelland, *The Achieving Society* (Princeton, 1961); Paul Baran, *The Political Economy of Growth* (New York, 1960); and Robert Heilbroner, op. cit.
29. For supporting evidence, see such writings as Michael Edwardes, *Asia in the Balance* (Baltimore, 1962); *Africa: Continent of Change*, edited by Peter Gould (Belmont, Calif., 1961); Barbara Ward, *Five Ideas that Change the World* (London, 1959); Jean and Simone Lacouture, *L'Egypte en mouvement* (Paris, 1962); and the various *Public Opinion Surveys* published by the Indian Institute of Public Opinion.
30. C. Wright Mills, op. cit. p. 395.

# 26

PAUL MEADOWS

## Industrial Man:
## Another Look at a Familiar Figure *

**I**

It was Arnold Toynbee who, after a generation of efforts by others to make plain and familiar the nature of the new society of the mid-nineteenth century, gave currency—appropriately enough the setting was London adult education—to the phrase "the industrial revolution," establishing thus in the political context of "revolution" the salient characteristic of the nineteenth century's economic world. Karl Marx had similarly heralded it in the *Communist Manifesto,* and so had many a writer of less economic and political sensibility than he. The Western world had become the stage of a new drama, "industrialization," and of a new character, "industrial man"; the vicissitudes and fortunes of this new society, "industrialism," have been the preoccupation, if not obsession, of generations of intellectuals since then.

The contours and dimensions of this new society have been caught in the webs of imagination which have held back the changing and mobile vitality unleashed in the new society. The expansion of Europe, the opening of the New World, the western

* This paper appears in somewhat different form in the author's forthcoming volume, *The Developmental Process,* to be published by the Syracuse University Press.

frontier, European colonialism, the rise of capitalism, the march of finance industrialism, the emergence of democratic man, the upsurge of humanitarianism, the tide of liberty, the passing of the European age—these and many other phrases have sought to capture the powerful energies and explosive creativity of this new "man" of the nineteenth century. Generally, the imagery of this industrial inquiry has succeeded in canonizing the "middle classes," the "bourgeoisie," the "entrepreneurs," though gaudy bouquets of praise have at the same time been tossed at that presumably ascendant occupational segment, the "proletariat."

Yet however redolent the phrase, however stirring the slogan, however poetic the historic license, the vocabulary and language of this new industrial literature, whether by savant or scientist, proclaimed that the advent and global sweep of description and explanation were in the grand tradition of metaphysical reports and reflections on the world, the great traditional models of cosmology, used by writers in the physical and social sciences to construct a rationale for the new dynamic social, political and economic landscapes. The "inscapes" of metaphysics, that is, formed the master perspectives of empirical and analytic theory. This metaphysical posture goes far in explaining the fact that each of the first two great phases of industrial inquiry reached a kind of cultural climax in a systematic theory: facts and theories organizing facts in time are placed together in master systems of thought which explain all the fascinating and fabulous parts in terms of no less fascinating and fabulous totality. It is as though industrial man, no less than his many ancestral "types," was moved and shaped by a strain toward "system." Although no such "systematics" of theory are as yet at hand in this present phase, there is abundant evidence that here, too, master systems of analysis are on the way to delivery in due time.

## II

Big-range industrial theory in the nineteenth century and in the first two decades of this century became very slowly aware that the reality behind the changing drama of social life was a giant technological shift. This insight, first formulated in a historical and philosophical mode, placed the source of change—initially, it must be stressed, with hostility and nostalgia, as in the Rousseauian romanticism of the first half of the nineteenth century and in the powerful romantic historical school of the later nineteenth century —in the mobile contexts of "process." Here was to be the Procrustean bed into which all accounts of the many revolutions of nineteenth-century societies were fitted, whether these accounts were phrased in terms of Newtonian mechanics, Hegelian idealism, Marxian dialectical materialism, Darwinian evolutionism, or persisting rationalist optimism (often called social progress theory). They held this process, by whatever name known, operated in history and that it did not transcend history (as most earlier metaphysical models invariably insisted) but embraced it; in fact they sought to discern in the sweeping spatio-temporalizations of historic experience the tell-tale, the generative, the unfolding "form" (or, as we like to say today, "pattern") beyond appearance. There was in such a quest guidance and comfort for there was in it the same certainty of the deliberate patterning of social fabrics which has characterized the technology and engineering of industrial equipment and techniques and activities. In consequence, engineering did not have to and indeed should not be confined to inanimate nature.

The romantic school of history and of economics was as sure that they had found in the impressive continuities of custom and tradition the stuff of selected destinies as were the Hegelians and the post-Hegelians (of either idealistic or materialistic breed). "History is on our side" has been the theme song of every metaphysics of immanent change since 1800. Whether "history" was conceived of in terms of the cosmos itself, or in terms of terrestrial evolution, or in terms of "Western civilization," or in terms of Condorcet's infinite capability of the human mind, inquiry about the new industrial society was shoved up against giant intellectual frames of reference, either in order to explain or promote, to analyze or agitate, to remember or predict.

Among the ethicists, for whom the underlying technological process was a problem of God and man, or at least a dialogue of man and man, the new technological age was seen as a function of an immanent axiological model: process must be judged, it must stand before judgment in terms of prevailing values and norms. Thus the Social Gospel movement, grounding its inherited transcendental eschatology in a search for a kingdom of heaven in this world, gloomily pronounced, as did the prophet Amos in the setting of the agrarian urbanism of his day, prophecies of doom—unless, of course, there should be a penitential turning of the tide of perversion of the technological process. The technological process itself was good; only man—and there is a Wordsworthian romantic overtone here—is evil. The Christian Socialist movement joined this hue and cry of human failure and institutionalized abuse. And so did the Social Welfare movement, as it spawned settlement houses, community centers, parks and playgrounds, charity organization, and a long, unending line of social legislation dating from the days of Bismarckian Germany. Sometimes the lyrics of this chorus were theocentric, sometimes plainly and sentimentally humanistic; but populism—the people count, they must be counted, and they must be served—proved to be the truly original and native political philosophy of the period. The earlier philosophies of history deified process itself, or reified it, and thus variously came to terms with the evil of the new society. Romanticists accounted for evil in terms of the disastrous break with the past; Hegelians of both breeds, in terms of the equally disastrous clinging to the past which must be broken if the future is ever to come; the Social Darwinists and social progressivists, in terms of the teleological unfolding of process toward expansive and unlimited and unlimiting goals.

All of the schools of big-range industrial inquiry sought to fence their intellectual domains about with the boundaries of "systematics." Always the outer structures of change were seen as functional responses to the inner structures of process, however the latter may be conceived. Another of these efforts at systematics renounced the realm of *process* and proclaimed the dominion of *substance*. Change must be seen in terms of the substance of change, not the how but the what of change. Here then emerges the "sociologistic" school, if we may borrow Sorokin's very appropriate title for it. For then the technological shift must be seen as a function of differing forms of institutionalization. These men—Tönnies, Sombart, Tawney, Durkheim, Weber, Veblen, among others—have had a lasting impact on the mental framework of the present mid-century of industrial thought. Technology is not *sui generis* but is itself part and parcel of an intricate meshwork of ideational and institutional systems. Today whether one invokes the Protestant Ethic of Sombart and Tawney, or Weber's cultural structures of "authority legitimation," or the cultural "thematology" (if this neologism may be allowed tentatively to stand) of Tönnies' *Gemeinschaft und Gesellschaft*, or Durkheim's mechanical and organic solidarity, or the national characterology of Geoffrey Gorer, whether he salutes the entrepreneurialism of Schumpeter, or the suggestion-imitation of a Tarde, or the social interaction patterns of a von Wiese or a Ross, or the institutions of invention and change of Veblen or Ayres, the *fin de siècle* days achieved the truly impressive cogency of system-bounded social empiricism. Indeed, the new society of industrial "contract"—there are so many such phrases in the industrial literature—managed to arrive at conceptual organizations ironically with far more unity and integration than the social reality itself. And it was just this gap between epistemic model and ongoing existence, between the historistic ideologies and the objective reality, that helped to push industrial inquiry in a new direction and onto a new level, that of the "middle range."

## III

It was, however, less the fallacies of historicisms noted above than their basic irrelevance to the daily round of life and problems in the local work places of industrial production that turned a generation of industrial inquiry to the study of the shop, the office, the firm, and the varieties of economic situations in and outside the industrial community. Taking their cue from the sociologistic models of the pre-World War I theorists, this new generation started with the proposition that the technological shift was basically a shift in the nature of human relations at work. Emerging from the studies which span the 'twenties and 'thirties are formulations about the technological shift of the new industrial society, formulations which phrase a meta-sociologistic model, that is, the theme that beyond the teeming and changing varieties of social life and differentiated functions there are social patterns generating and guiding the social work life. We may, in fact, distinguish three such meta-sociologistic models: the "human relations" approach, the "interactional" approach, and the "social systems" approach.

An after-thought child of the scientific management period in industrial production theory, nourished by the popularity of psy-

chology during the first World War and by its newly perceived
utility for sales as well as production, the human relations approach
viewed the industrial scene in terms of harmonious local inter-
group work relations, which were conceived in the best traditions
of natural harmony, rational choice, and competitive equality of
economic man. This view was solemnized in the marriage, as it
were, of Adam Smith economics and the Scottish moral philosophy
school, a marriage blessed by Fourierist associationist harmony, religious humanism, and social optimism. The work place should become an ethical culture society, and so must such belligerent interest groups as unions, trade associations, and professional institutes. The notion of democracy in the market and the work place
loomed large in this period. A "basic English" of motivation language appeared, deriving partly from perceptive psychologists such
as Walter Dill Scott or Ordway Tead, partly from the happy salesmanship of Dale Carnegie, partly from the luncheon club fraternalism of Rotary and other brethren, partly from the industrial experimentation that demonstrated "the social" as being a dimension
of work place existence equally with "the financial" or "the physical." The human relations contribution to industrial inquiry was
also greatly spurred by the discovery of the productivity thera-
peutics of general semantics. In general, it was as though this generation, having failed to save the world for democracy, would at
least try to save industry for it, or at least to save industry for
some solid, harmonious, and happy human relations.

Gradually, however, during the late 'twenties and with swelling
volume in the 'thirties another approach to industrial inquiry made
its appearance. The "interactional" approach, operating from a supply base in personality theory which was partly Freudian and
partly sociological, proposed a conception of industrial society
and of industrial man in terms of a meta-sociologistic model which
pointed to major patterns of human interaction as generating and
guiding human action in the industrial society.

This approach is interesting partly because it projected in the
arena of theory the pragmatic concerns of the world of work. Industrial enterprises had found during the 'twenties they had some
key operational problems involving human beings *qua* human
beings on the job. Unlike the human relations approach, which
stressed the interactivity of groups, this approach sought to deal

with the human being as a total person and with individual-to-group and group-to-individual interactions. *What's on the Worker's Mind?* was the question which Whiting Williams tried to answer through participant observation as a worker himself; others exploited survey-questionnaire methods. Indeed, industrial society became in the 'thirties the land of the Gallup Poll—"Galluputia"—as researchers, equipped with pencils, pads, and opinionnaires, sought to throw on the screen of national attention the bright beams of percentages and averages of mass opinions. All kinds of targets for interviewing were added—consumers, investors, families, regions, neighborhoods, ethnic groups, churches, prostitutes, and convicts. "If only we knew one another better," went the refrain, "we would avoid so many troubled human interactions." To this self-revealing prophecy was added another, this time from the strait-laced purity of semanticized communication theory: "if only we could talk with one another—communicate better—how vastly improved would be the lot of industrial man!"

The search for the "right" word was paralleled by the search for the right technique for selecting the "right" man. Just as we ignorantly employ the wrong word or the wrong motive in the right place, so likewise industrial society must avoid the placement of the wrong man in the right job, whether that man is worker or manager. The test and interview, the proper instructional formula, used wisely in worker and management personnel, can smash the barriers to the greater productivity of social harmony. People, whether as workers or managers, have productively appropriate and educable traits which can undergo quality control in selection, training, and general product improvement. Even corporations have personalities (in other than the long-established though fantastic juridical sense!) and certainly they have images, both body and ego, both public and private, as do industrial workers. The cult of personality, in other words, swept through the assembly line, into the front offices and to the board rooms of production and public relations executives. It was the day of "the new personality in industry."

But behind toothpaste smiles and jaunty, tilted heads was a vague something of grave anxiety—the fact of human "irrationality." Celebrated in ancient mythology as "demoniac possession," decried as a "fever" by the romantic counter-revolutionaries (e.g.

Taine and Chateaubriand), derogated as "herd," "crowd," and "mass" behavior by the aristocrats of industrial theory (e.g. Le Bon, Trotter, and Ortega y Gasset), the irrationality concept finally found a home in the mythology-modeled analytic paradigms of Freud. Locating the sources of human hostility, anger, violence, hate, and resistance in the unconscious *imperium* of unsocialized, primitive impulse, Freudian social theory provided the same kind of conservative blast at political and economic radicalism and non-conformity in the late 'twenties and early 'thirties which Malthusianism with its inevitable imbalance of food and reproduction ratios directed at the equally unpalatable radicalism and non-conformity of late eighteenth-century revolutionary Jacobins. This time, however, a new magic was added: the theme that irrationality is an illness, a behavioral not organic illness ordinarily, but illness nonetheless, and medical in jurisdiction. The "compleat" industrial man was thus in the making, via the fifty-minute couch and psychiatrized conformity masked as true individuality. To be sure, the "new personality in industry," seen in this light, turned out to be less happy than illusioned, and the fraternal bonds of the Scottish-Smithian economic model appeared to be as fragile as the Marxian historicists said they were. To these darkening counsels were added the equally pessimistic studies of those economists bravely specializing in monopoly and oligopoly and other consensual deviations from the perfect and free competition of rational equals. The house that Smith built seemed on the verge of becoming a mad house.

What saved the day, it now appears, was the hasty abandonment of happy fraternalism and neurotic conflict metaphors for the productive integrations of a very new metaphor. We may call it the "servo"-metaphor, after the discovery of the explanatory as well as technological benefits of servo-mechanisms. Although this model has not yet even begun to reach its zenith in full-scale "across the board" utilization in industrial theory, it began to make its impact felt in the social sciences only in the 'forties and the 'fifties. The way was prepared for it in the purely empirical discovery—later exploited in such dramatic theoretical achievements as information theory (e.g. Wiener's "cybernetics")—that reality occurs in existential systems, in functional unities of interacting members, persisting, bounded, organized. Whether as organisms, as communities, or enterprises, these interactive systems were actually made to serve industrial theory as their own epistemic models. The world famous Western Electric-Hawthorne studies of formal and informal work groups heralded this shift to the analytic systems approach to industrial inquiry, now unquestionably dominant in the literature of industrial research.

Two varieties of systems theory in industrial inquiry—other than the phenomenal use of it in engineering—may be identified. Typological system theory, following the Western Electric and Mayo-Barnard lead, sketched and limned the forms of interactional patterns occurring in the marketplace, which was conceived of as a relatively closed and invariably hieratic empirical social system of interdependent members. Four such empirical forms exist, as Dubin, one of the more recent exponents, has pointed out: formal, informal, nonformal, and technical. Similarly, national and regional economic analysis, using input-output mechanical models, have described the empirical system relationships of national economies and of metropolitan regional areas.

But typological system theory only prepared the way for both propositional system theory and meta-system theory. The former, utilizing the familiar functional equation, $X=f(Y)$, has formulated two different variables: industrial system structures (e.g. the factory, the corporation, the community) and industrial system processes (e.g. co-operation, collaboration, accommodation, conflict); and it has developed sensitive personal behavioral and social interactional correlations around these structural variances. These studies have pursued this theme in a widening variety of work situations—hospitals, research organizations, restaurants, campuses, unions—and in all of them, the integration of the rational-efficient and the sentimental-effective dimensions of productive effort have been underscored. When to this orientation in theory are added the huge donations of insights which role theory can make—as witness Erving Goffman's *Presentation of Self in Everyday Life*—one can easily predict a sure and long line of work-place system studies; less easy to predict is an enlargement of our stock of information much beyond what has already been produced.

Meta-system or general systems theory, bringing together industrial students from all over the industrial scene, is now in process of developing a meta-language of formalistic or axiomatic statements capable of generating theory of increasingly wide range— very probably the beginning of another period of "big-range" industrial theory in the nineteenth-century tradition.

## IV

There can hardly be any doubt about the resurgence, since the second World War, of big-range industrial theory. Reflecting the global involvements of Western nations, involvements in a politico-military as well as traditionally economic sense, this new orientation and scope of industrial theory is at the same time an essential implement in the global involvement itself. What is being suggested here is that the technological shift in the modern world is a function of a meta-political model, a model sharply different from the static, descriptive, and attenuated meta-political models of the nineteenth century. We are witnessing today the return to the grand theories of the past century, theories which bring together in an inclusive unity all the systems of industrial society—the technological, the institutional, the ideational. The units of perception are the great *Gestalten* of industrial experience, conceived sometimes as processes, sometimes as structures. And as is so often true in historic experience, the whole is seen in terms of synecdoche, the significant part which stands for the whole.

Thus, one variety of big-range industrial theory lays heavy stress upon industrialization, seen as a generic or transcultural process, but locally variable: this is the view that the change in the new society is a function of industrialization as a generic process. Marx, writing in the traditional dialectic of historical materialism, was one of the first, but certainly not the only early, theorists of the new society to see this. St. Simon understood it perhaps even more wisely because he was less garrisoned by an aprioristic and utopian philosophical system. Certainly a very large number of economic historians during the second half of the nineteenth century began to see that they were dealing not merely with transformation in productive techniques or production conditions, but with an interlocking meshwork of transformations revolving around the massed mechanization of men, materials, money, institutions, and communities. Some of them were especially interested in the stages of industrialization, others in its variable institutional and ideational forms, still others in cultural continuities which made it

possible, and yet others in the cultural discontinuities (or in-
congruities) which accompany its development. Whether there
are indeed invariant stages in industrialization is today much less
certain than that there are combinations of traits and variables
which are predictably present in some degree and in some "mix"
in industrializing societies everywhere. The search for generic relationships within the industrialization process will go on, despite
the polymorphic dynamic of this process. Moreover, the emergence of an international industrial economy in the twentieth
century is as phenomenal and as integral to the industrialization
process as was the emergence of national industrial economies in
the previous century. Whether this portends the onset in the future
of a neo-industrialism is of course hard to say. Certainly our
Western thought has been inclined to view industrialization as a
final cause, in almost Aristotelian terms; in so doing we have been
guilty of the most serious lapses into ethnocentrism. One of the
most inevitable consequences of African and Asian participation
in the industrialization process is not only to encourage many
modifications in its historic institutional morphology but to displace the concept itself in favor of some less Western-biased word.

"Development" may in time prove to be—and in this discussion
it is thought that it will be—a surrogate for "industrialization." For
this concept is also seen as a generic process, as a total process,
and, what is more to the point, also as a locally variable process.
Indeed, one of the cardinal traits of the new societies of the West
was their conception of themselves during the nineteenth century
as undergoing not merely some change, but total change in some
well-sensed direction. The productive process itself certainly became in a sense the new epistemic model of change. This is itself
a remarkable fact. Earlier conceptions of development dwelt on
historical patterns of change: the unfolding of latent tendencies
into manifest forms; the emergence of new forms in a natural
history sequence (as in Marxian historical materialism); historical
variations on a theme, as in succession of political systems (as in
Polybius); or mere growth in knowledge and wisdom (as in humanism). But in the industrial model of development transformation is viewed as being dictated by technological and institutional
imperatives inherent in the processes of industrial production: the
process is its own logic. The raw material to finished product

imagery provides a compelling metaphor: it is itself a visual and tangible demonstration of development.

Under the sway of such a persuasive model it is not surprising to find the literature of industrial inquiry focusing on stages in development as a generic process; on variables which affect the rate of growth; on institutional inventions which will or which might facilitate optimum if not maximum development; and on the possible presence of a universal dynamic to which can be geared the policies and programs of deliberate and managed change. There are many clues to the nature of this dynamic: the more technologically minded find it in the nature of the machine itself; the more anthropologically minded in the behavioral patterns of innovation and acceptance; the more psychologically minded in the dynamism of some master motive, such as "achievement"; and the politically minded, along with the sociologists, in rising standards of living—i.e. on the collective patterns of "insistences" and "urgencies"—which if they do not generate great winds of revolution, at least become potent agencies of such change.

There are a few, less optimistic observers who think they find in "development" a kind of anti- or counter-revolutionary theme, in somewhat the same way that some socialist theorists of the nineteenth century regarded parliamentary socialism. It is still not clear to many theorists of industrial change whether the apocalyptic or "spasm" model of change represents development at all. Yet still others agree, as did Marx in his brilliant and much neglected dispatches to the *New York Tribune* in the 1840's (collected in a volume and published near the end of the century as *The German Revolution and Counter-Revolution*), that unless there is a capture of the revolutionary tradition inherent in any country undergoing modernization, development may not prove in time to be at all possible. Be that argument as it may, it is now clear that development is indeed tied to national diplomatic and military self-interest, though it has been institutionalized in even more hallowed forms as international assistance and idealistic overseasmanship and development diplomacy.

From the beginning, as we have seen, the new society was the occasion and the target of hotly contested ideological strategies.

Here we are underlining a theme, suggested earlier, that the present "big-range" industrial theory period hinges on a functional assertion: the technological shift of the Western world is a function of a meta-political model. Some role by the state in the change processes of modernization is necessarily and inescapably stipulated in any theory of deliberate change. Some writers conceived that role in terms of the idealized or ideal-typical individual entrepreneur as against the political collectivity: individualism versus collectivism, or, as Lord Russell pointed out, freedom versus organization. Others, dialectically ingenious and impatient with dichotomies, viewed the role of the state as an organization for freedom, or as an organization of freedom, or as freedom within organization. The undeniable march of both Western and non-Western societies toward collectivism has changed the whole nineteenth-century argument, as Walter Lippmann argued in his memorable *The Good Society:* the debate now centers on such questions of how much and when, on what forms for the legitimation of power and for a state in which the due processes of administration will have the same respect and stability as due process of justice.

Meantime, the orbital flights of the space age have set the stage for another kind of industrial ideological conflict over the role of the state. A space age revolution is already under way, one in which the technological *Machtpolitik* of space conquest is also serving as a relatively moral equivalent for war. It is also serving as a fairly moral equivalent for depression. Through its powerful exploitation of the Keynesian economic multiplier principle the expanding margins of production for space age ventures can finance a whole generation of neo-Malthusian industrial societies as they try to win the race between development and reproduction.

Many observers of the industrial scene, of course, cannot take ideological strategy too seriously, since they hold that ideology, like political humor, is most effective when regarded lightly. A painful split exists in the very notion of ideological strategy: for some, ideology is a defense of the existential order, for others it is an instrument of attack on that order. In such a situation humor about ideology is an irrelevance, even an irreverence; and talk about "the end of ideology" is unforgivably humorous.

Meantime, there does not seem to be now a climax in this phase of industrial theory. Systematization, a cultural climax in theory, seems to await the assemblage of relevant but still highly scattered information. When it does come, it matures because a major rupture in the total culture—at this juncture in world history, a rupture in world culture not merely national cultures—forces the framing of a new rationale for existence. Then, as many times in the past, the literature of industrial inquiry will turn to a metaphysical or cosmological model (perhaps "unified field theory" is just such a model) as a means of achieving a tight, cohesive, and ultimately cogent conceptual organization of the then new society in crisis.

## V

For almost a generation now, economists, following Veblen's cue perhaps, have been bewailing the lack of conceptual model as apt and as persuasive for today's world as "economic man" was for the nineteenth century. The inept and obsolete psychology of that concept, its parochialism with respect to things institutional and global, and its simple-minded single dimensionality have been stressed in all of the obsequies for the departed. For a long time names have been hesitantly offered—"institutional man," "organization man," "political man." But slowly "industrial man" seems to be winning acceptance as the best device for bringing into focus the many stray but powerful beams of light among those complex structures which we call developed or developing societies. It is a familiar conventional device, as when we talk of Greek man when we mean Greek civilization, or Roman man, or French or English. The term "man" then becomes a personalized and tropological image of total experience in a whole society, or in fact the underlying and significant image of all modernizing societies: the face behind the polymorphic mask of change.

To be sure, it is risky and difficult to select a short-hand symbol for an elaborate and intricate and ever-variable system of experience. The procedure is less risky in such domains of inquiry as mathematics, as when Einstein's famous energy equation summarized an epoch of mathematical and physical probing. But here is a beginning, based on the century of industrial inquiry which we have just reviewed.

## VI

The concept culture, popularized by nineteenth-century romantic poets, historians, and philosophers, was made a captive of the anthropologists, who applied it to relatively undeveloped and small-scale societies on the edges of the industrial world in the nineteenth century. Franz Boas, the American anthropologist, was fond of describing the culture of such a people as an "ecotype" a unique social adjustment made by a people to a peculiar kind of physical environment. Earth-bound and kinship-structured, these hereditary organizations of life and meanings were the prevailing mode of the social life of man for a million years, until just yesterday (on the geological clock) when groups of kinsmen settled down in a favorable place and with a viable stock of tools and ideas began to grow and extend a settlement—in time a city, with a civic organization and an *emporium*. The growth and continuity of the urban organization saw the slow emergence of specialized institutions, at first religious-military-political, and then separated and secularized. The growth of a network of cities throughout a region and in time across the known world shifted the urban metropolis into a metropolitan or even megalopolitan cosmopolis, a world city, linked forever with the destiny of the globe itself, and in rapid transformation stripped of its local ecological uniqueness as it participated in a planetary ecology. Schematically, these shifts in the cultural experience of human beings, highly simplified, are suggested below.

TABLE I

CULTURE-AS-ORGANIZATION: HISTORIC TYPES

| BASES | CULTURE FOCUS | ILLUSTRATIVE SUB-SYSTEMS |
|---|---|---|
| 1. Ethnically based | Culture as Ethnos | Class, Villages, Crafts |
| 2. Territorially based | Culture as Demos | Demes, Polis, Emporium |
| 3. Institutionally based | Culture as Sacred Magisterium | Guilds, Burg, Nation-State, Weltanschauung or Dharma |
| 4. Trans-institutionally based | Culture as Universal Dynamos | Megalopolis, Imperium, Markets, Processes, Abstract Idea |

A century and a half in emergence and largely confined in its main expressions to the so-called Western world, it is the fourth developmental level of culture for which the term industrialism and industrial man are descriptive condensations. Here the bonds of localistic ethnicity and enshrined institutionalism—as in "the societies of command"—are being transcended by institutions of contract and speciality in "the societies of consensus"; here localistic structures are being shaped and reshaped, even displaced, by a universal dynamic. Thus the Protestant Ethic, so useful to Sombart, Tawney, and Weber in an understanding of the third level of culture, seems a hopelessly irrelevant normative system in a culture of interlocked metropolises, international emporia, abstract world markets, and magisterial processes and ideas characterized by a vast secularism of value and expectation.

The key phrase in the fourth level of culture viewed as the organization of human experience is the concept of trans-institutionalism, by which we refer to the synthesis of ideas and skills and customs in rationally articulated systems of life and meaning, not exclusively political any more than economic, neither religious nor esthetic: a true syncretism. Such syncretism is not totally new in history: Hellenism represented the same kind of trans-institutional fusion in post-Alexandrine days in the Middle East. But what is new here is the fact that the syncretism of industrialism derives largely from the universal dynamic which underlies and pervades it.

## VII

The key image of the new society has long been the "machine" —power attached to, linked with, an end tool. Through the decades of industrial revolution—the only "permanent revolution" which modern times has thus far really known—diversity and improvement have been responsible for an incredible elaboration of both the "power" and the "end tool" aspects of mechanization. Today, the term "machine technology" is a short-hand symbol for a very complex system of capital goods as well as institutional forms and human skills essential for the use and elaboration of this system of capital goods. "Industrialization" refers in part to the technical skills and productive technics developed and evolved in the processes of capital formation among a people turning to increased

## TABLE II

### SOCIAL DIMENSIONS OF INDUSTRIALISM: A SYSTEM ANALYSIS

| ACTION VARIABLES (CF. PARSONS) | SUB-SYSTEMS (CF. LESLIE WHITE) | | |
|---|---|---|---|
| | TECHNOLOGY | INSTITUTIONS | IDEOLOGIES |
| INSTRUMENTAL: | 1. "mechanization" <br> 2. "invention" <br> 3. science-capital-technology as ongoing concern <br> 4. economy and maximum of energy output <br> 5. selection by merit <br> 6. machine in series and in mass: seriated & massed mechanization | 1. "organization" <br> 2. "innovation" <br> 3. primacy and priority of "enterprise" and the "entrepreneurial unit" <br> 4. mobilization and proportioning of factors; diminishing returns <br> 5. competitive selection, modified by strain toward imperfect competition <br> 6. mass employment, mass markets, mass organization, mass communication | 1. "rationalization" <br> 2. "assimilation" <br> 3. "risk-taking" as dynamic; collective elaboration of behavior and interests; collective institutional, welfare <br> 4. "efficiency" <br> 5. competition as impersonal process; "market" as organon <br> 6. mass as measure: "mass production," "mass society," "masses," "mass politics" |
| CONSUMMATORY: | 1. machine & mechanization as source of gratification, of inspiration, of achievement, of "good things" | 1. industrialized institutions, via standardization (or routinization, bureaucratization) of things, people, ideas, actions and functions | 1. world as mechanism; "machine," as theoretical and as ideological model |

2. machine neutrality—universal adaptability; but nonetheless value-judgment of machine as synonym of good things (e.g., abundance)

3. new environmental unity through machine; mechanization as transformation process

4. "power"—mechanical, electrical, etc.

5. concept of tool as extension of man

6. dynamics

7. goods and services in growing volume and quality

2. optimism and perfectibility; doctrine of progress; varieties of historicism

3. organicism; internality; holism; gestaltism

4. "power" as *summum bonum*

5. technology as dominant ontological system

6. process

7. asserted identity of good with goods

mechanization. But the term also refers with equal cogency and relevance to the very complex institutional system of capital goods utilization among a people resorting to increased mechanization.

These two usages of the term industrialization point then to twin aspects of industrialization as a universal dynamic: its central aspect in the mechanization of economic functions and its auxiliary aspect in the rationalization of human behaviors and relationships. Mechanization constitutes the inner structure of industrialism, rationalization its outer structure. Here, then, is a meta-economic concept of industrialism: the essential and identifying process "behind" and "beyond" the apparent and surface processes and forms. It is the first—that "marriage of physics and technology," as Veblen called it—which has yielded the enormous and commanding universality of industrialism as a culture organization of experience. It is the second—the slow and ceremonially thwarted development of rationalized institutional behaviors adapted not to ethnicity or ecology, but to the logical imperatives of the machine process—which is responsible for the unending variability of industrialism. In a sense this is the philosopher's distinction between "logical entailments," as in science-technology, and "material embodiments," as in the politico-economic institutions of an industrial organization. It is the outer structure which is as yet so very troublesome, so laggard with respect to the clean and clear imperatives of mechanization. For here must occur the rationalization of human relationships to the machine process itself, of industrial men to one another, of industrial men to the institutional and psycho-social dimensions of their new society, and of inherited languages and customs, institutions and associations, and codes of rules and codifications of meanings.

But rationalization is a difficult thing, a slow and complicated affair of time and talent, for it means managing human beings for whom action, unlike the action of the machine, is both instrumental and expressive or consummatory, in Parsons' sense of these terms. Moreover, the logical (i.e. the efficient and effective) demands of rationalization require that instrumental and expressive rationalization must both occur in all three sub-systems, in Leslie White's distinction, of a total society—technological, institutional, and ideological. The preceding table seeks to portray, sketchily but suggestively it is hoped, the full scope of the rationalization process in the setting of developed industrial countries. Here, in miniature, is the dynamic of the underlying institution-building process of the new society. Here, it is suggested, one may glimpse the world of the "compleat" industrial man; but it is only a glimpse, not even a fragmentary map.

# 27

L. A. COSTA PINTO

## Portrait of Developing Man: The Processes of Social Changes in Latin America

It is no longer necessary to emphasize the importance of the subject of social development. There is a widespread consensus that some basic characteristics of social organization and the world order of tomorrow are being shaped in the developing world of today and in the processes of its transformation.

This applies to the entire, so-called "Third World." But it holds just as much for Latin America where, in fact, we do not find today the *emergence of new nations* in the strict sense of the word, as is the case in Africa or in some parts of Asia. The majority of Latin American nations have already celebrated their 150th anniversary of national independence. What they are trying to do at present is not to become members of a family of nations of which they have been the poor cousins for hundreds of years. What they are trying to do, and with definite evidence of success, is to change their position, their economic and political status in the structure of an international society.

Development arises as a natural consequence of the processes of industrialization and urbanization that today are the dominant trait and the predominant aspiration of the people of this part of the world. If we compare the processes of development now occurring in the social structure of the Latin American countries with the processes of social change that in the past have shaped the overdeveloped societies of our time, we may find a useful approach for understanding some basic aspects of the transition now in process in Latin America.

Perhaps the first prominent difference we find is the pioneer character of the development of England and Western Europe, and, in some sense, of the United States. They were creating pathways in history, modeling new patterns of social and economic organization. They never, in the current usage of the word at least, had been underdeveloped because they could not point to other countries more developed than themselves. Furthermore, they never participated in any international organizational activities in which the established relation with other more developed countries was sometimes the most important barrier to be surmounted in the historical processes of their own national development.

From this we may extract a second basic differential trait between the processes of modern and past development. Today, social change within the developing countries receives considerable impulse from exogenous sources, by means of so-called "demonstration effects." To varied extents, the patterns of material and social progress of the more advanced countries are emulated by the people of the developing countries. These exogenous factors, as compared with the endogenous patterns of development of the past, cannot always be conceived of as a positive force, since the "demonstration effect" often acts to intensify the mechanical application of some ideal model of development with which the policy makers may be fascinated. England became an industrial country while its working class was fighting to reduce its working day from 14 to 10 hours per day. Industrialization in Latin America must be performed simultaneously and in close connection with the preservation and the enlargement of the progress already obtained at the institutional level in the advanced industrial nations. It must anticipate the basic changes in the institutional framework of national societies, changes that in the past, and in other nations, occurred as an implication or consequence of economic and technological revolutions. In brief, development must now take place in an atmosphere of relatively enlightened labor legislation and management controls.

Perhaps the basic differential characteristic between the two processes of development is the "unnaturalness" of change, i.e. its "provoked" character. Modern development, at all levels, is not a spontaneous or gradual process of social change; it is, and sometimes must be, an induced, provoked, and intentional change. Development as a need has become an "act of faith." You may find obstacles and barriers, resistance and problems in the process of development, but at the national level the majority of these problems is concentrated in differences about the direction, rhythm, and model to be adopted. Little argument takes place over the worth of development as such. In these developing societies change appears as a value and the promotion of change is intentionally stimulated.

By this very fact, and as a consequence of this provoked character of modern development, we may find another quite distinct pattern of development when comparing past and modern trends. Here I have in mind the role of government as the leading force and source in the promotion of modern development as contrasted with private enterprise in the traditional pattern. In the past, national progress was conceived as a natural consequence of the prosperity of each part of the nation. In this liberal ideological framework the profit-making motive and achievement orientation had a function of utmost importance in the promotion of economic and social change.

Social change now takes place in a context that has also changed historically. Development appears as a chain of historical jumps in which the whole society is involved. The state, as the supreme agency of social control, is the only institution in a position to perform the role of basic agency of social change with authority and efficiency when development becomes the main goal of the whole nation. *En passant*, we find here another explanation for the importance of politics in the process of development in Latin America. This may help us to understand that the process of "politicalization" presented by some social institutions, such as the Church, the army, or the university, does not call only for a pejorative interpretation. In many instances it results from the fact that development in these countries is not only a technical operation but a living historical experience in which society as a whole, from bottom to top, is involved.

We have not exhausted the possible list of differential characteristics between the processes of social and economic change that have created the overdeveloped countries of our time, and the processes which the developing nations are now undergoing. But we may use the points thus far introduced to support this first basic conclusion: what is taking place in the developing world in our day is not a mere reproduction of the same process which occurred in the past in earlier phases of industrialization. Only if we start from a clear notion of the qualitatively different character and meaning of these two historical processes are we in a position to really understand the scope and importance of the experience that today is being lived by the people concerned.

Calling attention now to other aspects of the processes of development in Latin America, we begin with the problem of the *direction* of structural transformation. This is a problem of far-reaching significance. We observe that many people who agree about basic issues sometimes disagree when the issue is the definition of the direction or goals toward which a transitional society must be guided. Of course, a basic factor is the starting point at which a society is located when the process of development begins. Tanganyika, India, Guatemala, Brazil, are all illustrations of developing societies. But each one has initiated its process of development at a different starting point. All of them are marching into the future and turning their backs on traditional patterns of economic, social, and political organization. But these archaic patterns, whose destruction partially defines the very process of change, differ largely from one nation to the other. This circumstance makes a tremendous difference in all further steps of the process. This is important not only for the policy of development, but also at the conceptual level; i.e. for a better sociological understanding of the process of development. Great caution should be used in employing such expressions as "underdeveloped world," or "backward people," as a simplistic label for nations and peoples that are in fact extremely heterogeneous, and which have initiated the present rhythm of accelerated transformation starting from different points of the historical continuum. There exist different patterns of underdevelopment, as there are different patterns of development. Past as well as contemporary history offers quite different patterns and rhythms for moving from one situation to the other.

This is the reason why developing societies are, by definition, non-equally developed societies, in which we may find, from bottom to top, as a structural characteristic of these nations, the coexistence of two patterns of social structure: the old, traditional and declining pattern and the new, emergent, modern, developed one. This situation I propose to call structural marginality. Such marginality results from the fact that different parts of the traditional society do not change with the same rhythm, since each one offers various degrees of resistance to change. From this flows one of the basic characteristics of traditional societies. Their social structure is marginal in the sense that in it coexist two patterns of structural organization. The old, which although remaining, is not strong enough to dominate; and the new, which although already present, still does not predominate. This is the most important characteristic that results when development is *intensified* but not yet *generalized*.

This characteristic ambivalence or marginality is found in all epochs when societies are undergoing a process of accelerated transition. It stems from the fact that different parts of the social structure do not change with the same rhythm or speed. But in contemporary developing societies this appears as a most striking characteristic because of the provoked and deliberately induced character of the transition. Plans and policies of developments, at least in the first step, are always concentrated in the transformation of the economic structure. Industrialization is always the most explicit economic goal of the developing nations. Technological progress, rises in the indices of productivity, national product, and income *per capita*, etc., these are the fields toward which all social and political efforts move. Until recently the concept of *economic* development was predominant in the minds of most statesmen and scholars. *Social* development, in the broader sense of the word, was located, in this conceptual scheme, in the position of an "implication" of economic development.

All this affirms the statement that in the developing societies the contradictions between the rhythms of transformation of the different parts of the social structure are multiplied by the provoked character of the change and by the concentrated efforts for the promotion of an "industrial revolution." The intensification of this process of technological transformation, if it does occur simultaneously (and usually it does not), with equally accelerated changes in other levels and parts of the social structure, becomes the great source of social tensions, institutional problems, and political troubles in these societies. This is so because the consistent nature of the archaic pattern of social organization functions as a firm obstacle and barrier to development.

In the everyday life of developing societies all these contradictions form a situation which gives the impression that development itself is the great source of troubles. Defenders of tradition maintain that development is the essence of the problem and not the solution for the old ones. And, in some sense, this is true. The only difference being that not all social problems are necessarily bad problems. Since the archaic social and economic pattern with its rigidity, its inequalities, and its injustices is the basic social order that development intends to transcend, what logically results in the history of these nations is (not infrequently) disorder representing the beginning of a new social order. The fundamental goal of a dynamic approach to development in the emerging countries is to understand that development itself, in its very process, creates some new problems and intensifies some old problems that *only more development is able to solve.*

This is an unavoidable result of the fact that development is much more than a technical operation, a series of innovations forced upon a society from outside or from the top, affecting only the pattern of organization of economic activities, the expansion of industries, the use of new tools, and the rise of productivity. Development is a living historical experiment of tremendous scope in which the whole nation is involved. The laboratory of this experiment is history. The raw material is man. What is developing is a social structure as a whole and as each one of its parts: economic types, stratification systems, institutional patterns, values and norms, ideas and ideologies. What is involved is the shaping of a new structure of human relations in these countries, a new basic framework for the everyday life of each man and woman, a new pattern of relations between men and men, between men and things, between men and values, and the symbols of these values.

Development is not a moment, an issue, an event; development is a process—a historical process—with different stages, with partial results, each one with some definite goals. One of the results of this historical transformation is a man, a new type of man. One of the great mistakes and one of the great injustices that is usually done to pre-industrial man is to suppose that he should be developed first, and that afterwards he will deserve the comfortable life of a developed society. Quite the contrary, society is developing properly when men change themselves at the same time that they change the social structure.

In the contemporary history of developing countries, when we try to understand how social situations, emerging from processes of development, become *social actions* of concrete individuals or groups of individuals, we must begin by looking at the functioning of the class systems within these societies. It is in the system of social stratification that we find one of the basic links between economy and society. This applies with particular force to the class systems of the developing societies of Latin America. It is here that we find a basic link between economic development and social development. In the profile of the stratification system we observe a clear expression of the marginality of the social structure, the coexistence of old and new patterns, the presence of residual classes, and the maturation of new classes.

From the point of view of its internal process, development becomes an historical chain of conflicting situations. The objective analysis of these conflicting situations leads us to understand many implications of the process of development that are not usually mentioned in surveys. The first point which should be mentioned is the fact that government is the leading force of modern development. And since development is not only a technical operation, but a profound and live experiment in which the whole society is involved, the result is that in emerging societies everything is on the table for debate. And all debate is political in character. Development in Latin America today is not only a transition from plantation system to factory system. In fact, what is under debate is the whole heritage of the archaic society, economic, political, and intellectual, as well as the archaic society itself—its structure, its values, its prospects. Living in a transitional period of this scope, any decision is a political decision—in the highest meaning of the word. So too, social situations invariably are translated into social actions. And social actions soon become political decisions. This is the phenomenology of development.

In a transitional society the mark of transition is imprinted on every aspect of the social order. This is especially so in connection with the political game that always presents, in these societies, characteristic patterns of ambivalence. This ambivalence is rooted in the marginality of the social structure. Hence we may find simultaneous support for one decision or for the exactly opposite one. These dangerous alternations, potentially present in all developing societies, do not signify the incapacity for solid, equilibriated political life, but are often indicative of the newness of their political agencies. Another characteristic of political ambivalence in developing societies is the tendency to postpone major decisions. These societies are performing in a short time one of the most important experiments in social change ever known in history. However, if we closely analyze the decision-making process and how it functions in national policy, the impression is that the political elites of these countries are oppressed by two fears: the fear of the problem of development and the fear of its solution as well. Political inertia and political convulsion follow one another in surprisingly short periods. Sometimes changes in the dominant orientation concerning basic problems may occur in a short time because in a marginal society it is possible to find strong support, in the residual or in the emerging situations, for quite opposite decisions.

Compromise, an old and versatile Latin word, becomes in practice the basic pattern of the political game in many of these countries. Compromise may or may not take the form of "party alliances," depending upon different circumstances. It is nonetheless easy to find in the politics of Latin American development different examples and patterns of compromise.

The compromise between the commercial bourgeoisie and the urban proletariat was one of the basic conditions of "modernization" of political life in many countries of Latin America, especially during the first decades of the twentieth century. Fighting for control of power, that traditionally was in the hands of the old landed aristocracy, the rising industrial bourgeoisie developed a policy of compromise with the urban industrial working class. In this compromise, industrialists provided leadership, and the working class provided numbers and the popular "mass base." Industrialization, labor legislation, social security, protectionist legislation, development of an internal market for internal products, nationalism, etc., have expanded within this protectionist scheme of compromise. This has provided the social background and support for different types of political regimes, more or less authoritarian, more or less populist, in Latin America since the end of the First World War.

When the main goal of a compromise is achieved, and its main historical role is accomplished, this may signify, as so many times in past history, the end of the compromise itself. As a result of the first stages of development the new industrial and commercial elites establish control of political power and at times try to reduce the impetus of the process, becoming in some cases a force of resistance against the expansion of the developmental process. At the same time the working class begins to exhibit the capacity and aspiration for producing its own ideology and organized participation in the political game of the developing country. These two tendencies both move against the compromise. Different results may occur as a consequence of the disintegration of the compromise. In some countries the new ruling industrial and commercial classes have established a new compromise with the old landed aristocracy. This has been the basis for some well known oligarchical regimes in Latin America. In other countries the new ruling sectors and its power elite are trying not only to accept, but to take the initiative in revising the basis of the archaic agrarian structure, in order to bring the rural laborers out of their traditional apathy. With this added political element, a new compromise may be attempted in which, as was formerly the case with urban workers, the rural masses will now provide numbers and the ruling classes will provide the ideology and leadership.

Instead of changing the rules of the game, the ruling elites are now changing the terms of the compromise and are continuing to use the mechanism of representative government. This is so even when the price to be paid is at times a fight for values and programs in which they do not believe and which apparently they do not like. This contradiction is one of the most important characteristics of the political behavior of some sectors of Latin American societies in modern times.

In this same context another quite important aspect to be considered is the political implications of the rising middle sectors. For many observers, this was the great unrequited condition for the expansion of democracy in Latin America. Definitely, these expectations have not been entirely confirmed in the political sphere. The processes of development multiply the middle sectors in these societies. This is a fact. The multiplication of intermediary classes between extremely disparate top and bottom positions of the traditional profile of the "social pyramid" has a leavening effect on the social system. But it is another fact of the matter that development in Latin America historically presents, as a financial concomitant, a continuous process of inflation. One of the results of this inflation is its eroding influence on standards of living of these middle sectors, specifically white-collar groups, whose budgets depend upon fixed incomes. Development multiplies those groups in society whose income is destroyed by inflation. This creates instability and unrest among those sectors in whom it was supposed democracy would find its most solid roots. The crude fact is that it is the dissatisfaction of these middle sectors that causes many authoritarian regimes and anti-democratic trends in Latin America today. Only the future can determine if this is only a transitional fact or a deep-rooted trend. At any rate it is wise to avoid great expectations from the mechanical application to the newly developing countries of some schemes coming from other national and historical contexts in the past.

Another basic and wise approach to the study of the political problems in the developing countries is never to imagine that, after centuries of fighting for a better political organization, the creativeness of mankind in this field is exhausted. The present form of parliamentary, monarchical or republican regimes does not exhaust the possibilities of further political systems. The history of political institutions is still open to those new countries which exercise their creativeness.

The processes of development in Latin America are occurring in the midst of profound changes going on throughout the world. Developing countries are moving in a changing, not a static, context. The end of the colonial system and the emergence of new nations in Africa and Asia has brought about tremendous changes not only within each emergent nation, but also to the old Western colonial powers. The growing modernization of other nations, old or new, that either have political independence or others that are still in search of such independence has brought on a deep change not only for the peoples concerned, but also for the people of neighboring nations. Finally, internal changes are also occurring in the structure of the overdeveloped countries themselves, as a consequence of their own technological advances. These create for the peoples and governments of overdeveloped nations enormous problems of social reconstruction—as is happening in the United States, the Soviet Union, and the major countries of Western Europe. As a result of all these changes in process, a new world order is in the making. It is an objective truth, and not romanticism, which compels us to say that in the developing countries of Latin America some pieces of this future world are being shaped by the work, brains, and sometimes the blood, of these people.

From the fact that Latin America is now developing in an unequal, complex, changing and agitated world, flows the fact that different models of development are offered by historical experiences of other nations as guiding patterns for the newer developing areas. Development is, and must continue to be, a cumulative process. Latin American countries are trying to use not only their own experience but the experience and lessons of other nations. Their basic aspirations are to start from the results of these experiences, not to repeat them mechanically. This applies not only on the technological level but also to the techniques of modeling a new economic, social, and political order. During the first half of the twentieth century two great models of development were offered to the newer countries: the capitalist and the socialist models. For a great many generations ideological disputes within the developing nations were practically limited to reproducing in these countries one of these two models. After the end of the Second World War these two models changed enough in their internal structures (as compared with the ideal types from which they were derived) to make any mechanical or eclectic amalgamation impossible. Entirely new models of development have been inaugurated in Europe, in Asia, in Africa, and in America, which have multiplied the alternatives and enriched the historical examples available for inspection. There is no sound reason, of any magnitude, which compels any country of Latin America to accept only one of these existing models as its own desired pattern of development. First, historical circumstances which in the past, even in the recent past, have paved the way for the flowering of these patterns—the capitalist as well as the socialist—have very few chances of being entirely reproduced in the future with equal success. Second, all of them, as historical experiences, present advantages and disadvantages, and the recognition of this fact entails a search for something better than each model taken separately. Technologically as well as ideologically this is the way that history occurred in the developing countries of our age. This is not ideology. This is an objective diagnosis. Never forget that for developing nations, progress is the price of survival. If this statement appears too radical, the blame must be placed on history.

Some centuries ago a British soldier-statesman, Oliver Cromwell, said something about his own country that in my opinion correctly sums up the present situation of developing countries: they cannot wait until the iron becomes hot to begin to strike; they must heat the iron while striking. In the forge of history this is the action required of people of the developing countries. In so doing they will make their contribution to the shaping of a better world for tomorrow.

# 28

BYRON FOX

## The Emerging International Sociology

This paper is concerned with the increasingly international character of the subject matter of sociology, out of which is emerging
an international sociology displaying these characteristics: a commitment to mankind which transcends parochialism and nationalism, the development of "big-range" research and analysis with
emphasis upon the political aspect of developing international
institutions, the use of comparative sociology based on "relevant
areas" and significant variables, and the development of "outrageous hypotheses" to deal with mankind's effort to survive.

At the international level there is growing institutional structure in economic behavior, in education through the United Nations, and very importantly in the political area. This is properly
described as an emerging international society with political structure, communications structure, and professional structure. In the
developing international society discrete units of reference are
collectivities, particularly national collectivities, but also professional associations, international corporate associations, and international labor organizations. Sociology at the international level is
concerned with the study of these collectivities and the interaction
among them.

Of great significance to the sociologist, but only inadequately
studied up to the present time, is international political structure.

Increasing involvement in political structure at the international level is reflected in the governmental budgets of nations. For example, the United States allocates two-thirds of its federal budget for military purposes, of which the proportion spent for space development is rapidly becoming one of the most important single items in the military budget.

Involvement in the growing international political structure is reflected in the fact that many issues formerly entirely domestic, such as race relations, and mass communications in the United States, are now international in their effects.[1] C. Wright Mills referred to this interrelationship: "In our time problems of the Western societies are almost inevitably problems of the world. It is perhaps one defining characteristic of our period that it is one in which for the first time the varieties of social worlds it contains are in serious, rapid, and obvious interplay."[2]

Implied in the development of institutional structure at the international level is the need for adequate ideologies to meet the problems of unprecedented change. But as Mills pointed out, we have witnessed the collapse of traditional liberalism in the West and transmutation of Marxism in the Soviet Union. No new ideologies with power to confront the rapidly changing world have emerged.[3] In his discussion of the decline of the Left and the New Left, Mills has referred to the reconstruction of an independent Left as an effective intellectual force.[4] He finds no effectual criticism of the existing order within inherited ideological frameworks: "Where is the intelligentsia that is carrying on the big discourse of the Western world *and* whose work as intellectuals is influential among parties and publics and relevant to the great decisions of our time?"[5] The result, he shows, is support of the *status quo*—the postmodern order—in which reason and freedom are threatened.[6]

Mills many times referred to the "unorganized irresponsibility of a world of nation states."[7] Power at the world level must be considered in terms of acceptance of this obsolete framework within which power is exercised. This raises the question of who is to make decisions at the world level, and the basis for legitimating their authority and decisions which have world-wide effects. Though Mills does not clearly define the role of peoples outside the Western and Soviet camps, he indicates the lack of voice in decision-making at the world level affecting their interests. Someone has coined a slogan describing this: "No annihilation without representation."

The world Mills confronted was one in which reason and freedom were at loggerheads with one another. It was a world in which reason had become bureaucratic, and freedom had to be gained at the expense of progress. That was the dilemma that he referred to as the Fourth Epoch and in his essays, particularly in the essay "Culture and Politics," he has made a valuable contribution toward understanding that world in its post-modern form. Ideologically this post-modern world is explained by the fact that Marxism had opened up and liberalism had closed down. The void left by the closure of liberalism is really what we are now calling conservatism. As a matter of fact, liberalism has gone by default. It collapsed in its historic mission because it did not supply the necessary dialogue with Marxism. Liberalism in its classic form no longer interests or excites people; rather it is now Marxism which is provocative to the degree that there are splits within the Communist camp. Liberalism in this way is undergoing a renaissance within the socialist and third force blocs. This cogent point was introduced by Mills in his analysis of the Marxists.[8]

In proposing an international sociology having as its subject matter emerging structure and conflicting ideologies, it is maintained that this is in the mainstream of sociology as conceived by earlier sociologists. At present it requires reorientation of analysis from a parochial and national point of view to a world or universalistic perspective. This implies that tendencies toward ethnocentrism and temporocentrism be critically examined; and further, that political ideologies be located within a social context.[9]

At this juncture in history nothing less than a commitment of social scientists to the cause of man's survival and his avoidance of annihilation will suffice. It is required that there be a commitment to this struggle for survival, order, development, and improved life chances. The alternative to a reconsideration of social progress as well as process is annihilation. In this struggle of man against his environment, reaching out into space, the social scientist cannot be neutral. To attempt neutrality is to place one's weight on the side of the old order which is on its way out. The only alternative is to place sociological science at the service of the order which is being born.

Commitment to mankind clearly means that international sociology cannot become a professional establishment but must be free of ideological obligation to any Establishment, whether military or pacifist. Only a commitment to the "politics of truth" enables social science to meet the central demand of the community "to make clear the elements of contemporary uneasiness and indifference." [10] With this liberation, the social sciences are "becoming the common denominator of our cultural period, and the sociological imagination our most needed quality of mind." [11]

Ability of social scientists to escape from parochial and partisan commitments has special significance in relation to the present obsessive pre-occupation with the Cold War. Peoples of the world are flooded with propaganda emanating from the Soviet Union and the United States. Referring to this Mills said: "In the United States today, intellectuals, artists, ministers, scholars, and scientists are fighting a cold war in which they echo and elaborate the confusions of officialdoms. They neither raise demands on the powerful for alternative politics, nor set forth such alternatives before publics." [12] This description is equally applicable to the Soviet Union.

Commitment to mankind, transcending the patriotic goal will compel a shift from "winning" the cold war (at this point in history can any war be won?) to the idea of finding dependable ways for reducing tensions and resolving underlying conflicts. For most Americans and Russians this idea lies over the horizon. The sociological imagination is required to stimulate the dialogues which will result in basic shifts from cold war strategies, from the politics of oversimplification, to an emphasis upon conflicts which threaten mankind.

What is required is a change in stance and activities among social scientists. In relation to the greatly enlarged nature of the problem, there must be development of "big-range" research and analysis. This implies that social scientists use their know-how and research funds available, with the human energy involved, to redirect research to fit the needs of the post-modern era.

The social scientist in big-range research committed to mankind's survival has to deal with questions emerging in a new world situation. It may well be that the notion of commitment itself, rather than being a hindrance to research of the "big-range" sort, will open up new channels of thought; it depends upon what the social scientist is committed to. Energy devoted to "big-range" research and analysis guided by a commitment to mankind and its survival will result in useful knowledge. At any rate such an orientation is worth the effort, if for no other reason than the high stakes involved.

Sociology for the most part has not come to grips with the "big-range" implications of political power. This failure is the result of historical developments, especially in the United States. It is interesting to ask, what would have been the course of American sociology had it taken its departure from the Marxian concept of power in political terms, rather than from Sumner in the form of folkways? [13]

American sociologists have largely abrogated and abdicated the field of political power to the other social sciences, especially political science. This is an unwarranted surrender of valuable subject matter, and is evident if we consider the study of the development of norms in social groups as a crucial concept describing sociological subject matter. Sociologists have been concerned with norms in smaller groups up to the level of the nation state. But they have given little study to norms at the world level, nor have they projected the development of norms at the world level. [14]

In practice there is a double standard of definition operating between the nation-state level and the international level. American society is assumed to meet the requirements of a society-nation, and is taken to be a unity involving consensus. This plays down and overlooks cleavages and imperfect functioning of American society as a political entity. At the international level there is a tendency to minimize and even ignore existing political structure. This obscures the fact that there is a growing political structure at the world level. Further, the fact is overlooked that there are vast possibilities of co-operation among the nations represented in the United Nations. This double standard of definition arises from the blinding and distorting effects of nationalism operating on the perception of American sociologists. [15]

Mills made a substantial contribution to the sociological analysis of political power. Though primarily concerned with power at the national level, he provided useful insights applicable at the international level. His analysis in *The Power Elite* relates to the involvement of the United States in the world power struggle. When he describes the economic-political-military complex characterized as the power elite in the United States, it has significance for the international scene. Mills develops this in the textual material, showing that the political power of the elite, and, even more, the political power of the military elite, has been greatly and rapidly extended during recent decades.[16]

In a number of his essays, and especially those in the section on Politics in *Power, Politics and People,* Mills has given an excellent description of the power elite at the world level. For instance, in his description of the Fourth Epoch, where he finds uncertainty and doubt with reference to the role of reason and freedom in the post-modern world, he has delineated the outlines of the international power situation.[17] The Fourth Epoch is described in terms of the collapse of the two main ideologies—liberalism and socialism. Throughout his analysis Mills makes clear that what we have is a survival of eighteenth- and nineteenth-century philosophies into the middle of the twentieth century, where they confront conditions in the world very different from those in which they took root.

Mills calls attention to the enormous enlargement and the decisive centralization of the means of power and decision; that is, all the means of history-making: "In our time, international as well as national means of history-making are being centralized. Is it not thus clear that the scope and the chance for conscious human agency in history-making is just now uniquely available?" [18] Mills declares that "men can now make history." [19] However, ironically, the "ideologies which offer men the hope of making history have declined and are collapsing in the Western Societies." [20] It is the collapse of the expectations of the Enlightenment, "that reason and freedom would come to prevail as paramount forces in human history. And behind it there is also the intellectual and political default of the intellectual community." [21] The paradox is that at the very moment when human control of the social situation is most feasible technologically it seems to be out of reach politically.

Here we may extrapolate from the analysis of Mills in *The Power Elite,* where his description based on American society appears to fit at the international level. He calls attention to status striving and political opportunism in the mass society, and the permeation of the intellectual community by the conservative mood, comfortably timid in the midst of a new gentility. Then he adds that "we can readily understand why the power elite of America has no ideology and feels the need of none, why its rule is naked of ideas, its manipulation without attempted justification. It is this mindlessness of the powerful that is the true higher immorality of our time; for, with it, there is associated the organized irresponsibility that is today the most important characteristic of the American system of corporate power." [22]

Mills in his later and so far unpublished writings represents a considerable degree of sophistication with reference to the notion of power elites. He studied the power elites of the Soviet Union as well as those of the United States. He was aware that the world is a great welter of politics being transformed into policy-making. The world he confronted is breaking up into two world systems, with a world in between—a *Tiers Monde*.

Analysis of systems at the world level involves a comparative approach, and to undertake this Mills outlines in his later writings a cluster or "relevant area" analysis. This would subordinate politically oriented criteria reflecting the bias of Western culture. It was his idea to begin with the description of relevant areas, by which he meant an area such as Africa, Latin America, or Southeast Asia, replacing the common notion of American society criteria, which reflect the blinding effects of nationalism and parochialism. It is transnational, rather than international, in the sense that there is no international order yet. We can think in terms of areas of relevance factually, conceptually, economically, racially, and ethnically, and thus break out of ethnocentric and temporocentric problems.

Mills believed that comparative work, both theoretical and empirical, is the most promising line of development for social science today, and, further, that such work can best be done within social science unified as to its goals rather than as to its language.[23] He pointed out that comparative study and historical study are very deeply involved with each other. For example, "You cannot understand the underdeveloped, the Communist, the capitalist political economies as they exist in the world today by flat, timeless comparisons." [24] In his opinion, the historical viewpoint leads to the comparative study of societies. It is thus two-dimensional, and

Mills maintained that one cannot understand the major phases through which any modern Western nation has developed, or its present form, solely in terms of its national history. Not only has it interacted with other societies, but it cannot be understood without treating it as part of an area of relevance to be compared and contrasted with other areas of relevance.

The basis for comparative analysis would not be haphazard in terms of arbitrary national or society units; that is to say, simply by comparing nations without a systematic or methodological basis. Instead, Mills developed a theory of area clusters involving an exhaustive study of selected variables; for example, the study of 100 nations and 50 cities which might constitute five or six major world areas in terms of these major variables.[25] This would be one step in the direction of a sociology at the international level.

This would go far to make up for the present lack of a useful comparative sociology. Such a comparative study would be based on descriptions and relations of meaningful variables, with a bearing on crucial issues, including political, economic, and social problems. This might well result in a group of books about areas or clusters of economic, political, and social variables around the world. It would be more useful than the endless studies of individual societies classified on an arbitrary basis and having little relationship to each other. The nation is giving way to the region and the continent in fact—then why not in analysis?

Beyond the study of relevant areas and comparisons and contrasts among them is the analysis of the processes of group interaction; e.g. competition and conflict, co-operation, accommodation, negotiation or dialogue, and assimilation. The study of the process at the international level includes the conflict known under the euphemistic label of the cold war. Mills does not bring out clearly the issue of the cold war in terms of the commonly accepted notion of winning as against resolving the conflicts which underlie the relations between the United States and the Soviet Union. As noted above, the second alternative still lies over the horizon for the majority of the American people, and probably for a majority of the American sociologists as well. For sociology at the international level this is an issue of significance.

It is interesting that Mills did not develop the implications of the cold war by defining the historical dimension; that is, by defining the event in terms of the notion that like all social movements it has a life of some duration—whether short or long as measured in human  terms. This is illustrated by the seventeenth-century wars of religion between Catholics and Protestants which had the same sharpness and finality, and the distinctions between right and wrong, or between believers and heretics, as the U.S.-U.S.S.R. struggle has at present. It is necessary to delineate sharply the obsessive and emotional aspects of the Russian-American conflict, dressed up by each side in ideological terms favorable to itself.

There are sociologists who have contributed to the emerging world sociology. Among these are Riesman,[26] Sorokin,[27] Mills,[28] Parsons,[29] Horowitz,[30] Etzioni,[31] and others. However, the list is not a long one, and this kind of study is a recent phenomenon. There are few research grants for this kind of study and people interested in this kind of sociology are sometimes viewed as outsiders rather than insiders. Therefore, we have only a small number of social scientists following up in the development of world sociology, frequently working in relative isolation. There are a number of institutes, such as the Institute for Conflict Resolution at Michigan, headed by Kenneth Boulding, along with Anatol Rapoport. There are also the Canadian Peace Research Institute and the Peace Research Institute in Washington, D.C.

By contrast, it is interesting that there are many physical scientists who have shown a concern for the sociological issues of international problems, especially of nuclear warfare.. These remain relatively untapped phenomena within the social sciences. However, there is evidence of increasing awareness of the importance of sociology at the world level.[32] For example, at most of the regional and national sociological meetings, part of the program is devoted to what may be properly called emerging world sociology, often in the form of a panel or several papers. In some cases the treatment is narrow and even ethnocentric, but this aspect of sociology is being increasingly discussed at the present time. Peace research bureaus in the United States and Canada are now drawing sociologists into their orbit, with fruitful consequences for both sociologists and other professionals.

Following the lead of Robert Lynd, sociologists studying at the international level might boldly propose "outrageous hypotheses."

Exploring this line of inquiry sociologists may inquire whether an hypothesis such as that of a warless world is more outrageous than the hypothesis of a heavier-than-air craft was three quarters of a century ago. Or the hypothesis, ten years ago, that a European Economic Community would come into existence, in the face of strong national sentiments? The latter is now a reality, and an economic form of co-operation may well develop into political federation. This illustrates the dynamics of change which bring into view possibilities which could not previously be imagined or foretold.

Advancing the "outrageous hypothesis" that war can be abolished is a series of articles in the *Saturday Review* entitled "Toward a Warless World." [33] This is a serious inquiry by a group of social scientists into the problems of maintaining order and providing for change in a world where it is assumed that there has been voluntary disarmament of the great powers down to the level necessary to maintain internal order.

Arnold Toynbee [34] in one of the articles deals with a question that is probably in the minds of most Americans. Will such a world state work? Is a world government feasible? Toynbee makes the interesting point that at least six or seven world states have existed in the past; that is, if by world state is meant the inclusion of all the people that count, or are counted by the state that defines itself in universal terms. Among these states were China, Japan, India, Pakistan, and the Roman Empire. If Toynbee's analysis is accepted, world orders have existed and are not hypothetical, or "visionary" or "idealistic" or "impractical." Toynbee finds that these states, though maintained over a period of time, foundered on the problems of social change. Each attempted to maintain the existing order, and, while they did that successfully for a time through a system of enforceable law, they made the mistake of trying to freeze the social order. The crucial problem is directing change. An outrageous hypothesis is to assert that it is possible to establish a universal world order in which the processes of change will be provided for.

By advancing outrageous hypotheses sociology can encourage the discovery and consideration of cultural alternatives at the international level. This is what Mills had in mind: "What social science is properly about is the human variety, which consists of all the social worlds in which men have lived, are living, and might live." [35] As an illustration of cultural alternatives we may profitably examine several ways in which resources and technology can be used. There are two pairs of choices inherent in the relationship between technology (including space technology) and political structure in the world today. The first pair of choices relates to the allocation of resources and technology. One choice is what we call world development — economically and socially; an alternative choice is space development.

It may be that mankind cannot support the cost of both world development and space development. Grenville Clark recently pointed out in the *Saturday Review* in an article entitled "The Inhuman Equation: Can Arms Control End the Population Crisis?" that we probably cannot do both these things at the same time.[36] This assumes that space expenditures involve predominantly expenditures for military purposes. Clark argues that mankind cannot control population without the redirection of a major part of the $120 billion spent in the world for arms at the present time. His reasoning is simple and direct: unless a sizeable part of the money now used for armaments is channeled to raise the standard of living, incentive to limit numbers will be lacking. Increased economic production would thus be swallowed up by a rapidly increasing population, without population control. This narrows the choice to world development or space development.

A second pair of choices in the use of resources and technology is between the nation-state system and an international system for the exploration of space. Development of space through the nation-state system involves competition among the great powers. An important question is, can the nation-state sustain this kind of effort, or is it as inadequate and obsolete as a horse and buggy plodding down the New York State Thruway? The question is rhetorical, yet there is evidence that the job of retooling or discarding old social institutions has not been taken seriously.

In a world where the dominant emphasis is upon military advantages and development, it is evident that under the nation-state model the great powers will use space development for their own purposes. And indeed this is heady stuff that the Russians and Americans have seized hold of. Each is determined to win; when President Kennedy said, "While we cannot guarantee that we shall one day be first, any failure to make this effort will make us last," this seemed to express a clear-cut determination on the part of the President to achieve first place if at all possible.

Consider what kind of peace might emerge from the national development of space.[37] It is conceivable that we might reach a balance where there would be a peaceful world, but in the form of a Russo-American peace. It might be a devil's peace; for instance, peace on the terms agreed upon by these two great powers might be achieved at the cost of world development or at the expense of slowing down world development. Or it might be secured at the price of the sacrifice of the freedom and even the lives of two-thirds of the world. For instance, it might lead to ruthless policies for the reduction of overpopulation. Or, it might involve constant nuclear threats and even the use of nuclear weapons launched from space vehicles by Russians or Americans. This implies lack of representation in decisions by the other two-thirds of the world; that is, war without consent.

The second alternative is space development through the United Nations for peaceful purposes, with the benefits shared by all peoples of the world. Using these criteria, space development would be kept in perspective; and might be viewed as part of world economic and social development; e.g. extension of communications and weather control. Thus world development and space development would not be exclusive alternatives, but complementary parts of man's development of his total environment. Such a course might "make reason democratically relevant to human affairs in a free [world] society," in the words of Mills.[38]

We must recognize opposition to the position that has been outlined. Several forms of resistance can be identified: the pressures and momentum generated within American society toward the perpetuation and strengthening of the economic-political-military complex, as pointed out by Mills, and also, interestingly enough, by former President Eisenhower. Closely related is obsession with the cold war, and preoccupation with "winning" it at whatever cost. Lastly, there are pressures from within the social science establishment. The very growth of quantitative methods and empirical research on problems of small groups can be related to the attempt to ward off socialism by means of social reform. This is re-enforced at the present time through pressures against radical and unpopular positions taken by American social scientists, especially in the area of foreign policy.

The position of Mills vis-à-vis the opposition confronted by social scientists who venture into description and prescription at the international level is sharply stated in a concluding section of *The Sociological Imagination.* Here he asks for the answer "to the cultural and political question of The Cheerful Robot," and asserts that unless the problems are at least confronted no answers will be found. He asks, "Is it not obvious that the ones to confront them, above all others, are the social scientists of the rich societies? That many of them do not now do so is surely the greatest human default being committed by privileged men in our times." [39]

NOTES:

1. Byron L. Fox, "The Cold War and American Domestic Problems," *Social Problems,* 1, June 1953, pp. 10-12; Byron L. Fox, "International Cultural Relations," *American Sociological Review,* 15, August 1950, pp. 489-95; Byron Fox, "American Social Problems in a World Setting: the Role of U.S. Government Spending," *Social Problems,* 6, Fall, 1958, pp. 99-107.
2. C. Wright Mills, *The Sociological Imagination* (New York, 1959), p. 150.
3. C. Wright Mills, *The Marxists* (New York, 1962), pp. 19-22.
4. C. Wright Mills, "The Decline of the Left," Lecture on the British Broadcasting Company, *Contact,* No. 3, 1959. Also "The New Left," *New Left Review,* 5, Sept.-Oct. 1960. Both essays are included in *Power, Politics and People: The Collected Essays of C. Wright Mills,* edited and with an introduction by Irving Louis Horowitz (New York, 1963), pp. 221-35 and 247-59.
5. *The Sociological Imagination,* p. 183.
6. C. Wright Mills, "Culture and Politics: the Fourth Epoch," *The Listener* (published by the British Broadcasting Company), March 12, 1959, and reproduced in *Power, Politics and People,* pp. 236-46.
7. *The Sociological Imagination,* p. 9.
8. *The Marxists,* Ch. 1, *passim.*
9. See Irving L. Horowitz, *Philosophy, Science, and the Sociology of Knowledge* (Springfield, Ill., 1961).
10. *The Sociological Imagination,* p. 13.
11. Ibid.
12. Ibid. p. 183.
13. Richard A. Schermerhorn, *Society and Power* (New York, 1961), p. 13.

14. Increasingly there are exceptions; for example, a plenary session on world order was included in the program of the American Sociological Society meeting in Los Angeles, August 1963. A paper on "The Problem of World Order" was presented by Talcott Parsons of Harvard University and discussed by David Riesman, also of Harvard University.

15. Byron L. Fox, "International Cultural Relations," *American Sociological Review*, August 1950, p. 493.

16. C. Wright Mills, *The Power Elite* (New York, 1956). See the chapters on "The Warlords" and "The Military Ascendancy." Also C. Wright Mills, "The Structure of Power in American Society," *British Journal of Sociology*, IX, March 1958, reproduced in *Power, Politics and People*, pp. 23-38.

17. *Power, Politics and People*, pp. 236-46. Also *The Sociological Imagination*, pp. 165-7.

18. *The Sociological Imagination*, p. 183.

19. Ibid.

20. Ibid.

21. Ibid.

22. *The Power Elite*, p. 342.

23. *The Sociological Imagination*, pp. 150-51. This was further discussed in unpublished manuscripts. See Irving L. Horowitz, "The Unpublished Writings of C. Wright Mills," *Studies on the Left*, 3, No. 4, pp. 3-23.

24. *The Sociological Imagination*, pp. 150-51.

25. Irving L. Horowitz, "The Unpublished Writings of C. Wright Mills," *Studies on the Left*, 3, No. 4, pp. 3-23.

26. See many articles in the *Newsletter* of the Council on Correspondence.

27. Pitirim A. Sorokin, *The Crisis of Our Age: The Social and Cultural Outlook* (New York, 1942).

28. Mills demonstrated his concern in many of his writings. His thinking was crystallized in *The Causes of World War III* (New York, 1958), also in *Listen, Yankee: The Revolution in Cuba* (New York, 1960).

29. See note 14 above for his interest in the world order.

30. Irving L. Horowitz, *The Idea of War and Peace in Contemporary Philosophy* (New York, 1957); *The War Game* (New York, 1963); "Arms, Policies and Games," *The American Scholar*, Winter, 1961-62, pp. 94-107; and *Games, Strategies, and Peace* (Philadelphia, 1963).

31. Amitai Etzioni, *The Hard Way to Peace: A New Strategy* (New York, 1962); also see a review of this book by Byron Fox, *American Journal of Sociology*, Nov. 1962, pp. 398-9.

32. There may be a trend in the direction of using an international orientation in the writing of introductory sociology textbooks. For example, the British sociologist, T. B. Bottomore has published *Sociology: A Guide to Problems and Literature* (New York, 1963). This is an introduction to the comparative study of societies, with concentration on Indian-Asian social institutions and problems. Another example is Broom and Selznick, *Sociology*, third ed. (New York, 1963). This text includes materials on

world politics and world ideologies. Also Byron L. Fox and Irving Louis Horowitz, *Sociology: Human Behavior in a Changing World,* forthcoming. It is intended that this text will have an international orientation.

33.  This series of articles is edited by Arthur Larson, Director of the World Rule of Law Center at Duke University, and appeared in the *Saturday Review:* Arnold Toynbee, "How to Change the World Without War," May 12, 1962, p. 16ff. Walter Millis, "Order and Change in a Warless World," Sept. 15, 1962, p. 18ff. Kenneth E. Boulding, "Can We Afford a Warless World," Oct. 6, 1962, p. 17ff. Arthur Larson, "International Change in a Warless World," Nov. 17, 1962, p. 16ff. Grenville Clark, "The Inhuman Equation: Can Arms Control End the Population Crisis?" Feb. 16, 1963, p. 15ff. Margaret Mead, "Recapturing the Future," June 1, 1963, p. 10ff.

34.  "How to Change the World Without War," *Saturday Review,* op. cit.

35.  *The Sociological Imagination,* p. 132.

36.  *Saturday Review,* Feb. 16, 1963, p. 15ff.

37.  Lincoln P. Bloomfield (ed.) *Outer Space: Prospects for Man and Society,* The American Assembly, Columbia University (New York, 1962).

38.  *The Sociological Imagination,* p. 194.

39.  Ibid. p. 176.

# Name and Title Index

In these indexes the citation 48f., 356f. refers to the note on the page indicated.

# Subject Index

academic: community, 201; departments, 9; establishment, 62; freedom, 58, 59; life, 171; profession, 59-60
academicians, 159, 200
academicism, 19
academics, 86, 87, 158, 375
accommodation, 452, 483
Accra, 431
action, 120, 124, 229, 240, 289f., 310, 449, 462, 475; commitment to, 270; components of, 251; consequences of, 222, 271; determinants of, 236; elements of, 127; general theory of, 14, 15; and ideologies, 272; individual, 113-14, 116; interpersonal, 115; among Negroes, 307; organization for, 307; paradigm for, 15; and perception, 113, 127; political, 85, 300; among the poor, 291; possibilities of, 128; public, 304; self-satisfying, 129; social, 233, 235, 305, 370, 371, 374, 470; source of, 126; successful, 121; and thought, 377
administration: bureaucratic, 361; impersonal, 364-5
administrative elite, 357-69
administrators, 322, 357-69
affective neutrality, 385
affluence, 28, 261; consumer, 46

affluent: America, 101; economy, 299; society, 23, 265, 282, 290
Africa, 33, 154, 285, 436, 443f., 464, 473, 474, 482; rural, 430
Afro-Asia, 378
agencies: personnel of, 304; private, 304; social (service), 301-5, 310
agrarian structure, 474
agriculture, 441
alienation, 21, 30, 128, 130, 158, 179f., 272; and anomie, 253-67; as empirical problem, 126-8; and frustration, 244; Marx's concept of, 129; in mass society, 173; phenomenology of, 122-3; problem of, 108-33; and self-powers, 123; social sources of, 239-52; of workers, 241, 254; see also anomie
ambivalence, patterns of, 471
American Federation of Labor (AFL), 338, 349-51; and CIO, 308
American Plan, 351, 355f.
American Psychological Association, 208
American Sociological Association, 208
American Telephone and Telegraph, 318
Americanism, 333, 352; and consensus, 352
Americanization, 352, 356f.